KARL BARTH AND LIBERATION THEOLOGY

T&T Clark Explorations in Reformed Theology

Series Editors

Paul T. Nimmo
Paul Dafydd Jones

Editorial Board

Christophe Chalamet
David A. S. Fergusson
Angela Dienhart Hancock
Leanne Van Dyk
Matthias D. Wüthrich

KARL BARTH AND LIBERATION THEOLOGY

Edited by
Kaitlyn Dugan and Paul Dafydd Jones

LONDON • NEW YORK • OXFORD • NEW DELHI • SYDNEY

T&T CLARK
Bloomsbury Publishing Plc
50 Bedford Square, London, WC1B 3DP, UK
1385 Broadway, New York, NY 10018, USA
29 Earlsfort Terrace, Dublin 2, Ireland

BLOOMSBURY, T&T CLARK and the T&T Clark logo are trademarks of Bloomsbury Publishing Plc

First published in Great Britain 2023
Paperback edition published 2024

Copyright © Kaitlyn Dugan and Paul Dafydd Jones, 2023

Kaitlyn Dugan and Paul Dafydd Jones have asserted their right under the Copyright, Designs and Patents Act, 1988, to be identified as Editors of this work.

For legal purposes the Acknowledgments on p. xi constitute an extension of this copyright page.

Cover design by Anna Berzovan

All rights reserved. No part of this publication may be reproduced or transmitted in any form or by any means, electronic or mechanical, including photocopying, recording, or any information storage or retrieval system, without prior permission in writing from the publishers.

Bloomsbury Publishing Plc does not have any control over, or responsibility for, any third-party websites referred to or in this book. All internet addresses given in this book were correct at the time of going to press. The author and publisher regret any inconvenience caused if addresses have changed or sites have ceased to exist, but can accept no responsibility for any such changes.

A catalogue record for this book is available from the British Library.

Library of Congress Cataloging-in-Publication Data
Names: Jones, Paul Dafydd, editor. | Dugan, Kaitlyn, editor.
Title: Karl Barth and liberation theology / edited by Kaitlyn Dugan and Paul Dafydd Jones.
Description: London; New York: T&T Clark, 2022. | Series: T&T Clark explorations in reformed theology | Includes bibliographical references and index. |
Identifiers: LCCN 2022036231 (print) | LCCN 2022036232 (ebook) | ISBN 9780567698773 (hardback) | ISBN 9780567698827 (paperback) | ISBN 9780567698780 (pdf) | ISBN 9780567698803 (epub)
Subjects: LCSH: Barth, Karl, 1886-1968. | Liberation theology.
Classification: LCC BX4827.B3 K335 2022 (print) | LCC BX4827.B3 (ebook) | DDC 230/.0464–dc23/eng/20220906
LC record available at https://lccn.loc.gov/2022036231
LC ebook record available at https://lccn.loc.gov/2022036232

ISBN: HB: 978-0-5676-9877-3
PB: 978-0-5676-9882-7
ePDF: 978-0-5676-9878-0
ePUB: 978-0-5676-9880-3

Typeset by Deanta Global Publishing Services, Chennai, India

To find out more about our authors and books visit www.bloomsbury.com and sign up for our newsletters.

In the thought, speech, and action demanded of Christians, the issue is not just that of rejecting what they see to be a bad possibility but that of rising up and revolting against its actualization: a revolt that has positive meaning and inner necessity because another possibility stands with such splendor before the eyes of the rebels that they cannot refrain from affirming and grasping it and entering into battle for its actualization . . . Christians . . . exist under a binding requirement to engage in a specific uprising.

Karl Barth, The Christian Life, 207

The Good News takes a very concrete form. The central message is this: the situation cannot continue as it is; impoverishment and exploitation are not God's will; but now there is hope, resurrection, life, change. The reign of God, which is the reign of justice, is at hand.

Elsa Tamez, Bible of the Oppressed, 67

... For my Father (PDJ)
... For my beloved Grandparents, Georgia and Norman (KD)

CONTENTS

Acknowledgments — xi
List of Abbreviations — xiii

INTRODUCTION: KARL BARTH—ORTHODOX, MODERN, AND LIBERATIVE? — 1
    Kaitlyn Dugan and Paul Dafydd Jones

Chapter 1
KARL BARTH AND THE ORIGINS OF LIBERATION THEOLOGY — 15
    Luis N. Rivera-Pagán

Chapter 2
OF GODS AND MEN, AND WOLVES—THE "OTHER QUESTION": BETWEEN PROJECTION, COLONIAL IMAGINATION, AND LIBERATION — 33
    Hanna Reichel

Chapter 3
THE GENERATIVE FEMALE BODY AND THE ANALOGY OF FAITH IN KARL BARTH'S *CHURCH DOGMATICS* — 55
    Faye Bodley-Dangelo

Chapter 4
THE DISABLED GOD AND COVENANT ONTOLOGY — 69
    Lisa Powell

Chapter 5
KARL BARTH AND KOREAN THEOLOGY, PAST AND PRESENT — 85
    Meehyun Chung

Chapter 6
KARL BARTH'S THEOLOGY OF POLITICAL PARTICIPATION: AN EGYPTIAN APPROPRIATION — 99
    Hani Hanna

Chapter 7
KARL BARTH AND LIBERATION THEOLOGIES IN SOUTH AFRICA: THE DIFFICULTIES OF COMPARISON, CONVERSATION, AND CONSTRUCTIVE REFLECTION   117
   Rothney S. Tshaka

Chapter 8
LIBERATION THEOLOGY IN A SOUTH AFRICAN CONTEXT: DOES KARL BARTH HAVE ANYTHING TO OFFER HERE?   133
   Graham Ward

Chapter 9
USING BARTH "TO JUSTIFY DOING NOTHING": JAMES CONE'S UNANSWERED CHALLENGE TO THE WHITENESS OF BARTH STUDIES   147
   David L. Clough

Chapter 10
CLOTHED IN FLESH: THE ARTIST, LIBERATION, AND THE FUTURE OF BARTHIAN THEOLOGY   161
   Brian Bantum

Chapter 11
THELONIOUS MONK, ICON OF THE ESCHATON: KARL BARTH, JAMES CONE, AND THE "IMPOSSIBLE-POSSIBILITY" OF A THEOLOGY OF FREEDOM   177
   Raymond Carr

Chapter 12
TURNING BARTH RIGHT-SIDE-UP: JAMES CONE AND THE RISK OF A CONTEXTUAL THEOLOGY OF REVELATION   195
   Tyler B. Davis and Ry O. Siggelkow

Chapter 13
LIBERATION THEOLOGY AND KARL BARTH IN THE SHADOW OF THE ALT-RIGHT: WHITE SUPREMACISM, POLITICAL PROTEST, AND ECCLESIOLOGY AFTER CHARLOTTESVILLE   213
   Paul Dafydd Jones

Bibliography   235
List of Contributors   253
Index   255

ACKNOWLEDGMENTS

A number of chapters in this book had their origins in the 2018 Karl Barth Conference, "Karl Barth and the Future of Liberation Theology," held at Princeton Theological Seminary and cochaired by the editors of this volume. The intervening years, it seems fair to say, have been tumultuous. As political and social upheavals continue apace, racialized nationalisms, old and new forms of sex and gender-based discrimination, and disquieting trends toward totalitarianism—all backed by a global economic system that rarely fails to value profit over persons—seem to be gaining an ever-firmer grip on life in the northern and southern hemispheres. Meanwhile, those advocating for more just democratic processes and those pleading for a political reorientation that would enable the international community to reckon seriously with the interconnected challenges of mass migration, widespread socioeconomic precarity, and a deepening environmental crisis are struggling to make their voices heard. If one adds a devastating pandemic that has cost the lives of millions, a new and bloody conflict in Ukraine, and the prospect of an unprecedented assault on reproductive rights in the United States, there seems to be little reason for hope. And little time for the writing and reading of academic books.

We are convinced, however, that the obligation to engage in theopolitical reflection holds fast, and that the issues engaged in the following chapters remain pertinent. Christian communities, after all, ought never to pass up the opportunity to think again about what it means to follow one who was anointed "to bring good news to the poor . . . to proclaim release to the captive and recovery of sight to the blind, to set free those who are oppressed," and "to proclaim the year of the Lord's favor" (Lk. 4:18–19). It may be, too, that those holding other religious convictions—or, for that matter, those inclined to view religious commitments with a degree of wariness—will also find something of value in this book.

Although considerable time has elapsed since the conference in June 2018, we wish to thank Nicola Whyte and Thurman Barnes, former student assistants of the Center for Barth Studies, for their efforts in coordinating that event. We would also like to thank Amy Ehlin, Senior Director of Auxiliary Services at Princeton Theological Seminary, for her extensive work in overseeing various details of the conference. And we remain sincerely grateful to the advisory committee of the Center for Barth Studies for entrusting us with the responsibility of leading the conference. While this volume did not appear as quickly as we would have liked—the tumult described earlier hardly helped—it would not exist at all were it not for those who helped us to convene a rich array of scholars, ministers, and laypeople in New Jersey.

Although many colleagues and friends who supported this project are contributors to this volume, both editors want to express especial thanks to several individuals whose assistance and encouragement were crucial for bringing this book to fruition: Kendall Cox, Brandy Daniels, Charles Mathewes, Bruce L. McCormack, Paul T. Nimmo, Ry O. Siggelkow, Shelly Tilton, and Christian Collins Winn.

Finally, some more personal notes of gratitude.

Kaitlyn Dugan wishes to thank my family—Mom, Dad, and Jane—for their constant support and encouragement of my work at the Center for Barth Studies, to Peter Anders for setting me on this academic path, and to Chris Boesel for showing me how to do theology in the way that this volume tries to encourage.

Paul Dafydd Jones continues to be grateful for the warmth, wit, and wisdom of faculty and students in the Department of Religious Studies at UVa, who have provided me with an academic home since 2006. I am also, as ever, indebted to family members on both sides of the Atlantic, most of whom find my interest in Christian liberation theology only slightly more intelligible than my interest in Karl Barth. Extra special love and thanks go to my two children, Samuel and Tobias, and, of course, to Kate Becker, skeptical midwife extraordinaire.

Charlottesville and Princeton, May 2022

ABBREVIATIONS FOR WORKS BY KARL BARTH

CD   *Church Dogmatics*. Trans. G. W. Bromiley, T. F. Torrance, and others. Edinburgh: T&T Clark, 1936–1977.
CL   *Christian Life*. Trans. G. W. Bromiley. Edinburgh: T&T Clark, 1981.
GA   *Karl Barth Gesamtausgabe*. Zürich: TVZ, 1971–.
RII   *The Epistle to the Romans*. Trans. E. C. Hoskyns. London: Oxford University Press, 1933.
TET   *Theological Existence To-Day! (A Plea for Theological Freedom)*. Trans. R. Birch Hoyle. London: Hodder and Stoughton, 1933.
WGT   *The Word of God and Theology*. Trans. Amy Marga. London: T&T Clark, 2011.

INTRODUCTION

KARL BARTH—ORTHODOX, MODERN, AND LIBERATIVE?

Kaitlyn Dugan and Paul Dafydd Jones

I.

Recent engagements with the intellectual, cultural, ecclesial, and political contexts in which Karl Barth lived and worked have paid significant dividends in English-language scholarship. Bruce McCormack's "genetic-historical" interpretation of Barth's writings in the 1910s and 1920s, an invaluable counterpoint (and welcome *auf Wiedersehen*) to the final gasps of neo-orthodoxy, is a case in point. It is obviously legitimate to view Barth's early dialectical work as a repudiation of liberal Protestantism and a reassertion of the norms of the magisterial Reformation—something given dramatic expression in the first edition of the Romans commentary, when Barth declares a preference for the "old doctrine of inspiration" over "the historical-critical method of biblical research" (GA II.16: 4). But interpreters must also reckon with the local conditions that enabled the development of a "critically realistic dialectical theology." Marburg neo-Kantianism, Swiss religious socialism, the prophetic witness of Johann and Christoph Blumhardt, and, at the beginnings of the 1920s, the pressures of university teaching: each of these patently modern factors shaped Barth's dogmatic program.[1] Discussion of McCormack's work has also reignited interest in the pioneering research of Friedrich-Wilhelm Marquardt.[2] Although most scholars continue to resist Marquardt's early claim that Barth's theology was determined by socialist ideology (a central tenet of *Theologie und Sozialismus*), there is a growing awareness that Barth's theological output cannot be held at a distance from Barth's political convictions—or, for that matter, the multiple national and international crises that Barth sought to

---

1. See Bruce L. McCormack, *Critically Realistic Dialectical Theology: Its Genesis and Development 1909–1936* (Oxford: Clarendon Press, 1995). The reference to "genetic-historical" can be found on vii.

2. Friedrich-Wilhelm Marquardt, *Theologie und Sozialismus: Das Beispiel Karl Barths*, 3rd edn (Munich: Chr. Kaiser Verlag, 1985). For those seeking a useful English-language introduction to Marquardt's work, see *Theological Audacities: Selected Essays*, ed. Andreas Pangritz and Paul S. Chung, trans. Don McCord, H. Martin Rumscheidt, and Paul S. Chung (Eugene: Pickwick, 2010).

navigate. Barth's modern *philosophical* commitments, one might say, went hand in hand with equally modern *political* commitments, which extended from sharp denunciations of bourgeois complacency to prophetic broadsides against fascism, searching critiques of Western capitalism, and incisive analyses of the "lordless powers" (CL: 213–33) that haunt our lives.³

Granted that a new line of analysis has been opened by Christiane Tietz's recent biography of Barth, portions of which aptly scrutinize Barth's romantic entanglements,⁴ scholars have also sought to position Barth's writings in an increasingly broad intellectual environment. There has thus emerged a fresh sense of what one might call the deep context of Barth's theology, as well as laudable attempts to situate Barth in an ecumenical frame. In terms of the latter, mention must be made both of Hani Hanna's recent book, *The Christology of Karl Barth and Matta al-Miskīn*, and the important edited volume, *Correlating Sobornost: Conversations between Karl Barth and the Russian Orthodox Tradition*.⁵ In terms of the former, there have been incisive considerations of Barth's relationship to Schleiermacher and his liberal descendants that dispense with tired interpretative conventions, as well as fresh efforts to clarify Barth's relationship to Hegel and the tradition of German idealism.⁶ There have been new investigations of Barth's

---

3. See here, for instance, Paul S. Chung, *Karl Barth: God's Word in Action* (Eugene: Cascade, 2008); Timothy Gorringe, *Karl Barth: Against Hegemony* (Oxford: Oxford University Press, 1999); Angela Dienhart Hancock, *Karl Barth's Emergency Homiletic, 1932–1933: A Summons to Prophetic Witness at the Dawn of the Third Reich* (Grand Rapids: Eerdmans, 2013); and *Theo-Politics? Conversing with Barth in Western and Asian Contexts*, ed. Markus Höfner (Lanham: Lexington Books/Fortress Academic, 2022). On Barth's ability to charge doctrinal statements with political meaning, see Paul Dafydd Jones, "Karl Barth's *The Christian Life* and the Task of Political Theology," in *Theo-Politics?* 337–55; and idem, "Karl Barth," in *The Oxford Handbook of Political Theology*, ed. Shaun Casey and Michael Kessler (Oxford: Oxford University Press, forthcoming).

4. See Christiane Tietz, *Karl Barth: A Life in Conflict*, trans. Victoria J. Barnett (Oxford: Oxford University Press, 2021), 177–98.

5. See, respectively, Hani Hanna, *The Christology of Karl Barth and Matta al-Miskīn* (Lanham: Lexington Books/Fortress Academic, 2019) and *Correlating Sobornost: Conversations between Karl Barth and the Russian Orthodox Tradition*, ed. Ashley John Moyse, Scott A. Kirkland, and John C. McDowell (Minneapolis: Fortress, 2016).

6. On Barth, Schleiermacher, and Schleiermacher's descendants, see, inter alia, Matthias Gockel, *Barth and Schleiermacher on the Doctrine of Election: A Systematic-Theological Comparison* (Oxford: Oxford University Press, 2006); Bruce L. McCormack, *Orthodox and Modern: Studies in the Theology of Karl Barth* (Grand Rapids: Baker, 2008), esp. 21–105; Sung-Sup Kim, *Deus Providebit: Calvin, Schleiermacher, and Barth on the Providence of God* (Minneapolis: Fortress, 2014); Christophe Chalamet, "Barth and Liberal Protestantism," in *The Oxford Handbook of Karl Barth*, ed. Paul Dafydd Jones and Paul T. Nimmo (Oxford: Oxford University Press, 2019), 132–46; and Paul Dafydd Jones, "Schleiermacher, Neo-Orthodoxy, and Dialectical Theology," in *The Oxford Handbook of Friedrich Schleiermacher*,

commitment to and departure from the main lines of the Reformed tradition, extending from new studies of Barth and Calvin, in-depth considerations of Barth's engagement with post-Reformation Reformed scholasticism, and Barth's reception of magisterial confessions.[7] And, turning to earlier phases of Christian history, there have been instructive treatments of Barth and Aquinas, Barth and Anselm, and Barth and early church writers.[8]

This book, however, has a different object. It aims to complement a burgeoning tradition of historical-interpretive inquiry with a series of constructive theopolitical provocations. So, rather than looking back in history to understand Barth, its chapters attempt consistently to look forward, setting Barth's work in critical and constructive conversation with diverse theologies of liberation. And with this forward-looking orientation, Barth is treated less as a "founding father"

---

ed. Andrew Dole, Shelli M. Poe, and Kevin Vander Schel (Oxford: Oxford University Press, forthcoming). Although English-language scholarship still awaits a monograph committed entirely to Barth and Hegel, both Bruce McCormack and George Hunsinger have reflected on Barth's appropriation and critique of German idealism. Nicholas Adams has offered insights on their relationship in "Barth and Hegel," in *Wiley Blackwell Companion to Karl Barth*, ed. George Hunsinger and Keith L. Johnson, vol. 2, *Barth in Dialogue* (Oxford: Wiley-Blackwell, 2019), 519–34; and Sigurd Baark offers a number of fascinating claims in *The Affirmations of Reason: On Karl Barth's Speculative Theology* (London: Palgrave Macmillan, 2018).

7. On Barth and Calvin see, inter alia, Cornelis van der Kooi, *As in a Mirror: John Calvin and Karl Barth on Knowing God: A Diptych*, trans. Donald Mader (Leiden: Brill, 2005), and Randall C. Zachman, "Barth and Reformation Theology," in *The Oxford Handbook of Karl Barth*, 101–15. On Protestant scholasticism, see Rinse H. Reeling Brouwer, *Karl Barth and Post-Reformation Orthodoxy* (London: Routledge, 2015). And on Barth and a central confessional document, see Hanna Reichel, *Theologie als Bekenntnis. Karl Barths kontextuelle Lektüre des Heidelberger Katechismus* (Göttingen: Vandenhoeck & Ruprecht, 2015).

8. See, inter alia, Eugene Rogers, Jr., *Thomas Aquinas and Karl Barth: Sacred Doctrine and the Natural Knowledge of God* (Notre Dame: University of Notre Dame Press, 1995); Amy Marga, *Karl Barth's Dialogue with Catholicism in Göttingen and Münster: Its Significance for His Doctrine of God* (Tübingen: Mohr Siebeck, 2010); *Thomas Aquinas and Karl Barth: An Unofficial Catholic-Protestant Dialogue*, ed. Thomas Joseph White and Bruce L. McCormack (Grand Rapids: Eerdmans, 2013); Paul Dafydd Jones, "Barth and Anselm: God, Christ, and the Atonement," *International Journal of Systematic Theology* 12, no. 3 (2010): 257–82; idem, "Barth and Anselm," in *Wiley Blackwell Companion to Karl Barth*, vol. 2, 435–48; George Hunsinger, "Karl Barth's Christology: Its Basic Chalcedonian Character," in *The Cambridge Companion to Karl Barth*, ed. John Webster (Cambridge: Cambridge University Press, 2000), 127–42; Matt Jenson, *The Gravity of Sin: Augustine, Luther, and Barth on Homo Incurvatus Se* (London: T&T Clark, 2006); and Tom Greggs, *Barth, Origen, and Universal Salvation: Restoring Particularity* (Oxford: Oxford University Press, 2009).

of twentieth-century Protestant theology and more as a resource for thinking theologically, critically, and politically in the twenty-first century. Can *The Epistle to the Romans*, the *Church Dogmatics*, and related texts connect with scholarship that trains its sights on longstanding structures of oppression and discrimination and, concomitantly, affiliates the age-old project of faith seeking understanding with present-day struggles for justice? Are such texts a help or hindrance for those who would link the historic concerns of Christian faith with progressive politics? Or, to make the point more bluntly: What does Basel have to do with Black theology? What does Basel have to do with South American theology? With feminist, womanist, and queer theologies? With Latinx theology? With theologies that reckon with life in the Global South? With ecotheology? With theologies of disability? With new movements of radical political protest?

Liberationist projects, we hurry to add, clearly do not *need* Barth to succeed. Most often, they have flourished when taking leave of European authors and drawing inspiration from their own resources (exegetical, doctrinal, experiential, ethical, sexual, etc.). And certainly it would be a mistake to read this volume as suggesting that liberationist perspectives are quietly waiting for Barth's endorsement—an external affirmation that would finally secure them the ecclesial and academic "respectability" they have long sought after. Indeed, it is important to concede that liberationist theologians may well have sound reasons to hold Barth at a distance. The sheer volume of Barth's writings, with many installments of the *Gesamtausgabe* yet to be translated and over a dozen additional volumes to be added in coming years, is one factor. But that is hardly the only issue. Does not Barth studies appear, at least at first glance, to be a decidedly esoteric field of study, one that is more fascinated by intertextual analysis, metaphysics, and doctrine than concrete material conditions, injustice, and political activism? Does it not appear, at least at first glance, to be dominated by garrulous white males, often of a Reformed persuasion, whose readiness to voice opinions about the *Church Dogmatics* far outstrips their willingness to confront hegemonic operations of power? And is this not all in sync with Barth's regressive views on sex, gender, and sexuality, his uneven understanding of colonization, his reluctance to theorize race, and his sometimes-dismissive attitude toward non-Christian religions?

Complementary to these particular concerns, arguably, is a broader assumption that cuts across Barth studies and liberationist scholarship: namely, that Barth's theology and liberation theologies are too different to be brought into productive conversation—that these fields of study simply run along diverging tracks. On one side, it is supposed, one finds a deep wariness toward insights that originate from *any* particular community, paired with a determination to foreground the event of revelation as it is refracted through the biblical witness; on the other, one finds a determination to ground theological reflection in various kinds of "subjugated knowledge," birthed in the midst of communal struggle. On one side, it is supposed, there is an unembarrassed delight in extended dialogues with the "greats" of the Western philosophical and political tradition; on the other, a sense that conversation with such "greats" diverts attention from those often rendered voiceless in theological inquiry: the poor and the disenfranchised, women and children, the disabled, people of color, those who identify as queer and trans*. On one side, it is supposed, there is a frank embrace of "regular dogmatics" and the complex task of parsing and connecting doctrinal loci;[9] on the other, a deep suspicion of the protocols of what is sometimes dubbed T-theology—"theology that wants to impose and keep in place a sexual-economic-religious system that does not have the capacity to wrestle with the complexity of people's lives" and functions as a "grand imperial narrative of power."[10] And so on.

Needless to say, this volume cannot summarily dispel the misgivings that some have about Barth. And it will certainly not attempt to apologize for Barth's failings, just as it will not attempt to downplay his theological gifts—or, for that matter, the failings and gifts of any thinker considered in the pages to come. But it does seek to challenge the assumption that Barth and liberation theology have little, if anything, to say to another. There is no need to presume incommensurability here, nor any need to treat differences in theological "method" (a term that liberationists and Barth might well baulk at) as a reason to discourage a conversation before it has a chance to launch. We believe, in fact, that the following chapters disclose something of the exciting possibilities that arise when Barth and various kinds of liberationist inquiry are brought together. They demonstrate that Barth need not be fetishized as an ecclesial and academic "authority" but can rather be read as one voice that sounds among many others—received as an intellect whose determination to set about "thinking and speaking in responsibility and openness *to all sides*" makes him a worthy interlocutor for those who seek new kinds of responsibility and openness in the third decade of this fast-moving century.[11] And if, at the end of the day, many liberationist thinkers still choose to forgo Barth, we suspect that those in the world of Barth studies have a great deal to gain. After all, if the ongoing Barth renaissance in English-language circles has a meaningful future—which is to say: a future beyond parochialism, a future that contributes to the pluralization of the academy, and a future that renders Christian communities more engaged with the pursuit of justice and peace—it cannot just be orthodox and modern. It must be orthodox, modern, and *liberative*.[12]

II.

The chapters that comprise this book, of course, are not entirely without precedent. Over the last sixty years, several scholars with liberationist commitments have

---

9. Karl Barth, *Göttingen Dogmatics*, vol. 1, ed. Hannelotte Reiffen, trans. Geoffrey W. Bromiley (Grand Rapids: Eerdmans, 1991), 38.

10. Linn Marie Tonstad, *Queer Theology: Beyond Apologetics* (Eugene: Cascade, 2018), 85. Tonstad is drawing here on the pioneering work of Marcella Althaus-Reid.

11. Karl Barth, *Gespräche 1964–1968*, ed. Eberhard Busch (Zurich: TVZ, 1995), 545.

12. We are here expanding McCormack's formulation; see, of course, *Orthodox and Modern*.

engaged Barth's theology, and have done so with varying degrees of criticism, skepticism, and appreciation. And while the precise nature of the relationship between Barth and any given thinker or group cannot be tackled at length in this introduction, a brief glance at some sites of interaction may prove useful.

Looking beyond Marquardt's controversial thesis about the relationship between Barth's theology and socialism, a number of German theologians in the late 1960s and 1970s were alert to the possibility of connecting Barth and liberation theology. One can read Jürgen Moltmann's *Theology of Hope* as initiating a line of reflection that sought to draw out the liberative implications of Barth's theology, while simultaneously extending and developing a number of Barth's doctrinal claims. It seems possible, too, to read works by Ernst Käsemann, Hans Küng, and Dorothee Sölle as indirect, ad hoc attempts to develop a connection between Barthian motifs and political concerns—attempts that ran alongside a more direct appropriation of Barth's thought by Helmut Gollwitzer.[13] A little later, and granted that Dietrich Bonhoeffer was a typical point of reference for South African scholars, a number of theologians interacted with Barth's work in rich ways when engaged in their struggle against Apartheid: Allan Boesak, Charles Villa-Vincencio, Takatso Mofokeng, Dirk Smit, and John de Gruchy.[14] And this line of analysis continues

13. On Gollwitzer, who is finally becoming more well known in English-language circles, see the instructive text of W. Travis McMaken, *Our God Loves Justice: An Introduction to Helmut Gollwitzer* (Minneapolis: Fortress, 2017).

14. See here Charles Villa-Vicencio, *On Reading Karl Barth in South Africa* (Grand Rapids: Eerdmans, 1988); Takatso A. Mofokeng, *The Crucified Among the Crossbearers: Towards a Black Christology* (Kampen: J. H. Kok, 1983), 112–85; Dirk J. Smit, "Barmen and Belhar in Conversation: A South African Perspective," in *Essays on Being Reformed: Collected Essays 3*, ed. Robert Vosloo (Stellenbosch: SunMedia, 2009), 325–36; idem, "Barths Krisentheologie in Kontexten radikaler Transformation lesen? Eine südafrikanische Reflexion," in *Theologie im Umbruch der Moderne*, ed. Georg Pfleiderer (Zürich: TVZ, 2014), 158–68; John W. de Gruchy, "The Reception and Relevance of Karl Barth in South Africa: Reflections on 'Doing Theology' in South Africa After Sixty Years in Conversation with Barth," *Stellenbosch Theological Journal* 5, no. 1 (2019): 11–28; idem, "Toward a Reformed Theology of Liberation: A Retrieval of Reformed Symbols in the Struggle for Justice," in *Toward the Future of Reformed Theology*, ed. David Willis and Michael Welker (Grand Rapids: Eerdmans, 1999), 103–19. Allan A. Boesak, a prominent Reformed South African theologian, engaged Barth's theology in a much more ad hoc and critical way, but he was also heavily influenced by those who were shaped by Barth's theology through their own training in America and Europe. And he has offered some meaningful and constructive engagements with Barth's theology in recent years; see, for instance, "Poverty, Wealth, and Ecology: A Theological Perspective," in *Living Theology: Essays Presented to Dirk J. Smit on his Sixtieth Birthday*, ed. Len Hansen, Nico Koopman, and Robert Vosloo (Wellington: Bible Media, 2011), 569–84.

into the present, particularly in the writings of Rothney S. Tshaka (a contributor to this volume), Marthinus Havenga, and Martin Laubscher.[15]

With respect to North American scholarship, George Hunsinger's edited volume, *Karl Barth and Radical Politics* (1976), has often served as a valuable introduction to debates inspired by Marquardt's work and a starting point for discussions of Barth's (possible) contributions to progressive political theology.[16] While this volume was followed by some interesting work in the 1980s and 1990s,[17] it joined a broader conversation that bears intriguingly on the reception of Barth's work by a number of South American theologians. Prior to Hunsinger's volume, John MacKay, president of Princeton Theological Seminary from 1936 to 1959, had done much to strengthen the relationship between the Presbyterian Church and Latin America. MacKay was instrumental in bringing Paul Lehmann, the famous American friend of Dietrich Bonhoeffer, to Princeton Theological Seminary in 1947; and Lehmann, who later moved on to teach at Union Theological Seminary in New York City, taught and influenced several liberation theologians who formed their theologies in the context of concrete struggles in Latin America, sometimes with explicit reference to Barth.[18] If, as with Germany and South Africa, the lines of

---

15. See Rothney S. Tshaka, *Confessional Theology? A Critical Analysis of the Theology of Karl Barth and its Significance for the Belhar Confession* (Cambridge: Cambridge Scholars Publishing, 2010); idem, "'Doing Theology as Though Nothing Had Happened': Reading Karl Barth's Confessional Theology in Zimbabwe Today," *HTS Teologiese Studies/Theological Studies* 72, no. 1 (2016): a3028; Marthinus Havenga, "Worship as Primary Ethical Act: Barth on Romans 12," *HTS Teologiese Studies/Theological Studies* (2020): a5824; Marthinus Havenga and Robert Vosloo, "On Knowing the Time: Temporality, Love and Confession in Barth's *Der Römerbrief*," *Pistis & Praxis* 14, no. 1 (2022): 115-32; and Martin Laubscher, "Reforming Our Barth?" *Stellenbosch Theological Journal* 3, no. 2 (2017): 181-98.

16. See *Karl Barth and Radical Politics*, ed. George Hunsinger (Philadelphia: Westminster Press, 1976). For the revised and expanded second edition, see *Karl Barth and Radical Politics*, ed. George Hunsinger, 2nd edn (Eugene: Cascade, 2017). Also important are the essays collected in George Hunsinger, *Disruptive Grace: Studies in the Theology of Karl Barth* (Grand Rapids: Eerdmans, 2000), esp. 21-129; and *Conversational Theology: Essays on Ecumenical, Postliberal and Political Themes, with Special Reference to Karl Barth* (London: T&T Clark, 2015).

17. See, for instance, Daniel Migliore, "Jesus Christ, the Reconciling Liberator: The Confession of 1967 and Theologies of Liberation," *Journal of Presbyterian History* 61, no. 1 (1983): 33-42; George Hunsinger, "Karl Barth and Liberation Theology," *The Journal of Religion* 63, no. 2 (1983): 247-63; and Josiah Young, "Betwixt and Between Neoorthodoxy and Afrocentrism: A Simple Call to Freedom," *Journal of Religious Thought* 50, no. 1 (1994): 72-80.

18. See Sergio Martínez Arce, *Karl Barth y su Doctrina de Palabra de Dios* (Mantanzas: Seminario Evangelico de Teologia, 1957); idem, *La doctrina de justificación según Karl Barth*, Círculo Teológico no. 16 (Matanzas: Seminario Evangelico de Teologia, 1964); idem, "Cristo y la liberación Social," in *Teología en revolución, volumen I* (Matanzas: Centro

connection here are difficult to trace, those very lines have enormous importance, not least because they disturb easy assumptions about *who* engages in the study of Barth, and their reasons for doing so.

The most well-known point of connection between Barth and liberation theology in the United States, however, is James Cone. After writing his dissertation on Barth's anthropology, Cone's first two books drew frequently on Barth in order to challenge white supremacism, while also offering a Barth-like account of the ongoing lordship of the risen Christ.[19] Indeed, as Cone himself later noted (and this point is explored skillfully by Tyler B. Davis and Ry O. Siggelkow in Chapter 12), these works sought to reprise something of Barth's past in North America's present, albeit for different purposes: just as "Barth had turned liberal theology up-side-down, I [Cone] wanted to turn him right-side-up with a focus on the black struggle in particular and oppressed people generally."[20] And if Cone's later work does not engage Barth with comparable intensity, it is noteworthy that Cone's early engagement with Barth—as well as Cone's later decision to draw more from African American traditions and less from European scholarship—has not made much of an impact on Barth studies. Even so, a few scholars have continued to investigate Cone's early use of Barth, and some in-process research projects aim to re-connect Barth and Cone for constructive purposes.[21]

---

de Información y Estudio "Augusto Cotto," 1988), 45–56. José Míguez Bonino was Paul Lehmann's student at Union Theological Seminary (1958–60) who was heavily influenced by Barth's theology. See his "Introducción" to Karl Barth, *Introducción a la teologí evangélica* (Buenos Aires: Ediciones La Aurora, 1986), 11–25. See also Paul Louis Lehmann, "Karl Barth, Theologian of Permanent Revolution," *Union Seminary Quarterly Review* 28 (1972/1973): 67–81; and idem, *The Transfiguration of Politics* (New York: Harper & Row, 1975), 42–6. For more on Lehmann's theology and its contribution to radical politics and liberation theology, readers should consult *The Revolutionary Gospel: Paul Lehmann and the Direction of Theology Today*, ed. Nancy J. Duff, Ry O. Siggelkow, and Brandon Watson (Minneapolis: Fortress, forthcoming).

19. James H. Cone, "The Doctrine of Man in the Theology of Karl Barth" (PhD diss., Northwestern University, 1965); idem, *Black Theology and Black Power* (Maryknoll: Orbis, 1989 [orig. published 1969]); and idem, *Black Theology of Liberation* (Maryknoll: Orbis, 1997). See also Theo Witvliet, *The Way of the Black Messiah: The Hermeneutical Challenge of Black Theology as a Theology of Liberation* (London: SCM, 1987), 163–77.

20. James H. Cone, *My Soul Looks Back* (Maryknoll: Orbis, 1986), 45.

21. See Raymond Carr, "Barth and Cone in Dialogue on Revelation and Freedom: An Analysis of James Cone's Critical Appropriation of 'Barthian' Theology" (PhD diss., Graduate Theological Union, 2011) and Beverly E. Mitchell, "Karl Barth and James Cone: The Question of Liberative Faith and Ideology" (PhD diss., Boston College, 1999). Jason Oliver Evans, a PhD student at the University of Virginia, is working on a doctoral dissertation that draws on Barth and the early Cone for liberative ends: "If God Be For Us: Toward a Theology of Atonement and Christian Life from a Black Queer Perspective."

The contributions to this volume, then, do not emerge from a vacuum. There is a history here—a history, we suspect, that merits close and critical attention in years to come. And there are, of course, more recent works that engage Barth's theology in view of liberationist concerns, with particular interest in issues of race, gender, sexuality, and life in the Global South.[22] But it is clear that much more can and should be done. It is not particularly controversial to acclaim Barth as one of the most important European Christian thinkers of the twentieth century. Nor is it controversial, we think, to view the emergence of liberation theology as one of the most consequential developments in the world of late modern Christian thought. The challenge is to try and think Barth and liberation together, and to do so in a way that the distinctive contributions of both can factor into a theological imagination that is fitted to deal with the complexities of the present and future.

III.

Our first chapter, Luis Rivera-Pagán's "Karl Barth and the Origins of Liberation Theology," provides a historical and intellectual overview of liberation theology, broadly speaking, before engaging South American and North American Black liberation theologies at close quarters. Rivera-Pagán identifies several points of connection between Barth and later thinkers, while also pointing to the complex relationship between North American scholarship on Barth—particularly as undertaken at Princeton Theological Seminary—and theology in the Global South. Something of the benefits that accrue when Barth is read with a "forward-look" to the latter half of the twentieth century and the early decades of the twenty-first century, then, are found in the opening chapter to this volume.

---

22. See Jaime Ronaldo Balboa, "*Church Dogmatics*, Natural Theology, and the Slippery Slope of *Geschlecht*: A Constructivist-Gay Liberationist Reading of Barth," *Journal of the American Academy of Religion* 66 (1998): 771–90; Emmanuel Gerrit Singgih, "Toward a Postcolonial Interpretation of Romans 13:1–7: Karl Barth, Robert Jewett, and the Context of Reformation in Present Day Indonesia," *Asia Theological Journal* 23, no. 1 (2009): 111–22; J. Kameron Carter, "An Unlikely Convergence: W. E. B. Du Bois, Karl Barth, and the Problem of the Imperial God-Man," *New Centennial Review* 11, no. 3 (2012): 167–224; Daniel D. Lee, *Double Particularity: Karl Barth, Contextuality, and Asian American Theology* (Minneapolis: Fortress, 2017); Tim Hartman, *Theology After Colonization: Bediako, Barth, and the Future of Theological Reflection* (South Bend: University of Notre Dame Press, 2019); Willie Jennings, "Barth and the Racial Imaginary," in *The Oxford Handbook of Karl Barth*, 497–516; and Paul Dafydd Jones, "Liberation Theology and 'Democratic Futures': By Way of Karl Barth and Friedrich Schleiermacher," *Political Theology* 10, no. 2 (2009): 261–85. During the time this introduction was written, a journal volume was published in Portuguese on Barth's public theology from a global perspective, edited by Jefferson Zeferino, Waldir Souza, and Rudolf Von Sinner: "Karl Barth e a Teologia Pública," *Pistis & Praxis* 14, no. 1 (2022): 1–154.

In Chapter 2, "Of Gods and Men, and Wolves—The 'Other Question': Between Projection, Colonial Imagination, and Liberation," Hanna Reichel ruminates on the concept of "the other" in relation to projects of liberation. Through an extensive engagement with Ludwig Feuerbach, Reichel turns to Barth's infamous dictum of God as "the Wholly Other" and considers how Barth's doctrine of reconciliation might be refigured to encourage right relations between human beings. God emerges, hereby, as one who is "an Other othered both *for* us and *by* us; the one true non-othering Other othered for all others, so that we may other each other no more." Via an engagement with Enrique Dussel and Gayatri Chakravorty Spivak, among others, the old topic of Barth's relationship to Feuerbach thus gains new significance. It points toward a planetary vision of sociality and solidarity that challenges the dehumanizing agenda of colonialism.

Faye Bodley-Dangelo offers an incisive critical analysis of Barth's views of gender in Chapter 3, "The Generative Female Body and the Analogy of Faith in Karl Barth's *Church Dogmatics*." Through a series of close readings, Bodley-Dangelo shows how the female body is a persistent *problem* in Barth's descriptions of God's activity. Most vividly in Barth's doctrine of creation, but also quite evidently in his treatment of Mary, the mother of Jesus, Barth constantly stumbles over the reality and productivity of the female body. And this ought to occasion concern among those of us who hope to forge a positive relationship between Barth's work and feminist and womanist endeavors. Rather than offering a liberative word, Barth's reflections on this issue serve consistently to reinforce patriarchal and unjust social relations.

In Chapter 4, Lisa Powell places Barth into conversation with disability theology. In "The Disabled God and Covenant Ontology," Powell argues that Barth's theology shares many of the concerns found in theologies of disability, particularly Nancy Eiesland's famous text, *The Disabled God*. Recent debates over Barth's "theological ontology" prove particularly significant. If God elects not to exist without us, and if God's self-election is expressed through an act of divine self-determination that makes Christ's concrete history ingredient to the life of God *qua* Word, then it is possible to imagine the "electing God" and "elected human" as the God who receives—and embraces—the disability of the crucified Christ. For all eternity, God stands in solidarity with those whose bodies are non-normal, "broken," and, all too often, held in contempt.

In Chapter 5, Meehyun Chung reflects on the influence of Karl Barth's theology within a Korean context. "Karl Barth and Korean Theology, Past and Present" provides an overview of Barth's response to and navigation of a number of geopolitical conflicts, including the Cold War, the Korean War, and the Hungarian Revolution. Chung concedes that Barth's refusal of absolute moral principles and wariness toward ideological grandstanding frustrated some of his peers. But this stance was rooted in a laudable concern to protect the freedom of God, which went hand in hand with a desire to confront idolatry: an instance of "evangelical impartiality" that doubles as an expression of "prophetic reticence." And this stance, Chung argues, has much to offer Korean feminist theology as it strives to negotiate a divided country.

Hani Hanna offers a political reading of Barth's theology from an Egyptian perspective in Chapter 6, "Karl Barth's Theology of Political Participation: An Egyptian Appropriation." After an instructive overview of the contemporary situation within Egypt and reflections on the Arab Spring, Hanna argues that Barth's work can serve as a resource for rethinking Christian political participation in the Middle East. Barth's famed actualism, which encompasses divine and human beings, is important in this respect. Likewise, Barth's rich vision of human agency. Together, they support a Christian theology that is always-already a political theology—one that frees individuals, not least Egyptian Christians, to engage in meaningful and responsible political activity on behalf of the coming Kingdom.

Rothney S. Tshaka reflects on the potential for Barth to be a resource for current theological discourse in South Africa in Chapter 7. "Karl Barth and Liberation Theologies in South Africa: The Difficulties of Comparison, Conversation, and Constructive Reflection" identifies and praises Barth's socialist commitments, as well as Barth's renowned christocentrism, as vital resources in the fight against those who would justify the subjugation and oppression of Black Africans. But the chapter adopts a more critical line than that taken by Chung and Hanna. In an ecclesial and academic context that remains leery of indigenous African worldviews, Tshaka is not convinced that engaging Barth is the right path forward for South African liberation theology. If there *is* here a liberative word for today—and that is a big "if"—that needs to be set alongside, and perhaps subordinated to, rather different resources.

Chapter 8 is also ambivalent about the relationship between Barth's work and South African liberation theology. In "Liberation Theology in a South African Context: Does Karl Barth Have Anything to Offer Here?" Graham Ward considers at length the particular social context in which liberation theology has unfolded and developed in South Africa, while noting, like Tshaka, that Bonhoeffer's work has often been preferred to Barth's. Ward also identifies a fascinating dogmatic quandary. While Barth's doctrine of reconciliation bears witness to the reality of God's redemptive activity for all of humanity, that same doctrine underrates human negotiations of context—precisely what is needed to support those struggling for liberation in South Africa today. The wry question in Ward's title is thus left hanging.

Chapter 9, by David Clough, is "Using Barth 'to Justify Doing Nothing': James Cone's Unanswered Challenge to the Whiteness of Barth Studies." Clough opens by rehearsing Cone's critique of white theologians who ignored or trivialized the suffering of the Black community in theological reflection and shows that this critique has not—after over fifty years!—been taken seriously. For the most part, Barth studies remains captive to the ideology of whiteness. It continues to look askance at the concrete conditions of racial discrimination in the United States and, in so doing, lends support to a racist status quo. Gesturing toward what he hopes will be a rather different future, Clough then considers the complex relationship between Christian theology, race, and animals. He seeks to help readers to appreciate how disregard for nonhuman creatures goes hand in hand with racism toward individuals and communities of color, and he encourages scholars—

Barthian and otherwise—to recommit themselves to the task of dismantling the transnational project of white supremacism.

Brian Bantum's "Clothed in Flesh: The Artist, Liberation, and the Future of Barthian Theology," which comprises Chapter 10 of this volume, argues that Barth's commentary on the Epistle to the Romans offers a liberative-aesthetic approach to theological writing, one which might contribute to a "literary theology" that reckons seriously with the ambiguities of the quotidian. While Bantum initially develops this point through engagements with sculpture and painting, the later stages of his chapter take a constructive turn. Bantum moves closer to literature and poetry when he calls Barth studies "to rediscover its liberative hope and its constructive, performative modality and edge." Authors like Toni Morrison, he suggests, might join Barth in helping us to formulate a theology that attends to the everyday—a theology that begins "to chart a path or tender an invitation for theologies that can speak to violence, marginalization, and the world in general in ways that are not simply 'accessible' or simplified, but *incarnate*."

In Chapter 11, "Thelonious Monk, Icon of The Eschaton: Karl Barth, James Cone, and the 'Impossible-Possibility' of a Theology of Freedom," Raymond Carr provides a musical complement to Bantum's literary theology. He argues, specifically, that the rich musical output of jazz pianist Thelonious Monk might serve as a surprising bridge between Barth and James Cone: an inspiration for an outlook that attends both to the "objectivity" of God (which so fascinated Barth) and to Cone's interest in the "subjective" experiences of Black Americans. If this outlook is hard to imagine, the rewards on offer are significant: a theology that "joyfully engages in solidarity with Barth *and* Cone through the musical witness of Monk."

Tyler B. Davis and Ry O. Siggelkow continue to engage Cone and Barth in Chapter 12. "Turning Barth Right-Side-Up: James Cone and the Risk of a Contextual Theology of Revelation" reads the 1967 Detroit Rebellion as a decisive and life-altering event in Cone's theological development. The authors argue that this event complicated Cone's earlier, Barth-inspired aversion to natural theology, and prompted him to risk identifying God's being and action with certain concrete, worldly events. And that Cone adopted and maintained this line of thought despite the protestations of an otherwise-sympathetic crowd of "left-wing" Barthians discloses something of the challenge of doing Christian theology "in the midst of the world": the obligation to "hear the promise of the gospel in context" and to think clearly about how God is acting, in the here-and-now, to defeat evil and effect liberation.

In the final chapter, "Liberation Theology and Karl Barth in the Shadow of the Alt-Right: White Supremacism, Political Protest, and Ecclesiology after Charlottesville," Paul Dafydd Jones reflects both on the far-right violence inflicted upon the residents of Charlottesville in 2017 and on the brave resistance of religious and nonreligious activists. With a consideration of "religion" and an analysis of the place of experience in theological reflection in hand, Jones asks if Barth's ecclesiology—and also Barth's account of the Kingdom that is coming—might be reworked to include occasions of political protest, offered in opposition to far-right hate.

IV.

More could be said about many of the issues raised in this introduction. That is especially the case with respect to the history of Barth studies in the United States from the 1970s onward; it is also the case with respect to the way that Barth's work has been received, positively and negatively, in other regions of the globe. And more could be said, too, about dogmatic issues that are considered only briefly (or not at all) in the chapters ahead, yet which exercise Barth and liberationist thinkers alike: eschatology, prayer, baptism and the Eucharist, ecumenical and confessional statements, the relationship between Israel and the church, the scope of redemption, and so on. But it seems best to allow the chapters of this volume to set the terms for further discussion, multifaceted and multidimensional as it must be. So we will content ourselves with a concluding remark about the broader task of theological reflection in the present.

In refusing a sharp differentiation between systematic and liberationist thinking, one can read this volume as pursuing a new style of theological reflection—one that makes no apologies for combining forthright dogmatic claims with manifestly progressive ethical and political stances; one that supposes that theology "after Barth" must always be a theology that pursues liberation in all spheres of creaturely life. This style of reflection certainly does not presume that Western philosophical traditions are the most appropriate (or best) conversation partner for dogmatic work. Rather, it places those traditions alongside insights drawn from the social sciences, from critical studies of race, from new analyses of sex, gender, and sexuality, from the arts, and from the everyday. And this style of reflection does not presume, either, that the riches of the Christian tradition will always be found in "heights" of academic and ecclesial achievement. Rather, it juxtaposes and conditions those "heights" with the insights drawn from unstudied and undervalued communities and individuals, mindful that "God chose what is weak in the world to shame the strong" and cognizant that the "last will be first, and the first will be last" (1 Cor. 1:28 and Matt. 20:16). It does so, too, with due awareness of the churches' support for and entanglement in various structures of domination, while still believing, sometimes against the odds, that Christian faith and praxis might be reimagined, reinvigorated, and reworked in ways that render the world more just and peaceful. Finally, in that this style of reflection looks toward a time in which the "power of the Resurrection" brings about "the disturbing and the upsetting of the equilibrium" (RII: 207) and thus initiates "the absolute transfiguration of all creation,"[23] it lives on the hope that theological reflection today might, in fits and starts, be both troublesome and edifying— troublesome and edifying in ways that pay homage to Barth *and* the expanding tradition of liberation theology.

---

23. M. Shawn Copeland, *Knowing Christ Crucified: The Witness of African American Religious Experience* (Maryknoll: Orbis, 2018), 155.

Chapter 1

KARL BARTH AND THE ORIGINS OF LIBERATION THEOLOGY

Luis N. Rivera-Pagán

> We have for once learnt to see the great events of world history from below, from the perspective of the outcast, the suspects, the maltreated, the powerless, the oppressed, the reviled—in short, from the perspective of those who suffer.
>
> —Dietrich Bonhoeffer[1]

In this brief essay, I will consider four issues: the historical and intellectual context of liberation theology, early Latin American liberation theology, early North American Black theology, and, finally, Karl Barth as precursor of liberation theology. The goal is to show how Barth's work can be positioned within a somewhat different history of twentieth-century theology, one less interested in Barth's relationship with the Reformation, Friedrich Schleiermacher, and liberal Protestantism, and more interested in setting Barth in the context of reformist and revolutionary movements in the latter half of the twentieth century.

Liberation Theology: Its Historical and Intellectual Origins

Liberation theology was the unforeseen *enfant terrible* in the academic and ecclesial realms of theological production during the last decades of the twentieth century. It brought to the conversation not only a new theme—liberation—but also a new perspective on doing theology and a novel way of referring to God's being and action in history. Its project to reconfigure the interplay between religious studies, history, and politics soon became a meaningful topic of analysis and dialogue in the general theological discourse. Many scholars perceive in its emergence a drastic epistemological rupture, a radical change in paradigm, and a significant shift in both the ecclesial and social roles of theology.

---

1. Dietrich Bonhoeffer, *Letters and Papers from Prison*, ed. Eberhard Bethge (London: Folio Society, 2000), 16.

Its origins are diverse and reach beyond the realms of the theological and ecclesiastical. One important source, neglected by some accounts, was the complex constellation of liberation struggles during the 1960s and early 1970s. It was a time of social turmoil, when many things seemed out of joint: there was a strong antiwar movement (directed particularly against American military intervention in Vietnam and the global nuclear threat); a spread of decolonization movements, all over the "Third World"; the feminist struggle against patriarchy and sexism; a robust challenge to racial bigotry; the Stonewall rebellion (June 1969) against discrimination toward those who identify as queer; student protests in Paris, Prague, Mexico, and New York in opposition to repressive states of all stripes; and guerilla insurgencies and social unrest in many Latin American nations. Many agents of social protest adopted the title of "liberation movement" as a means of public self-presentation, while "Fronts of national liberation" flourished in the Third World.[2]

Another significant factor regarding the intellectual origins of liberation theology was the development of a nondogmatic Marxism that read Marx's texts as an ethical critique of human oppression and as a projection of a utopian, non-oppressive future, something akin to a kingdom of freedom. This heterodox reading of Marx, exemplified by authors like the German philosopher Ernst Bloch, made possible something considered largely unthinkable until then: a constructive and affirmative dialogue between theology and Marxism, located at the margins of church and of party hierarchies, as both looked beyond rigid forms of orthodoxy. Bloch's *Atheismus im Christentum* (1968) is particularly instructive on this front.[3] It set forth a hermeneutic that interpreted the biblical texts as a struggle between the voices of the oppressors and those of the oppressed, and provocatively asserted that whoever wants to be a good Marxist should constantly read the Bible (and, vice versa, whoever wants to be a good Christian should have Marx as bedside reading).

Other iconoclastic authors like Herbert Marcuse and Franz Fanon were passionately read from Buenos Aires to Berlin, from Berkeley to Nairobi, and

---

2. The most famous of them, and a model for many, were the Algerian Front of National Liberation, established in 1954, which led the revolt against French colonial domination (brilliantly depicted in Gillo Pontecorvo's 1966 film, *Battle of Algiers*); the National Liberation Front for South Vietnam, created in December 1960, which successfully fought against the division of Vietnam and the military invasion of the United States; and the Palestine Liberation Organization, founded in 1964 to organize the struggle for Palestinian statehood. See Alistair Horne, *A Savage War of Peace: Algeria 1954–1962* (New York: Penguin, 1987); Frances Fitzgerald, *Fire in the Lake: The Vietnamese and the Americans in Vietnam* (Boston: Little, Brown and Company, 1972); and Helena Cobban, *The Palestinian Liberation Organisation: People, Power and Politics* (Cambridge: Cambridge University Press, 1984).

3. Ernst Bloch, *Atheismus im Christentum* (Frankfurt: Suhrkamp Verlag, 1968).

1. Karl Barth and the Origins of Liberation Theology

with eyes that looked far beyond the walls of the academy.[4] Exiled from Brazil, Paulo Freire delivered scathing critiques of traditional educational systems and promoted a pedagogy for the liberation of the oppressed.[5] Martin Luther King, Jr., and Ernesto "Che" Guevara, meanwhile, became emblematic icons and martyrs of those turbulent times. Paul Éluard's poem *Liberté*, recited and sang in many languages, became a poetic hymn that captured the passions and intentions of many:

> By the power of the word
> I regain my life
> I was born to know you
> And to name you
> Liberty[6]

Within the churches, important processes were also underway. To the surprise of many, Pope John XXIII summoned the Second Vatican Council. Progressive Roman Catholic theologians now consider Vatican II an important turning point in the modern history of their church.[7] According to their interpretation, the council had three main objectives:

(a) To change the attitude of the Roman Catholic Church toward the modern post-Enlightenment intellectual world from censure and condemnation to openness and dialogue. The Italian word *aggiornamento* ("bringing up to date") became the watchword of those seeking to reform the church.
(b) To heal the fragmentation of Christianity by positioning the Roman Catholic Church within the emerging ecumenical movement. Delegates from Protestant and Orthodox churches were invited to observe the proceedings of the council.[8] A series of bilateral and multilateral dialogues began between Rome and other Christian denominations.
(c) To face the plight of a world marked by suffering violence, oppression, and injustice with honesty and compassion. The council took place in a global context sundered by national liberation struggles, civil wars, and the painful gap between the haves and the have-nots. The quest for peace and justice,

---

4. Herbert Marcuse, *An Essay on Liberation* (Boston: Beacon, 1969); Franz Fanon, *The Wretched of the Earth* (New York: Grove Press, 1965).

5. Paulo Freire, *Educação como prática da liberdade* (Rio de Janeiro: Paz e Terra, 1967). See also idem, *Pedagogía del oprimido* (Montevideo: Tierra Nueva, 1968).

6. "Et par le pouvoir d'un mot/Je recommence ma vie/Je suis né pour te connaître/Pour te nommer/ Liberté."

7. See *Vatican Council II: The Basic Sixteen Documents: Constitutions, Decrees, Declarations*, ed. Austin P. Flannery (Northport: Costello Publishing, 1996).

8. See *Dialogue on the Way: Protestants Report from Rome on the Vatican Council*, ed. George A. Lindbeck (Minneapolis: Augsburg, 1965).

concomitantly, was conceived as an essential dimension of the church's presence in the world.

Indeed, John XXIII's 1963 encyclical *Pacem in terris*, published in the context of that conciliar process, seemed to be another sign of renewal, favoring a shift away from anathematization and hostility toward the modern world and promoting a spirit of dialogue and solidarity. Such ecclesiastical openness was accompanied by several theological projects that seemed to shape an alternative way of looking at social conflicts.[9] An attempt was made to configure a "political theology" as a way to facilitate a creative dialogue with Marxism and post-Enlightenment secular ideologies.[10]

Latin American Liberation Theology

Vatican II was followed by regional synods of bishops. The most famous of them was the general meeting of Latin American Roman Catholic bishops that took place from August 26 to September 6, 1968, in the Colombian city of Medellín. To the amazement of many observers, the Roman Catholic Church, which the radical intelligentsia of the continent had considered an ideological bulwark for maintaining social inequities, now made a decisive pastoral shift. It identified solidarity with the poor and destitute as a central concern.

If Vatican II opened a theological dialogue with modern rationality, then, Medellín was perceived as a prophetic convocation that challenged poverty, inequality, and oppression. If Vatican II was mainly concerned with the gap between the church and secular modernity, Medellín was more concerned with the scandal of social injustice in a Christian continent. In a crucial section of their final resolutions, the Latin American bishops explicitly linked Christian faith with the project of historical and social liberation:

> The Latin American bishops cannot remain indifferent in the face of the tremendous social injustices existent in Latin America, which keep the majority of our peoples in dismal poverty that in many cases becomes inhuman wretchedness.... A deafening cry pours from the throats of millions of men and women asking their pastors for a liberation that reaches them from nowhere else.... Christ, our savior, not only loved the poor ... he centered his mission in announcing liberation to the poor.[11]

---

9. See esp. Jürgen Moltmann, *Theologie der Hoffnung* (München: Chr. Kaiser Verlag, 1966) and Johann Baptist Metz, *Zur Theologie der Welt* (Mainz: Matthias-Grünewald Verlag, 1968).

10. See Dorothee Sölle, *Politische Theologie. Auseinandersetzung mit Rudolf Bultmann* (Stuttgart: Kreuz-Verlag, 1971).

11. *Liberation Theology: A Documentary History*, ed. Alfred T. Hennelly (Maryknoll: Orbis, 1992), 114 and 116. Translation slightly amended.

To be sure, the Medellín conference was a meeting of bishops, not theologians. But several Roman Catholic theologians perceived the final documents and the general tone emerging from the conference as allowing the possibility of rethinking the theological enterprise from the perspective of the liberation of the poor and downtrodden.[12] Prior to the Medellín meeting, in July 1968, Gustavo Gutiérrez gave a lecture in Chimbote, Peru, significantly titled "Toward a Theology of Liberation," that established a close connection between spiritual salvation and human liberation.[13] This lecture proved to be a pioneering text for Latin American liberation theology. It also inaugurated Gutiérrez's five decades of fertile theological production. (Indeed, he was already eighty-two years old when, on July 17, 2010, he gave a lecture at Princeton Theological Seminary at the invitation of the Hispanic Theological Initiative.)

In 1971, the first edition of Gutiérrez's most famous book, *Theology of Liberation*, was published. It remains a towering achievement of Latin American theological writing. His triadic understanding of human liberation—liberation from social and economic oppression, history as a process of self-determined humanization, and redemption from sinfulness—quickly gained classic status.[14] Hugo Assmann's book *Opresión-Liberación: Desafío a los cristianos* was also published the same year. Assmann placed the emerging liberation theology in the wider context of the Third World: "The contextual starting point of a 'theology of liberation' is the historical situation of domination experienced by the peoples of the Third World."[15] And Gutiérrez and Assmann were followed by waves of other theologians—Leonardo Boff, José Porfirio Miranda, Juan Luis Segundo, Jon Sobrino, Pablo Richard, Jorge Pixley, among others—whose writings were conceived as expressions of a new intellectual understanding of the faith: liberation theology.[16] Two particularly notable texts, which rocked the placid realm of theological production during the early years of Latin American liberation theology, were José Porfirio Miranda's *Marx y la Biblia* (an important contribution to a liberationist hermeneutics and also sort of a theological companion to Bloch's *Atheismus im Christentum*) and

---

12. See Gustavo Gutiérrez, "The Meaning and Scope of Medellín," in *The Density of the Present: Selected Writings* (Maryknoll: Orbis, 1999), 59–101.

13. This lecture is translated and reproduced in Hennelly, *Liberation Theology*, 62–76.

14. Gustavo Gutiérrez, *Teología de la liberación: perspectivas* (Salamanca: Sígueme, 1973), 67–9.

15. Hugo Assmann, *Opresión-Liberación: Desafío a los cristianos* (Montevideo: Tierra Nueva, 1971), 50.

16. See the important book on the origins of the Latin American liberation theology by Samuel Silva Gotay, *El pensamiento cristiano revolucionario en América Latina y El Caribe: Implicaciones de la teología de la liberación para la sociología de la religión* (Salamanca: Ediciones Sígueme, 1981), translated into Portuguese as *O pensamento cristão revolucionário na América Latina e no Caribe (1960–1973)* (São Paulo: Edições Paulinas, 1985) and into German as *Christentum und Revolution in Lateinamerika und der Karibik: Die Bedeutung der Theologie der Befreiung für eine Soziologie der Religion* (Frankfurt: Peter Lang, 1995).

Juan Luis Segundo's *Liberación de la teología*. Both books offered a direct challenge to scholastic ways of doing theology.[17]

What could be considered the main tenets of this theological movement? I would identify five:

(a) *The retrieval of "subversive memories,"* inscribed in sacred scriptures, sometimes hidden below layers of cultic regulations and doctrinal orthodoxies but never totally effaced. This theological movement also gives hermeneutical and exegetical priority to the Exodus story, understood to be a paradigm of the liberating character of God's actions;[18] to prophetic denunciations of injustice and oppression;[19] and to the confrontations of the historical Jesus with Judean religious authorities and Roman political powers, alongside Jesus' solidarity with the "nobodies" of Judea and Galilee.[20]

(b) *A historical understanding of Jesus's proclamation of God's kingdom.* The kingdom is conceived as referring not to some otherworldly, postmortem realm, but rather to the unceasing hope of a social configuration characterized by justice, solidarity, and freedom. Leonardo Boff and Jon Sobrino, in particular, identified Jesus as the Liberator, thereby recovering the semantic roots of the term "redemption" (the deliverance of a captive or slave).[21] There emerged a Christology attuned to the plight of the indigents and, to use Frantz Fanon's term, to the "wretched of the earth."[22]

(c) *The divine preferential option for the poor, the excluded, and the destitute of this world.* The church must become the church of the poor by sharing the poor's sorrows, hopes, and struggles. Initially the emphasis of the preferential option was socioeconomic, but it was gradually widened to include other categories of social exclusion (indigenous communities, racial and ethnic minorities, women, and sexual orientation).[23]

---

17. José Porfirio Miranda, *Marx y la Biblia* (Salamanca: Ediciones Sígueme, 1972); Juan Luis Segundo, *Liberación de la teología* (Buenos Aires: Ediciones Carlosd Lohlé, 1975).

18. See José Severino Croatto, *Exodus, a Hermeneutics of Freedom* (Maryknoll: Orbis, 1981) and Jorge V. Pixley, *Exodo, una lectura evangélica y popular* (México, DF: Casa Unida de Publicaciones, 1983).

19. Walter J. Houston, *Contending for Justice: Ideologies and Theologies of Social Justice in the Old Testament* (London: T&T Clark, 2006).

20. Jon Sobrino, *La fe en Jesucristo: ensayo desde las víctimas* (San Salvador: UCA, 1999).

21. Leonardo Boff, *Jesus Cristo libertador; ensaio de cristologia crítica para o nosso tempo* (Petrópolis: Editôra Vozes, 1972); Jon Sobrino, *Jesucristo liberador: lectura histórico teológica de Jesús de Nazaret* (San Salvador: UCA, 1991).

22. See here Jules Martínez-Olivieri, *A Visible Witness: Christology, Liberation, and Participation* (Minneapolis: Fortress, 2016).

23. Leonardo Boff, *Igreja, carisma e poder: ensaios de eclesiologia militante* (Petrópolis: Vozes, 1981).

(d) Theology cannot be reduced to an intellectual understanding of the faith; *it must also be a practical commitment for historical transformation.* The category of praxis, partly borrowed from Paulo Freire's pedagogy of liberation, partly an adaptation of Marx's eleventh thesis on Feuerbach ("philosophers have only interpreted the world in various ways; the point, however, is to change it"), acquired normative status.[24] History, understood increasingly as the realm of the perennial struggle against oppressions and exclusions, emerged as the locus for Christian praxis.[25]

(e) God is reconceived not as an immutable and impassible entelechy but, in line with the biblical narratives, as a compassionate Eternal Spirit who hears and pays close attention to the cry of the oppressed and whose action in human history has the redemption of the downtrodden and excluded as its ultimate telos. Herein might be located liberation theology's main theoretical epistemological rupture and reconfiguration: a novel way of thinking about God's being and action in history.[26] Instead of contriving arcane scholastic definitions of the divine essence, *God is named as Liberator.*

Latin American liberation theology also strove to forge a new way of being the church in the world: the base ecclesial communities were understood as seeds for reconfiguring the church as "the people of God." These congregations were considered expressions of the church's solidarity with the poor and oppressed in their aspirations for liberation and the promotion of human flourishing. They produced an impressive wealth of liturgical, musical, exegetical, homiletical, ethical, and literary resources in order to promote social and human emancipation. Their key theme was historical transformation. Leonardo Boff even advocated for a new genesis of the church.[27]

However, many in the hierarchical church, including some members of the Roman Curia, viewed these potential disruptions of episcopal authority with marked distrust and moved to restrict the autonomy of some Latin American theologians. Rome was also concerned about the consequences of this new theological perspective for orthodoxy. A protracted confrontation emerged, which continues into the present.

The political backstory to this confrontation, moreover, should not go untold, because it draws the connection between the broad theological currents I have described and a number of important historical occurrences. Since their colonial

---

24. Karl Marx, "Theses on Feuerbach," in *The Marx-Engels Reader*, 2nd edn, ed. Robert C. Tucker (New York: W. W. Norton & Co., 1978), 145.

25. See *Praxis cristiana y producción teológica*, ed. Jorge V. Pixley and Jean-Pierre Bastian (Salamanca: Ediciones Sígueme, 1979).

26. Jonathan Pimentel Chacón, *Modelos de Dios en las teologías latinoamericanas* (Heredia: Universidad Nacional de Costa Rica, 2008).

27. Leonardo Boff, *Eclesiogênese: as comunidades eclesiais de base reinventam a Igreja* (Petrópolis: Editôra Vozes, 1977).

inception, an official linkage between the state and the Roman Catholic Church has characterized Latin American nations. The royal patronage exercised by the Iberian crown entailed the acknowledgment by the church of the sovereignty and authority of the metropolitan state, but it was paired with the state's recognition of the Roman Catholic Church's primacy in religious affairs. It was sometimes the source of acute conflict, especially when the ethical conscience of bishops, priests, missionaries, and theologians clashed with the severe exploitation of the native communities. Bartolomé de las Casas, to whose historical significance Gustavo Gutiérrez devoted a magnificent book, perhaps remains the most astute theological analyst of such conflicts.[28] Even so, it was a convenient arrangement for both partners, since it conferred a sacred aura upon metropolitan sovereignty and, conversely, provided the church with state protection.

The governments of the new states that emerged after the nineteenth-century wars of independence promptly recognized the advantages of papal patronage and tried to preserve it. This heritage forged a particular brand of Latin American Christendom, closely linking the state and the Roman Catholic Church—a condition juridically inscribed in several national constitutions and Vatican concordats.

However, if the official connection of church and state was venerable, it was also vulnerable. The prophetic and evangelical subversive memories inscribed in the Christian scriptures and traditions surfaced powerfully during the somber and violent times of Latin American military dictatorships (1964–89), shaking the alliance between political powers and church authorities. The most famous of the ensuing conflicts took place in the midst of the violent civil war in El Salvador, a nation where nuns, priests, lay workers, and even the Primate of the Roman Catholic Church, Archbishop Oscar Arnulfo Romero, were assassinated by the military or their right-wing allies.

Archbishop Romero, famously, tried to steer his church to become a defender of the poor and persecuted. He recognized that the forbearance of the ruling clans was as limited as their economic interests were great. Two weeks before his assassination, in an interview conducted by a Mexican newspaper, Archbishop Romero foreshadowed his death and gave a theological and pastoral interpretation of his personal destiny:

> I have frequently been threatened with death. . . . If God accepts the sacrifice of my life, then may my blood be the seed of liberty, and a sign of the hope that will soon become a reality. . . . May my death, if it is accepted by God, be for the liberation of my people, and as a witness of hope in what is to come.[29]

---

28. Gustavo Gutiérrez, *Las Casas: In Search of the Poor of Jesus Christ* (Maryknoll: Orbis, 1993).

29. Oscar Romero, *Voice of the Voiceless: The Four Pastoral Letters and Other Statements* (Maryknoll: Orbis, 1998), 50–1.

Romero's assassination, arguably, convinced many church authorities that liberation theology was seriously jeopardizing the social status of the Roman Catholic Church, and that a convenient, long-standing church-state covenant was endangered by the radical political interventions of some members of the clergy. Those church authorities thus moved decisively to suppress liberationist thought.

Ecclesiastical and social political considerations were not the only issues of concern for Vatican authorities. Doctrinal orthodoxy obviously matters for the Roman Catholic Church. Under the prefecture of Cardinal Joseph Ratzinger, the Sacred Congregation for the Doctrine of the Faith strongly criticized what it considered liberation theology's ominous doctrinal deviations. On August 6, 1984, with the approval of Pope John Paul II, it issued the rather censorious "Instruction on Certain Aspects of the 'Theology of Liberation,'" followed by an admonition to Leonardo Boff and another general critique, "Instruction on Christian Freedom and Liberation" (March 22, 1986). Liberation theology was accused of borrowing improperly from Marxist thought, emphasizing historical and social liberation to the detriment of spiritual salvation, promoting class struggle instead of reconciliation, disdaining the church's social doctrine, and politicizing biblical hermeneutics, Christology, and the church. The goal of the authoritative reprimands, moreover, was

> to draw attention . . . to the deviations and risks of deviation, damaging to the faith and to Christian living, that are brought by certain forms of liberation theology . . . the "theologies of liberation" especially tend to misunderstand or to eliminate . . . the transcendence and gratuity of liberation in Jesus Christ, true God and true man. . . . One needs to be on guard against the politicization of existence, which, misunderstanding the entire meaning of the kingdom of God and the transcendence of the person, begins to sacralize politics and betray the religion of the people in favor of the projects of revolution.[30]

Traditionally, indictments like these were able to silence the accused theologians. But not this time. Prompt reactions by Gustavo Gutiérrez, Leonardo Boff, and Juan Luis Segundo were evidence that Rome had lost the capability to repress this new theological movement.[31] On April 9, 1986, John Paul II sent a letter to the Brazilian bishops, which several scholars interpreted both as an attempt to quell the growing dispute and thereby to avoid a sharp rupture with the Latin American church, given a measured endorsement of the claim that the concept of social and political liberation is an important dimension of the church's pastoral mission.[32]

---

30. "Instruction on Certain Aspects of the 'Theology of Liberation'"; see Hennelly, *Liberation Theology*, 394 and 411–12.

31. See, for instance, the strong response of Juan Luis Segundo, *Teología de la liberación: Respuesta al Cardenal Ratzinger* (Madrid: Ediciones Cristiandad, 1985).

32. Pope John Paul II, "Letter to Brazilian Episcopal Conference" (1986); see Hennelly, *Liberation Theology*, 498–506.

Since then, several Roman Catholic theologians have endeavored to convince Rome that liberation theology is a valid and legitimate rethinking of the apostolic tradition and to demonstrate that this new form of theology does not constitute a threat to the church's orthodoxy or integrity.[33] However, some influential sectors of the Roman Curia still look askance at liberation theology, as evidenced by the Sacred Congregation for the Doctrine of the Faith's scathing critique of Jon Sobrino's Christology ("Notification on the works of Father Jon Sobrino, SJ"), offered in November 2006.[34]

As a final note, it is worth mentioning that Roman Catholic narratives often disregard other sources that contributed to the birth of liberation theology. In the 1960s, several Latin American Protestant churches were undergoing similar processes of rethinking the relationship between salvation, history as the sphere of divine-human encounter, and liberation.[35] In fact, the first extensive monograph that focused on historical and social liberation as the central hermeneutical key to conceptualize the Christian faith was the doctoral dissertation of Rubem Alves, a Brazilian Presbyterian. In May of 1968, Alves successfully defended his dissertation at Princeton Theological Seminary, entitled *Towards a Theology of Liberation*.[36] Alves wrote it under the direction of Richard Shaull, who for a good number of years had been working in theological education in Latin America, first in Colombia and later in Brazil, and who was crucial for the development of a liberationist theology in Protestant Latin American circles.[37] Shaull had also been instrumental in the 1970 English publication of Paulo Freire's *Pedagogy of the Oppressed*, a key text in the development of Latin American liberation theology.[38]

---

33. See *Mysterium liberationis: Conceptos fundamentales de la Teología de la Liberación*, ed. Ignacio Ellacuría and Jon Sobrino (Madrid: Editorial Trotta, 1990). On November 16, 1989, Ellacuría (then rector of El Salvador's Central American University), five other Jesuits priests, and two domestic servants were assassinated by a group of soldiers.

34. See http://www.vatican.va/roman_curia/congregations/cfaith/documents/rc_con_cfaith_doc_20061126_notification-sobrino_en.html. Also noteworthy is the defense of Sobrino by almost forty theologians in *Bajar de la Cruz a los Pobres: Cristología de la Liberación*, ed. José María Vigil (México: Ediciones Dabar, 2007).

35. See Alan P. Neely, "Protestant Antecedents of the Latin American Theology of Liberation" (PhD diss., American University, Washington, DC, 1977).

36. Rubem Alves, "Towards a Theology of Liberation: An Exploration of the Encounter Between the Languages of Humanistic Messianism and Messianic Humanism" (PhD diss., Princeton Theological Seminary, Princeton, 1968).

37. Richard Shaull, *Hombre, ideología y revolución en América Latina* (Montevideo: ISAL, 1965). See also Neely, *Protestant Antecedents*, 253: "It is doubtful if any theologian has more consistently and directly contributed to the shaping of the contemporary Protestant theologians of liberation than Richard Shaull."

38. Paulo Freire, *Pedagogy of the Oppressed*, trans. Myra Bergman Ramos (London: Continuum, 2000).

Alves's dissertation is a powerful text, written in a splendid literary style. It was published as a book in 1969, two years before Gutiérrez's, but with a significant change in the title: *A Theology of Human Hope*. Apparently, the publishers believed that the concept of "hope," with its obvious connotations to the writings of Jürgen Moltmann, would be more commercially attractive or relevant than "liberation." Yet, despite the change of title, Alves conceptualizes the temporal dialectics proper to theological language in terms of a historical politics of liberation. He writes:

> The acts of remembering and hoping that determine the language of the community of faith, therefore, do not have any reality in themselves but in the engagement in the ongoing politics of liberation which is the situation and condition of theological intelligibility.[39]

Black Liberation Theology

If it is wrong to locate the birth of liberation theology exclusively in Roman Catholic circles, it is also a mistake to situate it solely in Latin America. During the times of slavery and racial discrimination in the United States, Black churches were communities of solidarity and hope for enslaved peoples of African ancestry. In this context, the exodus story, prophetic denunciations, and the story of the crucified and resurrected Jesus were sung, preached, and hoped, sustaining the narratives of the suffering Black communities. Bodies might have been in bondage to white masters, but hearts and minds were nourished and comforted by stories of retribution and redemption.[40]

African American churches became important protagonists in the civil rights movement for the elimination of racial discrimination. Across the South, Black preachers became leaders in spreading the challenging message and gospel music acquired a sharper political edge. The speeches of Martin Luther King, Jr., are saturated with the cadences, intonations, and biblical images typical of African American preaching.[41] The lyrics of "We Shall Overcome," the emblematic hymn of the civil rights movement, is a variant of a prior hymn, "I'll Overcome Some Day," written in 1901 by Charles Albert Tindley, one of the founding fathers of African American gospel music. The melody of this song is based upon an even

---

39. Rubem Alves, *A Theology of Human Hope* (Washington, DC: Corpus Books, 1969), 163. On the theological trajectory of Alves, see Leopoldo Cervantes-Ortiz, *Serie de sueños: la teología ludo-erótico-poética de Rubem Alves* (Quito, Ecuador: Consejo Latinoamericano de Iglesias, 2003).

40. See Albert Raboteau, *Slave Religion: The "Invisible Institution" in the Antebellum South* (Oxford: Oxford University Press, 1978); and idem, *A Fire in the Bones: Reflections on African-American Religious History* (Boston: Beacon, 1995).

41. *A Call to Conscience: The Landmark Speeches of Dr. Martin Luther King, Jr.*, ed. Clayborne Carson and Kris Shepard (New York: Warner Books, 2001).

earlier, defiant Black song: the nineteenth-century spiritual, "No More Auction Block for Me," revived in the twentieth century, first by the powerful voice of Paul Robeson and later by Bob Dylan:

> No more auction block for me
> No more, no more
> No more auction block for me
> Many thousands gone
>
> No more driver's lash for me
> No more, no more
> No more driver's lash for me
> Many thousands gone
>
> No more whip lash for me
> No more, no more
> No more pint of salt for me
> Many thousands gone

In this social and ecclesial environment, some African American theologians began to rethink their intellectual role in the epic struggle of their people. Black liberation theology, rooted in the historical experience of slavery and racism, took on an important role in theological dialogue, bringing the issues of racial and ethnic discrimination into the conversation. The foremost thinker among African American liberation theologians was the recently deceased James Cone. In his 1969 book, *Black Theology and Black Power*, Cone wrote that "the work of Christ is essentially a liberating work, directed toward and by the oppressed."[42] This was but a foretaste of his groundbreaking text of 1970, *A Black Theology of Liberation*. Cone was not one to mince words in his radical transformation of theology:

> It is my contention that Christianity is essentially a religion of liberation. The function of theology is that of analyzing the meaning of that liberation for the oppressed so that they can know that their struggle for political, social, and economic justice is consistent with the gospel of Jesus Christ. Any theology that is indifferent to the theme of liberation is not Christian.
>
> Christian theology is a theology of liberation. It is rational study of the being of God in the world in light of the existential situation of an oppressed community, relating the forces of liberation to the essence of the gospel, which is Jesus Christ.
>
> In view of the biblical emphasis on liberation, it seems not only appropriate but necessary to define the Christian community as the community of the oppressed which joins Jesus Christ in his fight for the liberation of humankind.[43]

---

42. James H. Cone, *Black Theology and Black Power* (New York: Seabury Press, 1969), 42.
43. James H. Cone, *A Black Theology of Liberation* (Maryknoll: Orbis, 1970), v, 1, and 3.

It is fair to say, in fact, that Black theology of liberation soon became an important partner of theological discourse in the academic, ecclesiastical, and public social realms in *all* places where African peoples have been subjected to dominion or control.[44] This theology has been able to dwell very creatively with the cultural and artistic traditions of Black communities.[45] And, in times like ours, when racism has had a violent political reawakening and African American communities have to proclaim that "Black Lives Matter," it is essential to remember and retrieve James Cone's superb theological analysis of the link between the cross and the lynching tree.[46]

Karl Barth: Precursor of Liberation Theology

With this backdrop in view, I want now to suggest that Karl Barth, in some of his writings, was a key precursor of liberation theology.[47] This claim can be substantiated, in a preliminary way, by taking into consideration the following cardinal points in Barth's texts—points that will help to set the stage for the later chapters of this volume.

(a) *The correlation between theology and politics.* In a conversation that took place on May 4, 1962, at Princeton Theological Seminary, Barth firmly asserted that theology requires and demands political action:

> If Christians serve the King of kings, then politics is something straightforward. Thus theology is itself political action. There is no theological word, no theological reflection or elucidation, there is no sermon . . . that does not imply political action.[48]

Previously, at a conference of the World Student Christian Federation, held in Strasbourg on July 19, 1960, Barth was even more emphatic and radical:

> There is no possibility for a Christian to retreat from the political aspects of life . . . we must take seriously the question of politics, peace, and justice in the

---

44. This includes the Caribbean, with its long and dense tradition of Black slavery. See Noel Leo Erskine, *Decolonizing Theology: A Caribbean Perspective* (Trenton: Africa World Press, 1998).

45. See James H. Cone, *The Spirituals and Blues* (New York: Seabury, 1972).

46. James H. Cone, *The Cross and the Lynching Tree* (Maryknoll: Orbis, 2011).

47. See George Hunsinger, "Karl Barth and Liberation Theology," in *Karl Barth and Radical Politics*, ed. George Hunsinger, 2nd edn (Eugene: Cascade, 2017), 193–209.

48. Eberhard Busch, ed., *Barth in Conversation, vol. 1, 1959–1962* (Louisville: WJKP, 2017), 91.

world.... A Christian is asked to take full responsibility for what happens in the world.⁴⁹

(b) God's preferential option for the poor. In December 1949, in the Swiss paper *Atlantis*, Barth published a brief but strong and categorical essay affirming God's preferential option for the poor, one of the main tenets of liberation theology:

> [God] in no wise takes up a neutral position between the poor man and the rich man. The rich may take care of their own future. He [God] is on the side of the poor ... The gospel was proclaimed to the poor, while on the contrary the rich are often shown in suspiciously close proximity to the mighty evildoer, whose pride goes before a fall....Thus the Bible is on the side of the poor, the impecunious and the destitute. He whom the Bible calls God is on the side of the poor.... [P]overty ... is not a natural condition of life in this world, but is part of the evil which dominates that life. It is perhaps the most striking result of human sin ... Christ was born in poverty ... and He died in extreme poverty, nailed naked to the Cross. He is, then, the companion, not of the rich men of the world, but of the poor of this world.... Not wealth but poverty is the mark of heaven, the mirror of eternal salvation.⁵⁰

This is a theological principle that Barth also reiterates in the *Church Dogmatics*:

> He [Jesus] ignored all those who are high and mighty and wealthy in the world in favour of the weak and meek and lowly.... In fellowship and conformity with this God who is poor in the world the royal man Jesus is also poor, and fulfils this transvaluation of all values.
>
> [T]he hungry and thirsty and strangers and naked and sick and captives are the brothers of Jesus in whom He Himself is either recognised or not recognised (Mt. 25:32f, 42f). Those whom He calls to Himself are always the weary and heavy-laden (Mt. 11:28) ... this way of the man Jesus is a reflection of the way God Himself went from those who have all things to those who have nothing. (CD IV/2: 168–71)

(c) God's righteousness and the rights of the dispossessed; justification and justice. In the *Church Dogmatics*, Barth correlates God's righteousness with the rights of the poor and dispossessed, and associates the doctrine of justification with the travails that spur the pursuit of justice for the indigent and displaced:

> [T]he human righteousness required by God and established in obedience—the righteousness which according to Amos 5:24 should pour down as a mighty

---

49. Ibid.
50. Karl Barth, "Poverty" (1949), in *Against the Stream: Shorter Post-War Writings 1946–1952* (London: SCM, 1954), 244–6.

1. Karl Barth and the Origins of Liberation Theology

stream—has necessarily the character of a vindication of right in favour of the threatened innocent, the oppressed poor, widows, orphans and aliens. . . . God always takes His stand unconditionally and passionately on this side alone: against the lofty and on behalf of the lowly; against those who already enjoy right and privilege and on behalf of those who are denied and deprived of it.

God's righteousness, the faithfulness in which He is true to Himself, is disclosed as help and salvation, as a saving divine intervention for man directed only to the poor, the wretched and the helpless as such, while with the rich and the full and the secure as such, according to His nature He can have nothing to do. . . . The man who lives by the faith that this is true stands under a political responsibility. . . . He can only will and affirm a state which is based on justice. By any other political attitude he rejects the divine justification. (CD II/1: 386 and 387)

(d) The church's preferential option for the poor. Barth also affirmed the church's political obligation to side unequivocally with the poor and dispossessed, and to work to effect their vindication:

The Church is witness of the fact that the Son of man came to seek and save the lost. And this implies that—casting all false impartiality aside—the Church must concentrate first on the lower and lowest levels of human society. The poor, the socially and economically weak and threatened, will always be the object of its primary and particular concern.[51]

This is especially relevant to the condition of poor workers under a capitalist economic system, as Barth points out in the "special ethics" of *Church Dogmatics* III:

the only choice [they] often have is between starvation and doing work which either does not benefit the cause of mankind, is detrimental to it, or is completely alien, being performed in the service of a sinister and heartless and perpetually ambiguous idol. (CD III/4: 532)

The church's duty, accordingly, is to denounce that system of exploitation and side with those who have been subjugated, even as the church hopes and aspires to a future of freedom and justice. As Barth puts it: "The Church must stand for social justice in the political sphere. . . . And in choosing between the various socialistic possibilities . . . it will always choose the movement from which it can expect the greatest measure of social justice."[52]

(e) In some of his writings, Barth expressed an inclination toward socialism. When he was a pastor of a congregation in Safenwil, Switzerland, Barth gave a

---

51. Karl Barth, "The Christian Community and the Civil Community" (1946), in *Against the Stream*, 36.
52. Ibid.

speech to an assembly of workers in which he affirmed socialism as the hope of the dispossessed, displaced, and marginalized:

> Jesus felt himself sent to the poor and the lowly . . . Jesus is more socialist than the socialists . . . Jesus really wanted to say that a rich person, a possessor of worldly goods, does *not* enter into the kingdom of God. . . . Solidarity is the law and the gospel of socialism. . . . For Jesus there was only a social God, a God of solidarity; therefore there was also only a social religion, a religion of solidarity.[53]

Lest one think that these sentiments were offered the flush of youth, in later years Barth was still willing to raise the question of whether Europe might be able to leave behind capitalism and to begin designing a new kind of socialism after the Second World War:

> [T]he consciences of us Europeans should be clear as far as this problem is concerned. But is there any hope here? Evidently only if Europe still has the power to take up the challenge . . . by instituting a form of socialism of its own.[54]

This claim was not limited to occasional writings, either. In the *Church Dogmatics*, Barth eulogizes Karl Marx's criticism of the iniquities of capitalism and his promotion of resistance by the oppressed workers:

> Above all, perhaps as the main force behind the [workers] movement, and against the background of the great and radical analysis, questioning and criticism of the system particularly associated with the name of Karl Marx, there has been the awakening of the working class to consciousness of its power when properly organized, and its internationally directed self-defence and self-assistance both politically and in the form of trade unions and co-operative societies. (CD III/4: 543)

Although, to avoid confusion, Barth distances himself from Marxism as a form of a dogmatic creed, he will also assert that,

> As man believes in God, even in the form of his belief in providence he can believe in God, and only God. This object cannot be confused with any other. . . . Nor can we believe, as Karl Marx did, in a purpose of history worked put in the clash and counter-clash of the economic classes culminating in the victory and liberation of the economically oppressed. (CD III/3: 22)

---

53. Barth, "Jesus Christ and the Movement for Social Justice (1911)," in *Karl Barth and Radical Politics*, 5, 10, and 13.
54. Barth, "The Christian Message in Europe Today (1946)," in *Against the Stream*, 171.

(f) *Barth strongly criticized the church's historical lack of solidarity with the poor.* He writes:

> The church has . . . accepted social misery as an accomplished fact in order to talk about the Spirit, to cultivate the inner life, and to prepare for the kingdom in heaven. That is the great, momentous apostasy of the Christian church, her apostasy from Christ.[55]

The church should follow and obey God's command to struggle for social justice. In his *Church Dogmatics*, Barth affirms this divinely mandated duty in stark terms: "The command of God . . . is self-evidently and in all circumstances a call for counter-movements on behalf of humanity . . . and therefore a call for the championing of the weak against every kind of encroachment on the part of the strong" (CD III/4: 544).

(g) Barth also dared to affirm *gender equity and the rights of women*. In one key text, he wrote the following regarding women's rights:

> As the fellowship of those who live in one faith under one Lord on the basis of a Baptism in one Spirit, the Church must and will stand for the equality of the freedom and responsibility of all adult citizens . . . it is all the more important for the Church to urge that the restrictions of the political freedom and responsibility not only of certain classes and races but, supremely, of that of women is an arbitrary convention which does not deserve to be preserved any longer.[56]

This claim, of course, was not unambiguous; other parts of the *Dogmatics* show a deep wariness toward feminism and offer a worryingly hierarchical account of the relationship between "man" and "woman" (this polarity, unfortunately, being the only option given for human beings). Moreover, Barth's censure of "homosexuality" in the *Church Dogmatics* has provoked deep and widespread controversy in many ecclesial and theological circles, especially among those who seek a robust affirmation of the LGBTQIA+ community. On homosexuality, Barth critically (and unfortunately) asserts the following:

> This is the physical, psychological and social sickness, the phenomenon of perversion, decadence and decay . . . The decisive word of Christian ethics must consist in a warning against entering upon the whole way of life which can only end in the tragedy of concrete homosexuality. . . . The real perversion takes place, the original decadence and disintegration begins, where man will not see his partner of the opposite sex. . . . This is the place for protest, warning and

---

55. Barth, "Jesus Christ and the Movement for Social Justice (1911)," 7.
56. Barth, "The Christian Community and the Civil Community," 175.

conversion. The command of God shows him irrefutably . . . homosexuality can have no place in his life. (CD III/4: 166)

Conclusion

What Barth's strong condemnation of queerness pertains for the future of theology and the church is hard to predict. My hope is that in the contingencies of posterity, it will simply be forsaken, forgiven, and forgotten. Whatever its fate, I hope that it does not detract from recognizing Barth's contributions to the emergence of a radical theology of liberation. I thus end this chapter with the following words of the young Karl Barth:

> He [Jesus] came from the lowest social class of the Jewish people at that time . . . Jesus felt himself sent to the poor and the lowly . . . what he brought was good news to the poor.[57]

Karl Barth can be considered as a prophet and predecessor of the theology of liberation, in several of its dimensions. This is important and meaningful always to remember and to recognize. I have established a skeletal account of connections between Barth and liberation theology; other contributors will add details in subsequent chapters.

---

57. Barth, "Jesus Christ and the Movement for Social Justice," 5.

Chapter 2

OF GODS AND MEN, AND WOLVES—THE "OTHER QUESTION"
BETWEEN PROJECTION, COLONIAL IMAGINATION, AND LIBERATION

Hanna Reichel

Karl Barth and the Future, Past, and End of Liberation

"Karl Barth and the Future of Liberation Theology" was the illustrious and ambitious title of the conference that led to this volume. Barth is decidedly part of liberation theology's past—in fact, that is something that has been held against liberation theology by some postcolonial critics[1]—but is he part of its future? Barth himself might have answered, "The future of liberation theology is Jesus Christ." It is both the strength and the weakness of Barth's theology that this answer is so predictable.

We might reframe the question about the future of liberation theology as, "What is the end of liberation?" The answer may be freedom from marginalization and destitution, oppression and subjugation, violence and structural sin. More positively, the answer might be justice, right relations, and human flourishing. A "preferential option for the poor" never meant a romanticization of poverty or marginalization; it always sought to overcome them. This option was also not a call for a mere inversion of relations between oppressors and oppressed. Latin American liberation theology was particularly aware of the fact that oppression dehumanizes all parties involved. True liberation can be achieved only when not only the oppressed but also the *oppressors* are disentangled from the effects of sin, with the oppressed in their struggle for their own humanization becoming "restorers of the humanity of both."[2]

Since the end of "dependence" theory and with increasing attention to intersectionality, it has become even clearer that a mere inversion of relations is not a viable option. What is necessary for true liberation is the overcoming of

---

1. Rasiah S. Sugirtharajah dismisses liberation theology due to its servitude to the "two Karls" (Marx and Barth). See *Postcolonial Criticism and Biblical Interpretation* (Oxford: Oxford University Press, 2002), 116.

2. Paolo Freire, *Pedagogy of the Oppressed*, trans. Myra Bergman Ramos (London: Continuum, 2005), 44.

humanity's division into the categories of privileged and marginalized, center and periphery, and a host of other hierarchical relations. In the broadest sense, the end of liberation would lie in the achievement of full humanity in right relations for all, in a comprehensive, material, political, and spiritual sense—right relations with others, the world, ourselves, and God. In classical terms, the doctrine of reconciliation comes into view, particularly in terms of a literal vision of atonement as making "two parties one . . . to reconcile two parties one to another"[3] and justification as an "affirmation of the life of all."[4]

From the broad vision of right relations, the question I want to tackle in this chapter is the question of the "other" that is so central in many contemporary projects of liberation—that is, the question of the constitution of a self vis-à-vis an other, and the question of how God as "wholly Other" bears on this relationship. I will first turn to liberation theology's left Hegelian past, starting with Ludwig Feuerbach (a somewhat lesser-known contemporary of Marx) who articulated one of modernity's most incisive criticisms of religion. Espying in religion a deprecating form of self-alienation, Feuerbach advocated for liberation from religion's projected other, in order to bring about the reconciliation of humanity with itself and the realization of a universal humanism.

I will then draw on postcolonial and feminist analyses of oppressive "otherization" to argue that Feuerbach was overly optimistic, thus substantiating Barth's theological suspicion that Feuerbach failed to take seriously the ways in which death and sin obstruct our pursuit of humanity. Blind to the ugly underbelly of modernity, the identity and solidarity that animate Feuerbach's passionate vision are constituted at the price of the otherization, dehumanization, and structural oppression of others.

Conceptualizing God as humanity's "wholly Other" with Barth seems like the theological riposte to such otherization and dehumanization.[5] It allows Christ's death on the cross to be interpreted as God vicariously taking upon Godself the sin of otherization. The question remains, however: Is such a theological vision

---

3. James Atkinson, "Atonement," in *A Dictionary of Christian Theology*, ed. Alan Richardson (London: SCM, 1969), 18.

4. Elsa Tamez, *The Amnesty of Grace: Justification by Faith from a Latin American Perspective*, trans. Sharon L. Ringe (Eugene: Wipf & Stock, 2002), 141–54.

5. It is somewhat surprising, given the extensive engagement of liberationist theology and postcolonial theory with alterity and "the other," that there has been relatively little direct engagement by both fields with Barth's notion of the "wholly Other." Mayra Rivera's postcolonial *The Touch of Transcendence* (Louisville: WJKP, 2007) is a notable exception, but she only cites Barth in passing to formulate her own notion of divine otherness and incarnation. Some of the contributors in this volume, however, have paid close attention to Barth's conceptions of God's alterity from a liberationist perspective; I think here particularly of Graham Ward and David Clough.

ultimately redemptive? It *fulfills* the law, but does it overcome it? Does it not ultimately reify and validate otherization?[6]

Humanity and Its Others

"Homo homini Deus est!" Liberation from Religious Self-alienation to Universal Humanism?

At the height of modernity, Ludwig Feuerbach dreamed of the realization of universal humanity, without division, discrimination, or limitation. Love for the other was the highest principle of this dream. The Christian imagination, Feuerbach claimed, rightly posited the end of religion to consist in the good of humankind—its salvation and well-being—but its projection of an idealized image of human perfection onto a divine other ultimately impeded the achievement of this end.[7]

For Feuerbach, the possibility of religious projection is grounded in the highest human capacities of reason, will, and affect. However, their natural inclination to be directed "outwards" toward an object makes the human being susceptible to misapprehension. When contemplating human nature itself, the human tends to construe that which is contemplated as a separate, distinct reality outside of itself. "Man—this is the mystery of religion—projects his being into objectivity, and then again makes himself an object to this projected image of himself thus converted into a subject; he thinks of himself, is an object to himself, but as the object of an object, of another being than himself" (29–30). The characteristics of this objectified self, attributed to the divine, are thus merely the characteristics of human nature, elevated beyond the limitations of the individual. Feuerbach's project, then, is to show that "this differencing of God and man, with which religion begins, is a differencing of man with his own nature" (33); to demonstrate that the "divine being is nothing else than the human being, or, rather the human nature purified" (14). Faith in a God who cares about humanity has always been about *humanity*—but religion, failing to understand this, clings to its projected other over against its real, human other.

First, faith creates God in the image of humankind. But by projecting this image, faith depreciates the real human being in relation to God. God becomes the perfect "antithesis" of humanity, to the detriment of humanity: "God is not what man is—man is not what God is. God is the infinite, man the finite being; God is perfect, man imperfect, God eternal, man temporal; God almighty, man weak; God holy, man sinful. God and man are extremes: God is the absolutely

---

6. For the honing of these critical questions after presenting my initial lecture, I am deeply grateful for critical feedback from R. C. Jongte, Thomas Renkert, and Benedikt Friedrich.

7. Ludwig Feuerbach, *The Essence of Christianity*, trans. George Eliot (Amherst: Prometheus Books, 1989). Subsequent references are included in the body of the text.

positive, the sum of all realities; man the absolutely negative, comprehending all negations" (33). The logic of differentiation through projection, on this reckoning, carries a negative implication: "To enrich God, man must become poor; that God may be all, man must be nothing" (26). Religion thus "sacrifice[s the human being] to God! The bloody human sacrifice is in fact only a rude, material expression of the inmost secret of religion" (272).

Second, religion establishes an internal division within humankind, differentiating between believers and unbelievers: "faith is essentially a spirit of partisanship" (255). Feuerbach thus sides with love against faith:

> Faith isolates God, it makes him a particular, distinct being; love universalizes; it makes God a common being, the love of whom is one with the love of man. Faith produces in man an inward disunion, a disunion with himself, and by consequence an outward disunion also; but love heals the wounds which are made by faith in the heart of man. (247)

Third, the religious illusion justifies atrocities against humankind, while immunizing itself against rational criticism:

> Wherever morality is based on theology, wherever the right is made dependent on divine authority, the most immoral, unjust, infamous things can be justified and established. . . . To place anything in God, or to derive anything from God, is nothing more than to withdraw it from the test of reason, to institute it as indubitable, unassailable, sacred, without rendering an account *why*. (274)

The externalizing "otherization" of the self in the form of the God-projection, then, is not merely a misapprehension. False consciousness results in self-alienation, and that is not only obstructive to the achievement of human potential but "profoundly injurious" (274). Criticism of religion is thus not just a matter of intellectual transparency; it is a humanistic imperative. The love and unity to which humanity is destined must be liberated from its religious bond, liberated toward a true universal love for the other.

In continuity with Immanuel Kant's motto to see the human person as an end in itself rather than as a means to another end, Feuerbach therefore postulated that "love should be immediate" (268), that there should be no detour via an imagined divine being. The true end of religion—human love for the human other—will be reached directly and fully only when the false consciousness of religion is overcome, transforming the Christian belief that "God is love" into the notion that *human* love is divine.

"Homo homini lupus est!" *Liberation from Oppressive Otherization—to the Other?*

Enrique Dussel: Inventing Amerindia as Modernity's Other Programmatically, Feuerbach turned the analytic phrase, *homo homini Deus est*, into a "great practical principle" (271). The human being is—and thus should be!—God to the human being. Those familiar with this phrase might find its classic corollary, *homo homini lupus est*, curiously absent from Feuerbach's account. Thomas Hobbes insightfully differentiated both aspects: "The former is true of the relations of citizens with each other, the latter of relations between commonwealths."[8] Human beings have a generous and loving attitude toward others in their "in-group," while acting aggressively and violently toward outsiders.

Feuerbach may truly have believed modernity's ability to include everyone under the "in-group" of a shared humanity, such that there would be no more outsiders and the second half of the proverb would be nullified. Even as Feuerbach read Hegel in a distinctly materialistic way, his belief was that the critical reflection of human self-consciousness would not only establish the rational subject but lead also to emancipation, progress, democracy, morality, and universal love. This perspective remains curiously idealistic, and emblematic of the problems of the Enlightenment's self-accrediting optimism. Unfortunately, and arguably in unprecedented ways, modernity has manifested the other side of the proverb, revealing how much the human being is really a proverbial wolf to the human other. So it may turn out that, even as he appreciated half of the truth about the human, Feuerbach was altogether *wrong*.

We know today that Western modernity was and is blind to mechanisms that exclude others from the "humanity" it celebrates. Modernity's lofty ideals have an invisible, violent underside. And, as liberation philosophies have pointed out, this is not an unfortunate coincidence of history: modernity and modern subjectivity is not first and foremost founded in introspection but is deeply tied to colonialism and imperialism, the rise of capitalism, slavery, and exploitation. As Enrique Dussel put it: "*Homo homini lupus* is the real—that is, political—definition of the *ego cogito* and of modern and contemporary European philosophy."[9] He argues that the possibility of an *ego cogito* was grounded in the *ego conquiro* of the Americas. "The experience not only of discovery, but especially of the conquest, is essential to the constitution of the modern ego, not only as a subjectivity, but as subjectivity that takes itself to be the center or end of history."[10]

Modern subjectivity is often portrayed as self-consciousness—that is, as not primarily defined by its relation to an external Other (like God) but by self-reflective transparency, rationality, and identity. But this perception masks its own underside: the process of conquest, domination, and erasure that enables the constitution of a self-sufficient subject. The modern subject does not establish

---

8. Thomas Hobbes, *De Cive: The Latin Version Entitled in the First Edition Elementorum Philosophiae Sectio Tertia de Cive, and in Later Editions Elementa Philosophica de Cive*, ed. and trans. Howard Warrender (Oxford: Clarendon, 1983), 3.

9. Enrique Dussel, *Philosophy of Liberation*, trans. Aquilina Martinez and Christine Morkovsky (Maryknoll: Orbis, 1985), 9.

10. Enrique Dussel, *The Invention of the Americas: Eclipse of "the Other" and the Myth of Modernity*, trans. Michael D. Barber (New York: Continuum, 1995), 25.

a unity of humankind through its shared love for one another, as Feuerbach dreamed it would; rather, it establishes itself in, by, and through the subjugation and even eclipse of the human other. Dussel points particularly to the Amerindian "others" who were all but wiped out by the conquistadors who "otherized" them as uncivilized, non-Christian, subhuman. In his historical writing on this conquest, Dussel sees the modern subject as constituting itself "in Europe's confrontation with the Other. By controlling, conquering, and violating the Other, Europe defined itself as discoverer, conquistador, and colonizer of an alterity likewise constitutive of modernity. Europe never discovered (*des-cubierto*) the Other as Other but covered over (*encubierto*) the Other as part of the Same: i.e., Europe."[11]

Dussel draws on Feuerbach, specifically, making him a critical objector to the modern ideals he championed. Eurocentrism has not projected and divinized humanity. It has made the European subject into a "system," a "prevailing totality," and a "God-fetish." Dussel thus calls for the overthrow of this God-fetish, merely a veiled apotheosis of the European subject. In his analysis, universal humanity and belief in God as its divine other are not mutually exclusive. On the contrary, the Other "has an analogous meaning: it can be the anthropological Other . . . or it can be the absolutely absolute Other: other not only than the world but than the very cosmos."[12]

This analogous meaning translates into a theopolitical hermeneutic: God as the transcendent Other, who stands beyond human reach, can best be found in "those persons who, as victims of the world/system, have been excluded from the world-system and thus remain invisible to the 'center.'"[13] Rather than requiring the sacrifice of the human to the divine, then, religion can help to establish the worth of the *human* other through their identification with the *divine* other. A defense of true humanity, attentive to those on the underside of history, "can be articulated theologically only in the form of analogically-related liberation theologies which proclaim the irreducibility of both God and the person to any system."[14] Only a "conversion to the Other," in both senses, can lead to "the beginning of the process of liberation."[15]

This supplement, which Dussel provides to Feuerbach, illuminates the story of modernity at large. The idealized *homo homini deus* is only half the truth. The elevation of the human is also effected through the *homo homini lupus*, through

---

11. Ibid., 12.

12. Enrique Dussel, *Filosofía Ética Latinoamericana*, vol. 5, *Colección Filosofía y Liberación Latinoamericana* (México: Editorial Edicol, 1977), 51.

13. Roberto Goizueta, "Toward a Transmodern Christianity," in *Thinking from the Underside of History*, ed. Linda Alcoff and Eduardo Mendieta (Lanham: Rowman & Littlefield, 2000), 185, citing Dussel, *Filosofía Ética Latinoamericana*, 5:77.

14. Roberto Goizueta, *Liberation, Method and Dialogue: Enrique Dussel and North American Theological Discourse* (Atlanta: Scholars Press, 1988), 166.

15. Rivera, *Touch of Transcendence*, 69, citing Enrique Dussel and Daniel Guillot, *Liberacion latinoamericana y Emmanuel Levinas* (Buenos Aires: Editorial Bonum, 1975), 26.

the assertion of this self over and against the other to the point of their erasure. Translated into theological language, we arrive at a classic insight of hamartiology: the attempt to divinize the human in fact leads to the dehumanization of the human.

Variations in Otherization: Culture, Race, and Gender Amerindia is not the only example of an other invented and othered in the self-constitution of the modern *ego*. Similar analyses have been proposed in different projects of liberation as well, although not all exhibit theological concerns. In his groundbreaking work, *Orientalism*, Edward Said lucidly exposes how the "Orient" was invented for the benefit of "Western" identity.[16] The self-definition as "Western" posits an identity conceived in contrast to an "Eastern" counterpart, subsuming everything from the Maghreb to China as a variation of the "Oriental" other. The Orient is positioned as Europe's exterior, but in this specific positioning, it in fact constitutes "an integral part of European *material* civilization and culture" (1) that "has helped define Europe (or the West) as its contrasting image, idea, personality, experience" (3). Both conceptually and geopolitically, "European culture gained in strength and identity by setting itself off against the Orient as a sort of surrogate and even underground self" (3).

Said meticulously elucidates how the Orient was constructed as a negative projection of Europe's self-construction. "To the Westerner . . . the Oriental was always *like* some aspect of the West" (67) while, at the same time, set off as different and distant. The Orient was effectively rendered a variation of the European self, as its inferior reverse image, in order to enable to an understanding of the Western self. The characteristics attributed to "the Orient" oscillate between intrigue and repulsion, but the pattern is clear: "The Oriental is irrational, depraved (fallen), childlike, 'different'; thus, the European is rational, virtuous, mature, 'normal'" (40).

Beyond questions of malign intentions, Said discerns in these dynamics a human need for order, which "is achieved by discriminating and taking note of everything, placing everything of which the mind is aware in a secure, refindable place, therefore giving things some role to play in the economy of objects and identities that make up an environment" (53). Even the ensuing tendency to "impose corrections upon raw reality, changing it from free-floating objects into units of knowledge . . . is perfectly natural for the human mind" (67). For Said, it becomes problematic when the ordering of reality is part of a development of self-identity—or, to put it differently, when this process of representation is part of a process of projection.

Orientalism as a discourse and a field of knowledge was and is intertwined with European conquest and domination in complex ways, both deriving from it and, in turn, legitimizing it. Said points out how "the Orientalist reality is

---

16. Edward W. Said, *Orientalism* (New York: Random House, 1978). Further references are included in the body of the text.

both antihuman and persistent" (44) to the present. The quasi-divinization of Western identity continues to result in inhumanities against non-Western people and nations, informs prejudice and discrimination, and justifies hegemony and military intervention. Said thus poses the question, "Can one divide human reality, as indeed human reality seems to be genuinely divided, into clearly different cultures, histories, traditions, societies, even races, and survive the consequences humanly?" (45) Can one, indeed?

This question can be drawn out further to include the persistent division of humanity into sexes and genders, some of which are particularly prone to oppression and subjugation. Feminist critiques have long analyzed how humanity has been defined by othering half of it. Simone de Beauvoir uncovers how the invention of "the second sex" implies that by default, "humanity is male and man defines woman not herself but as relative to him." Woman is "determined and differentiated in relation to man, while he is not in relation to her; she is inessential in front of the essential. He is the Subject; he is the Absolute. She is the Other."[17] To achieve this, the essence of woman is formulated again as the inverse mirror image of the self-definition of man.[18] Man is rational and strong, defined by his mind, and succeeds by seeking transcendence and being active in the public realm. Women are irrational and weak, defined by their body (erotic, reproductive and caregiving functions), and are limited to immanence and private spaces.

De Beauvoir insightfully observes that the underlying structures go beyond material or social issues of gender into the realm of epistemology and subject formation. "The category of Other is as original as consciousness itself.. . . [A]lterity is the fundamental category of human thought. No group ever defines itself as One without immediately setting up the Other opposite itself" (6). Like Dussel and Said, De Beauvoir seems to indicate that Feuerbach's celebration of the *homo homini deus* missed the underside of human nature, the *homo homini lupus* that manifests itself in otherization, subjugation, and oppression on the way to self-assertion. She points out:

> These phenomena could not be understood if human reality were solely a *Mitsein* [being-in-fellowship] based on solidarity and friendship. On the contrary, they become clear if, following Hegel, a fundamental hostility to any other consciousness is found in consciousness itself; the subject posits itself only in opposition; it asserts itself as the essential and sets up the other as inessential, as the object. (7)

---

17. Simone de Beauvoir, *The Second Sex*, trans. Constance Borde and Sheila Malovany-Chevallier (London: Vintage, 2015), 6. Further references are included in the body of the text.

18. Interestingly, de Beauvoir compares the oppression of Jews as well as of "American blacks" to the situation of "the woman" throughout her seminal text.

In Need of an Other? Theologizing Otherization

Feuerbach rightly discerned that "othering," which sows divisions in humanity, arises from a fundamental self-alienation and has devastating effects. And because he saw religious illusion as the foundational problem, Feuerbach sought to overcome the religious self-alienation of humanity. Postcolonial and feminist scholars share Feuerbach's assumption that human beings are "intended toward the other."[19] Against Feuerbach's enlightened optimism, however, they highlight the othering side of this relation: the dehumanizing impulse of humanity. Theologically, they point not to the quasi-divinity of humanity, but rather to humanity's sinfulness.

The analyses of the previous section—and, of course, more variations in the theme could easily be furnished—suggest that the anthropological roots of the problem may lie deep within the epistemological and political structures of identity construction. Every universalism rests on an act of exclusion. Every totality requires an exteriorized "other." Of course, in principle, the epistemological and political dialectics of identity construction might result in the *recognition* of the infinite worth of such the other—not their subjugation.[20] However, reality obtrudes at this very point, as different camps of critical theory can confirm. Identity construction does not automatically result in recognition; it results, typically, in oppressive otherization.

In the hermeneutical process of subject formation, the needed other is not simply a *given*, to be encountered and described. In order to be able to read it *as* an other for purposes of self-constitution, it has to be hermeneutically rendered as an other; *therefore*, it has to be materially turned into an other. The material effects of this process stymie those who are subjected by the othering gaze in their freedom to see themselves (or the dominant othering other) outside of the projected gaze, while those who force their gaze and view on the othered assert their dominance precisely in their own not-being-subjected to the gaze of that other. To secure the identity thus established, the othered will not only have to *become* the projected self's negative mirror, but it will also be forced to *adopt* this constructed image for its respective subject-formation—a subject-formation that, from the outset, is marked by internalized inferiority and ontological dependence on the one who dominates. The structural violence emanating from such unequally mutual subject-formation ranges from stereotyping through discrimination and oppression, all the way to genocide.

---

19. Gayatri Chakravorty Spivak, *Death of a Discipline* (New York: Columbia University Press, 2003), 72.

20. And such proposals exist, of course. The I-Thou paradigm of Martin Buber and Emmanuel Levinas's philosophy of the other may be cited. In a different, but similarly positive vein, recent postcolonial proposals situate a different nonhuman other under the banner of "planetarity" or creaturely kinship. See Gayatri Chakravorty Spivak, *A Critique of Postcolonial Reason: Toward a History of the Vanishing Present* (Cambridge: Harvard University Press, 1999) and Donna Haraway, *Staying with the Trouble: Making Kin in the Cthulucene* (Durham: Duke University Press, 2016).

It may seem, then, that through religious projections, there is a pervasive human tendency not only to constitute self-identity in opposition to an other, but also to generate dynamics of otherization in order to achieve this end, even as noble goals (humanity, solidarity, etc.) are invoked. Feuerbach's idea of universal humanism thus reveals itself as one of homosolidarity by way of homosociality:[21] a solidarity built on a commonality, which in turn depends on the sustained otherization of and domination over an ostracized other. The well-documented role that Christian religion has played and continues to play in colonial and patriarchal enterprises only makes the problem more acute, since Feuerbach's dream of overcoming the religious illusion proves illusionary itself. It is not the "detour" through faith in God that prevents true humanity from prevailing. Unity relies on exclusion and the appreciation of difference on some common ground. Such appears to be the dialectic of humanity: as we try to get to the other human being directly, we project things upon them that no human being can bear, positively and/or negatively. Thus, both the *homo homini deus* and the *homo homini lupus* disfigure true humanity.

As it stands, it seems there is no direct way for us to reach universal humanity. The theologian therefore might infer that Feuerbach was right in diagnosing projection as the heart of religion but wrong in thinking that overcoming the religious mediation of projective self-constitution would serve to advance humanity. This was indeed Barth's criticism of Feuerbach: Feuerbach had been too optimistic in regard to the human being, and his critique of religion was not radical enough. To be sure, Barth appreciated Feuerbach's attention to materiality and historicality as well as his serious intention to liberate the whole human being. Barth understood Feuerbach's determination to uncover the core of religion to be "as positive as that of any theologian. He is not merely a skeptic or Nay-sayer."[22] Indeed, given this shared vision, Barth does not even care to challenge Feuerbach's denial of God. Nevertheless, Barth critiques Feuerbach's insufficiently realistic account of the human being.

What Feuerbach deems suggestive of divine qualities in the human, Barth ascribes to humanity's sinfulness (29). Feuerbach's one-sided optimism convicts him; he was "ignorant of death" and

---

21. The term was theorized by Eve Kosofsky Sedgwick, referring to "social bonds between persons of the same sex" as a social mechanism that maintains hegemonic masculinity. See *Between Men: English Literature and Male Homosocial Desire* (New York: Columbia University Press, 1985), 1. My own usage follows Marcella Althaus-Reid, who conceives of a broader (i.e., not exclusively gender-based) logic of "homosolidarity" in *Indecent Theology* (London: Routledge, 2002), 91.

22. Karl Barth, "Ludwig Feuerbach. Mit einem polemischen Nachwort," *Zwischen den Zeiten* 5 (1927): 11–40; reprint of *Ludwig Feuerbach*, ed. Erich Thies (Darmstadt: Wissenschaftliche Buchgesellschaft, 1976), 1–32 at 7. Translation my own. Further references are included in the body of the text.

misapprehend[ed] evil. . . . Indeed, he who knew that we human beings are evil from head to toe, and who reflected on the fact that we are mortal, would surely recognize it as the most illusionary of illusions that the essence of God should be the essence of humankind; he would leave God—even if he thought him just a dream—alone with such confusions with ourselves. (22)

Like Feuerbach, Barth sees religion as a false solution to humanity's condition. But where Feuerbach sets out to liberate the human being from its religious self-alienation, Barth views his optimism as persisting in an underlying self-delusion. So he proposes to invert Feuerbach's solution. The path to liberation will be "to comprehend the human being in God, not God in the human being" (28).

Barth's Wholly Other—the God of Substitutionary Otherization?

The Wholly Other . . .

Whether we associate the examined phenomenology of "othering" with a specific logic underlying Western modernity or with some cognitive mechanisms of evolutionary psychology at large, there seems to be strong evidence that the human being is indeed directed toward an other and constitutes itself in relational opposition to that other. This idea, in itself, is ripe with theological implications. If otherization is structurally necessary for the constitution of subjectivity and the political building of (homo)solidarity, God's otherness comes into view, as does God's potential to unify rather than divide, and anchors a redemptive (and thus not alienating) perspective. Given the insights drawn from critical theory, we would almost have to say the following with Voltaire: if there was no God, we would have to invent one—true humanism might only be found via a detour to the wholly Other.

This is precisely the lens through which I will read Karl Barth's theology. The otherness of God was a central notion of Barth's thought, and it afforded him an almost Archimedean point for his interventions into ethical and theological debates. In his theological debut of his commentary on the epistle to the Romans, Barth declares: "If I have a system, it is limited to the recognition of what Kierkegaard called the 'infinite qualitative distinction' between time and eternity . . . 'God is in heaven, thou art on earth'" (RII: 10).[23] At the time, Barth tended to construe this claim in the polarizing manner that Feuerbach critiqued. The human being's identity is found in contrast and opposition to this wholly Other who remains incommensurably different and radically exterior.

---

23. Following Barth's term *Mensch*, which denotes the individual human being as well as the species without reference to gender, I replace the English "man/men" with "human being" or "humankind."

Barth sets this idea of God as wholly Other in the context of a critique of religion that is at least as scathing as Feuerbach's. Like Feuerbach, religion is a thinly veiled enterprise of egoism. In further continuity with Feuerbach, Barth denounces the way in which religion sows division in the individual human being as well as and between different groups of people, promoting "disruption, discord, and the absence of peace" (RII: 266). Religion is almost like a disease, "not a thing to be desired or extolled; it is a misfortune which takes fatal hold upon some men and is by them passed on to others" (RII: 258), with devastating consequences. As Barth boldly declares, "Death is the meaning of religion" (RII: 253).

Unlike Feuerbach, however, Barth does not believe that humankind can overcome its religious condition, which is marked by a similarly conspicuous entanglement between the epistemological and hamartiological dynamics that shape the power-play of otherization. Indeed, what Feuerbach judged to be humankind's true essence, in need of being saved from the illusory form of religion, was precisely the illusion that Barth denounces—humankind making itself its own God. For Barth, religion may be a lie, but it is not merely a matter of false consciousness. Instead, "The meaning of religion is that it reveals how powerfully sin rules over the human being in this world: even the religious human being is a sinner, *especially* as a religious being is he a sinner!" (RII: 257 rev.).[24] The lie that is the sin of religion lies in the creation of an illusion different from the one Feuerbach exposed—namely, that precisely in the attempt to know and relate oneself to God, the human being is attempting to grasp God, to construct God in their own image, and work out their own salvation. In this sense, Feuerbach's proposal for overcoming the religious illusion would *still* be "religious" for Barth. The way out—the human being becoming God to the human being—is simply the reification of what Barth calls "the religious possibility."

Barth's notion of the wholly Other thus enables a powerful critique of ideology. It intervenes against the human attempt at self-constitution through direct relation to human others, and against the human attempt to appropriate God. In fact, *every* notion of God that is constructed by comparing God to the human being, i.e., by othering projection, is unmasked and torn down by the uncompromising alterity of the wholly Other. In the human subject's external constitution through God as its wholly Other, Barth finds the potential for a universal humanism akin to the kind Feuerbach sought, if initially in a predominantly negative way. The reality of the wholly Other marks first and foremost a border and a barrier, a "No" to the human being's religious logic and quasi-divine pretensions, a "sentence of death" for this religious human being (RII: 181). But in this way, the reality of the wholly Other also constitutes the positive identity that the human being cannot provide for itself: "that the human being is the human being—this is a strangely humiliating fact that one cannot tell oneself. It must *be* told, it must *be* given as an answer, before one cries out" (RII: 271; cp. GA 47: 424).

---

24. This sentence is rather garbled in the Hoskyns translation of the second edition of Romans. For the original, see GA 47: 353.

The revelation of the wholly Other God is thus not only judgment. In its unalienable external givenness it is also grace and peace, and it signals the promise of reconciliation not only between God and the human being but within human life itself. God's alterity radically disrupts all interhuman relationships, whether of fellowship or antagonism. The "infinite qualitative distinction" between heaven and earth is the one and only relevant categorial difference. Its "radical dissolution of all physical, intellectual, and spiritual achievements of men" effects the "all-embracing 'relativization' of all human distinctions" (RII: 78) and contests any hierarchizing otherization—whether in the name of religion or with respect to the "merits" of culture, education, race, gender, etc.

The alterity of God thus tears down the human commonalities that previously afforded homosocial in-group cohesion at the expense of ostracizing outsiders. "Grounded upon a negative" (RII: 101), it constitutes the kind of solidarity and universal human fellowship that no positive commonality could ever guarantee. Furthermore, the shared relation to the wholly Other places them *positively*—if indirectly—in universal fellowship with each other (RII: 446). Indeed, the dialectics of God's negative alterity (as the wholly Other) and God's positive alterity (as the concrete Other to the human being in the incarnation) funds the unspoken universalism of Barth's soteriology as much as his political advocacy for universal human rights, even at a time when both options were far from the theological mainstream.[25]

Spelling out Barth's conception of the human-divine relationship along the lines of the logic of otherization, we arrive precisely at Barth's mature anthropology. As a creature, human beings are indeed intended toward an other—"created by God (*von Gott*) for God (*für Gott*)" (CD III/2: 243). Our being as creatures is not independent and self-sufficient; it is constituted in, by, and through our relationship to our Creator in whom we live and move and have our being. Constituted by this Other, the need of an other for our own self-constitution will indeed emerge as an anthropological constant.

It is then no surprise that, absent recognition of the existentially constitutive directedness toward God, humans will draw on *other* others to fulfill this constitutive need. But since the goal, end, and meaning of human life is not found within the created sphere, no creature can truly substitute for that constitutive relationship, and no creature can ground our existence and identity in the same way as the Creator.[26] The "true need of every creature for another" is thus attended by a "profound ultimate dissatisfaction with every relationship between creature

---

25. See, for example, Karl Barth, *The Humanity of God*, trans. John Newton Thomas and Thomas Wieser (London: Collins, 1961).

26. The slippage between Barth's framing of this relationship as "true humanity" and "creatureliness" indicates in an important way that God's alterity surpasses the intra-human distinctions such that it ultimately relativizes any anthropocentrism within creation. The only theologically relevant difference is that between Creator and creature, not between human and nonhuman creation, thereby fundamentally relativizing claims of human

and creature, as also with the relationship between the individual creature and the creaturely cosmos as a whole." Only the "true 'wholly Other' in distinction from every partial and relative other ... has the power to satisfy the creature as a partner" (CD III/4, 478–9).

In terms of hamartiological implications, the loss of God as our constitutive Other will not only result in alienation from God, human others, self, and our own finitude; it will also engender harm and suffering within these fundamental relationships. In effect, the humanity of both the othering and the othered self is lost. But loss is not, as Feuerbach thought, due to the religious illusion. It arises when one does not accept the reality and irreducibility of our relation to God. A direct affirmation of humanity, apart from God, in other words, seems unable to escape inhumane, dehumanizing relations. Rather than divinizing the human other, it results in their exploitation and oppression. Rather than bringing about liberation, the loss of God means the loss of our shared humanity. When the human being aspires to become divine, it becomes a wolf to another instead.

For Barth, it is thus only the almost-frightening reality of this wholly Other that can break through the lie of religion. The uncompromising alterity of the wholly Other cannot be objectified in our attempt to gain control of our self-constitution. This is the first substantial difference between this wholly Other and all the "little others" we insist on othering. And because the uncompromising alterity of the wholly Other is *God's* being—God, who is not "in need" of an other in the same way as we are—God cannot be made to adopt our otherization of Godself as God's own identity and remains unaffected by our problematic tendencies to that end. This is the second substantial difference between this wholly Other from the little others, who cannot escape navigating our othering projections in their own identity construction.

Barth believes in the objective reality of this wholly Other. He is, however, uniquely attentive to the fact that such an account stands in stark contrast to our actuality, in which we continue to engage in theological projection and to persist in dividing humankind. While some might infer that only our conversion and return to right relation with God will allow us to create non-othering relationships with fellow creatures, Barth's theology does not in fact allow for such a resolution. It would discern here instead only another cycle of religious self-delusion. No amount of "getting it right," theologically, breaks the cycle of hubris and otherization.

Barth's conception of God as the "wholly Other" is therefore not just some kind of "neo-orthodox" reaction against Feuerbach, one that calls for a return to a supposedly premodern religious relationality. In its critical grasp of the ambivalences inherent to modernity, Barth's notion of God is rather postmodern. Barth recognizes (a) that the human being may not be able to liberate itself from its othering condition; (b) that even the best parts of the Christian religion are not immune to this tendency; and (c) that we may indeed need a *different* other

---

superiority at the expense of the rest of creation. See David Clough, *On Animals*, vol. 1, *Systematic Theology* (London: T&T Clark, 2012).

to liberate us from our tendency to other human others. The deep historical complicities between Christianity and colonial, patriarchal, and heteronormative otherizations that have become subject to much scholarly theorization in the meantime can only further substantiate the relevance of Barth's theological rejection of undue optimism regarding modernity's optimism.

Amid the manifest, ongoing devastation caused by such othering processes, the theologian might indeed infer that "only a God can save us" from objectifying our fellow creatures, rendering them objects of worship or aggression.[27] Barth already sees quite clearly that no solution can be found in reverting to some projected original (prelapsarian or premodern) state. Barth clearly sees, in fact, the need for *redemption* from this logic. In short, and again in classical theological language, his proposal looks for liberation not in a protological ethics but in substitutionary atonement. Only God can bear the weight of being this other for us.

. . . Othered for Us

Building on these claims, one might go on to ask: what if the righting of relations consists in the fact that God stepped in to be the ultimate Other humankind needs, not only the Other to be worshipped and adored, but also the Other who bears the weight of our othering self-assertion? Barth spells out a Christologically mediated anthropology, which subsequently culminates in a substitutionary theory of atonement in "The Judge Judged in Our Place" (CD IV/1: §59.2). It will not be difficult to translate this forensic language into the language of "the wholly Other, othered in our place"—an Other othered both *for* us and *by* us; the one true non-othering Other othered for all others, so that we may other each other no more. In Jesus Christ, the Lord becomes the suffering servant, the master becomes the slave, and the wholly Other becomes a concrete other, allowing us to objectify him to the point of victimization in our self-affirmation over and against others.

The wholly Other, then, has to be more than an abstract category or a being *only* completely distinct and separate from humankind. Already in his early work, Barth emphasizes that there is no wholly Other God apart from the revelation of Jesus Christ as the "wholly other human being" (RII: 255). From within the logic of otherization, the absolutely "wholly other" God who becomes the concrete, victimized other in Christ seems like the natural-theological solution in an understanding of atonement as vicarious. Only a *divine* Other can bear the sin of our perpetual othering, which is the cost of any homosociality, and only a *human* other can be othered in this way. Only in its overcoming can the fundamental difference between Creator and creature thus also be rightly discerned, and only

---

27. Martin Heidegger coined this phrase in his famous interview on his involvement with Nazism—which might also give a first indication of why the logic must eventually be criticized. See "Only a God Can Save Us," in *Heidegger: The Man and the Thinker*, ed. Thomas Sheehan (Chicago: Precedent, 1981), 45–67.

thus can relationships in danger of misconstrual be righted. Humanization is only possible through the mediation of this divine Other.

Barth asserts that the humanity of Christ is not an abstract human nature, but the concrete fulfillment of what it means to be human, spelled out in his particular and singular existence. Christ's humanity consists in the kind of direct love that Feuerbach prized: his being-for-others.

> In His existence [Christ] is referred to humankind, to other human beings, His fellows, and this not merely partially, incidentally or subsequently, but originally, exclusively and totally. When we think of the humanity of Jesus, humanity is to be described unequivocally as fellow-humanity (*Mitmenschlichkeit*). In the light of the [hu]man Jesus, the human is the cosmic being which exists absolutely for its fellows. (CD III/2: 208 rev.)

Barth calls this fulfillment of what it means to be human "obedience": conformity with the end and goal of humanity, enacting right relations between God and humankind.

Stepping into the place of being-for-others and doing the truly human thing for the human being (which the human cannot do for itself) makes Christ the ultimate other. It effectively renders him an object of our otherization. In his being-for-others, Jesus does not resist; instead, he becomes the projection of everything that is weak and despised in the eyes of humankind, so that humankind might set itself over and against him. He stands in the place of that othered, subjected one, unto death on the cross. In Christ, we thus also recognize the profound cost of such otherization: Christ's death is not merely the historical end, but also the logical culmination of incarnation. His being-for-others can be all but reduced to his otherization. Indeed, Barth himself affirms that it is not *anything* that Jesus did or said, neither his teaching nor his ministry, neither his ethics nor his personality, that is constitutive of his identity; rather, "the concepts *passus, crucifixus, mortuus, sepultus* [say] everything that is decisive about the human Jesus" (CD IV/1: 165 rev.).

According to Feuerbach, the substitutionary role that Christ plays in reconciling humanity, in his love for humanity and for the good of humanity, ought to be overcome by overcoming the illusory otherization of divine being from human being, thus reconciling humanity with itself. Wherever a human being

> loves [the hu]man for the sake of [the hu]man, who rises to the love of the species, to universal love, adequate to the nature of the species, he is a Christian, is a Christ himself. He does what Christ did, what made Christ Christ. Thus, where there arises the consciousness of the species as a species, the idea of humanity as a whole, Christ disappears, without, however, his true nature disappearing; for he was the substitute for the consciousness of the species, the

image under which it was made present to the people, and became the law of the popular life.[28]

As the human being steps into the role formerly reserved to the divine other, then, emancipation and humanization follows. However, in light of the critical and theological analysis established, we may find that the opposite obtains. Humanity continues to need *God* to step into this space, to take the place of the other, so as to ensure that no further human others need to become victims in the process of othering. And in Christ, God graciously determines Godself to be human for humankind, to be the Other whom we colonize, otherize, and even kill.

God does not need the incarnation or the cross in any way. But we do. And this is what permits the constitution of our subjectivity in universal solidarity, if initially only in negation. Before the cross, for one second, we find a humanity strangely united in ostracizing this Other. Roman and Jewish law, religious authorities and revolutionary activists, the crowds and Jesus' intimate friends, they all stand united against this concrete Other instead of standing against one another.[29] As God steps in, not only to be an absolute, unattainable other, but vicariously to become the concrete, relatable, and therefore other-able other, God suffers the violence of othering-unto-death, fulfilling that scapegoat-like function to the redemption of humanity. Against critiques of such vicarious atonement as a validation of submission and suffering, Barth vigorously maintains that Christ's being is not a being-for-others that we can or should strive to *imitate*, even as we are asked to *follow* him. Substitution means that Christ submits to suffering *instead* of us, and in *place* of us, rather than in solidarity with us. The cross is the "end of sacrifice"; it is not a model for human imitation or discipleship.

Only one who is God has the ability to bear the weight of that otherization that no human being can. We might thus conclude with Barth against Feuerbach that in fact, **Deus** *homini deus est*: God is and therefore becomes God for the human being precisely by standing in the place of *homo* **deo** *lupus est*, allowing the human being to rage like a wolf against him.

Wolves, incidentally, are among the most gregarious and cooperative animals. What may sound like a random side note reveals once more how persistent the structural sin of otherization is. By advocating for "humanity" and for "universal humanism" with and beyond Feuerbach and Barth, I have once more reiterated the problematic logic I denounced. I have established a unity, a universality through the exclusion of another other—in this case, the nonhuman creation we continue to objectify, commodify, and exploit. What might have already dawned on the attentive reader at some point deserves to be spelled out explicitly: even as it diagnoses the problem, the proverb itself engages in the same kind of self-asserting otherization. Certain nonhuman others are here defined as less-than-human,

---

28. Feuerbach, *Essence of Christianity*, 269.

29. See Michael Welker, *Gottes Offenbarung: Christologie* (Neukirchen-Vluyn: Neukirchener, 2012), 174.

as inhumane others, by way of distinction from human beings who assert their humanity at the expense of wolves. While the resultant image of the animal may bear little resemblance to actual existing wolves, it has effectively informed human treatment of wolves for centuries, who have suffered the consequences of human homosolidarity acutely and, in many regions, up to the point of their extinction.

This side note serves to indicate a crucial point. Just like with all good intentions of overcoming sexism, we may fall into racism and culturalism, even the apparently more universal category of "humanity" might only be shifting the site of violence once more. In our context, it may be common to assert that the word did not become "man" (that is, male, excluding women) but human. We may, accordingly, eventually come to the realization that the word becoming *flesh* might invite us to theologically expand our homosolidarity further than we realize in our sustained anthropocentrism. The decisive "infinite qualitative distinction" that Barth talks about is, after all, the difference between heaven and earth, between creator and created. Therefore, all distinctions and differences within the creaturely realm must surely be relativized in the same way as the distinctions between human beings. Furthermore, I believe it would be possible to reformulate my proposal in the light of this insight, even if Barth did not draw this conclusion.[30] For now, let me conclude with a few reflections on how my rereading of Barth's response to Feuerbach in light of insights into othering might speak to the "the future of liberation theology."

The End of Redemption and the Beginning of Liberation— Putting Otherization in Divine Parentheses

"The wholly Other, othered for us." In the reading proposed here, Barth's notion of divine alterity and substitutionary atonement is the logically consistent and anti-ideologically effective *theological* solution to the othering problem.

However, this solution has its own share of problems. It might be argued that it is bought at the price of reifying and sanctioning the issue it set out to solve. In order to overcome the toxic logics of othering in the "horizontal" plane, it cements those logics in the "vertical." At the root of this redemptive model lies a metaphysics of recognition that can only be achieved through submission, an understanding of the subject that can only establish itself through domination and subjection, and a reductive ontology that can only conceive of difference in terms of binary opposition: God positioned over against the world and its creatures. Furthermore, this solution postulates the necessity of violence for a healing of the social fabric

---

30. This opens points of convergence with emergent conversations about "deep incarnation." See Niels Henrik Gregersen, "Deep Incarnation: Why Evolutionary Continuity Matters in Christology," *Toronto Journal of Theology* 26, no. 2 (2010): 173–87; and *Incarnation: On the Scope and Depth of Christology*, ed. Niels Henrik Gregersen (Minneapolis: Fortress, 2015).

and, in its account of Christ's vicarious atonement, elevates redemptive suffering. We would not be the first ones to ask: is such a conception of redemption really liberating? How does othering God save us and our fellow human beings from our acts of othering and subjugation? How does it bring about justice and enable right relations? Moreover, does it not reproduce and perpetuate the twisted logics of otherization by positing these dynamics as necessary and inescapable, even divine?

Moving with Barth and beyond Barth, I would propose that divine otherness is not enough. It cannot effectuate liberation, and it does not do justice to the full range of the canonical witness to Christ's redemptive significance. If there is to be any hope for actual, realized liberation, God has to do more than fulfill anthropological logics. A different redemption is necessary. And a different redemption is indeed possible—we see indications toward such a vision already in Barth's own Christology, which have been worked out further by liberationist scholars drawing on biblical and systematic insights. While the cross may continue to stand at the center of theological epistemology, its problematic aspects are also bracketed by the incarnation and resurrection, as if put in a divine parenthesis.

We have already seen that Barth significantly developed his notion of divine otherness from "the wholly Other" toward the *concrete* Other, the incarnate "one who is there for others." Barth also shifted the emphasis away from a theological epistemology in the shadow of the cross to a fuller appraisal of Jesus' history, witness, ministry, and resurrection in the final volumes of *Church Dogmatics*. Even within the architecture of Barth's doctrine of reconciliation, substitutionary atonement is only one of three movements. It appears in combination with two other movements—the uplifting of the servant to become the master in the incarnational existence of Jesus, and the prophetic quality of the true witness—that may well fund a more comprehensive and more effectively liberatory perspective. All three movements, too, are framed from the standpoint of the resurrection rather than the cross. The strength of Barth's theology is shown in the fact that his dialectics are multilayered and remain highly dynamic right to the end. But, as Barth explicitly acknowledged (WGT: 190–5), God is ultimately beyond dialectics.

So we might revisit the incarnation and find that in Jesus' history, God already fleshes out, in and for the world, an offer of a *different* difference than the one that alterity affords. This different difference is defined by conviviality and concrete solidarity and is excessive rather than oppositional. It is one of passionate witness and existence, restless rather than determinative. It is one of receiving shelter and of healing, empowering rather than dominating. It is one of reading new meaning into old inheritances, subversive rather than agonistic in its commitment. It is one of being touched and of sharing bread, open to encounter rather than exclusive. It is one of expectation, which entails holding both betrayal and promise beyond the confinements of projection. It is one that is powerful and actualistically transformative, for it remains inconclusive and irresolvably ambiguous.

The world does not recognize such a different difference. It can only otherize. Recognition fails here, precisely as it affirms its dominance: it casts difference into the role of fulfillment or revolution, supersession or failure, and it ultimately crucifies God as its other "outside the gates" of logical closure. If the world insists on its aspirational dominance, othering and being-othered are the only possible modes of relation. God takes upon Godself the role that we would encourage every victim of othering to escape: God *allows* Godself to be othered as the only means to be in relationship with this othering world, and God suffers the consequences.

The crucifixion is thus the end of the logic of othering, its necessary conclusion which allows it to reveal itself as a fatal and utterly *non*-redemptive mechanism. God reveals the anthropological dynamics of subjection and othering, identity and alterity, recognition and exclusion to be what they are: dynamics that bring death and destruction, rather than life and humanity. God's redemptive self-othering in Christ does not overcome this logic. Instead, by *fulfilling* it, its violence is unmasked, as well as the utter futility of achieving redemption by way of vicarious self-othering. Even God's self-othering cannot end the cycle of othering violence, which has continued to rage ever since the death of Jesus, and in many iterations has even been fueled by Christian supremacist imaginations.

Even in the historical process of Jesus, neither the Jews nor the Romans, neither law nor common opinion are justified. And even what little homosolidarity is achieved at the cross is short-lived: no community emerges from that crowd, and no revolution is started. Even those who mourn are not effectively united by this death: they scatter, flee, and fight. And, as is painfully obvious, this "ultimate" sacrifice has not brought an end to sacrifice. Unless one either adopts an intellectualism bordering on gnosticism (i.e., if we would just properly understand this one sacrifice, then we would have no need to further sacrifice other others—therefore, what is lacking for the actualization of reconciliation is the educational work of the theologian) or defers to a very strong eschatology (i.e., judgment will come!), the cross, in and of itself, is not redemptive.

The cross, in other words, is not enough. Its theological significance is primarily revelatory. As liberation theologians often point out, the cross reveals God's deep solidarity with the victims of othering throughout history. The crucified God performs solidarity with the crucified peoples of the world, and what we see on the cross is who God is. In the crucified peoples of the world, we can thus also recognize the face of God. The cross as the end of othering logics also reveals profound if uneasy truths about the human being (in this sense it is epistemically relevant), and it constitutes an essential solidarity (in this sense it is political). But salvation comes from somewhere else. True salvation cannot achieve universality by way of exclusion and will not erase difference in a homogenous totality. Neither does it fund a politics of recognition in subjection and dominance, nor is its solidarity built on homosociality. Rather, it moves across the radical yet nonbinary difference between God and the poor.

As I have tried to establish in this chapter, the cross reveals that *not even* God can salvage alterity, convicting its logic as onto-theology and its redemptive desire as—a projection. But if not even God's self-othering can do this, should we not look for a different kind of redemption altogether? While the first wave of Latin American and Black liberation theologians drew strongly on the theology of the cross and redemptive suffering,[31] such a focus has been ferociously critiqued by others who saw in it a problematic validation of divine and human suffering. Womanist theologians, especially, have since prompted a return to the breadth of Christological reflection, foregrounding instead the life and ministry of Jesus, the incarnation, and, more recently, the resurrection as the source of Christian hope.[32] These constructive reappropriations of what is in fact ingrained in the Christian tradition urge us to overcome the narrow modern fixation on theologies of forensic justification, substitutionary atonement, and politics of recognition.

Forensic theologies were profoundly emancipatory for the Reformers in the sixteenth century in their critique of institutional mediation. They also remain central to theological hermeneutics, and to critiques of supremacy, subjection, and domination. Ultimately, however, they do not move beyond issues of recognition and epistemology, which remain constitutively fraught with ambiguity. From a systematic perspective, the cross may be the—irrevocably and irreducibly!—the culmination of Jesus' earthly ministry and revelation of who God is and how God relates to the logics of the world. Yet it is by no means the only word that is to be said about Jesus, God, or the human being. In both a systematic and a liberationist perspective, the cross acquires significance only when it is viewed in the light of resurrection and understood as the consequence of Jesus' life, rather than being tied exclusively to a dialectical metaphysics.

In the end, then, the beginning. The resurrection breaks the logic of alterity, not the cross, and leads us back to the promise of God in Jesus' life. The resurrection discloses that God can be othered, but not conclusively, terminally, and fatally—that God cannot, ultimately, be confined to the role of Other. God is beyond otherness, even though we might not have categories for what that means. Life is beyond death, even as this may not seamlessly materialize into our projected liberational aspirations. And universal humanism might not, in the end, be the end of liberation or of theological reasoning. But maybe such disillusionment is in fact auspicious, for us, for God, and even for the wolves.

---

31. See here Ignacio Ellacuría, "The Crucified People," in *Mysterium Liberationis: Fundamental Concepts of Liberation Theology*, ed. Ignacio Ellacuría and Jon Sobrino (Maryknoll: Orbis, 1994), 580–603; Jürgen Moltmann, *The Crucified God*, trans. R. A. Wilson and John Bowden (London: SCM, 1974); Jon Sobrino, *Jesus the Liberator*, trans. Paul Burns and Francis McDonagh (Maryknoll: Orbis, 2003); and James H. Cone, *The Cross and the Lynching Tree* (Maryknoll: Orbis, 2019).

32. See here Delores Williams, *Sisters in the Wilderness: The Challenge of Womanist God-Talk* (Maryknoll: Orbis, 1993); M. Shawn Copeland, *Enfleshing Freedom: Body, Race, and the Human Being* (Minneapolis: Fortress, 2010); Eboni Marshall Turman, *Toward a Womanist Ethic of Incarnation: Black Bodies, the Black Church, and the Council of Chalcedon* (New York: Palgrave Macmillan, 2016); and M. Shawn Copeland, *Knowing Christ Crucified: The Witness of African American Religious Experience* (Maryknoll: Orbis, 2018).

Chapter 3

THE GENERATIVE FEMALE BODY AND THE ANALOGY OF FAITH IN KARL BARTH'S *CHURCH DOGMATICS*

Faye Bodley-Dangelo

> It is essentially right when John of Damascus . . . describes Mary's ear as the bodily organ of the miraculous conception of Christ.
> —CD 1/2: 201

> By being called the work of the Holy Spirit the conception of Christ is actually withdrawn from any analogy save the analogy of faith.
> —CD 1/2: 201

Karl Barth's radical relationalism is built upon the irreducible alterity of the God who is revealed in Christ, and it serves as a promising site for inquiries into the political potential of Barth's theology to resist ideologies that seek to harness God's power in order to efface the differences and multiplicities of the many creatures surrounding us. Yet a nagging set of questions continues to trouble the waters of this resource. Does Barth's God create a space for creaturely alterity, or does his God make space only for lesser copies of Godself? Can Barth's theological imaginary accommodate multiple sites of creaturely difference and agency without constructing them as potential threats to divine power—threats that must be neutralized, rendered abjectly dependent on God in order to have any kind of relationship with God? These sorts of questions arise rather persistently when it comes to Barth's account of sexual difference and his subordination of women, and indeed all of creation, to men. Does the dominating God, whose raw power to act, to create, save, and redirect, call into existence imitative men—men who reiterate this power in their control and domination over all other creaturely beings? Does Barth's radical relationality ever really get off the ground? Or does it flounder upon a repetition and legitimization of unjust social arrangements?

Barth's doctrine of creation is an obvious place where these sorts of worries arise for critics such as Catherine Keller. She appreciates that "Barth meant to honor the creation-complex of finite and uncertain relations precisely by proclaiming the 'infinite qualitative difference' of its Creator" and recognizes that, "in a limited sense . . . Barth sought what feminism has since found: a radical relationality, or intersubjectivity, in which difference is not swallowed up by the self, but enhanced."[1]

---

1. Catherine Keller, *Face of the Deep: A Theology of Becoming* (New York: Routledge, 2003), 87.

Yet Keller uncovers in Barth's reading of Gen. 1 a phallocentric logic that swallows up difference, distorting and undermining the liberative potential of his project, and a dominating intimacy of a hypermasculine God whose self-sufficiency heightens in direct proportion to human self-sufficiency. "Is the (self-)possessive modern subjectivity that Barth denounces merely displaced upward, projected onto the propertied Lord in heaven?" she asks. She goes on to suggest that, "in his attempt to put Modern Man in his place, Barth seems to have transferred to the Lord's account our most modern claims to certainty and property." She suspects that Barth's "gender logic," with its dominating language of order, "only make[s] explicit and literal motives that otherwise remain metaphorically indirect, to be teased out of the small print of bigger matters."[2]

Graham Ward shares some of these worries when looking at Barth's reading of the creation and naming of Eve in Gen. 2. Here he finds an economy of the same that effaces difference—a phallocentrism in which no genuine sexual difference can be established because the other sex is always interpreted from the perspective of the one, monolithic male sex. Barth, he argues, has merely "reaffirmed the socio-sexual *status quo*," since "the female is only a variant of the male" and "she functions as complement, not difference." Yet Ward also finds resources in Barth that recover the political potential of Barth's radical relationality in another economy of desire based not on the lack that drives Adam to seek a partner, but on "the very excess of love in God that pours itself out towards the other," lavished upon creatures, overflowing from God's internal Trinitarian economy.[3]

Like Ward, Willis Jenkins finds an economy of excess and overflow in the Garden of Eden of Gen. 2. However, unlike Keller, he also finds imagery of maternal generativity that, he suggests, stands in dialectical relation to what Keller takes to be the hyper-phallic language of Gen. 1. God creates a garden that (like God's self) overflows in abundant gift-giving aid to other creatures, in water, mist, and bountiful fruit. Moreover, in contrast to Barth's many ecologically oriented critics, Jenkins discerns in Barth's reading of Gen. 2 a resource for ecotheology and environmental ethics that cultivates responsive practices, calling readers to recognize their situatedness in a cosmos that is the special place of God's indwelling. Even so, Jenkins suspects that Barth's account of divine creative action might require some reconfiguration: its lordship/service paradigm, appropriated from the modernist subject, leads humans—and males in particular—to assume for themselves an administrative responsibility for the proper order of creation and social relations, which they then order to serve their own ends.[4]

In this chapter, I engage these criticisms by focusing on the often-subtle ways that Barth attempts to neutralize female bodily imagery. I look at two

2. Ibid., 89–90 and 95.
3. Graham Ward, "The Erotics of Redemption—After Karl Barth," *Theology and Sexuality* 8 (1998): 66, 67, and 58.
4. Willis Jenkins, *Ecologies of Grace: Environmental Ethics and Christian Theology* (Oxford: Oxford University Press, 2008), 153–87.

doctrinal loci—the virginal conception of Christ and the doctrine of creation—and show how Barth adopts different strategies for addressing what seems to represent an unspecified threat to his way of conceiving divine activity upon creatures: the generative female body. I will point, specifically, to places where this body surfaces momentarily as a threat to divine creative potency that must be neutralized. I argue that this threat has much to do with an analogy that might be drawn between the female body's role in sexual reproduction and the capacity of the creature to contribute to or collaborate with God's creative and saving activity on behalf of creatures. At stake for Barth is his analogy of faith, wherein the human creature brings no capacity and offers no contribution to the revelatory and saving work that God enacts. We will see that the generative female body, in its very capacity to reproduce, is a vexing site of creaturely activity, one that Barth ultimately fails, perhaps even refuses, to incorporate into his doctrine of creation.

The Virgin Mary

Mary of the annunciation scene in Lk. 1 appears at several points in the first volume of *Church Dogmatics* as a model for the obedient response to the revelatory address—a model, that is, of the human being's participation in the revelatory event. The participation of her virginal body in the conception of Christ functions as an analogy for the lack of resources that she (or anyone else) brings to an encounter with God. In both Mary's capacity for the revelatory address and her capacity to conceive as a virgin, Barth argues, there is nothing for the theologian to see.

Barth is especially interested in Mary's remark, "be it unto me according to thy word" (Lk. 1:38, KJV). With these words, Mary exercises her free decision to acknowledge, embrace, and vocally profess/confess what she has heard in the revelatory event—namely, the angelic promise that she will conceive as a virgin. She is one of many biblical figures that Barth uses to argue that human beings have no resource or capacity in and of themselves to hear the revelatory address spoken through creaturely media. If we are to hear God speak in the words of scripture and proclamation, if we are to know something of God by way of creaturely media, it can only be through the miracle of a divine act wherein human concepts and words temporarily communicate knowledge of God's will and nature as it has been revealed in Christ. We bring nothing to the table, so to speak, with respect to intellect, will, or a feeling that can cooperate with God's revelatory address. We have no intrinsic capacity for God's self-revelatory work upon us. Indeed, the figure of Mary is an especially helpful model in refuting both Roman Catholic and Protestant configurations of a human being who collaborates with or is well suited to respond to God's revelatory work. A model hearer of God's divine address, Mary brings no inherent quality, worth, or piety to the event of divine revelatory encounter; she supplies nothing that makes her intrinsically worthy of the grace for which she is elected. And at times, her very body functions for Barth as an analogy of this lack of capacity. I turn now to three different occasions in which Mary plays this role for Barth.[5]

The first is a brief passage in *Church Dogmatics* I/2, §22, where Barth evokes Mary's words, "be it unto me," as a model for preachers and dogmaticians. As would-be hearers of the divine address, mediated through scripture, the task of proclamation is to re-speak what one has heard, with the hope that in this proclamation, others will hear the divine address. Barth writes:

> If the human word of Christian preaching is to perform the service of leading to the hearing of God's Word, it must obviously have the quality of creating obedience to the Word of God, as it is itself obedient. It must be a selfless human word, a human word which will not say this or that in a spirit of self-assertion, but devote itself only to letting God's own Word say what must be said. *Like a window, it must be a transparent word; or like a mirror, a reflecting word.* The

---

5. Besides the passages mentioned in this section, Barth discusses the virgin birth also in GA II.14, 365–7; and *Göttingen Dogmatics: Instruction in the Christian Religion*, vol. 1, trans. Geoffrey W. Bromiley (Grand Rapids: Eerdmans, 1991), 160–7. Literature on the virgin conception in Barth's theology includes William A. Mueller, "Karl Barth's View of the Virgin Birth," *Review and Expositor* 51, no. 4 (1954): 508–21; L. Gordon Tait, "Karl Barth and the Virgin Mary," *Journal of Ecumenical Studies* 4 (1967): 406–25; Andrew Louth, *Mary and the Mystery of the Incarnation: An Essay on the Mother of God in the Theology of Karl Barth* (Fairacres: SLG, 1977); Geoffrey W. Bromiley, *An Introduction to the Theology of Karl Barth* (Grand Rapids: Eerdmans, 1979): 26–7; Paul S. Fiddes, "Mary in the Theology of Karl Barth," in *Mary in Doctrine and Devotion: Papers of the Liverpool Congress, 1989, of the Ecumenical Society of the Blessed Virgin Mary*, ed. Alberic Stacpoole (Collegeville: Liturgical Press, 1990), 111–27; Volker Strümke, "Die Jungfrauengeburt als Geheimnis des Glaubens—ethische Annmerkungen," *Neue Zeitschrift für systematische Theologie und Religionsphilosophie* 49, no. 4 (2007): 423–41; and Tim Perry, "What is Little Mary Here For?" *Pro Ecclesia* 19, no. 1 (2010): 46–68. Dustin Resch's *A Sign of Mystery: Karl Barth's Interpretation of the Virgin Birth* (Burlington: Ashgate, 2012) provides the most extensive treatment of Barth's understanding of the virgin birth. He finds that, beginning with *The Great Promise* of 1934 and most clearly articulated in CD I/2, §15, Barth shifts from giving the virgin birth a constitutive role in the incarnation to presenting it as a sign with the purely noetic function of unveiling the identity of Christ. He notes that this development enables Barth to avoid the many criticisms typically directed at the Augustinian approach to the virgin conception, for Barth can now affirm the virgin birth without having to affirm a particular view of original sin, its transmission, and human sexuality. Resch only briefly describes and does not critically engage Barth's assumptions about gender. However, Resch does show that by CD I/2, §15, Barth had distanced himself from his earlier appreciation for scholastic discussions of the Holy Spirit's role in the conception of a sinless Christ, along with their antiquated views of procreation, wherein the female seed receives its form from the male seed.

more it repudiates and rejects anything which might intervene as a third element between God's Word and the human hearer, the less it obtrudes itself in its own solidity between God and the hearer, the more it is positively an indication, pointer and compulsion to hearing the Word of God itself, and negatively a hushing of all the possible notes of false idolatry and human exaltation—the better it will be. (CD I/2: 764; emphases added)

For scriptural examples of such speech, Barth directs readers to Mary's response to the annunciation and also to Christ's words in the Garden of Gethsemane:

We may be permitted to remind ourselves at this point that in mediaeval art a frame of clear cut glass was used for symbolic pictures of the Virgin. This was an implied allusion to Lk. 1:38: "Behold the handmaid of the Lord, be it unto me according to thy word." We may also recall Mt. 26:39: "Not as I will, but as thou wilt." It is pure vessels like this which the divine Logos seeks, creates and finds in the proclamation of the Church as well. (CD I/2: 764)

Let us keep this image of the vessel Mary in mind as we move forward. Mary, not only with her words of proclamation but also her body as an object of artistic representation, must be rendered a translucent pane of glass—lacking anything visible or vocal that would obscure the activity of the divine self-revelatory Word.

The second occasion is found in Barth's Advent lectures.[6] Here Mary's role as a model agent is fleshed out in an extended reading of Lk. 1, and again her words exemplify the obedient hearing of the divine address to Barth's audience of theologians and preachers. Gabriel appears first to Zechariah and then to Mary, promising impossible pregnancies: both the postmenopausal Elizabeth and the virgin Mary will conceive. In his description of the scene in which the pregnant Elizabeth and Mary greet one another, Barth finds a place for the imagery of pregnant bodies, connecting the women's fellowship and their pregnant bodies with the community of the church and the presence of the divine Word within it:

Where there are such people who have received the promise, such a Mary and such an Elizabeth, where the *Church* is, there is what is called pregnancy in physical life, there is expectancy and the presence of what is expected; there is not only a knowledge of grace but there is grace itself. Where the Church is, there is he in the midst of them, there is he who is the hope of the Church, without whom there would be no Church, *as little as the world which God has created from nothing*.[7]

---

6. Karl Barth, *The Great Promise*, trans. Hans Freund (New York: Philosophical Library, 1963). The preface to *The Great Promise* provides an account of the context in which these lectures were delivered.

7. Ibid., 39. Emphases added.

However, the pregnant bodies of Mary and Elizabeth only find a figurative place in Barth's retelling of this scene once any possible capacity to conceive has been fully neutralized. Their bodies, in other words, have first to be turned into a transparent pane of glass through which the divine Word might be seen, now displaced by a church-vessel, impregnated through the Spirit by the Logos. It would seem that the imagery of pregnancy itself is not threatening so much as the specific generative activity that the bodies of women play in sexual reproduction, a problem that will become clearer as we proceed. Barth's reference to the world created from nothing, incidentally, is also noteworthy: God's raw power to create out of absolutely nothing is frequently on Barth's mind when he speaks of these miraculous conceptions.

The third occasion is Barth's most extended discussion of Mary, in *Church Dogmatics* I/2, §15, where he attends more closely to the miracle of the conception than to Mary's words. Mary's body's contribution, or lack thereof, to God's activity serves as an analogy to what the human does not bring to the revelatory event. Christology is the focus of §15, specifically the doctrine of Christ's two natures, encapsulated in the creedal formula, *vere deus vere homo*. And Barth gives the virginal conception a prominent place in his discussion. His focus is the virgin Mary both as a referent of the creed (*natus ex Maria virgine*) and as a character in the Lucan annunciation scene, but he seems most preoccupied with the former issue. Barth argues that the virgin conception is a *necessary* doctrine because it serves as a sign that points beyond itself to the mystery of the incarnation, to the union of the Logos with an individual human nature. "Born of a virgin" does not explain that mystery, but rather casts a light on its very inexplicability by foregrounding the utter incapacity of the creature for the work God that does with it.

Barth draws analogies between (a) the incapacity of Christ's human nature for its union with the Logos, (b) Mary's incapacity to conceive without a male partner, and (c) the reader's incapacity to acknowledge and confess the creedal claim that Christ is both very God and very man, born of a virgin. At each level, divine activity overcomes human incapacity. Mary's profession of faith ("be it unto me according to thy word") exemplifies for readers the faithful hearing and response as they consider two creedal declarations (CD I/2: 172–3): that Christ is very God and very man and that Christ was born of a virgin.

Barth shows no interest in Mary's maternal fecundity or in any aspect of her maternal relationship to Christ—say, his gestation, his birth. Anything other than the miracle of the conception itself, it seems, would cloud the sheet of glass. Rather, Barth's interest in Mary's conceiving body resides precisely in what it *lacks*. First, "Virgin birth means birth without previous sexual union between man and woman. Speaking generally, it is what it lacks that distinguishes the birth of Christ, that marks it as the mystery of God" (CD I/2: 190). Second, the virgin conception excludes the activity and desire of the male to be master of history and culture.

Regarding the first point of absence, Barth writes:

> The event of sex cannot be considered at all as the sign of the divine *agape* which seeks not its own and never fails. It is the work of willing, achieving, creative,

sovereign man [*Mensch*], and as such points elsewhere than to the majesty of the divine pity. Therefore the virginity of Mary, and not the wedlock of Joseph and Mary, is the sign of revelation and of the knowledge of the mystery of Christmas. (CD I/2: 192)

While, positively, the virgin conception means Christ was born of a mother's body and blood like any other son, thereby receiving something from his *mother* (so CD I/2: 185-6), Barth acknowledges, gesturing to Mary's bodily fecundity, that its theological significance resides in inability and incapacity. Whatever Mary "does" as the conceiving virgin, she does not do it as a female partner in sexual reproduction. Mary's incapacity to conceive precisely "as a virgin," instead, directs attention to the incapacity of the human nature itself for the incarnation and thus for God's revelation. Barth makes this connection explicit:

It is declared that in any other way, i.e., by the natural way in which a human wife becomes a mother, there can be no motherhood of the Lord and so no such entrance gate of revelation into our world. In other words, human nature possesses no capacity for becoming the human nature of Jesus Christ, the place of divine revelation. It cannot be the workmate of God. If it actually becomes so, it is not because of any attributes which it possessed already and in itself, but because of what is done to it by the divine Word, and so not because of what it has to do or give, but because of what it has to suffer and receive—and at the hand of God. (CD I/2: 188)

With this same concern in mind, Barth detaches the conception of Christ by the Holy Spirit from any analogy with sexual reproduction, given that such an analogy would suggest a collaboration or cooperation between God and creature in the saving work of God. "We should not imagine the Holy Spirit . . . fulfills the function of the male," for the Holy Spirit is no "apotheosised husband," and there is no marriage between the two (CD I/2: 200-1); "Joseph is completely set aside, while God takes his place, not in the creative function of a creative father, but simply as God, as the Creator who performs a miracle, creating and instituting something new" (CD I/2: 194). In this final quotation, we see once again that the doctrine of creation is never far from the surface of Barth's discussion of the virgin conception.

With these concerns in view, Barth proposes Mary's ear as the orifice that is "penetrated" in the conception of Christ:

It is essentially right when John of Damascus . . . describes Mary's ear as the bodily organ of the miraculous conception of Christ. "The operation of the Holy Spirit at the conception of Jesus is one mediated through Mary's faith. Mary believes . . . and by believing in the Word of God spoken by the angel she is thereby enabled to take the eternal Word into herself and independently to bring about the beginning of the Redeemer's life (Ed. Böhl, *Dogmatik*, 1887, 311)." (CD I/2: 201)

With this passing slippage between Mary's ear and vagina, Barth evokes sexual intercourse as an analogy for the purpose of displacing it, thus *again* refusing any place for an analogy between human copulation and the Spirit's relation to Mary. "By being called the work of the Holy Spirit the conception of Christ is actually withdrawn from any analogy save the analogy of faith and, like every genuine miracle, from any explanation of its How" (CD I/2: 201). Whatever Mary's fecund body might bring to the event of conception must be bracketed by our dogmatician, with the reader's gaze redirected from her sexed, material specificity to an ear—that part of the body in which Barth can see a reflection of his own orifices for the entry of the Logos.

Barth glances again at the doctrine of creation when suggesting that this miraculous conception is a new creation. The conception *ex Maria* is not a creation ex nihilo, for what is conceived of the virgin is a "new creature." The virgin's body is the old humanity, out of which God miraculously fashions something new (CD I/2: 186). Any part that Mary's body might play could only obfuscate the miracle of divine potency, and this is precisely what is at stake for Barth in refusing the imagery of female fecundity and capacity here as in *Church Dogmatics* III/1, which I will consider shortly. Indeed, it is *only* in this way that the virgin conception can function for Barth as a sign barring any recourse to a natural theology: "Against the creaturely self-glorification which might creep in here and interpret man with his existence as God's partner, against all natural theology, the *ex virgine* with its positive background in the *conceptus de Spiritu sancto* will provide the necessary safeguard" (CD I/2: 187). Human nature bears no more capacity for its assumption by the Logos than does Mary's body for the miraculous conception of Christ.

The connection between Barth's worry about Mary's fecundity in conception and his analogy of faith becomes clearer when he sets Mary's incapacity to know God, in and of herself, as a supporting parallel to her bodily incapacity. Barth rejects a Roman Catholic reading that sees in Mary's words evidence of a piety that makes her worthy of the conception for which she is selected. Her response to Gabriel is neither indicative of a "receptive readiness," nor a "living, passive and active receptivity to regenerating grace," nor "the creature's openness or readiness for its God"; she is not in any way "disposed to possess the grace of the motherhood in question" (CD I/2: 144–5). In her piety, she is no more capable of contributing to this divine work than her body is capable of conceiving without a male partner.

It is precisely (and only) in her response of faith, in her verbal acknowledgment and embrace of the revelatory disclosure through Gabrielle, that Mary participates in God's work and transcends the role of a spectator. Barth aligns Mary's "let it be" with figures like John the Baptist, arguing that she points beyond herself to Christ:

> the greatness of the New Testament figure of Mary consists in the fact that all the interest is directed away from herself to the Lord. It is her "low estate" (ταπείνωσις, Lk. 1:48), and the glory of God which encounters her, not her own person, which can properly be made the object of a special consideration, doctrine and veneration. Along with John the Baptist Mary is at once the personal climax of the Old Testament penetrating to the New Testament, and

> the first man of the New Testament: "Behold the handmaid of the Lord; be it unto me according to thy word" (Lk. 1:38). She is simply man to whom the miracle of revelation happens. (CD I/2: 140)

As with the human being's experience of the revelatory event, so also with Mary's conceiving body and faithful response. There is nothing to see here, only something to see *through*—a transparent pane of glass. Once again, Barth connects Mary's "be it unto me" with Christ's "not as I will," reading both as an acquiescence to divine judgment accepted in trepidation (CD I/2: 187).

The significance of the virgin conception lies not only in its exclusion of the sexual activity of male and female, but also in the exclusion of the male from any role whatsoever. Here Barth assumes the power and dominance of men in history, society, and culture and notes specifically the humbling effects of the exclusion of this power and activity from God's work. "So it is the male who must be set aside here," Barth writes, "because he is peculiarly significant for the world history of human genius. What takes place in the mystery of Christmas is not world history and not the work of human genius" (CD I/2: 194). Barth attributes male predominance to a consequence of the Fall—the curse that Adam should rule over Eve, and the male tyranny that follows (a view that he no longer holds when he reaches his doctrine of creation). In this way, Barth uses the virgin conception to humble the self-exalting "master" of human history yet also, and in the same breath, to silence feminist criticism of that mastery:

> If woman demands justification and rehabilitation in face of the significant pre-eminence of the male for world history—and it is better that she should not—let her keep to this sign. By its limitation of man and his sin it means at the same time the limitation of male pre-eminence. The sign declares that if Christ were the son of a male He would be a sinner like all the rest, and that therefore He cannot be the son of any male. (CD I/2: 194)

These words are typical of Barth's references to the feminist movement. Women ought to make no demands, they ought not to revolt, protest, or show any sort of critical self-assertion; they ought rather to restrain themselves and their complaints, however legitimate the complaints might be, and they ought to take comfort in the fact that God has condemned the proud in the figure of Mary (who, recall, is a transparent pane of glass through which we might see God's raw power to act).

Earth and Rib

While creation out of nothing is close to the surface in passages about the virgin conception, Mary does not make an appearance in Barth's reading of the creation narratives of Gen. 1 and 2. Perhaps surprisingly: we might expect her to play a supporting role, given the sort of narrative parallels in divine activity of which Barth is usually fond of highlighting—for as God creates something new out of something old in the conception of Christ, so God does also in the creation of Adam and of Eve, using material (earth and rib) with no inherent capacity for the work that God does with it. But in Barth's earlier discussions, as we have seen, the generative capacities of Mary's body had first to be neutralized by the exclusion of any sexual partner (human or divine). In these Genesis scenes, something of a follow-up can be discerned, with the generative capacities associated with the female body evoked only to be evicted from the narrative altogether, lest any analogy should compromise God's creative potency. Barth is at pains to emphasize the sterility, the abject incapacity, of the materials that God uses for the creatures God makes.[8]

We see this first in Barth's paraphrase of Gen. 1:2: "And the earth was formless and void; and darkness was upon the face of the deep; and the Spirit of God moved upon the face of the waters" (CD III/1: 102). In a disturbing move, at least for those who find in v. 2 beautifully suggestive imagery for God's relation to creation, Barth reconfigures these primeval waters as the nothingness, the threat of all that God has not chosen: death, chaos, and disorder; all that God has rejected with the words "Let there be light" in v. 3. The Spirit of Elohim, hovering over these waters, represents for Barth the sort of being that God has elected not to be in the moment of the divine utterance of v. 3: a God who is impotent and utterly powerless to effect the chaos. Barth therefore follows commentators who find in v. 2 the residue of a mythic cosmology that gestures to a matriarchal worldview in which mother figures took center stage. Unlike these commentators, however, Barth argues that the biblical narrator evokes mythical worldviews in order to critique and reject them. The hovering Spirit, in fact, is not sufficiently virile to represent God. Rather, "the Spirit of *Elohim* is condemned to the complete impotence of a bird hovering or brooding over shoreless or sterile waters," an activity Barth finds akin to a "passive-contemplative role and function" (CD III/1: 107). Catherine Keller captures the gendered dimensions of this idiosyncratic treatment when she writes that,

> the gender of the bird itself slides menacingly between mother and male.... Barth bats a double-whammy for Protestant virility. An inadequate masculinity "flutters" above an abortive femininity.... Any concept... of a generative chaos, a spontaneous natality, must be sterilized. As to any God who demonstrates queer male or any female propensities—Barth kills both birds with a single stone.[9]

Barth evokes generative female bodies several times when discussing this verse for the purpose of excluding them from any contribution to his interpretation. He

---

8. For an extensive analysis of gender and maternal imagery in Barth's readings of the Genesis creation narratives, see Faye Bodley-Dangelo, *Sexual Difference, Gender, and Agency in Karl Barth's Church Dogmatics* (London: T&T Clark, 2020), 61–110.

9. Keller, *Face of the Deep*, 94.

speaks of this water as a boundless chaos, as sterile and barren, completely lacking in resources for the production of the orderly world that God creates. He objects to interpreters who see in the waters "a world-egg" or "a mother-womb which bears the future," over which a dove-like Spirit hovers: "All explanations of the origin of the world in terms of divine conception and birth are superseded when the 'And God said' is put at the beginning" (CD III/1: 104 and 114). This imagery in v. 2 Barth finds to be completely antithetical to the Old Testament Elohim for whom "creation means the irruption and revelation of the divine compassion" (CD III/1: 110).

In Gen. 2, which opens with earth already created, Barth depicts this earth as barren, sterile, desert-like and arid, susceptible to dissolution into chaos apart from the sustained will of God to reject the latter. When God fashions both animal life and human life from this earth, Barth insists that the material that God uses disallows any analogy to maternal fecundity, neutralizing the same threat he found in Mary's virgin body and the fecund chaos of Gen. 1:2. Regarding the emergence of animals from the earth on the sixth day (Gen. 1:24), Barth declares: "We are spared the thought of a bearing 'mother earth' as the principle of the world" (CD III/1: 179). Of God's fashioning of Adam from the dust, he offers the same disavowals:

> There is no place here, of course, for the idea of "mother earth" . . . It is quite impossible both in the sense and course of the saga and in the rest of the Old Testament. It is not the earth but God who produces man, and He does so according to His plan and decree, in the free choice of a lump of earth and in the sovereign formation of this lump. The Pauline association of creation with the resurrection of the dead (Rom. 4:17) is very much to the point in relation to Gen. 2:7. . . . For the sake of clarity it is best not to speak of a "deep sleep of creation" which man originally slept, "resting on virgin soil . . . in full surrender to the blessed earth" . . . What existed prior to the event described here was not man, either in the womb of mother earth or sleeping on the earth. It was merely a lump of earth like others, but one out of which man was creatively fashioned by God. (CD III/1: 244–5)

In God's work of creating new entities from already-created entities, then, the earth's role reflects that of Mary's virginally conceiving body—especially once Barth has carefully removed any threatening capacity to collaborate with the divine creative act, any metaphorical association with the fecund female body.

When turning to the creation of Eve in Gen. 2, Barth is again eager to emphasis Adam's incapacity. Adam's rib has nothing to contribute to the life-generating work of God in fashioning Eve from it, and Barth emphasizes that Adam "did not actively participate in the creation of woman" (CD III/1: 294), since *God* put Adam to sleep before surgically extracting the rib from his side. However, Adam, like Mary in *Church Dogmatics* I/2, *does* have a role to play—in his free decision to accept and embrace the work and gift of God upon and for him. Barth depicts Adam's naming of Eve as a response to the divine revelatory event, just as earlier he depicted Mary's response to the angel in *Church Dogmatics* I/2. Yet while God's creative activity was evoked in *Church Dogmatics* I, when Barth spoke of the virgin conception, Mary and her "let it be" are not mentioned in Barth's retelling of this Edenic scene. We are instead presented with an Eve whose narrative silence in Gen. 2 is transfigured by Barth into a transparent pane of glass. Barth declares that Eve does not herself participate in her own creation as Adam does by naming her, and Barth sees through her silence her unspoken consent to Adam's decision to choose and name her for himself (CD III/1: 303).

Genealogies

In his treatment of maternal bodies and in the attention given to patrilineal succession, Barth again evokes mother figures for the strict purpose of robbing them of any theological contribution. While Barth detaches sexual reproduction from the theological significance of sexual difference and the relationship between the sexes and downplays the divine command to human beings to be fruitful and multiply, he does secure a figural function for parenthood in the patrilineal genealogies of the Old Testament. In the relational function of fatherhood and motherhood (but explicitly *not* the sexual encounter itself), Barth finds a prophetic anticipation of the coming of Christ. And yet, he makes a point of claiming that mothers do not appear in any scriptural genealogies. Thus while Barth has disassociated sexual reproduction from theological significance, he smuggles male generativity back into view by drawing attention to the patrilineal succession where what matters for the theologian is a father reproducing himself in a son—while woman, he declares, "is not mentioned in Gen. 5:3, in the table which follows, or—significantly—in any of the genealogical tables of the Bible" (CD III/1: 199). So dire is the threat of female generativity to Barth that, in this statement, Barth must efface the genealogy of Matt. 1 where five women appear in a lineage ending in none other than Christ himself. It would seem that Barth's anxiety over the female body has temporarily interfered with his recollection of what is, for his own dogmatic purposes, one of the two most important genealogies in all of Scripture. Or, perhaps, the generative female bodies of these noteworthy biblical figures (Tamar, Rahab, Ruth, Bathsheba, and Mary) have become so translucent to Barth that he fails even to notice their presence in this particular genealogy—peering right through them down the long lineage of fathers reproducing sons—fails even to see the displacement of a father by the virgin mother.

Only a few pages earlier, we see a repetition of this maternal elision when Barth finds a prefiguration of covenant history in the divine command to fish and birds to be fruitful and multiply (Gen. 1:22): he suggests that this command points to "a God-like creature ordained for fatherhood and sonship and continuing its existence in the relationship of fatherhood and sonship" (CD III/1: 170). He makes no mention of female birds, fish, or human beings whose generative capacities are necessary to secure creaturely sonship, nor is there any reference to the birthing of daughters.

Only the generativity of male human bodies is allowed into view, a chain of filiation, reflecting the Trinitarian Father and Son, in a covenantal history that moves forward genealogically toward the birth of the messiah. Barth writes:

> Jesus Christ ... is the man whose existence was necessary for the perfecting of the earth; *for the redemption of its aridity, barrenness and death*; for the meaningful fulfilment of its God-given hope; and especially for the realisation of the hope of Israel. He is the man who, *taken from all creation, all humanity and all Israel*, and yet belonging to them and a victim of their curse, was in that direct, personal and special immediacy of God to Him a creature, man, *the seed of Abraham and the Son of David*. . . . He is the man who did not return emptyhanded, but with the spoils of hope, to the earth from which He was taken but for which He was also given. (CD III/1: 239; emphases added)

At this point in the *Church Dogmatics*, Mary is nowhere in sight, not even as a transparent pane of glass. She is not named; her body is now displaced by the barren earth. Indeed, Barth is no longer interested in Jesus' lack of a human father, for there is no acknowledgment whatsoever of the disruption of father–son lineage by the virgin conception, nor any mention of God's exclusion of the role of male "master" of history from any contribution to the conception of Christ. It is Mary and all women with her who are now excluded from the prefiguration and movement of covenant history that rests upon the effacement of any role of female bodies.

Conclusion

I have shown that the fecund female body appears as a problematic site in Barth's *Church Dogmatics* at key junctures in God's creative and saving activity, coming into view only in the form of refusal and rejection. In these contexts, the capacity of the female body to produce offspring surfaces as a threat to the potency and miracle of the divine act. It is marked as risky: as an occasion to smuggle into view a natural theology, wherein the creature makes a contribution or brings its own resources to the work God does to and for it.

From the vantage point of these texts, it would seem that Barth's doctrine of creation allows no welcoming home for female bodies in his doctrine of creation. The relationship of mother and child poses a problem for a theological imaginary running on an economy in which the divine Father begets a Son, then reproduces a copy of that filial relationship in the production of a creature, who in turn reflects this relation in his generation of a son and inauguration of a patrilineal succession leading up to the Christ. The "gap" that Mary's virgin conception produced in patrilineal succession in *Church Dogmatics* I has become so translucent in *Church Dogmatics* III that Barth no longer acknowledges its presence. Generative third parties interfere with his picture of divine creative potency and creaturely incapacity. Arid, barren, dead-like material is required in order to secure the miracle and potency of God's creative work. In the virgin conception, the fecundity of the female body had to be neutralized in order to secure God's miracle. In the creation scenes it must be eradicated.

My intent has been to show, then, that feminist interpreters such as Keller have good cause for finding in Barth's theological imaginary a hyper-masculinist God, a phallocentric logic, a reproduction of the same, and an elision and effacement of maternal bodies. Such criticisms cannot be readily dismissed by scholars hoping to find in Barth's theology resources for liberative and inclusive ends, nor can the passages to which these critics point be bracketed as if they were merely a poor choice of wording on Barth's part or evidence of a momentary oversight. Rather, they require careful interrogation. As fleeting as Barth's references to and treatment of female bodies are, they continue to raise broader questions about the ways in which Barth's theology legitimizes patriarchal social relations. How do women find a home in a theological imaginary where female fertility poses such a threat to the creator? What kind of God is envisioned here, when "his" power, love, and will to create and sustain creaturely existence is so readily undermined by the very capacities of the creatures God has lovingly created? Why, in the creative acts of God, must creaturely resources and agencies be rendered barren, infertile, dead-like in order for God's grace, love, and creative majesty to be duly recognized and adored? How deeply ingrained is this theologian's anxieties in his construal of divine and creaturely relations and the role of the miracle in those relations? With such questions in view, it is not surprising that Barth's radical relationality comes at a price that some are unwilling to pay.

Chapter 4

THE DISABLED GOD AND COVENANT ONTOLOGY

Lisa Powell

Theological Reflection and the Disabled God

I begin with this confession: I am relatively new to the study of Barth. I avoided it as much as I could as a theology student at Princeton Theological Seminary, where it was debated with heat and sometimes vitriol in our seminar rooms by male colleagues. The whole scene felt like a manifestation of masculinist hegemony, stifling to this Wesleyan woman with an emerging commitment to liberation theology. I came across the fierce debate in Barth studies over the logical priority of election to triunity because a friend and colleague got mixed up in it all, and I was curious. So I read Bruce McCormack's "Seek God Where He May Be Found," as well as a series of articles written in response.[1] I was shocked to find myself moved by the account of God outlined in that original essay. I did not care in the least which was the "truer" reading of Barth, or whether or not a significant shift in Barth's thought was demonstrable. I simply found that McCormack's position articulated an understanding of God that resonated with the liberation theologies that had rescued my faith, while offering a precision of doctrinal explication for which I longed.

In this essay, I will sketch some of the promise that I see in this conception of God for the concerns of liberation theology, particularly disability theology as introduced in Nancy Eiesland's *The Disabled God*.[2] How, you may ask, could debates about the primordial "ordering" of God's being bear on the pressing concerns of the oppressed in our world? Or you may resonate with Ivone Gebara's summary of a common lack of interest in the Trinity: "It seems to take place far from us, far from our own flesh and concerns. And besides, it seems to be a sharing among 'persons' who are totally spiritual and perfect. It is, after all, a divine

---

1. Bruce L. McCormack, "Seek God Where He May Be Found: A Response to Edwin van Driel," *Scottish Journal of Theology* 60, no. 1 (2007): 62–79.

2. Nancy Eiesland, *The Disabled God: Toward a Liberatory Theology of Disability* (Nashville: Abingdon, 1994).

communion that barely affects us."³ Certainly, there is no policy proposal or action plan for social change in this essay. However, liberationists have long asserted that our God-talk matters, and I believe there is a way of reading Barth, through the lens of disability theology, that helps one to understand more fully that the divine life is neither "far off from our own flesh" nor "totally spiritual."

Another confession is warranted: I am not currently disabled, although chronic illness played a significant part in my childhood, and I know that at any moment, my physical, cognitive, and mental status may change. So I am writing, in effect, as an outsider. I receive the social and structural benefits of being abled-bodied and being perceived as such. Even so, disability theory and theology have been vital to my formation as a liberation theologian. The critiques that disability studies bring to feminist theory and theology, for example, expose the ways in which even the best-intentioned ideas can replicate social values that denigrate the gifts of others. And disability is a crucial perspective in liberation theology, because it crosses every context with the force of intersectionality. The disabled are twice as likely to be poor in the United States, and people of color are disproportionately disabled. Disability is the largest "minority" population, too, and most people are impacted by disability at some point in their lives—through a parent who becomes physically or mentally impaired as they grow older, a sibling in the home with a mental illness or physical impairment, or through a temporary or enduring disability acquired at birth or through an accident, illness, or aging. And yet disability is the most overlooked perspective in our liberationist conversations, including at the conference from which this book sprang, where scholars repeatedly critiqued the assumption of normativity given to the white heterosexual male, yet often failed to remember that this norm is also an able-bodied one.

Notwithstanding its critiques of feminist theology, disability theology shares many common commitments with liberation theologies. For example, one finds skepticism of divine transcendence in favor of an emphasis on immanence, as well as a critique of divine omnipotence, seen as the divinization of "masculinist" or able-bodied power. Shared also is a critique of the supremacy of the independent, self-sufficient individual identified in much Western theology, and a rejection of anthropologies that posit humanity as primarily "mind" or "spirit," and their concomitant binaries that differentiate normal and abnormal, that value males over females, and that denigrate embodiment. Disability theologies also share a rejection of the corresponding image of God as the ultimate perfection of this Western ideal human, which would figure God as supremely autonomous and self-sufficient and refuses divine vulnerability, interdependence, and mutuality. Much like Mary Daly's famous dictum "If God is male, then the male is God,"⁴ if divine freedom is utter independence, those who live independently are figured closer to

---

3. Ivone Gebara, *Longing for Running Water: Ecofeminism and Liberation* (Minneapolis: Fortress, 1999), 138.

4. Mary Daly, *Beyond God the Father: Toward a Philosophy of Women's Liberation* (Boston: Beacon, 1985), 19.

God than those whose embodiment renders them in need of care or assistance (be it a prosthetic, a care-giver, a drug to manage mental illness, or social assistance like food stamps and housing shelters). Because disability theologians reject self-sufficiency and independence as ultimate values, these qualities are not given supreme status as attributes of God.

Disability studies as an academic discipline in the United States sprang from the disability rights movement and activism of the 1960s and 1970s, which achieved a series of advances in legislation, including the Architectural Barriers Act of 1968, the Rehabilitation Act of 1973, and the Education for All Handicapped Children Act of 1975. This social movement for civil rights and access gained a significant victory in the Americans with Disabilities Act (ADA) of 1990. Perhaps the most well-known text of disability theology, too, dates to the early years of the movement: Nancy Eiesland's *The Disabled God: Toward a Liberatory Theology of Disability*, published in 1994 in the wake of the ADA victory. This work situated disability theology in the stream of liberation theologies, which proliferated rapidly in the 1980s and 1990s, and its work relied upon similar methodologies: it utilized minority group theory and stigma theory to advance an argument (an appropriate move for a professor of sociology of religion, which Eiesland was at Candler School of Theology at Emory University until her death at only forty-four). Eiesland's book, written originally as a master's thesis, is somewhat limited in terms of doctrinal development, but has proved tremendously influential in the field of disability theology. As Deborah Creamer notes in *Disability and Christian Theology*: "almost every text or article on religion and disability published after Eiesland's book in 1994 includes a reference to *The Disabled God*."[5]

Eiesland says her book was inspired by a kind of vision she had of God in a puff-chair, the sort of wheelchair used by those with quadriplegia that is controlled by the breath of the user. For Eiesland, this vision does not disclose a pitiable god or suffering servant, but an active God, one who is on the move. So while Eiesland rejects traditional notions of God's omnipotence, her theology does not leave God without power and ability. She offers an icon that resists the projection of idealized human power and unrestrained force. She explains that when she saw God this way, "I beheld God as survivor, unpitying and forthright. I recognized the incarnate Christ in the image of those judged 'not feasible,' 'unemployable,' with 'questionable quality of life.' Here was God for me."[6] She goes on to qualify her use of "survivor" to describe God, because the word is culturally "contaminated with notions of victimization, radical individualism, and alienation, as well as with an ethos of virtuous suffering. In contradistinction to that cultural icon, the image of survivor here evoked is that of a simple, unself-pitying, honest body, for whom the limits of power are palpable but not tragic."[7]

---

5. Debra Creamer, *Disability and Christian Theology: Embodied Limits and Constructive Possibilities* (New York: Oxford University Press, 2009), 87.

6. Eiesland, *The Disabled God*, 89.

7. Ibid., 102.

I am not going to argue here that it would be apt for people to consider God disabled because it is a beneficial image for people with disabilities—and neither is that Eiesland's argument, although she does find comfort in God so imaged. She challenges us to move away from divinized abstractions of self-sufficiency and independence. I want to argue, instead, that her perspective derives from the revelation of God in Jesus Christ. Put more directly: Eiesland's claim that God is disabled ultimately rests on the resurrection accounts found in Luke and John's Gospels, where Jesus invites his disciples to touch the wounds in his hands and feet. In these accounts, the resurrected Christ *retains* the impairment of his body endured at his crucifixion. His resurrected body is not a perfected body; it is not an idealized, perfectly "able" body without brokenness or impairment. Rather, the resurrected body with which Jesus returns to the Father is a disabled body. Eiesland further supports this conclusion with a discussion of the Eucharist in which, according to some traditions, Jesus' body continues to be broken.

Eiesland makes four constructive theological claims worth mentioning, and each hinges upon the significance of the resurrected Jesus and the physical impairment visible in his hands and feet and hidden on his side.[8] (a) Theological Anthropology: Jesus reveals true humanity, and thus, as one with physical impairment, both discloses "the reality that full personhood is fully compatible with the experience of disability" and demonstrates that persons with disabilities are created in the *imago dei*.[9] (b) Christology: Jesus as God incarnate, who retains the wounds of his crucifixion into the Resurrected Life, means that God in God's second person is disabled, which simultaneously reinforces the claim that people with disabilities are created in the image of God. (c) Ecclesiology and sacraments: Jesus, the disabled God, remains bodily present in the church and "broken anew in each Eucharistic reenactment."[10] Our central symbol and sacrament, the "bodily practice" of Eucharist, relies upon the impairment of the flesh of Jesus. Eiesland writes, "The dissonance raised by the nonacceptance of persons with disabilities and the acceptance of grace through Christ's broken body necessitates that the church find new ways of interpreting disability."[11] Likewise, the church as the body of Christ is also a body impaired or, rather, as Eiesland calls it, a "community of struggle." (d) Eschatology: Jesus is the "first fruits" of the Resurrected Life, the first to receive the resurrected body, and because he retains his impairment, one can expect the resurrected life to include disabled bodies. This means that "resurrection is not about the negation or erasure of our disabled bodies in hopes of perfect images, untouched by physical disability; rather Christ's resurrection

---

8. She makes the connection here to visible disability and those disabling conditions that are often hidden, like chronic pain, which may not be visible in the physical comportment of the one enduring it, or the way in which some can, often with much effort, "pass" as able-bodied for a time in certain situations.

9. Eiesland, *The Disabled God*, 100.

10. Ibid., 23.

11. Ibid.

offers hope that our nonconventional, and sometimes difficult, bodies participate fully in the imago Dei and that God . . . is touched by our experience."[12]

For Eiesland, the life of the disabled God is one of interdependence, although this way of being is not "willed from a position of power" but is a "necessary condition for life."[13] She explains: "To posit a Jesus Christ who needs care and mutuality as essential to human-divine survival does not symbolize either humanity or divinity as powerless. Instead it debunks the myth of individualism and hierarchical orders, in which transcendence means breaking free of encumbrances and needing nobody and constitutes the divine as somebody in relation to other bodies."[14]

In what follows, I want to explore what it means for an interdependence to be a "necessary condition" for God's life by engaging an unlikely group of interlocutors in the field of Barth studies. I hope that by exploring the debate about Barth's theological ontology I may lay additional theological foundations for Eiesland's *Disabled God* and extend her contribution to our understanding of the nature and being of God.

On Disability and Barth Studies

Covenant Ontology

Those familiar with recent Barth studies in the United States are well aware of the rather heated exchanges among theologians over divine ontology and the relationship between the triunity of God and God's election. Many articles and essays have summarized the debate, and I will not rehash it here.[15] I will instead consider how this understanding of God advances the concerns raised by liberation theologies, specifically theologies of disability, that reckon with the meaning and legacy of Eiesland's *Disabled God*.

This debate was ignited by the publication of Bruce McCormack's now-famous essay, "Grace and Being," in *The Cambridge Companion to Karl Barth*.[16] A passionate barrage of publications followed: some repudiating McCormack's position, others defending it, and others attempting to mediate. Of course, McCormack also contributed, with continued clarifications and developments of his position.

---

12. Ibid., 107.
13. Ibid., 103.
14. Ibid.
15. A collection of articles central to the debate and a few additional essays are gathered in *Trinity and Election in Contemporary Theology*, ed. Michael T. Dempsey (Grand Rapids: Eerdmans, 2011). Dempsey's introduction to the volume provides a good summary of the development of the debate; see 1–25.
16. Bruce L. McCormack, "Grace and Being: The Role of God's Gracious Election in Karl Barth's Theological Ontology," in *The Cambridge Companion to Karl Barth*, ed. John Webster (Cambridge: Cambridge University Press, 2000), 92–110.

A key point in the debate is the question of whether God self-determines as triune, or whether subsistence as triune is necessary to God; or, put differently, whether Barth's remarks about divine self-determination refer to God's decision to *constitute* Godself as the triune God, or whether such remarks are simply a way of identifying God as the God of creation, covenant, and reconciliation. McCormack favors the former position: God self-determines God's eternal being, which makes triunity a logical "consequence" of God's decision to be a God of covenant. Obviously the language here is tricky; there is no real temporal "before" with respect to God's triunity. Yet we can still speak of an origin or that which is logically "prior," and that which founded what follows, much like one might say the Father is "prior" as the origin of Son and Spirit, and yet all three simultaneously exist as the eternal God. McCormack's stance, then, is that God's existence as three hypostases is logically consequent to God's determination to exist as one directed to the covenant of grace.[17]

This is a shift. Most traditional theologies take God's triunity as "given," and not as a result of a self-determining decision. God's triune identity as Father, Son, and Spirit in loving union is necessary to God, original and "prior" to God's decision to enter into covenant relationship outside Godself. That is to say: God exists in interpenetrating, abundant love "before" God determines Godself to be a God of covenant. God's triune nature grounds God's decision to create and be a God of relationship with something other than Godself. Yet Barth's references to God's self-determination seem to point back not only to God's self-determination to be a God-for-us, but God's initial primordial determination of God's very being as triune.

Before *Church Dogmatics* II/2, Barth affirms triunity as logically prior to election, with statements like the following:

> God would be no less God if He had created no world and no human being. The existence of the world and our existence are in no sense vital to God, not even as the object of His love. The eternal generation of the Son by the Father tells us first and supremely that God is not at all lonely even without the world and us. His love has its object in Himself. (CD I/1: 139–40)

Such statements correspond well with the views of many earlier thinkers and with the image of God as utterly independent of the world, existing in perfect triune love without and apart from the world. If we take Barth's idea of revelation as *self*-revelation seriously, however, we may find a gap between this triune God who loves himself in utter freedom and the "later" decision to determine his being for incarnation and covenant. McCormack discerns in the early volumes of the *Church Dogmatics* a move to close this gap, even though the moves are tentative,

---

17. Although in early publications McCormack seemed to give ontological priority to election, he has since indicated that he is only speaking of a logical priority—this is one act with two terms.

since "[t]alk of an 'ontological priority' of Trinity over election must inevitably result in an abstract, wholly metaphysical conception of the triune being of God that stands behind the event in which God chooses to be God 'for us' in Jesus Christ."[18] But, in these same volumes, Barth did not seem to linger over this issue.

In *Church Dogmatics* II/2 and subsequent part-volumes, however, a different way of thinking about God's triune existence comes into view. Barth opens the door to understand God's triunity as the *consequence* of God's eternal self-determination to be a God of covenant. God constitutes God's being as triune in God's gracious electing decision. Here, God's free decision to be in covenant relationship with that which is not God determines God's triune identity, and that means that God's very eternal being is primordially shaped by this "prior" decision. God is triune for the purpose of relationship with that which is other than God. Or, as McCormack puts it in "Grace and Being": "God is triune *for the sake* of his revelation," and God's eternal being is "knowable because it is constituted by the act of turning toward us."[19] Thus, the gap of knowing God before or behind the God of revelation shrinks in size, if not closes entirely.

At the center of this understanding of God's self-determination, of course, is Barth's Christology. Tradition locates Jesus within the economic Trinity, within the context of God revealing Godself in time, but not in God's primordial life. The Son, yes; Jesus, not yet. But Barth makes a mysterious claim that stands at the heart of this splintering divide in Barth studies: "Jesus Christ is the electing God. . . . In no depth of the Godhead shall we encounter any but Him" (CD II/2: 115). He calls Jesus not only the object of election, but also the subject of election. He says there is no "Godhead in itself . . . there is no such thing as a will of God apart from the will of Jesus Christ" (CD II/2: 115). The "Godhead," accordingly, has always been determined by the becoming of Jesus Christ. But how does one make sense of this? How can the historical, embodied, human being be present in the primordial being of God? Barth's answer, according to McCormack, is as follows. In the electing decision, which shapes the eternal divine life, the God-human Jesus Christ is present by way of anticipation. The second mode of God's being is eternally determined "toward" incarnation, and there is no other reality to the Son behind this eternal determination.

Why is this account of the originating elective decision, for triunity and for the sake of covenant, promising for disability theology (and, perhaps, other theologies of liberation too)? It may not be a surprise that the most attractive aspects of this account are exactly the points most targeted by critics who wish to preserve elements of "classical theism" (a perspective that many liberation theologians reject or reconfigure).[20] That is to say: it introduces "need" into the being of God;

---

18. Bruce L. McCormack, "Election and Trinity: Theses in Response to George Hunsinger," in *Trinity and Election in Contemporary Theology*, 119.

19. McCormack, "Grace and Being," 101 and 99.

20. See for example, Karen Baker Fletcher, *Dancing with God: The Trinity from a Womanist Perspective* (St. Louis: Chalice Press, 2007); Mayra Rivera, *The Touch of Transcendence: A*

it establishes an ontological connection between God and the cosmos—and not just by a decision to relate, but a connection that is eternal and necessary to God's second way of being; it positions God as vulnerable, since God risks the "fulfillment" or "completion" of the divine life in the humanity of Jesus; it makes humanity and embodiment necessary to the being of God; and it posits a posture of ontological receptivity for the Son, a kind of interdependence within the being of God, beyond a perichoretic interdependence of the Trinitarian hypostases.

The traditional position insists that triunity precedes God's electing decision for covenant, and defenders of this position believe that this affirmation is essential to protect the freedom of God. Since God's being is eternally self-sufficient, talk of the priority of election is unacceptable: it postulates an eternal God as "needing" that which is not God, an eternal God who is originally not self-sufficient. Aaron Smith describes the traditional view thus: "there is that eternity in which God is in himself, as he exists in triune seclusion, utterly free and not contingent, able to assign himself his being with recourse to none but himself, happily alone in unfettered autonomy and perfect contentment apart from all that is not he."[21] This is an image with which most readers of liberation theology are familiar, and it is an image of God that has been critiqued by feminists, postcolonial theologians, and others. In a covenant ontology, by contrast, God's eternal being is bound to creation not just through a "subsequent" decision to create and covenant with Israel; God is bound to creation in the very founding of God's triune eternal being. If God determines God's being for the sake of revelation and creation is necessary for revelation, then God needs creation. And if God in God's second way of being is begotten for the purpose of incarnation, God needs humanity, God needs "fulfillment" in the hypostatic union.

Most theologians would be comfortable saying that creation is a precondition of the self-communication of God's triune life—that creation is "necessary" for revelation, in the trivial sense that there needs to be creation for God to reveal Godself to some number of creatures. But we are saying something much more here, and this additional layer of meaning is what stirs great anxiety among Barth scholars who, for various reasons, want to affiliate Barth with the tradition. God self-determines to be triune in anticipation of fellowship with creation. Because the intention for creation is the precondition of God's self-determination, it would seem to make creation not only necessary for God's self-revelation, but for the fulfillment of God's very being. God is never "unfettered"; deep within God's eternal being, God needs—God needs that to which God will covenant Godself, and the Son needs the humanity of Jesus (and thus embodiment) to fulfill and complete the Son's identity as the God-human. McCormack does not shrink from

---

Postcolonial Theology of God (Louisville: WJKP, 2007); Catherine Keller, *Face of the Deep: A Theology of Becoming* (New York: Routledge, 2003); and Elizabeth Johnson, *Quest for the Living God: Mapping Frontiers in the Theology of God* (New York: Continuum, 2007).

21. Aaron T. Smith, "God's Self-Specification: His Being Is His Electing," in *Trinity and Election in Contemporary Theology*, 217.

acknowledging the necessity that this perspective places on creation for the being of God: "Given the divine will to redeem, creation was made 'necessary'; God had to become the Creator. There exists an 'ontic connection' between Jesus Christ and creation."[22] The cosmos, then, is not an add-on to a self-sufficient God who existed in primordial loving relation within God's own life. Rather, God's very immanent life is determined to be for this cosmos to such a degree that God determines to be triune for the purpose of this relationship. Not vice versa. God is not triune and then makes use of that triunity to enable the revelation and the economy of salvation. God self-constitutes as triune in order to be in covenant and to embrace that creation within God's very being. Barth even declares that in this electing decision, God determines not to be "entirely self-sufficient" (CD II/2: 10). In response to this quotation from Barth, Kevin Hector voices the terror many Christians may feel over such a thought: "God—not self-sufficient? From eternity?!"[23]

An important result of this shift in our understanding of God's primordial decision pertains to the concept of the pre-existent Word, the *logos asarkos*. If McCormack's reading of Barth is correct, there is no abstract "Son" who preexists the determination to become incarnate as this particular God-human. God's second way of being, as Son, is begotten as the one to become enfleshed. The *logos asarkos* is thus most properly named the *logos incarnandus*, the logos anticipating enfleshment. God's second way of being "needs" enfleshment, "needs" human nature to fulfill this eternal identity of God. And the incarnation and history of Jesus is constitutive of the identity of the second person of the Trinity, without metaphysical remainder. We can identify Jesus Christ as the second person of the eternal triune life of God; we can say that God in God's second way of being just *is* Jesus Christ in his human history.[24] McCormack summarizes: "That Jesus has his being in the Logos *eternally* can mean only that the Logos is never without Jesus and that therefore God is a human God."[25]

All of this, then, allows the formulation of two summary claims. First, God is not, in essence, autonomous. Aaron Smith puts it thus: "The reality that Jesus Christ

---

22. Bruce L. McCormack, "The Identity of the Son: Karl Barth's Exegesis of Hebrews 1:1–4 (And Similar Passages)," in *Christology, Hermeneutics, and Hebrews: Profiles from the History of Interpretation*, ed. Jon C. Laansma and Daniel J. Treier (New York: T&T Clark, 2012), 170, quoting CD III/1, 49, 58, and 51.

23. Kevin Hector, "God's Triunity and Self-Determination: A Conversation with Karl Barth, Bruce McCormack, and Paul Molnar," in *Trinity and Election in Contemporary Theology*, 42.

24. In his doctrine of God, Barth talks about God's being as "its own, conscious, willed, and executed decision" (see CD II/1: 271 and CD II/2: 175). And it is on these grounds that there is no "Godhead in itself . . . there is no such thing as a will of God apart from the will of Jesus Christ" (CD II/2: 115).

25. Bruce L. McCormack, *Orthodox and Modern: Studies in the Theology of Karl Barth* (Grand Rapids: Baker, 2008), 246.

is the subject of election precludes the possibility of . . . eternal autonomy, since in this event, as this event, a nonautonomous deity is fully revealed."[26] Second, if Jesus truly is identified as the second person of the Trinity, humanity is not foreign to the being of God; rather, humanity can even be said to be constitutive of the life of God in God's second way of being. As Darren Sumner writes, "What seems to us a contradiction—that a created essence is made essential to the Creator—is maintained by the freedom of God."[27] Embodiment and humanity thus become essential to the being of God. And this is a massive departure from the account of God often critiqued by liberation theology. Here, embodiment does not just occur at a point in time, via the incarnation of the Word; embodiment, rather, is essential to God's being from all eternity because of the original act of God's self-determination to be *this* triune God, in *this* way.[28]

The Eternal Identity of the Disabled Christ

A number of people in this debate consider what the eventual suffering of Jesus means for the eternal identity of the Son. Paul Dafydd Jones writes, "God qua Son is never not humanized; God *qua* Son is never not the Christ who undergoes suffering."[29] Barth himself writes: "The New Testament describes the Son of God . . . not only as the servant, but rather as the *suffering* servant of God. Not accidentally and provisionally does He *also* suffer—perhaps to the end of testing and preserving His basic conviction, perhaps for the attainment of a concrete goal through struggle, perhaps as a foil for emphasizing His glory in another way, but necessarily and to a certain extent, essentially" (CD IV/1: 216 rev.).[30] McCormack comments: "On Barthian soil, the statement that God is 'essentially' a suffering God is not an abstract metaphysical assertion. It is a concrete affirmation of a concrete reality—Jesus Christ as the One who suffers in time is what God is 'essentially.'"[31] However, what Barth and multiple commentators recognize but fail to name,

---

26. Aaron T. Smith, "God's Self-Specification," in *Trinity and Election in Contemporary Theology*, 225.

27. Darren Sumner, *Karl Barth and the Incarnation: Christology and the Humility of God* (New York: T&T Clark, 2016), 204.

28. To be sure, debate persists as to whether one can speak of a *logos asarkos* and a *logos incarnatus* simultaneously. Can we say there is "more" to the second hypostasis than the union between God-human in Christ? That is, does Jesus Christ exhaust the identity of the second hypostatis, or could one speak of a "more," that retains some sense of the Logos that remains "outside the flesh"? Is there any meaning to the old idea of the *extra Calvinisticum*?

29. Paul Dafydd Jones, *The Humanity of Christ: Christology in Karl Barth's Church Dogmatics* (New York: T&T Clark, 2011), 148–9.

30. See here McCormack, *Orthodox and Modern*, 216 (fn. 43).

31. Ibid., 218.

is that God as Son is, at essence, from God's primordial self-determination, the *disabled* God. God as Son is never not the disabled Christ.

We regularly read accounts of the suffering of Christ and the suffering of God, but it often remains somewhat vague and abstract—just "suffering." What Eiesland's bold identification of a disabled God accomplishes, among other things, is a reminder that this suffering is a particular suffering body, and although the suffering of Christ is not limited to his bodily suffering, it is in part the very impairment of his body to which we are referring. Moreover, as disability literature stresses, the suffering of people with disabilities is not limited to physical pain or struggle; it is also tied up with social stigma, lack of access, social barriers, and dehumanization. The *logos incarnandus*, then, is specifically the Logos anticipating the assumption of a broken flesh, a broken flesh that is outcast, rejected, and persecuted by social, religious, and political institutions. This, in the final analysis, is specifically who the Logos *is*, and this identity is the original free decision of God's self-determination and constitution: to be a human on the fringe, a human stigmatized, one who suffers in the body, and one who suffers the psychological and emotional pain of rejection and isolation. So it is the real suffering of Jesus, the disabled God, that is central to the very nature of the Christian faith. This is the flesh anticipated from eternity. It is not just that Jesus retained a broken body, so that the humanity of God is ever after a wounded, enfleshed humanity. Jesus is the lamb that was slain from the foundation of the world. God in God's second way of being has always been anticipating a disabled body. The eternal identity of the Son is not the *logos asarkos*, and not even the *logos incarnandus*, but more specifically is the *logos incarnandus fractus* (the Word who will be incarnate as broken flesh).[32]

Another promising feature of McCormack's approach is the ontological receptivity of the Son. Although liberation theologians are rarely concerned to retain the concept of divine immutability, it serves here not to preserve God's impassibility. Rather, because Jesus' suffering is eternally anticipated as *logos incarnandus fractus*, it does not introduce change in God. McCormack thus retains a commitment to God's immutability, understood in terms of God's faithfulness: we can trust God's revelation to demonstrate truly God's nature. Immutability means, then, that the nature of God as Son does not change when drawn into union with the full individual humanity of Jesus. One can affirm that the incarnation does not introduce change into God by (a) affirming this divine-human unity as the eternal identity of the Son, and (b) by understanding the role of the Son in a receptive posture, one who is always receiving the humanity, the real human action, and the guidance of the Holy Spirit.

McCormack further supports this understanding of the Son's receptivity through a form of kenotic Christology that understands the humbling of the Word as the addition of a full human nature to the divine person. Kenosis, here,

---

32. I am grateful to my colleague and friend Father Bud Grant for helping me with the Latin needed to describe the eternally anticipated, impaired, and stigmatized humanity of Jesus.

does not refer to the Son setting aside majesty in order to enter into this state of receptivity, but the Son eternally existing as receptive, anticipating "addition."[33] While Christologies have often preserved the divine-human unity of Jesus through the absolute activity of the Son over a passive and receptive human nature, here the Son receives *from* the human nature. McCormack explains, "Here the man Jesus acts and the Logos receives those acts as his own. The man Jesus experiences suffering and the Logos takes that suffering . . . into his own being."[34] While most discussions of the incarnation describe the Logos actively taking the human nature unto itself, then, McCormack stresses the ontological receptivity of the Logos such that the Logos does not actively assume the human nature, but instead the Logos *receives* the humanity as a work of the Spirit.[35] And so the fulfillment of God's triune life in the incarnation is not produced by the direct activity of the Logos (although, indirectly, the Son does breathe forth the Spirit together with the Father); the Son's identity is fulfilled in receiving the humanity through the Spirit.[36]

One might say, then, that the Son "surrenders" eternally for the sake of the humanization of God. This is a slightly different emphasis than that found in *Church Dogmatics* IV/1, which supposes that the Son just is eternally obedient to the Father because that is the Son's eternal identity. Instead of thinking in terms of obedience, the identity of the Son is understood as a *reception* of true humanity and embodiment. And the divine nature of Jesus responds in receptivity to the action of the human nature and in reliance upon the Spirit. There is within God a mode of being whose identity is in receptivity, dependence, and reliance on others—the Son who receives the humanity of Jesus, who acts in the power of the Spirit.

This relates to another promising feature: the introduction of an element of risk or vulnerability into the being of God. The Son relies upon the Spirit to empower the Son's own humanity. So too the Father risks, relying on the Spirit to guide Jesus in obedience toward the will of God, which ultimately is the fulfillment of the being of God, the very purpose set forth in the self-constitution of God. So it is not

---

33. For a fuller exposition of McCormack's thought on this matter, see Bruce L. McCormack, *The Humility of the Eternal Son: Reformed Kenoticism and the Repair of Chalcedon* (Cambridge: Cambridge University Press, 2021).

34. Bruce L. McCormack, "Kenoticism in Modern Christology," in *Oxford Handbook of Christology*, ed. Francesca Aran Murphy (Oxford: Oxford University Press, 2015), 455.

35. Bruce L. McCormack, "The Lord and Giver of Life: A Barthian Defense of the Filioque," in *Rethinking Trinitarian Theology: Disputed Questions and Contemporary Issues in Trinitarian Theology*, ed. Guilio Maspero and Robert Wozniak (New York: T&T Clark, 2012), 230–53.

36. McCormack explains that Puritan theologian John Owen held that "the only active use of divine omnipotence on the part of the Word vis-à-vis His human nature lay in the assumption itself. All other works performed by Him were performed humanly, that is to say, in the power of the Spirit. . . . I would not even make the assumption itself a direct work of the Son. I would say that all the Son's work is indirect, mediated by the Spirit who is at work in His human nature" (ibid., 251).

only the identity of the Son that is risked. God hazards God's own being (so CD II/2: 161). Or as Paul Dafydd Jones puts it: "God gives up thoroughgoing control over God's own being."[37]

Although McCormack pushes the ontological receptivity of the Son further than most, he does not assume this posture of receptivity to be as risky as other commentators. For example, considering the chance that the Son's identity as eternally obedient may be thwarted if Jesus does not enact perfect obedience, McCormack comments: "But a God who has exhaustive foreknowledge will know what the man Jesus will do. Therefore, there is no 'dependence' in God on temporal events and if no 'dependence,' then no 'need' (in the customary sense of the word)."[38] Others, however, find in Barth real risk in this venture. For example, Jones disagrees with those who claim God "fixed the outcome" of Jesus' life. According to Jones, Christ must "humanly achieve, enact and maintain obedience."[39] And, quoting Barth, he emphasizes that the history of the Son "plays itself out . . . under the entire burden and in the entire danger of world history" (CD IV/1: 215 rev.). Although today we may see victory as assured, this does not alter the risk in the real history of Jesus' lifetime. "Christ had to effect this victory—and . . . were he to have faltered, things would have turned out quite differently."[40] Jones asserts that there is "no assured path from cradle to cross" and movingly describes the risk of God's own heartbreak in this venture: "God took and takes the original risk of patience, the risk of having God's own heart permanently broken—shattered, even—when the Son assumes human flesh, and constitutes himself in terms of the life of Jesus Christ."[41] J. Kameron Carter makes a similar case for the risk of God in *Race: A Theological Account*, albeit without reference to Barth. He writes: "For when Mary gives birth to Christ, God not only becomes incarnate in a human being, but, more specifically, God's life is staked or dependent on woman. Dependent on Mary of Nazareth's fiat, the second Adam's human condition and potential to enact human redemption rests on the second Eve."[42] Which is to say: beyond God risking the fulfillment of God's identity in the human activity of Jesus, God also risks Godself to the care of Mary.

Of course, this understanding of the eternal receptivity of the Son can also be described in other terms, as with the distressing concept of the eternal command of the Father and eternal submission of the Son. And Barth's comparison of this

---

37. Jones, *The Humanity of Christ*, 98.

38. Bruce L. McCormack, "Processions and Missions: A Point of Convergence between Thomas Aquinas and Karl Barth," in *Thomas Aquinas and Karl Barth: An Unofficial Catholic-Protestant Dialogue*, ed. Bruce L. McCormack and Thomas Joseph White (Grand Rapids: Eerdmans, 2013), 124.

39. Jones, *The Humanity of Christ*, 225.

40. Ibid., 226.

41. Ibid., 98.

42. J. Kameron Carter, *Race: A Theological Account* (Oxford: Oxford University Press, 2008), 348.

event with the institution of heterosexual marriage, offered passingly in *Church Dogmatics* IV/1, is worse than absurd; it is deeply dangerous and entangled in the systemic evils of misogyny and patriarchy.

This matter is taken up richly in discussions in feminist theology over kenotic Christologies and whether or not the language of surrender, humility, and submission is at all redeemable in Christianity.[43] I cannot engage that debate here, but I want to be clear.[44] Yes, it may seem that I am suggesting the eternal receptivity of the Son is a desirable concept because those who are disabled are receiving care from able-bodied individuals, and thus it remains an image of able-bodied giver and disabled receiver, perpetuating a hierarchical image of charity and pity. But my point is otherwise. It is not the fact of receiving care, but rather the fact that everyone has gifts to give as well as needs to be met or responded to. I see this also in God as Father, the divine person who receives his identity as Father through the Son. Even so, by placing the receptivity on the divine side of the story in Jesus, it shifts the valuation away from the binary of giving care *versus* receiving care. If God is the receiver of gifts, and not only the giver of gifts, does that not begin to change the way we prioritize the two, such that we more easily recognize the agency of the receiver of care and value our interdependency as we see this within God's own identity in Christ?

Conclusion

Debra Creamer writes of Eiesland's proposal: "The memorable image of the Disabled God, as one who intimately knows and even experiences disability, is especially important: in addition to calling for change, it irrevocably changes the way one encounters the Christian story. How can one be a Christian and not value experiences of disability? The image necessarily leads to changes in understanding and in action."[45] I believe that Barth's approach to the ontology of God gives significant doctrinal support to Eiesland's image of God.

I would grant that I have some reservations, as well as some ongoing questions. What does treating the Logos as a placeholder for the name Jesus do to all of the rich work developed around Sophia Christology?[46] More specifically, what does the claim that Jesus is identical with the second mode of God's being mean for already overly-masculinized depictions of the being of God? Do we now have a

---

43. See for example Sarah Coakley, *Powers and Submissions: Spirituality, Philosophy, and Gender* (Oxford: Blackwell, 2002) and Anna Mercedes, *Power For: Feminism and Christ's Self-Giving* (New York: T&T Clark, 2011).

44. I will take up this issue more thoroughly in my forthcoming book on the disabled God.

45. Debra Creamer, "Theological Accessibility: The Contribution of Disability," *Disability Studies Quarterly* 26, no. 4 (2006). Available at https://dsq-sds.org/article/view/812/987.

46. Of course, the intensely Christocentric nature of this proposal may not be acceptable to some postcolonial theologians, and to others who are pushing for a more pluralist theology.

literal human male identified as an eternal hypostasis? How can this possibly help? Eiesland may offer us some assistance; she stresses, as do feminist theologians Rosemary Radford Ruether, Elizabeth Johnson, and others, that the significance is on the real *flesh*, the physicality of the humanity taken into God's own life, not the (apparent) maleness of the physical body.[47] So we ought not choose a disembodied God out of fear of the concrete sexed embodiment of Jesus. It is more important to say that God has taken real human flesh as God's own, that God determined the very shape of God's existence for this inclusion of human life, the particular life and broken body of Jesus and all that it reveals to us about God's solidarity with oppressed humanity. This fact of physicality is important to Eiesland and almost all disability theologies. She explains: "deliberate attention to the physical body is necessary in order to prevent it from becoming socially erased or subsumed into notions of normal embodiment."[48]

I also suspect that the position I have articulated does not quite measure up to the boldness of Eiesland's claims. As radical as God's identification with humanity is here—God's self-determined need and interdependence with creation being necessary to God's own being, from all eternity—it may still suggest a power *behind* that decision that is similar to conceptions of power, traditionally construed, for Eiesland and others. She writes: "The disabled God embodies practical interdependence, not simply willing to be interrelated from a position of power, but depending on it from a position of need."[49] Nonetheless, the proposal I have sketched moves toward real ontological need and interdependence in God, and real humanity, embodiment, and limitation in God, and thus—with Eiesland—takes leave of the classical theism that she and so many others critique from perspectives of marginality. I have not abandoned the image of a God who is free to self-determine, but by understanding God's primordial decision for covenant as that which constitutes God's triunity, it is possible to say that God is never other than the God shaped for interdependence. No trinity stands "behind" this God, deciding to establish the covenant and incarnate; we have no access to a knowledge of the omnipotent God, classically construed. There is only this God, self-constituted for this, fulfilled by this incorporation of the disabled humanity of Jesus into the divine life. Eiesland imaged God in a puff-chair; perhaps I have only qualified this as God *qua* Son as the chair-user, one who is neither a pitiable suffering servant, nor a divinized ableist force, but a God eternally constituted to need creation, to receive human embodiment, and to depend upon others to achieve the full life intended at that primordial moment.

---

47. Eiesland, *The Disabled God*, 102. See also Rosemary Radford Reuther, *Sexism and God-Talk: Toward a Feminist Theology* (Boston: Beacon, 1993), esp. 116–38; Elizabeth Johnson, *She Who Is: The Mystery of God in Feminist Discourse* (New York: Crossroad, 1992); and Sandra Schneiders, *Women and the Word: The Gender of God in the New Testament and the Spirituality of Women* (New York: Paulist, 1986).
48. Eiesland, *The Disabled God*, 22.
49. Ibid., 103.

Chapter 5

KARL BARTH AND KOREAN THEOLOGY, PAST AND PRESENT

Meehyun Chung

Liberation theology is an attempt to do theology in the context of a particular situation, and sometimes in the context of a particular region. In the Korean peninsula, liberation theology is related to the political separation of the two Koreas and the implications for Christian life that follow. When addressing this political situation, Barth's theology serves as a helpful conversation partner, especially when it is interpreted and understood as a European version of liberation theology that engages a range of economic, social, political, and cultural matters. As Barth himself said, "wherever there is theological talk, it is always implicitly or explicitly political talk also."[1]

This chapter examines how Barth articulated a European form of liberation theology in the context of Nazism, the Second World War, and the Cold War. Barth's response to the Cold War, in particular, bears on both the Korean War (1950–3) and the Hungarian crisis (1956) and discloses the possibility of a liberation theology that focuses attention on the Word of God. Reckoning with these issues sets the stage for a conversation between Barth and Soon-Kyung Park, arguably Korea's first explicitly feminist theologian. So the chapter begins by comparing Barth's position during the Cold War with the position he adopted during the Nazi regime. It then explores how Barth's theology has been adopted and adapted in Korea, with particular reference to Soon-Kyung Park. I show that Barth's thought, while not uncritically embraced, was received and transformed in support of feminist and liberative ends. Finally, I return to Barth, reading him alongside Soon-Kyung Park, and offer some remarks about Christian theology, peace, and justice in a globalized world.

Barth's Theology during the Cold War[2]

There is a well-known quotation that speaks to Barth's determination to connect Christian conviction and social context: "Take your Bible and take your newspaper,

---

1. Karl Barth, "To Students in Leiden, 27 February 1939," quoted by Eberhard Busch in his *Karl Barth: His Life from Letters and Autobiographical Texts* (London: SCM, 1976), 292.

2. This section reprises material in Meehyun Chung, "Barth's Theology for Peace," *Korean Journal of Systematic Theology* 8 (2003): 54–73.

and read both. But interpret newspapers from your Bible."[3] It is instructive to consider Barth's sociopolitical activity in light of this claim, with particular reference to Korea.

Although one can hardly deny the force of his theological and political protests against Nazism in the 1930s, Barth is often viewed as politically reticent during the Cold War, given a refusal "to indulge in wholesale condemnation of communism."[4] This reticence has been attributed to diverse factors: Barth's growing older, a dulling of his prophetic edge, even a diminution of the critical capacity exhibited in his early work. Emil Brunner and Reinhold Niebuhr number among those who leveled such criticisms. Why didn't Barth offer a stronger response to Soviet totalitarianism? Why did he not show a passion comparable to that demonstrated in debates with Brunner in the 1930s, when they argued about natural theology in relation to Nazism? Did Barth hereby reveal himself to be an uncritical socialist? Did his prophetic gifts fail?

In what follows, it will become clear that Barth did not respond to the Cold War with a lack of passion or prophecy, even given his eschewal of the rhetoric employed in previous decades. Quite the contrary: Barth developed an antiwar, pro-justice, and pro-peace stance, and articulated a theological perspective that is peculiarly germane to our current geopolitical situation.

Barth, the Korean War, Soviet Communism, and Anticommunism

The Cold War severely threatened world peace in the 1950s, and the Korean War numbers among the gravest manifestations of this troubled time. While there is little material available regarding Barth's views on the Korean War, thus making his views a bit difficult to discern, Barth's thoughts can be indirectly inferred through an analysis of his theology and an engagement with scattered remarks in his writings.[5]

The Korean War began on June 25, 1950, when North America and Western European nations deemed North Korea's unilateral invasion of South Korea an act of aggression, reflective of a growing threat from the Soviet Union and its allies. In the autumn of 1950, Western Europe and the United States discussed the possibility of forming an "European Defence Community" (EDC). But the EDC was quickly mired in controversy when the chancellor of West Germany, Konrad Adenauer, made participation in the EDC conditional upon parliamentary approval.

---

3. "Barth in Retirement," *Time* 81, no. 22, May 31, 1963.

4. George Hunsinger, "Karl Barth and Liberation Theology," *Journal of Religion* 63, no. 3 (1983): 250.

5. See Meehyun Chung, *Karl Barth, Josef Lukl Hromádka, Korea. Das Verständnis von Offenbarung und Geschichte im Denken Karl Barths: ein Vergleich mit dem Offenbarungs- und Geschichtsverständnis Josef Lukl Hromádkas in bezug auf ihre theologische und politische Tätigkeit* (Berlin: Alektor Verlag, 1995), 114–24.

Representatives of the Confessing Church sharply criticized Adenauer in an edition of the German Christian magazine, *Christ und Welt*, published on October 12, 1950. Gustav Heinemann, a member of the Confessing Church and the head of the Evangelical Church in Germany, resigned from his position as Minister of the Interior. It was during this time that one of Dietrich Bonhoeffer's students, Wolf-Dieter Zimmermann, a pastor and editor of the Berlin magazine, *Unterwegs*, requested a public statement from Barth in his capacity as the "spiritual father of the Confessing Church" (GA V.15: 203). Referencing Barth's letter to Josef L. Hromádka in the 1930s, which called on Czech soldiers to resist Nazism, Zimmermann expressed the hope that Barth would write a similar public letter in light of the Cold War.[6] Both Heinemann and Zimmermann felt that Barth's encouragement was needed, given the similarities between the threats to peace posed by Hitler and Stalin. Indeed, Zimmermann supposed that a written statement would go some way to justifying Germany's rearmament. By updating his earlier letter, Barth could underscore the need for the "free world" to rise up against communism.

Barth viewed the issue differently. In response to Zimmermann's request, Barth wrote a public letter, "Fürchtet euch nicht!" ("Fear Not!") on October 17, 1950, which was published on November 1. In this letter, Barth explains why the Cold War cannot be compared to the political situation of the 1930s—and why his letter to Hromádka after the 1938 Munich Agreement could not simply be recycled to address the Cold War. Three points in the letter are especially noteworthy: (i) During Hitler's rule, Barth contends, European churches and citizens were unable to face reality. There was a widespread failure to think clearly about the political and theological situation. Barth sought therefore to address this failure directly. But Stalin's version of communism amounts to an altogether different situation. Since the West is *already* united against Stalinism, there is no point articulating Christian principles in support of resistance, as Barth did in the Barmen Declaration. Indeed, the oppositional nature of the Cold War means that such an articulation would not ease tensions, only heighten them. Christians should proceed differently: offering consolation, defusing political tensions, and comforting the fearful. (ii) Barth does not deny the Soviet threat or the problem of aggressive propaganda. But he does not view the invasion of Korean as a new manifestation of Soviet belligerence. Up to this point, the Soviet Union has "not issued an ultimatum to anyone—I do not see Korea in such terms—or proved itself guilty of corresponding aggression."[7] The Cold War, again, must be viewed differently than the Nazi threat. The best defense against Soviet communism is not military preparation, but rather righting the social system to benefit *all* classes in the Western world. "Those who do not

---

6. See Meehyun Chung, "Letter of Barth to Hromádka," *Korean Journal of Systematic Theology* 2 (1996): 155–76.

7. Karl Barth, "Fürchtet Euch nicht!" in *Der Götze wackelt. Zeitkritische Aufsätze, Reden und Briefe von 1930–1960*, ed. Karl Kupisch (Berlin: Käthe Vogt, 1961), 153; see also GA V.15: 209.

want communism—and we all do not want it—must not defy communism, but stand up for true socialism."[8] Equally: "The way to prevent communism is not by hastily denying it and raising fear in the Western world, but to instill a 'better realization of economic justice.'"[9] (iii) What about German rearmament? While Barth does not condemn armed defense, he fears that German rearmament would mean a reintroduction of militarism, and that militarism could transform itself into totalitarianism—which, in turn, would make the advance of social justice impossible.[10]

This stance on Soviet communism as it relates to Korea speaks also to Barth's attitude toward *anti*communism, and a broader concern to alleviate the ideological conflicts of the Cold War. Milan Machovec has written instructively on this point, arguing that "[m]ost of Western Europe's simple Christians did not understand Barth's motives. It was even harder to understand his profound doctrinal system. However, his distinctive words—and even his silence—gave the people room to break their Cold War hostility and prejudices."[11] This amounts to a useful gloss on Barth's own words:

> Since World War II, the East-West problem has haunted me and many others. In fact, this problem has prevented me and others reaching a consensus. It is not because I hold an affinity for Soviet or North Korean communism. I feel very fortunate that I do not have to live in that region. I hope that others will not be forced to do so. Yet I do not believe that my resistance should further sharpen the political and theological conflict of Western society, which has continued for the past fifteen years. I believe that anticommunism, in principle, is worse than communism itself.[12]

One of Barth's motives for this claim was his critique of Western capitalism's worship of mammon—a new deity, and one that ought not to be obscured through Western Christian appeals to "liberal democracy." Just as Barth did not seek to criticize atheists who denied the existence of God, but worried more about so-called believers in liberal democracies who lived without knowing God,[13] so he wanted the West to think critically about *itself* before rushing to judgment about the Soviet Union. None of this means that Christians should look upon worldly

---

8. Ibid., 154; see also GA V.15: 210.

9. Karl Barth, "How My Mind Has Changed," in *"Der Götze wackelt": Zeitkritische Aufsätze, Reden und Briefe von 1930 bis 1960* (Berlin: Vogt, 1961), 197.

10. See Karl Barth, "Politische Entscheidung in der Einheit des Glaubens," *Theologische Existenz heute* 34 (1952): 7.

11. Milan Machovec, "Praktische Konsequenzen der dialektischen Theologie," in *Marxismus und die dialektische Theologie* (Zürich: EVZ-Verlag, 1965), 118.

12. Barth, "How My Mind Has Changed," 201.

13. See Barth, "Die christliche Kirchen und die heutige Wirklichkeit," in *"Der Götze wackelt,"* 103.

events and conflicts with a neutral or uncritical mindset. It means, rather, that Christians should recognize God's work in the world and engage in the practice of self-critique and self-reformation. In the final analysis, that alone is the basis for the church's mission of witness and outreach.

In 1948, Barth traveled to Hungary, a country that the Soviet Union liberated from German control that now exposed the enmity between the Soviet Union and the United States—nations that were, of course, allies for the latter half of the Second World War. He subsequently delivered a lecture in 1949, entitled "The Church between East and West" ("Die Kirche zwischen Ost und West").[14] He argues here that this conflict between two major world powers is a *political* power struggle, with differing ideologies pitted against one another. In this context, the church should not add fuel to the fire by exacerbating disagreement, much less by taking sides. The church must instead understand that this kind of conflict is not one in which Christians should engage. Certainly one cannot promote "Western" values as compatible with Christian faith. Nor, for that matter, is Christian action in opposition to this conflict appropriate. That would be but one more ploy for power, and one that could risk moving the world toward another war.[15] A third way is possible: a posture of mutual self-critique; a posture that embraces neutrality in order to bear witness to the gospel that stands above and beyond all ideologies. This kind of impartiality—one might well call it *evangelical* impartiality—is more important than lending support to the project of so-called Western democracy.

But perhaps "impartiality" is not the best word? Worldly events can themselves be viewed as an *appeal*, an occasion for the church to decide where it stands. I refer to the "church" purposefully at this juncture, for neither the appeal nor the decision is the responsibility of autonomous individuals; and I use the term "appeal" to underscore how Barth was seeking to negotiate his context in a faithful way, paying attention to what it is that God was and is doing. Both the appeal and the church, moreover, arise in light of the event of revelation. It is a matter of the Christian community listening to God's Word and considering it anew. When the time of decision comes, the church may not deny reality; it must instead *respond* to God—sometimes in silence, sometimes through active participation in the world.

This brings me back to the Korean War, the onset of which occasioned multiple ecclesial responses. The World Council of Churches (WCC), for its part, adopted the Toronto Statement, which roundly condemned North Korea. Bishop Albert Bereczky of the Reformed Church in Hungary (also a member of the WCC's Central Committee) immediately remonstrated. On August 14, 1950, Bereczky met with Barth in Zürich, Switzerland, where they shared mutual criticism of the Toronto Statement and the policies of the WCC.[16]

But as Barth learned more about political dynamics within the Hungarian reformed church through German newspapers, he became apprehensive about

---

14. See *"Der Götze wackelt,"* 124–43.
15. Ibid., 129 and 134.
16. See Chung, *Karl Barth, Josef Lukl Hromádka, Korea*, 119.

the Hungarian church's rosy estimate of the political situation. Somewhat similar to the mood of German Christians in the 1930s, it seemed that many in Hungary viewed the communist forces as a kind of second revelation. As a result, Barth sent a public letter to Bereczky. Continuous with the convictions outlined in the Declaration of Barmen, Barth asserts here that no political event or movement, in any shape or form, can be accepted as a revelation of God.[17] There can be no "coordination" or identification of political ideologies with the gospel. Taking a further step, Barth goes on to caution Western European Christians, who, of course, live in a capitalistic society, about the dangers of anticommunism and its idolization. Concomitantly, he cautions Eastern European Christians against confusing communist ideology with the gospel. At every turn, Barth criticizes absolute statements with respect to any and all forms of political ideology.

Barth's and Brunner's disagreements during the Cold War disclose a similar mindset. Of course, the two theologians were known for their differences in the 1930s. But Brunner was newly skeptical of Barth after the latter's report regarding his visit to Hungary in "The Reformed Church Behind the 'Iron Curtain'" ("Reformierte Kirche hinter dem 'eisernen Vorhang'"). Upon reading the report, Brunner penned a public letter, which led to a new public debate.[18] With the title "How Are We to Understand?" ("Wie soll man das verstehen?"), the letter argues that the church should reject totalitarianism in the 1950s with the same immediacy and vehemency found in Barth's *No!* to natural theology in the 1930s. Without this clear "no," according to Brunner, Barth risks justifying totalitarian communism and endorsing complacent, indifferent theologians who act "as if nothing had happened (*als ob nichts geschehen wäre*)" (TET: 9).

On June 6, 1948, Barth responded to Brunner's critiques in a public letter titled "Theological Existence 'Today'" ("Theologische Existenz 'heute'"). He reused the title of his pamphlet of 1933 to emphasize, again, how theology should relate to contemporary life: as an act of free obedience to the Word.

> [The Church] must not concern itself eternally with various "isms" or systems, but with historical realities seen in light of the Word of God and of the Faith. Its obligations lie, not in the direction of any fulfilling of the law of nature, but towards its living Lord. Therefore, the Church never thinks, speaks, or acts "on principle." It makes judgments spiritually and by individual cases. It refuses any participation in political society in light of a "system." For that reason it rejects every attempt to systematize political causes. Therefore, it preserves the freedom to judge each new event afresh. If yesterday it spoke from its position of responsibility, then today it should be silent if in this position it considers silence to be the better course. The unity and continuity of theology will be best

---

17. See here GA V.15: 280 ("Brief an Bereczky 16, September 1951").

18. See Emil Brunner, "Wie soll man das verstehen? Offener Brief an Karl Barth," in GA V:15, 149–58.

preserved if the Church does not let itself be discouraged from being up-to-date theologically.[19]

Upholding the first article of the Barmen Declaration, for Barth, was more important than criticizing totalitarianism.[20] And, again, he insisted that Soviet communism be handled in a different manner than Nazism, not least because a conflictual mindset raised the prospect of nuclear war. Rather than expressing opinions through political parties, the proclamation of the Kingdom of God has paramount importance. And, in the context of the Cold War, the church's principal task is to help with the reformation of society by pursuing social justice and upholding human rights. *That*, one might say, is what "liberation" meant in the middle of the twentieth century, in a fraught geopolitical context.

To be sure, many never endorsed Barth's differentiation of German Nazism and Soviet communism. Especially within Switzerland and among the Swiss press, many believed anticommunism was the highest national virtue and criticized Barth's left-wing leanings. The "Red Pastor of Safenwil" thus retained his name well into the 1950s. But one can discern here a genuine consistency with respect to the Cold War and (anti)communism—one that speaks to Barth's determination to balance commitment to the gospel with a sensitivity to local conditions, and with a determination to bring about genuine political change.

Barth and the Hungarian Revolution

Prior to moving on Korean feminist theology, it is worth mentioning that Barth also remained quiet about the Hungarian Revolution of 1956. This led again to criticisms and accusations of inconsistency. Reinhold Niebuhr asked: "Why is Barth silent on Hungary?"[21] Was this not a time to reiterate something of the opposition that was shown to Nazism in the 1930s? Was this not a time in which the prophetic vanguard of the Confessing Church needed to return to the fray? Barth did not provide an immediate response to the Hungarian conflict, nor did he broach the subject in a public debate with Niebuhr. (The two theologians, of course, had already engaged in debate regarding the problems of theology in Europe in 1948, after the founding of the WCC.[22]) Once again, Barth did not want to feed the already-burning fire of anticommunism—a Western posture that he

---

19. Karl Barth, *Against the Stream: Shorter Post-War Writings, 1946–1952* (New York: Philosophical Library, 1954), 114. For the original, see GA V:15, 159.

20. Meehyun Chung, "The Problem of the Natural Theology in Connection with the First Article of Barmen's Confession," *Korean Journal of Systematic Theology* 1 (1995): 85–101.

21. Reinhold Niebuhr, "Why is Barth Silent on Hungary?" *The Christian Century* 74 (1957): 108–10.

22. See Karl Barth, "Präliminäre Gedanken zu Reinhold Niebuhrs Darlegung über die 'kontinentale Theologie,'" 20–9; and Reinhold Niebuhr, "Wir sind Menschen und nicht Gott,"

regarded as self-righteous, hypocritical, irresponsible, and ultimately irrelevant.[23] Barth certainly rejected the Soviet communist system and its totalitarian methods, but opposing communism was not the right way forward. Again: systematic anticommunism was worse than communism itself.

In a 1958 letter, Barth confided in an East German pastor, and in a manner that nicely summarizes his stance. He would not answer questions Christians asked who did not genuinely wish to exchange thoughts, nor would he take up questions posed by politicians who fixated on the fall of the "enemy" (GA V.15: 412). Doing so would either present him as anticommunist *or* procommunist: precisely the polarization he wanted to avoid. Barth's determination to do his part to reduce tensions and to seek peace and justice certainly allowed the view that he was a thinker who had abandoned progressive politics and become a negligent, cowardly, old theologian. With the benefit of historical distance, however, one must again say that this was *not* the case. Barth simply did not accept the Cold War dichotomy. He could support neither the morbid anticommunism of the West nor the antiwestern sentiment of the East; he thought it imperative to chart his own course, and to live as a Christian who read the signs of the times and responded accordingly. Adherence to God's Word, spoken in a particular context, was preferable to political partisanship. Indeed, while a prophetic voice can be expressed loudly, reticence is also a prophetic option. And Barth's reticence was not indifference. It was a strategy intended to promote justice and peace in the light of Christ. It was, I hazard to say, an attempt to promote *liberation*, albeit in a style that is somewhat unfamiliar today.

Korean Feminist Theology

From its beginnings, Korean feminist theology has been shaped by various influences. Western feminist theology was certainly important, and it led to the formation of the Korean Association of Women Theologians (KAWT) in 1980. At the same time, feminist theology, feminist consciousness, democratic awareness, and national awareness come together in specific ways in Korea, and they have particular relevance to life in a long-divided country.

Soon-Kyung Park, the foremost pioneer of feminist theology in Korea and one of the founders of KAWT, is very influenced by Barth, particularly with respect to the notion of divine freedom, God's rule over history, and the need to promote social justice.[24] She belongs to the first generation of scholars who introduced

---

in *Gespräche nach Amsterdam*, ed. Jean Daniélou, Reinhold Niebuhr, and Karl Barth (Zollikon-Zürich: Evangelischer Verlag, 1949), 11–19.

23. See, for instance, Barth, *Against the Stream*, 116–17, 129, 131, 138–41, 146, and 170–1.

24. For more about her theology, see Meehyun Chung and Lisa Sedlmayr, "Soon-Kyung Parks feministische Theologie als koreanisches Beispiel reformierter Theologie im 20.

Barth to Korean theological discourse and is often considered a "left-wing Barthian."[25] Even so, Park has moved beyond Barth in various ways. Most notably, she has elaborated the concepts of Minjung and Minjok for Korean feminist liberation theology with an eye to challenging narrowminded nationalism.[26] "'Minjok' includes the people's entire history with its religio-cultural heritage, and is at present to be concentrated on the unification question. The word 'Minjung,' however, is more specific: it refers "to the downtrodden class of the Minjok."[27] Both terms, then, speak to Korea's relationship to imperialism and wider power struggles since the nineteenth century as well as life "within" Korea, even though the latter has especial pertinence for liberationist thought. And both are construed by Park in ways that challenge Christian nationalism and support a constructive posture that is attuned to the experience of victims.

These terms gain further meaning when one reckons with life in a *divided* Korea. After the war, many Christians escaped the North and migrated to the South. Subsequently, a number of American fundamentalist and evangelical groups gained prominence in the South. Not coincidentally, and granted that the "mainline" National Council of Churches in Korea (NCCK) has encouraged different movements for social justice and reunification, the Korean churches have often presumed the triumph of capitalism and retained a reflexively anticommunist mindset. Even the WCC was accused of harboring procommunist views in the 1950s. Sharp divisions among Presbyterian churches emerged, and tensions remain today, hindering an ecumenical spirit. So with her account of Minjok and Minjung, Park aims to address challenges stemming from the division of Korea, while also contributing to feminist theology. Hers is a feminist theology that does not only concern itself with women but occupies itself with the problem of the people—even though Park is aware that women are acutely oppressed.

An intriguing continuity with Barth comes into view at this juncture. On one level, Park seeks peaceful coexistence between North and South through a system of federation and reunification that moves beyond a dualistic opposition of capitalism and communism. Indeed, after the end of the Cold War, Park nurtured the hope that Korea could overcome division in terms of a broader perspective of a unified world, liberated of borders through the activity of women and men who rejected the narrow straits of jingoism and nationalism. She promoted self-

---

Jahrhundert," in *Reformierte Identität*, ed. Marco Hofheinz and Matthias Zeindler (Zürich: TVZ, 2013), 191–210.

25. See Soon-Kyung Park, "My Theological Search," in *The Kingdom of God and the Future of Minjok* (Seoul: Christian Literature Society of Korea, 1985), 13–24 and 70–186.

26. On which, see Soon-Kyung Park, "The Problem of Minjok and the Task of Theology," in *The Kingdom of God and the Future of Minjok*, 367–412; and idem, "Korean Minjok and the Task of Feminist Theology," in *Unification of Minjok and Christianity* (Seoul: Hangilsa, 1986), 187–262.

27. Soon-Kyung Park, "The Unification of Korea and the Task of Feminist Theology," in *On the Journey of Theology of Unification* (Seoul: Hanwool, 1992), 307.

criticism, self-correction, and a "third way," all combined with the concepts of Minjok and Minjung. And this perspective continues to hold great potential, even if it appears idealistic in a world that continues to be marked by ideological conflicts and military tensions. On another level, Park criticized the tendency of South Koreans to exalt "free" democracy, arguing that this tendency is more rooted in Western capitalist bourgeois individualism than Christian convictions. Her thinking was continuous with Barth's: she viewed "anticommunist and anti-North Korean ideology [as] the product of errors contained in Western Christian civilization"[28] and sought to correct anticommunist ideological tendencies in Korean theology and Korean churches, which often gained notoriety (a move that led to Park herself suffering significant hardship).[29] Much in the spirit of Barth, too, Park formulated critiques of capitalism, military power, and US-centered globalization, with an emphasis on the eschatological dimensions of God's Kingdom. She even insisted on allowing North Korean communism to feature in the discourse of reunification, and she attempted to establish a dialogue between North Korean communist ideology and Christian theology.[30] Male-centered and anticommunist-oriented Korean Christian leaders, however, neither understood nor accepted these efforts.

Just as strikingly, Park has also developed some of Barth's ideas to nourish feminist theology in Korea. Her Mariology, which emphasizes that Jesus' birth did not involve a male contribution, aims to show that God's transcendent power to intervene does not amount to an endorsement of patriarchal activity. Quite the contrary: it challenges this activity by circumventing it, thereby opening space for new visions of maleness and masculinity. Concomitantly, Park has adapted Barth's critique of neo-Protestantism as bourgeois religion, predicated on a naively positive evaluation of human experience and rationality that bolsters European imperialistic ideology. Park has used this critique to put some distance between her own work and certain feminist theological discourses, especially those that elevate and idealize women's experience, while drawing fresh attention to God's freedom and subjectivity.

South Korea is still deeply affected by the Cold War—socially, ecclesially, and theologically. Park's feminist theology, then, is an important tool that enables one

---

28. Soon-Kyung Park, "The Kingdom of God, The Ultimate Revolutionary Power of World Society and History," *Korea Journal of Christian Studies* 41, no. 1 (2005): 80.

29. Soon-Kyung Park was imprisoned in 1991 for 106 days due to her lecture, "Perspective of the Korean Church and Reunification," delivered in Tokyo in July 1991. A number of theologians and pastors accused her of identifying God with the North Korean leader through North Korean Church ideology.

30. Soon-Kyung Park, "Theological Significance of Korean People's Unification Liberation Movements Under the Yoke of National Division and Global Capitalization," in *Sustaining Spiritualities with Living Faiths in Asia in the Context of Globalization: Proceedings of the 5. Asian Theological Conference of the Ecumenical Association of Third World Theologians (EATWOT), January 9–16, 2000, Lewella, Kandy, Sri Lanka*, ed. Sookja Chung and Marlene Perera (Colombo: Centre for Society and Religion, 2002), 29.

to advocate for justice. It combines Barth's delicate negotiation of context, while also offering new resources for thinking about liberation. And the continuation and refinement of this project can contribute to the transformation of both church and society, witnessing to the reign of God over both.

Promoting Peace and Justice in a Globalized World

In *Church Dogmatics* III/4, Barth writes about the ethics of life with respect to the doctrine of creation. Under the heading "Freedom for Life," Barth prioritizes "Respect for Life" in light of Christ's birth. This event is itself a command of revelation, a call for reverence for life. In "Defense for Life," Barth emphasizes the sixth commandment, "You shall not murder," to underscore the problems of violence and killing—problems that include suicide, abortion, homicide, euthanasia, self-defense, capital punishment, and war. Except for a few circumstances, Barth argues that war is impossible to accept as part of a political order that approximates to God's intentions. Peace must be the norm.

At the same time, Barth argues that the prohibition of war is not absolute but relative, and that war can be avoided, not according to principle, but through a "sane intelligence." He writes: "The Church must not preach pacifism, but it must see to it that this sane intelligence is voiced and heard so long as this is possible, and that the many ways of avoiding war which now exist in practice should be honestly applied until they are all exhausted" (CD III/4: 460). As such, the church should support educational initiatives for peace, oppose militarism, and consistently challenge the idea that war is unavoidable. Rejecting the "absolutism of radical pacifism" (CD III/4: 468), however, Barth acknowledges that the rejection of wartime duties is wrong. Since peace grounded in justice has utmost importance, an absolute pacifism is impossible. It could lead to an internally degraded, superficially tranquil peace. Rather than an ethic of pacifism that does not relate to a concrete situation and opposes all military action, then, Barth favors a situational ethic. The Christian must be attentive to the particular circumstances of any given situation and discern God's command, rather than holding to certain principles that determine action in advance.

Over the years, Barth adopted slightly different perspectives on war and pacifism.[31] However, with the experience of two world wars and in light of the growing threat posed by nuclear weapons, Barth revisited the Barmen Declaration and admitted problems with the theory of "just war" (*bellum iustum*) in the *Dogmatics*.[32] He had, of course, previously stated his willingness to oppose Hitler

---

31. While John Howard Yoder's detailed analysis on Barth and pacifism cannot be engaged in this chapter, it remains relevant. See *The Pacifism of Karl Barth* (Washington, DC: The Church Peace Mission, 1964).

32. See Karl Barth, "Die These 5 der Barmer Erklärung und das Problem des gerechten Krieges," in *Texte zur Barmer Theologischen Erklärung*, ed. Martin Rohkrämer (Zürich: TVZ, 1984), 196.

by taking up arms. But he now considered the position outlined in the *Dogmatics* to be insufficient, given the actual process of war in the contemporary age. Nuclear war overwhelms the theory of a just war. As such, if nuclear war—a form of war that is, by definition, unjust—is inevitable, Christians should refuse military service. Such a war can be joined neither for the sake of protecting one's country nor in light of a divine order, since it will simply lead to total destruction. One can only offer a strict "no."[33]

Barth therefore adopts a position of outright pacifism. He writes: "To believe that war is a solution to restore broken rights is paradoxical in the era of nuclear weapons ... Today, when someone refers to war, they mean nuclear war. If it comes to this, the only thing left for us to say is that we must not go to war!"[34] Christians cannot take part, either, in the conflict between two kinds of imperialism—which, again, is precisely what Barth deemed the relationship between the Soviet Union and the United States to be: "a mere power-conflict."[35] So while Barth's ideas about just war shifted in the 1930s and 1940s, he became insistent on peace in the context of a dangerously militarized 1950s. And his belief that the use of nuclear weapons cannot be justified in any circumstances remains pertinent for the twenty-first century, not least because of a dangerous combination of neoliberalism, militaristic action, and borderless, profit-driven capitalism has the potential to claim countless lives.

To be sure, Barth continued to highlight God's freedom and continued to underscore the importance of grounding human knowledge of God in God's revelation in the 1950s. He would stand by his earlier words:

> Revelation is not a predicate of history, but history is a predicate of revelation. Of course, we can and must speak of revelation first of all in the principal statement, in order subsequently to speak of history by way of explanation. But we may not first of all speak of history in order subsequently or by epithet to speak with force and emphasis about revelation. When the latter happens, we betray the fact that we have gone our own way in interpreting, valuing, absolutizing. We have not gone the only possible way, the way of obedience. (CD I/2: 58)

God is only known through God, who has revealed Godself in love through Jesus Christ. This revelation is the Subject of history, and history is the object of revelation. So while it is important to keep one's eyes on political affairs, these affairs cannot be absolutized. Politics is important, but Christian theology must always go its own way. Put differently: in light of Jesus' person and work, one can and should reflect on political matters. But one must not absolutize any event or context, especially in the context of capitalism, which Barth considered an "almost

---

33. Ibid., 208.
34. Ibid., 206.
35. Barth, *Against the Stream*, 131.

unequivocally demonic process" (CD III/4: 531), that exacerbates the worst aspects of human nature, debases culture, and obscures its own injustices.

It is precisely this emphasis on God's freedom that afforded Barth the ability to respond to different contexts in nuanced, ad hoc ways. His thought was not fixed in place by ideology. In the 1930s, his principal object of criticism was the false religious belief of the "German Christians" who, distorting the insights of some nineteenth-century liberal theologians, believed in the possibility of finding a new revelation in Hitler. Later, Barth declined the requests of colleagues and followers who wanted him to raise his voice during the Cold War, and showed the value of restraint. In a context in which the threat of nuclear weapons loomed, his actions made evident a deep yearning for peace. While Barth in the 1930s was a theologian of prophetic outspokenness, Barth in the 1950s was a theologian of prophetic restraint.

On one level, then, Barth tried hard to promote peace and justice instead of increasing destructive tensions and justifying war. He is aptly read as a liberation theologian in a European context—and, given the ever-increasing economic and political disparity between rich and poor in the twenty-first century, a theologian whose voice is needed more than ever. On another level, Soon-Kyung Park can be read as a worthy interpreter of Barth's theology, drawing particularly on Barth's vision of divine freedom to challenge idolatry and to promote peace and justice in Korea. If "feminist theology" takes up the task of vigilance "to ensure that theology does not turn into a male-dominated ideology," Park's work strives to bring peace and justice to the Koreas by defusing tension when possible, enabling critiques of entrenched ideology, and promoting gender justice.[36] *Both* voices, I would contend, are needed in a globalized era of technocracy, militarism, and capitalism savagery. A liberation theology that spans Europe and Korea is more relevant than ever.

Closing Remarks

Although the military operations of the Korean War ended seventy years ago, work toward peace is an ongoing task. Koreans live in a fragile and unstable space with merely a ceasefire agreement, not a peace treaty. Violence could thus recommence at any time, and tension, threats, and anxiety emanate from South and North. Indeed, in recent years, due to successive nuclear weapons tests in North Korea and the establishment of the Terminal High Altitude Area Defense (THAAD) weapons system in South Korea, militaristic and diplomatic tensions in northeast Asia have heightened considerably. Both national security and worldwide peace cannot be guaranteed, unless the conflict between the Koreas and the surrounding nations,

---

36. Soon-Kyung Park, "Korean Theology: The Value and Task of Feminist Theology Regarding Salvation Historical Significance," in *On the Journey of Theology of Unification*, 356.

including the United States, is resolved.[37] The pursuit of a complete, verifiable, and irreversible dismantling of nuclear weapons, I would suggest, should not be required only from North Korea; it must be treated as part of a mutual, communal act of peacemaking by all nations in the world.

Barth's theology was a liberation theology written during, between, and subsequent to war that encouraged release from the ideological tensions of the Cold War. It might contribute to a similar posture today vis-à-vis the Koreas. It could support evangelical impartiality and prophetic reticence, and, when combined with the insights of Soon-Kyung Park, it could form an integral part of a Korean liberation theology.

A final comment: in a letter to Christians in Southeast Asia, Barth wrote: "There is no need to be European, Western, or, even more Barthian, to be a good Christian and theologian" (GA V.15:55). These words adverted to a vision of Christianity developing outside of the European continent and gave encouragement to Christians who were growing in number in the southern hemisphere. A similar remark: "There may be a religious West, but there is not a Christian West.... It could well be that one day true Christianity will be understood and lived better in Asia and Africa than in our aged Europe."[38] Those of us who are reformed theologians have a duty to preserve the identity of the gospel while simultaneously engaging the contexts in which we are placed. To be connected to Barth's theological legacy, in critical solidarity, holds promise for negotiating an era of ever-more complex crises, while holding fast to the imperative to promote liberation across the world.

---

37. For more about the culture of militarism in Korea, see Meehyun Chung, "Revisiting the Issue of US Military Prostitution and Culture of Militarism in Post Korean War," *Madang* 27 (2017): 43–69.

38. Karl Barth, "Das Christentum und die Religion," in *Kirchenblatt für die reformierte Schweiz* (1963): 181. Quoted by Eberhard Busch in *Karl Barth*, 468.

Chapter 6

KARL BARTH'S THEOLOGY OF POLITICAL PARTICIPATION

AN EGYPTIAN APPROPRIATION[1]

Hani Hanna

During the 2011 revolution in Egypt, I visited Taḥrīr Square twice. That time had a certain fullness to it. Once, I went there with friends. After a while, the crowd's excitement shuffled us into different groups. I found myself standing with strangers. I soon discovered that none of them had known the others before, either. It was 15°C (about 60°F), which is cold—at least for an Egyptian. A middle-aged man had a big thermos of tea. His wife grabbed disposable cups from her large handbag. They began offering all of us strangers drinks. We moved to the fringe of the crowd and sat down on the ground in a circle. We drank the tea and chatted about what had led things to escalate thus far. Suddenly, a young man pulled out his guitar and began to play. Everyone immediately recognized the music of the famous Egyptian folk song. We stopped chatting and could see the tears in each other's eyes as the lyrics began:

> Ṭil'it yā māḥla nūrhā shams al-shammūsah! (The bright sun rose; How sweet the light is!)

> Yallah bīnā nimlā w-niḥlib laban al-jāmūsah. (Let's milk the cow; Let's bottle the milk in.)

This song describes the daily life of Egyptian villagers who wake up to the sunrise and start their day with optimism and deliberation, knowing that they have a say in their future, even if that future is only one day ahead at a time. This romantic picture captured the hopes of the Egyptian people who had been suffering from social injustice, political mediocrity, and corruption for a long time. We all joined in, as did neighboring groups. We did not think of our religious affiliations. Nor did we discuss our political orientations or aspirations. Yet we felt hope, we felt unity, and we felt common citizenship. I felt the presence of God.

---

1. I am grateful to Darren Kennedy, Safwat Marzouk, Nesreen al-Sayegh, Paul Dafydd Jones, and Kaitlyn Dugan who read a draft of this chapter and provided valuable comments.

This experience also speaks to the hopes that the Arab Spring produced in other countries in the Middle East, especially those in which the only political options had been military or religious rule. These options necessarily controlled political outcomes and jeopardized the integrity of political life. They led to an inhibition of personal freedom and cultural creativity, and they encouraged polarization based on religious affiliation. The result has been an attenuated sense and/or exercise of citizenship and an absence of genuine political life, not only for Christians but also for most Muslims. The Arab Spring aimed to alter this reality.

In such a situation, one wonders what the role of the church could be in the midst of it all. How can Christians read the signs of time? Should Christians adopt a quietistic path, seeking self-preservation in a predominantly nondemocratic and non-Christian Middle East? Should Christians act more riskily, adopting an activistic attitude that defies the status quo? Egyptian Christians have historically opted for the first strategy in relation to the regime. This is understandable, at least to an extent. After all, there are verses in scripture that emphasize obeying the government (Mk 12:17) and praying for it (1 Tim. 2:1–3). However, there are also biblical texts that emphasize the identity of Christians as light in the darkness (Matt. 5:13–16) and command Christians to obey God, rather than human beings (Acts 5:29). This biblical prioritization—obeying God over obeying people—is to be honored through praying for the realization of God's kingdom in the world (Lk. 11:2) and working toward that end through promoting justice on earth (Mic. 6:8; Matt. 25:34–46). Obeying the government and praying for it is thus undertaken in the context of witnessing to God's kingdom and promoting its realization (1 Tim. 2:4). And scripture makes it clear that seeking self-preservation ultimately results in self-annihilation (Matt. 10:39). In light of these diverse and complex biblical commands, how can Christians exercise responsible political participation?

Paul Dafydd Jones argues for a "theopolitical imagination" that is "open-ended" and "flexible."[2] This chapter is an attempt to explore such a possibility in the Egyptian context. My claim is that Karl Barth provides a theological framework for a form of Christian political participation that is relevant to the Egyptian setting in particular and the wider Middle East in general. This theological framework trades on an actualistic ontology grounded in God's covenantal election, revealed in Jesus Christ. It engenders a covenantal moral vision that avoids the binary of activism or quietism, thus providing an alternative pathway to responsible political participation. I want to suggest, still more specifically, that political participation entails *quiet activism* whose heart is *improvised praxis*, grounded in a Trinitarian view of reality that overcomes the negative dynamics threatening the identity of Christians in Egypt.

To elaborate these claims, I will first outline the general features of the Egyptian context. I will then present Barth's political participation in his time to show the organic relation of his theology and political activity. Next, I will consider Barth's

---

2. Paul Dafydd Jones, "Liberation Theology and 'Democratic Futures,'" *Political Theology* 10, no. 2 (2009): 278–82.

actualistic theology as it bore on his political activity. Finally, with Barth's theology in view, I will address some important theological issues, so as to promote a genuine, contextually relevant political option for Egyptian Christians.

The Egyptian Context

The aim of this section is to paint a general picture of the contemporary situation in Egypt. While many details are omitted, I want to suggest that the Arab Spring expressed the frustrations and hopes of many in the twenty-first-century Middle East. It was the climax of historical developments in economic, sociopolitical, and religious spheres.

The economic dimension is the most important and most tangible. The inflation rate in Egypt has increased exponentially, which has caused the middle class to suffer greatly. The middle class has in fact shrunk, leaking members into the lower class or losing them through immigration. There have arisen chasms between a too-thin, extremely rich upper class, a "thick" lower class, and a diminished middle class, whose members are closer to the poorer end of the economic spectrum. To be sure, prior to the Arab Spring, Egypt had adopted an economic reform policy that resulted in the growth of national income. But growth in personal income was minimal and the distribution of income was unbalanced. Such an imbalance was due to an unstable increase in productivity to maintain sustainable economic growth, an incompetent handling of the social dimensions of economic policy, an inability to sustain a mature social market economy, a failure to curb exponential population growth, and a distortion of the democratic processes essential for development.[3]

The economic reality in Egypt is also grounded in sociopolitical challenges, with the legacy of colonization and the struggle for independence being especially significant. The British colonized Egypt for seventy years, until the Free Officers of the army took over in 1952 and put an end to the monarchy of Muhammad Ali's descendants.[4] Since then, Egypt has been ruled by indigenous presidential leaders from the army. The quest for liberation in the Middle East, more broadly, has been connected to freedom from a foreign oppressor/exploiter—which is to say that it has often been a quest for national autonomy. The upside of this quest is a celebrated independence, which changed the structure of the Egyptian state from a kingdom to a republic and restored national pride. The downside, however, is that independence did not help the economic reality much in the long run. And a main reason for this is that Egyptians have been caught up in a pendulum that oscillates between hearing the voice of a colonized mind, effected by the monarchy

---

3. On which, see *The Egyptian Economy: Current Challenges and Future Prospects*, ed. Hanaa Kheir-El-Din (Cairo: The American University in Cairo Press, 2008).

4. Robert L. Tignor, *Egypt: A Short History* (Princeton: Princeton University Press, 2010), 256.

of the past, and hearing the voice of a true desire for participatory democracy that looks to the future. Such an oscillation has led to frustration in the long run, as the following analysis will show.

Given the extravagance and profligacy of kings and aristocrats in Egypt's monarchical period (i.e., prior to 1952), demands for social justice have often emerged. Jamal Abdul-Nasser, Egypt's second president from 1956 to 1970, had socialist inclinations, yet he autocratically led a movement that nationalized industrial resources and redistributed aristocrats' land. He also abolished various political parties, which weakened political life. In addition, Nasser severed Egypt's relationship with the West, which resulted in the cessation of financial aid. Two wars (the Tripartite Aggression against Egypt in 1956 and the war with Israel in 1967) were then detrimental to the economy. Finally, Nasser installed in government posts loyal army leaders who were incompetent civic officials.[5]

Given the strong religious consciousness of many in the Middle East, the pursuit of liberation is often framed in terms of discrete traditions and systems of belief. Particularly notable is an Islamic socialist movement, initiated by Hassan al-Banna in the 1920s and developed and intellectually enhanced by Sayyid Qutb in the 1950s: the Muslim Brotherhood (MB).[6] However, Nasser imprisoned many MB leaders and a militarist-religionist antagonism has existed ever since. This antagonism hardened into the MB's cultivation of a militant arm, known as al-Jamā'āt al-Islāmiyyah (The Islamist Groups [IG]), which has received religious inspiration and financial support mainly from the regressive Wahhabism found in Saudi Arabia.

Anwar al-Sadat (Egypt's third president, serving from 1970 to 1981) autocratically adopted capitalism. However, his religious inclination led him to accept MB and IG, and he used them to neutralize Soviet influence, while accommodating the foreign policy of the United States. Egypt then became one of the principal allies of the United States in the Middle East. Multiple consequences followed. First, the economic gap between rich and poor expanded. A tiny percentage of people became extremely rich while many fell into poverty—even as, given Egypt's small population, the severity of that experience was considered bearable. Second, Sadat's capitalist strategy helped MB to thrive economically. (Ironically, it effectively rendered MB a capitalist group, despite its originally religious-socialist orientation: this was the only way that MB could survive under the new socioeconomic/political conditions.) Third, IG grew stronger and threatened the peace of Egyptian society through terrorist activity, mainly directed against Christians, and sought to create a wedge between Christians and Sadat's regime. This all contributed to the eventual assassination of Sadat in 1981.[7]

---

5. Ibid., 257, 259, 266–7 and 270–1.

6. See Sayyid Qutb, *Social Justice in Islam*, trans. John B. Hardie, ed. Hamid Algar (New York: Islamic Publications International, 2000).

7. Tignor, *Egypt*, 276 and 278–80.

Hosni Mubarak, Egypt's fourth president, serving from 1981 to 2011, kept MB and IG in check without harming them (unlike Nasser). The result was that MB continued to gain power, both economically and socially. The IG, for its part, committed repeated atrocities against Christians and largely got away with it. Meanwhile, the population increased and misconduct continued to plague government offices. Elections were rigged; the constitution was violated and amended at whim; there was a tawdry marriage between money and politics. There followed a wider surge of corruption, poverty, and illiteracy.[8] In light of all this, and in view of the fact that Mubarak intended to pass the presidency to his son, the 2011 revolution took place following the self-immolation of a Tunisian man in protest against social injustice.[9] At this point, liberation became defined as freedom from indigenous oppression. The Arab Spring thus shifted from a quest for national autonomy to a quest for the dignity of individuals, for citizens who participate in a democratic process.

Throughout this time, the church as an institution and most individual Christians tended to ally with the state, fearful of the prospect of a regressive Islamist regime. Yet the Arab Spring also showed that an increasing number of people could no longer tolerate corruption and poverty. Given a feeling of political hopelessness and the religious propensity of many Egyptians, MB came to power in 2012. But only for a year. MB showed political immaturity and ineptitude by aspiring to impose a religious autocracy, one that simply used democracy as a ladder that could be thrown away once power had been gained. Many Egyptians therefore felt that they had jumped out of the frying pan into the fire. So a second revolution, which occurred in June 2013, brought the military back to power and kicked the MB out of the political picture.[10]

The aggregate effect of these developments was frustration and disengagement among many Egyptians who hoped for change. This served to confirm three main interpretations of the Arab Spring. The first is that the Arab Spring was a fiasco, because it neither involved a major shift in the structure of the state nor resulted in a redistribution of power. The second interpretation is that the Arab Spring was never a true revolution, given it lacked a leader or a revolutionary vanguard. The Arab Spring was, at most, a call to reform, which led only to minimal political changes. The third interpretation is that the Arab Spring was indeed a revolution, in terms of mobilization, but one that created only minor reforms. This interpretation is suggested by Asef Bayat and strikes me as the most persuasive, offering the most comprehensive account of historical facts as well as confirming

---

8. Ibid., 285–91 and 295–300.

9. Ibid., 308–10.

10. Noah Feldman, *The Arab Winter: A Tragedy* (Princeton: Princeton University Press, 2020), 30–76. See also Eric Trager, *Arab Fall: How the Muslim Brotherhood Won and Lost Egypt in 891 Days* (Washington, DC: Georgetown University Press, 2016).

my firsthand experience.[11] And this interpretation proves helpful as I begin to reflect theologically on the political responsibility of Egyptian Christians, given their Christian calling as a religious minority in a context marked by political absolutism and social injustice. The Arab Spring was an event geared toward realizing human agency in a manner that enables self-determination and effects historical change; hence the call to *praxis*. Since agency has to be realized in a complex sociopolitical context, *praxis* must take the form of moral *improvisation* via established social channels, relativizing the immoral factors at work and creating openings for sociopolitical reform.

Barth's Theology and Political Participation

Paul Tillich criticized Barth's theology for proclaiming the gospel as if it were thrown from heaven like a stone, without regard for the setting in which it might land.[12] This critique is invalid. While it is true that Barth's theology involves a movement from grace to law, rather than from law to grace (the ordering favored in Tillich's and some Lutheran theologies), it does not follow that Barth does not reckon with context in his theology. Quite the contrary: Barth considers dogmatics to be the right kind of apologetics (so CD I/1: 31), undertaken in view of life in the here-and-now. He writes:

> [D]ogmatics must orientate itself to the actual situation in the light of which the message of the Church must be expressed . . . i.e., to the Word of God as it is spoken by Him, and must be proclaimed by the Church in the present. . . . Therefore, . . . [dogmatics] must throw itself into this contemporary situation. . . . It will itself enter into this solidarity with the action, labour, struggles and sufferings of the Church of the present. What is required is that it should persist in this attitude, that its whole thinking and speaking should be a consequence and application of it. . . . A Church attitude precludes the possibility of a dogmatics which thinks and speaks, as it were, timelessly. (CD I/2: 840–1)

Since the Word of God became flesh, God's self-revealing act in the history of Jesus Christ is the basis of Barth's theology of political participation. But Barth clearly emphasizes that the concrete situation is relevant for theological work. Concreteness, moreover, does not simply mean that dogmatic "theory" is applied haphazardly. Rather, dogmatics is itself "a consequence and application" of practical engagement with the current situation. Put differently, dogmatics is the church's proclamation of the Word of God, spoken anew to the situation of the present.

---

11. Asef Bayat, *Revolution without Revolutionaries: Making Sense of the Arab Spring* (Stanford: Stanford University Press, 2017).

12. Paul Tillich, *Systematic Theology*, vol. 1 (Chicago: The University of Chicago Press, 1951–1963), 7.

Even so, what Barth emphasizes here is witness *in action*, not the articulation of theory. The difference between Tillich and Barth, then, is not best described in terms of attending to, neglecting, or marginalizing the "setting" in which theology happens. The difference pertains to engaging context in terms of theory or in terms of praxis. Tillich represents the former option; Barth, the latter.[13] Barth's emphasis on contextual praxis, moreover, points to the actualism of his theological outlook (about which I will have more to say soon). Tillich's critique, by contrast, misses or misunderstands the significance of Barth's political involvement for his theology. While a pastor, Barth developed a socialist orientation for his preaching and led poor workers in Safenwil, Switzerland, to form a union to attain their rights. In 1934, Barth also led the effort to draft the Barmen Declaration, declining an oath of loyalty to the Nazis and affirming Jesus Christ as the sole *Führer*. Upon being dismissed from his university position, Barth moved back to Basel and continued to encourage the Christians of Europe to serve God by resisting National Socialism.[14] Such political engagement is consistent with the concern for the "contemporary situation" referenced in the excerpt above, showing again that Christian praxis is integral to Barth's actualistic ontology.

Friedrich-Wilhelm Marquardt was among the first to understand the political core of Barth's thought.[15] Marquardt argued for Barth's political thought in a short essay with four theses: "Barth was a socialist. Barth's theology has its life setting in his socialist activity. Barth turned to theology to seek the organic connection between the Bible and the newspaper, the new world and the collapsing bourgeois order. The substance of Barth's turn to theology was the construction of a concept of God."[16] Given the quotation from the *Church Dogmatics* earlier, I agree with Marquardt, with the caveat that socialist experience is not understood as the *source* of dogmatics.[17] Experience is the setting or medium through which the Word of

---

13. On which, see Friedrich-Wilhelm Marquardt, "Socialism in the Theology of Karl Barth," in *Karl Barth and Radical Politics*, ed. George Hunsinger, 2nd edn (Eugene: Cascade, 2017), 24–49.

14. Eberhard Busch provides a biography of Karl Barth's life in his book *The Great Passion: An Introduction to Karl Barth's Theology*, trans. Darrell L. Guder and Judith J. Guder (Grand Rapids: Eerdmans, 2004).

15. See Friedrich-Wilhelm Marquardt, *Theologie und Sozialismus: Das Beispiel Karl Barths*, 3rd edn (Munich: Chr. Kaiser Verlag, 1985).

16. Marquardt, "Socialism in the Theology of Karl Barth," in *Karl Barth and Radical Politics*, 24.

17. Barth's thought developed from the early period of his ministry in Safenwil through a break with liberalism after the First World War. This development did have some impact on his political views, which were initially a matter of "ethical idealism" (see Bruce L. McCormack, *Karl Barth's Critically Realistic Dialectical Theology: Its Genesis and Development 1909–1936* [Oxford: Clarendon, 1995], 87). However, there is no doubt that Barth maintained a generally socialist orientation. On this point, see Helmut Gollwitzer, "Kingdom of God and Socialism in the Theology of Karl Barth," in *Karl Barth and Radical Politics*, 51–85.

God is heard and to which it is proclaimed, as attested in Scripture and in dialogue with the Christian tradition (so CD I/2: 840); it cannot be equated with the Word as such. With this caveat in view, Marquardt's thesis nevertheless draws attention to Barth's determination to engage his own context.

Barth's political engagement ought also to be understood as prophetic, as an act of witnessing to the kingdom of God. He writes:

> The Christian community both can and should espouse the cause of this or that branch of social progress or even socialism in the form most helpful at a specific time and place and in a specific situation. But its decisive word cannot consist in the proclamation of social progress or socialism. It can consist only in the proclamation of the revolution of God against "all ungodliness and unrighteousness of man" (Rom. 1:18), i.e., in the proclamation of His kingdom as it has already come and comes. (CD III/4: 545)

Four claims are advanced here. First, the goal of Christian political participation is to proclaim or bear witness to the kingdom of God as it happens on earth. Second, the happening of the Kingdom is the act of God, not of humans; it is always "the revolution of *God*." The world is God's, and God comes to it in a transformative manner. So Christian political work requires correspondence with God's act in history, speaking against the injustices that resist the coming of God's kingdom, and, as God wills it, making way for the coming of kingdom. Third, this participation is concrete and not abstract; it has a specific content, whether that be socialist or something else. Fourth and finally, God's kingdom is not to be essentially and timelessly identified with a specific ideology. The objection to this identification stems from the recognition that God is transcendent and, as such, free to act graciously in history. (As Barth says elsewhere: "God may speak to us through Russian Communism, a flute concerto, a blossoming shrub, or a dead dog . . . or a pagan or atheist" [CD I/1: 55].) The Christian community must hear the Word of God anew in every age and give witness to the Word of God through prophetic action.

Barth, clearly, was neither an anarchist nor a quietist: he did not want to absolutize revolution or legitimize the status quo. He sought instead to render *all* forms of political life subservient to the kingdom of God whose manifestation in history is justice and freedom. The church

> must be to the world . . . a reminder of the law of the kingdom of God already set up on earth in Jesus Christ, and a promise of its future manifestation. . . . In relation to those who are without it can and should demonstrate, as well as say, that worldly law, in the form in which they regard it as binding, and outside which they believe that they cannot know any other or regard any other as practicable, has already ceased to be the last word and cannot enjoy unlimited authority and force; that there are other possibilities, not merely in heaven but on earth, not merely one day but already, than those to which it thinks that it must confine itself in the formation and administration of its law. It cannot produce any perfect

or definitive thinking or action on this question of law. It can produce only a thinking and action which are defective because provisional. (CD IV/2: 721–2)

For Barth, the church is a parable of the kingdom of God. As such, the church proclaims the gospel: the world does not have to imprison itself in old ways of thinking and doing, because its freedom was accomplished in Jesus Christ. At the same time, the world is allowed to live out its reality in light of God's gracious act. The world is invited and enabled to engage in grateful self-criticism, with grace forming the basis of historical transformation.

All this means, further, that the church's prophetic role regarding the kingdom of God is not complementary to its being as church. Rather, the church *is* church in this *act*: "The Christian community is either the place of this great anticipatory joy in relation to all [people] and all creation, or it is not the Christian community" (CD IV/3: 812). Given the connection between Barth's dogmatic conceptions and praxis, I now turn to Barth's actualistic ontology in order to discuss what kinds of dogmatic commitments undergird his views of politics.

Barth's Actualism

Barth's view of political participation is grounded in his actualistic theology. *Actualism* refers to Barth's understanding of the reality of God and humanity on the basis of God's definitive *act*, that is, the history of Jesus Christ in which the reality of both God and humanity is disclosed (so CD IV/2: 61; see also CD III/2: 132). And what is disclosed is that both the divine being and the human being are what they are *in* and *by* their shared history (CD IV/3: 43). Indeed, actualism is the reason that, for Barth, the Christ event is itself God's self-revelation to us. Note the order inherent in these statements. *God* grounds and maintains the creaturely reality with which God interacts; *God's* triune being is the unique eternal event of God's free determination of God to be the God of humanity, and of humanity to be God's elect in Jesus Christ. It is for this reason that Barth identifies Christ's history as *Urgeschichte* ("primal" or "original" history), insofar as it is eternity's presence in time. "In no depth of the Godhead shall we encounter any other but [Jesus Christ]. There is no such thing as Godhead in itself" (CD II/2: 115). Yet this original history always bears on life in the present. "God is not *in abstracto* Father, Son and Holy Ghost, the triune God. He is so with definite purpose and reference" (CD II/2: 79); and the history of God and humanity in Jesus Christ, ontologically grounded in eternity and revelatory of eternity, cuts into creaturely existence in the here-and-now.

The event of eternity breaking into time in Jesus Christ by the power of the Holy Spirit is also the basis of humanity's hope. *Urgeschichte*, by these lights, implies "revolutionary history."[18] God's gracious interaction with the world is actual;

---

18. Marquardt, "Socialism in the Theology of Karl Barth," 31.

therefore, sociopolitical change is possible. Humans are allowed and enabled to have hope. Moreover, since God reveals Godself as the gracious covenant partner of humanity, in Christ and by the Spirit, "the dogmatics of the Christian Church, and basically the Christian doctrine of God, is *ethics*" (CD II/2: 515, emphasis added). Theology cannot be an abstract or speculative enterprise. Its subject matter is the God who reveals Godself as the covenantal God who concerns Godself with God's creation. This is the basis of Barth's Trinitarian ethics in *Church Dogmatics* II/2, III/4, and IV/4.

With these claims in play, Barth's assertion that Christ reveals human nature as a *social* history, as well as a history with God, comes into view. The human subject is a being in encounter with both God and other humans; to be human is to be both "for God" and "for others," positioned within a "history which shows how one of God's creatures, elected and called by God, is caught up in personal responsibility before Him and proves itself capable of fulfilling it" (CD III/2: 55). The human being, more specifically, is an *agent*, and agency is exercised in response to God's calling, the material center of which is God's Word as Jesus Christ.

Barth's affirmation of human agency has two main dimensions. First, the human being is not static or self-enclosed, much less tied to an abstract substratum that underlies his or her historical existence. The human being *is* in their self-transcending act of responding to God's calling. They are as the event of God's gracious relating to them and their free response to God's Word, that is, Jesus Christ, in the power of the Spirit (a point made vividly in CD III/2; see 365). The human being, in fact, is constituted by a twofold act of gracious divine communication. The first is God's speaking to humanity by God's Word. The second is God's enabling the human being to respond to God's Word, the human acting in self-transcendence toward God, by grace. In this openness lies the freedom in which the human being is oriented to the future and enabled to enter it. Accordingly, if political participation is an exercise of freedom in which one has a say in one's future, it represents one way of responding to God's calling—engaging a future that is neither abstract nor indeterminate but marked by definite content: Jesus Christ who is the beginning and end of all God's ways (so CD II/2: 1–3).

Second, responses to God's calling in Jesus Christ, by the Spirit, bear on the ethical character of the human in relation to God. To be human is to be moral, and morality consists in obeying God's command. But God's command is not a matter of static moral rules (i.e., what Barth calls *casuistry* ethics). Casuistry ethics, as Barth construes it, may take either the heteronomous extreme of legalistic moralism of the traditional divine-command theory (e.g., Tertullian) or the autonomous extreme of romantic and idealist ethics (CD III/4: 6–14).[19] In contradistinction, Barth's ethics is *covenantal* in nature, with its material center being the person and work of Jesus Christ. It is for this reason that Barth thinks of a gracious divine

---

19. For contemporary versions of the divine-command theory, see Philip L. Quinn, *Divine Commands and Moral Requirements* (Oxford: Clarendon, 1978) and Linda Trinkaus Zagzebski, *Divine Motivation Theory* (Cambridge: Cambridge University Press, 2004).

command that does not simply constitute the human being, but also *frees* them, in the Spirit, to relate to God and others. A couple of implications follow. On one level, God's commands always have a revolutionary effect on humanity since those commands aim at liberating humanity from sin. On another level, Christian ethics has a Trinitarian (and thus revelational) structure. God's command invites the human being to a future defined by Christ, the Son of the Father, and the Holy Spirit frees human beings to move toward that future. Our creaturely reality and history, then, is always caught up with God's command. This is the reason why Barth emphasizes the dynamic character of the ethical decision; this is the reason, too, that Barth's ethics may be called *graced improvisation*. They focus attention on creative, Spirit-enabled activity that has a christological orientation and addresses a unique situation involving others. This *improvisation* corresponds to what Barth calls "training in Christianity, and . . . keeping the command" (CD III/4: 31).

A covenantal morality is flexible and open-ended. Such flexibility and open-endedness relativize anthropocentric morality in its absolutistic and legalistic forms, creating a space for change. The dynamism of such a covenantal ethical, I would also suggest, is an improvisation that creates room for political engagement that is not dictated by or married to a certain ideology. *Any* part of creation could serve, at least in principle, as a medium for God's addressing us. And such ad hoc-ness emphasizes the gracious character of God's address to humanity (which, of course, is why Barth can so emphatically assert God's ability to speak through shrubs, flutes, communism, etc.). The order of creation is not separate from human life; it is a "graced" reality that exists under God's reign. "Creation [is] the outer basis of the covenant" and "Covenant [is] the inner basis of creation" (CD III/1: 94 and 228), and Christ is the One in whom "all things in heaven and on earth were created, things visible and invisible, whether thrones or dominions or rulers or powers—all things have been created through him and for him. He himself is before all things, and in him all things hold together" (Col. 1:16–17). Political participation is thus human engagement in the covenantal drama that is the ground, meaning, and telos of history. It is at once unavoidable and an acknowledgement of the covenantal character of reality. And since Christians are essentially called to witness to Jesus Christ as the realization of God's kingdom on earth, political participation becomes an important Christian act.

To be human is not only to be "for God" in the human freedom of obedience but also to be "for man [and women]," to coexist with and for others. In other words, Barth's covenantal morality has a horizontal as well as a vertical dimension. Improvised praxis is a covenantal act because humanity is *co*-humanity. Barth writes:

> the word "Thou," although it is a very different word, is immanent to "I." . . . The word "I" with which I think and declare my humanity implies as such humanity with and not without the fellow-man. I cannot say "I" even to myself, without also saying "Thou," without making that distinction and connexion in relation to another. . . . What does "I am" mean on this presupposition? Who and what am I myself as I confirm my being in this way? What kind of a being is it in the

freedom and necessity of which I, posit myself, distinguishing and connecting myself, projecting myself outwards? One thing at least is certain. A pure, absolute and self-sufficient "I" is an illusion, for as an "I" even as I think, and express this "I," I am not alone or self-sufficient, but am distinguished from and connected with a "Thou" in which I find a being like my own, so that there is no place for an interpretation of the "I am" which means isolation. (CD III/2, 245–6)

Relating to others is not an addition to human existence; it is essential to it. In fact, in a sense, co-humanity *precedes* individual existence. Humanity is essentially relational in the horizontal plane as well as the vertical plane. And, as always, the web of human relations is grounded in Jesus Christ, the "Royal Man," who defines what humanity is and to whom we are called by God's gracious and freeing command (so CD IV/2: 185).[20]

The horizontal dimension of human relationality that Barth points out is not an abstract property that underlies our individuality or particularity, much less is it reducible to a kind of interiority that one could access through a particular kind of religious practice. It is the actual event of relating to and being related to by others, and to such an extent that we are human in and by the act of relating, and we are human in and by our history with others. Barth's actualistic/historical view of humanity is in view here again, but he gives it specificity by identifying four basic features of human life, which he takes to be ingredient to actual I-Thou encounters: the joyful acts of seeing, hearing, speaking, and assisting (see CD III/2: 222–84). Clearly, these acts are all directed outward, and they disclose self-transcendence toward the Other (God) and others (fellow humans). The *joyful* quality of these acts also underscores the fact that they are intentional and responsible acts in response to grace, undertaken within the web of human relations. They are responsive to God's gracious, freeing command, while also being grateful and obedient acts that witness to Jesus Christ.

These four features accentuate Barth's moral and sociopolitical understanding of humanity, with each act opening a future for others. They are an occasion for each person to affirm another's existence, and to welcome, promote, and celebrate it. Moreover, such acts help to create room for others to have a say in who they are and what they want. They open a space for others to share their dreams and frustrations, and to make decisions toward changing the oppressive status quo. Or, to move back to a temporal register: such acts are *future-opening* acts in the simplest yet deepest sense. And, since politics is an act of having a say in our future, so again is political participation brought into view.

A final note: it is important to notice that the doctrine of providence overarches Barth's theological anthropology and ethics. It ensures that the question of the relationship between divine and human action is located in *history*. Providence, I hurry to add, is not an abstract doctrine about a general worldview, be it

---

20. On this last point, see also Karl Barth, *Christ and Adam: Man and Humanity in Romans 5*, trans. Thomas Allan Smail (New York: Macmillan, 1968), 86–94.

determinism, libertarianism, and so on. For Barth, it is concretely grounded in the covenant of grace in Jesus Christ. It pertains to God's dynamic interaction with humanity in light of, and for the sake of, the realization of God's covenant of grace in justice and freedom. Accordingly, Barth defines preservation, concurrence, and governance of history in ways that uphold human agency. As one finds consistently in the *Church Dogmatics*, God's sovereignty does not compromise human freedom. God is the Trinitarian other who grounds human life, and God's act in the world happens *through* humans who are graciously permitted to participate in God's work as partners created for a covenant with God and other fellow humans in Jesus Christ by the Spirit. Once again, then, free human responses to God's gracious calling through political acts can be understood as participation in God's liberating act in history. Humans are permitted and called to activity that proclaims, bears witness to, and celebrates God's salvation in the context of time and space.

The Political Import of Barth's Actualistic Theology

Needless to say, Barth's context was predominantly Christian. The Egyptian context, by contrast, is predominantly Muslim—a difference that often pushes Egyptian Christians toward self-marginalization, which impedes political participation. Barth's context was also highly dynamic: a time marked by world wars and a time that promoted (if not necessitated), social change, transformed the meaning of secularity, and engendered a good deal of intellectual upheaval. By contrast, Egypt's life setting is less politically informed and predominantly religious. These two differences occasion a third. If Barth's Trinitarian understanding of the God-world relation and God's action in history was immediately legible in a Christian and political context, thereby encouraging him and his contemporaries to participate politically, the Egyptian context is quite different, being marked with a belief in an eternity-time dualism, a fatalistic worldview, and a self-marginalizing attitude, which together downplay the importance of political participation. With that said, in this final section, I want to argue that Barth's theology provides the Christian community in Egypt with a basis for addressing these conceptual challenges. It encourages what I call *quiet activism*, which fits Egypt's life setting and the need for reform.

Both the monotheism of Islam and Christian classical theism presume an eternity-time dualism. This is evident in the classical doctrine of timeless eternity, according to which God is not temporally conditioned.[21] A correlate of this doctrine is a dualism of spirit and matter, some forms of which assign less value to the material aspect of reality. Both of these factors can lead to a devaluation of political activity, especially in a context shaped by the political history outlined

---

21. Thomas Aquinas, *Summa Theologiae*, trans. Fathers of the English Dominican Province, 5 vols. (New York: Benziger, 1948), I.10.1. See also George Leonard Prestige, *God in Patristic Thought* (London: SPCK, 1952), 3–7.

above, wherein a colonized-mind syndrome followed in the wake of imperial rule and an absence of democracy. On the one hand, a timeless view of eternity can complicate talk of God's presence in history. This complication depresses the hope for historical change, insofar as it places humanity in utter loneliness, isolated from God. On the other hand, a dualistic view of reality paves the way for an escapist eschatology that downplays materiality and makes spiritualization the meaning and goal of history. This dualism also builds a wall between religion and culture and imperils hope for sociopolitical transformation. This is especially true insofar as many Egyptian Christians are inclined toward a dispensationalist interpretation of scripture, wherein the eschatological consummation of God's work is always deferred. These factors make Egyptian Christians prone to political resignation and discourage active participation in political life.

Barth provides the beginnings of a way out. His christocentric, actualistic theology is covenantal and Trinitarian in character. Transcendence, by these lights, is not a fate to which God must submit; the incarnation provides evidence of God's freedom. And Barth asserts the *fellowship* of eternity and time: he supposes that God grounds time, accompanies time, enters time, and eschatologically receives time in virtue of the resurrection of Jesus Christ that inaugurates a new creation. The reality of this fellowship, of course, is revealed in the history of Jesus Christ: a history that reveals that God is "for us," and humanity is "for God," and that grounds the possibility of historical change. Humanity is not God-less, because God graciously is not human-less.[22] Correspondingly, Barth's historical understanding of humanity in terms of I-Thou encounters, grounded in a divine action and relationship that graciously constitutes the human, moves us from interiority to exteriority. The four basic acts (joyful seeing, listening, speaking, and helping) that constitute human being give shape to this exteriority. And the direct implication of this move is that the "realization" of humanity, which happens in obedient response to God's command, *requires* interaction with others. Withdrawal is simply not an option. Equally obligatory is political engagement, in moral obedience to God's command, for the goal of proclaiming God's kingdom and, in a sense, "making way" for that kingdom in history. The actualistic ontology operative in Barth's christocentric theology thus addresses the challenge of dualism in the Egyptian context and promotes responsible political participation.

What of the fatalistic worldview that shapes much Egyptian religiosity? Fatalism is the view that, no matter our decisions or actions, God always ensures a predetermined outcome. Within the bounds of an eternity-time dualism, which affirms a timeless eternity and grounds a separation between the orders of creation and reconciliation, the genuineness of human agency is jeopardized.[23] It therefore casts a shadow over the feasibility of any social or political undertaking. In Egypt,

---

22. See, of course, Karl Barth, *The Humanity of God*, trans. John Newton Thomas and Thomas Wieser (Richmond: John Knox Press, 1960).

23. Nasr Abu Zayd, *Reformation of Islamic Thought: A Critical Historical Analysis* (Amsterdam: Amsterdam University Press, 2006), 23.

this has resulted in laxity, complacency, and extreme dependency, all of which have encouraged a mediocre work ethic and superficial political participation. In Barth's hands, by contrast, the Christian doctrine of the incarnation challenges fatalism. It presents the human being as

> active, engaged in movement. . . . The gift of God which characterizes the creatureliness of man, namely, that as His creature he may be himself, is not a gift to be hidden away in a napkin. It is certainly given him to possess, so that he could not be at all unless he found himself in this possession. But freedom cannot be possessed otherwise than by being seized and won. Hence the fact that man is subject is not to be understood in the sense that man is first a passive idler and then becomes active, as if his life were in the first instance a blank sheet on which is later written what he knows, wills and does. The freedom which constitutes man's being is not to be thought of as the mere latent possibility and capacity of man which is then realized in this or that particular use of freedom. We recall the point that it is not merely a question of man's static but of his active responsibility before God. If his being in this responsibility has the character of freedom, then freedom too means the actualization of this responsibility—the event of the knowledge of God, his obedience to Him and his asking after Him. The word "freedom" might easily be misunderstood in this connection, since as an abstract noun it can suggest a passive condition. But it must not be taken in this way. Man is, as he knows God; he is, as he decides for God; he is, as he asks after God and moves to His judgment. Thus he is, as he lives. And now, we have only to summarize the lessons learned. Who is the man of whom all this had to be said? We have defined him as the free creature of God; the subject posited by God for free self-positing; the recipient of the divine gift, who in his creaturely sphere may be himself no less than God may be Himself in His sphere. (CD III/2: 195)

By these lights, freedom has a positive orientation, marked by grateful obedience to God's freeing grace. The grace of God is experienced and occurs in a context of revelation where God makes Godself available to be known in the web of relations that constitutes humanity and empowers human beings to *act*. God, crucially, does not coerce us; God waits on our response to God's commands. An actualistic and covenantal view of humanity thus conceives of human beings as agents of sociopolitical change who work toward realizing justice and freedom in service to fellow humans and in witness to the kingdom of God. Barth's theology, one might even say, aspires to *mobilize* individuals and groups who bear witness to and realize God's kingdom (so CD IV/3: 488–9).

To be sure, one can affirm human agency without recourse to an actualistic ontology or a covenantal theology. But understanding reality in covenantal terms helps one to realize that even when humans fail, they can have faith that God is always at work. Barth's actualism does not only empower human agency; it also enables people to let go when evil overpowers them, in order to hope for and work toward continued *rounds of improvised praxis*—rounds of training oneself to obey God in the complex web of co-humanity.

That Egyptian (and Middle Eastern) Christians constitute the smaller percentage of the population is, of course, indisputable. What is disputable, though, is whether this means Egyptian Christians cannot play a vital and significant role in the political life. The final challenge to be discussed, then, is self-marginalization. Self-marginalization or, as Najib George Awad would put it, "self-minoritization," is an attitude of self-belittling and self-ghettoing in fear that inhibits sociopolitical participation.[24] The challenges of dualism and fatalism have contributed to forming and informing this attitude. But the essence of this attitude is also an identity-citizenship complex. This complex has been created by a historical absence of participatory democracy and the presence of religious discrimination. In addition, a manipulative militarist-Islamist politics has led to innumerable terrorist attacks by Islamist extremists on Christians during the last century.[25] One such attack took place in August 2013, subsequent to Muhammad Morsi (an MB president of Egypt after the Arab Spring) being ousted. Christians effectively turned the other cheek in the wake of these attacks in an act of self-sacrificial peacemaking. Christians viewed unjust and brutal consequences without reprisal as an act of self-giving. And this was indeed one of the main factors that kept the country together at such a difficult time. It revealed the love that Egyptian Christians have for their country. However, the Egyptian constitution still has an article stating that Islam is the religion of the country and the principal source of legislation. Every Egyptian is reminded of this article when looking at their national ID card which includes their religious affiliation. These factors make self-marginalization an enforced proposal and a continuous temptation.

Currently, there is nothing Christians can do to alter the legal situation. However, steps may be taken toward alleviating pressure and achieving progress toward a society of equal citizenship. Those steps necessarily require sociopolitical participation and initiatives. Such activity must not be done in a self-serving manner; otherwise, many citizens would not see the promise and hope awaiting these actions. It must be a participation in which citizenship *happens*. Citizenship, one might say, must be defined actualistically, as a historical enactment of identity. It would stand in direct contrast to Egyptian sloganeering, which trivializes actions and sacralizes social and political hypocrisy, and defines citizenship in static terms apart from concrete historical relationships and commitments. It is not enough endlessly to chant, "Egypt is my mother; Her Nile is my blood," yet do the bare minimum in one's vocation to the detriment of one's neighbor. It is not enough to say, "Christians and Muslims constitute the one fabric of the Egyptian nation," yet still let the constitution and civic documents implicitly and explicitly treat

---

24. Najib George Awad, "Social Harmony in the Middle East: The Christian Contributions," in *Christian Citizenship in the Middle East: Divided Alliance or Dual Belonging?* ed. Mohammed Girma and Cristian Romocea (London: Jessica Kingsley, 2017), 80.

25. See S. S. Hassan, *Christians Versus Muslims in Modern Egypt: The Century-Long Struggle for Coptic Equality* (Oxford: Oxford University Press, 2003).

Muslims as *the* true citizens. The love of God must not be abstracted from the love of neighbor, and faith must not be reduced to doctrinal battles within the church.

Barth's covenantal view of humanity helps us define identity in a concrete, inclusive, and relational manner, rather than in a static and exclusive way. We are human as we relate to others (e.g., Christians, Muslims) in hospitable ways that open up the future for them by freeing them and bringing justice into their lives (CD IV/3: 493). What we do counts more than what we say, for we are constituted by and in what we do. Christians, accordingly, must not engage in politics for self-serving purposes. They should participate in political action in witness to the Kingdom of God that has already broken into history in Jesus Christ. Equally, Christians must not want to be equal citizens in order merely to receive their rights. They must want to receive their rights in order to serve others in their witness to Jesus Christ here-and-now, in their particular context. And this goal necessarily requires including others in the web of other-serving humanity, lest the act of other-serving become unidirectional—perhaps resulting in a perpetuation of oppression. Inclusion is essential to a covenantal understanding of humanity, and the goal is to transform culture. Sociopolitical action, then, becomes a concrete realization of citizenship. It is true to Christian identity, without which the church would cease to be church. And while Egyptian Christians are fewer than non-Christians in number, an actualized vision of human life ensures that Egyptian Christians can be what and who they are in a *history* that includes others. It becomes possible for self-marginalization to be conquered in both theory and praxis.

Conclusion

Barth's actualism supports a moral ontology that provides a robust theological framework for responsible political participation in witness to God's kingdom. Furthermore, Barth's emphasis on the radical distinction between God and world enables a mode of political participation that does not identify the gospel with any ideology. It frees Christians to work within—or for that matter, outside—the bounds of sociopolitical conventions. The orientation of a theologically based sociopolitical action, moreover, is to realize freedom and to bring justice to fellow humans, to those who constitute the historical web of co-humanity. There is thus real hope for change in God's work through human actions and relations, empowered by the Spirit in witness to Jesus Christ.

Barth's actualism, more particularly, provides a theological basis for a sociopolitical perspective that prizes responsible action. In an Egyptian context, that perspective is best framed as *quiet activism*. It is quiet *activism* insofar as it denotes action toward realizing freedom and justice. It is *quiet* activism insofar as it does not subscribe to any ideology, but instead relativizes all ideologies in witness to the kingdom of God. The paradoxicality of the name denotes this very relativization. Barth's actualistic ontology, equally, enables an *improvised praxis*, a witnessing to and celebrating of the fragmentary realization of God's kingdom in history whenever it happens through the church or the state, while also supporting critiques of church and state whenever they engage in actions that undermine the realization of God's kingdom in history. This improvised praxis helps to break the vicious cycle of choosing between the false political options whose dictated outcome continues to restrict Egyptian citizens. It achieves those ends by addressing detrimental religious and cultural barriers (dualism, fatalism, and self-marginalization) that inhibit Egyptian Christians from actively participating in sociopolitical life; by providing the church with a way of affirming its Christian identity as a parable of the kingdom of God; and by nourishing a realistic strategy for a post-Arab Spring Egypt that is predominantly Muslim and hopes for the emergence of an authentic participatory democracy.

Chapter 7

KARL BARTH AND LIBERATION THEOLOGIES IN SOUTH AFRICA

THE DIFFICULTIES OF COMPARISON, CONVERSATION, AND CONSTRUCTIVE REFLECTION

Rothney S. Tshaka

Introduction

My interest in Karl Barth started purely by chance. I was a young student of theology at the University of the Western Cape in the mid-1990s. South Africa had just had her first democratic election, and the new dispensation had clearly caught South African critical theology by surprise. Which is to say: critical theology, or *liberation theologies*, most of which can be considered guerrilla enterprises, had not done enough to imagine a mode of reflection that affirmed the total humanity of Black people beyond Apartheid. In a way, this was to be expected: Apartheid had become so entrenched in society that to imagine its demise seemed pointless.

Conversations with my peers during this time revolved around the question of what theological reflection in a postapartheid world might look like. It was almost impossible to approach this question without thinking about Allan Boesak or the radical Desmond Tutu, as well as other likeminded theologians. The idea of a theology "from the underside" invariably engaged these figures. If we looked farther afield, Dietrich Bonhoeffer was invoked most frequently. His seminal work, *The Cost of Discipleship*, became a key text in informal theological conversations.[1]

The fourteen part-volumes of the *Church Dogmatics*, however, were another matter. It was always a threatening sight to those of us who spent the majority of our time in the library for fear of failing the course and the consequent threat of having to return to our villages after being excluded academically (and therefore financially).[2] Additionally, at that time, the *Church Dogmatics* was largely available

---

1. Dietrich Bonhoeffer, *The Cost of Discipleship* (New York: Simon & Schuster, 1995).
2. Tertiary education in South Africa is not free. Most of those who study at universities are admitted on the grounds that they have scholarships and personal loans. Scholarships require that you pass all modules and remain in good standing.

only in German. Knowledge of the German language was essential to read and engage with the text, but in African universities it was Hebrew, Greek, and Latin that needed to be mastered.[3] Mastery of these languages, in fact, was an accolade for the few who made it to university and thereby came to be seen as distinguished members of Black communities, even as others were deprived of tertiary education due to its exorbitant costs.

Still, during my studies, I stumbled on a text by Eberhard Busch titled *Karl Barth: His Life from Letters and Autobiographical Texts*, translated into English by John Bowden.[4] This text became a compass that helped me to navigate the *Church Dogmatics*. What got me hooked on Barth was my sense of his engagement with politics. I was a student of the Black Consciousness Movement, and something in Barth's masterwork spoke to my interests and commitments.[5]

I open this chapter with these reflections because they are connected to three commitments that, in combination, might appear irreconcilable—and, in fact, might just be irreconcilable. First, I have a sustained interest in the theology of Karl Barth, who insisted radically on the centrality of Christ for theological inquiry and who linked theological and political reflection in innovative ways. In the context of mainstream European historical theology, Barth's christological focus is so well known as to be a commonplace; but for the colonized Christian, fed on a diet foreign to her context in hope that she would deny the essence of her being, it is simultaneously an invigorating and ambiguous matter—or, at least, that is what I have come to believe. Second, I am fascinated with Black liberation theology as a theological hermeneutic that is suspicious of the Christ who has often been presented to the suffering and marginalized people of South Africa. Third, I believe the lessons that I have learned from African worldviews and deem important have been deliberately ignored by the broader academy, in an attempt to depict African insights as "backward" and useless, and that Barth's theology does not really help remedy this problem. Each of these commitments, too, converges around a tension between theological inquiry and political activity—a tension I find particularly significant to academic discourse in South Africa today and, I daresay, the world at large.

---

3. Reflecting today on the languages imposed upon us as students makes me realize how a total onslaught on African cultures was engineered in a way that befuddled even some of the smartest students. In that context, one can appreciate why talk about "Africanization" was perceived to be out of sync with the times.

4. Eberhard Busch, *Karl Barth: His Life from Letters and Autobiographical Texts* (London: SCM Press, 1976).

5. Nyameko Pityana gives an overview of Black Consciousness. He lists at least four basic tenets, one of which is that the Black man must reject all value systems that seek to make him a foreigner in the country of his birth and reduce his basic human dignity. See Nyameko Pityana, "What Is Black Consciousness?" in *Black Theology: The South African Voice*, ed. Basil Moore (London: C. Hurst & Company, 1973), 61.

As will also become evident in the following pages, the *image* of Christ cuts across these three commitments. Early on, this image was presented to South Africans in an idealized fashion, and it functioned as exclusionary on racial grounds. Black theology, by contrast, is rightly commended for challenging the captivity of Christ's image; and, at least in my view, its presentation of Christ is pregnant with theopolitical potential, as Barth himself realized. But, again, there remains constructive work to be done. Toward the end of this chapter, I draw on wisdom taken from African theology (a term I use in place of the more conventional "African Traditional Religions," in order to affirm its intellectual significance), challenging a theological hermeneutic concocted by those who thought there is nothing to learn from "African savages."[6]

Barth's Socialism and Its Relationship to His Theology

Let me open proceedings with some reflections on Barth. In my reading of his early work, it seems clear that Barth was always interested in politics. Frank Jehle grasps this point: while Barth was fascinated by theology from his student days onward, that fascination always went hand in hand with an engagement with contemporary issues—something made evident by Barth's membership in the Swiss Zofinger Union.[7] Research on Barth's later writing has shown the same trend. Barth's theology was always shot through with political concerns.

The idea of a nonpolitical or even antipolitical Barth, of course, has frequently been raised. Reinhold Niebuhr supposed that Barth viewed the political terrain from "an eschatological airplane," soaring at such "very high altitude" that his theology was "too transcendent to offer any guidance for the discriminating choices." Charles West surmised that Barth neglected empirical analysis and failed to pay attention to "the facts of human experience." And Emil Brunner challenged Barth's lack of zeal in condemning Soviet communism. He asserted that Barth's critical sympathy stemmed from beliefs residing "in his subconscious but not his conscious approach to things."[8]

But it is impossible to deny that Barth's socialism colored his theology. This was the basic insight of Friedrich-Wilhelm Marquardt, who sparked a crisis in Barth scholarship in 1972 when he argued that Barth's political commitments were fundamental for his theology and its interpretation. This claim resulted in the

---

6. Kwesi Dickson insists that any reflection on this subject must accept that the culture of a people embraces its economy, politics, legal systems, and other societal systems and arrangements. These aspects are interwoven and form the foundation for African theology. See Kwesi A. Dickson, *Theology in Africa* (Maryknoll: Orbis, 1984), 47.

7. Frank Jehle, *Ever Against the Stream: The Politics of Karl Barth, 1906–1968* (Eugene: Wipf & Stock, 2002), 18.

8. Quotations taken from George Hunsinger, "Towards a Radical Barth," in *Karl Barth and Radical Politics*, ed. George Hunsinger (Philadelphia: Westminster, 1976), 181–2.

Theologische Hochschule in Berlin rejecting Marquardt's thesis. Eberhard Jüngel refused to act as an external examiner, which in turn resulted in the resignation of Helmut Gollwitzer from his chair in protest.[9]

The reluctance to read Barth as a scholar working in a political context and tendering political claims spurred George Hunsinger to raise important questions in the mid-1970s. These questions remain apposite. Having provided some background for understanding Marquardt's supposedly "controversial" work, Hunsinger challenged those disinclined to read Barth as a contextual and political theologian:

> If politics is peripheral to his theology, then why did Barth so often insist that there was a political thrust to his formal thought? If his theology actually leads to such complacency, then what accounts for Barth's leadership in the resistance to Nazism? If his theology is incapable of discriminate political choices, then what explains his subtle, if controversial, discrimination between Communism and Nazism?[10]

Timothy Gorringe has deepened this point in recent years, arguing that Barth, perhaps more than any other theologian of his time, was a political animal.[11] Indeed, to my mind, one of the reasons that the early Barth, as well as the Barth of the *Kirchenkampf*, gradually became interesting to Black theologians in South Africa was because they were engaged in a struggle of their own against the theological justification of Apartheid.[12] As noted above, Dietrich Bonhoeffer was initially assumed to be more relevant. But the few Black students who developed an interest in Barth did so because of his staunch opposition to the fusion of state and church—an opposition that gained powerful expression in the Barmen Declaration.[13]

As suggested earlier, Black South African interest in Barth was a complex matter. Students who welcomed the rise of Black theology, a thought-provoking hermeneutic that had recently landed on South African shores, tended to favor the integration of Marxist analytical tools in the development of Black theology.[14] And while we knew that Barth had been a lifelong socialist, we were also aware that he

---

9. See Timothy J. Gorringe, *Karl Barth: Against Hegemony* (Oxford: Oxford University Press, 1999), 5.

10. See Hunsinger, "Toward a Radical Barth," 184.

11. Gorringe, *Karl Barth*, 11.

12. See Robin M. Petersen, "An Analysis of the Nature and Basis of Karl Barth's Socialism" (Unpublished master's thesis, University of Cape Town, 1985).

13. See also Ramathate Tseka Hosea Dolamo, "The Relevance of Karl Barth's Theology for Church and State for South Africa" (PhD diss., University of South Africa, Pretoria, 1992).

14. See Itumeleng Mosala, *Biblical Hermeneutics and Black Theology in South Africa* (Grand Rapids: Eerdmans, 1990).

was averse to a direct combination of socialism with theological claims—something demonstrated in the Tambach address of 1919, which showed that Barth did not position himself in the tradition of Hermann Kutter and Leonard Ragaz.[15] It must also be said that the issues that preoccupied those on the "underside of history," in South Africa, were not issues that Barth engaged directly. Yet Barth's views on the encroachment of state-sponsored ideology into theological discourse, rightly noted by R. T. H. Dolamo and others, have their own significance—even if, as Dirk Smit notes, it is apt to do theology in Africa by speaking only of Barth in parentheses.[16]

As Hunsinger points out, Barth was always aware that "a viable relationship between theology and politics" requires "mutual clarification in which neither discipline is reduced to the terms of the other.... Theology must not be politicized, nor politics theologized."[17] He goes on to complicate Marquardt's perspective in useful ways. Hunsinger rightly contends, for instance, that Marquardt's reading of Barth's insistence on God's otherness makes the cardinal mistake of reducing Barth's doctrine of God to its political function.[18] Hunsinger also grants that there are statements made by Barth which can lead readers to suppose that his move away from liberalism occurred for exclusively theological reasons. Barth's unsparing christocentrism, for instance, can sometimes come across as a "methodological" claim—not a theopolitical claim. And Barth himself can describe his theological development rather narrowly. (A good example: "I was a pastor for twelve years... and *had* my theology; not my own, of course, but that of my unforgettable teacher, Wilhelm Herrmann... I have been pushed by various and sundry circumstances more and more strongly toward the specific *pastoral* problem of the *sermon*" [WGT: 105–6].) So, again, it is crucial to exercise interpretative care. It is one thing to honor Barth's socialism; it is another to elevate socialism over everything else.

Even so, that Barth came to be the "Red Pastor of Safenwil" was itself a function of his time as pastor of a small church. As Timothy Gorringe points out, Barth's context moved him to study literature on socialism, for "in the class conflict which I saw concretely before me in my congregation, I was touched for the first time by the real problems of real life." While engaged in "the careful preparation of sermons and classes . . . [w]hat I really studied were factory acts, safety laws and trade unionism, and my attention was claimed by violent local and cantonal struggles on behalf of the workers."[19] Arguably, it was the *interplay* between theology and

---

15. Gary Dorrien, *Social Democracy in the Making: Political and Religious Roots of European Socialism* (New Haven: Yale University Press, 2019), 243.

16. Dirk J. Smit, "On Karl Barth: Dogmatics after 'Barth'? South African Challenges," in *Remembering Theologians—Doing Theology: Collected Essays 5*, ed. Dirk J. Smit (Stellenbosch: Sun Press, 2013), 17–27.

17. Hunsinger, "Towards a Radical Barth," 181.

18. Ibid., 188.

19. Gorringe, *Karl Barth*, 30–1. Gorringe is here quoting from *Karl Barth—Rudolf Bultmann, Letters 1922–1966*, trans. Geoffrey W. Bromiley (Grand Rapids: Eerdmans, 1981), 154.

praxis, discerned by Barth in the 1910s, that prompted his overcoming of liberal Protestantism.

And we should not forget that this interplay extended to Barth's later life. During his only visit to the United States, Barth gave a series of lectures at Princeton Theological Seminary on "evangelical theology." In a question and answer session, Barth was asked to say a little more about how evangelical theology relates to politics. The forthrightness of his response is notable:

> politics is an aspect of what we have just called culture. Politics means the human attempt to create and uphold some sort of order and peace in the world. Even at best, politics will create only some sort of order and some peace, no more. The purpose of politics is to realize in some degree something like a human commonwealth. . . . Christianity has to do with politics. If Christians serve the King of Kings, then politics is something straightforward. Thus theology is itself political action.[20]

To be sure, politics as it bears on the "commonwealth" is not uncontroversial. We have seen in South Africa how the selective application of the notions of "politics," "culture," and "theology" can adversely affect the lives of those communities that are not aligned with dominant powers. One can easily have a reformed theology that excludes and becomes fixated on race—even as there is *also* a reformed theology struggling against the illegitimate use of the Bible and the justification of Apartheid. Dirk Smit is quite right to speak of the reformed faith in South Africa as a story with many dimensions.[21]

In this section I have sought to demonstrate that Barth was always a contextual theologian with a close interest in politics. It is true that the relationship between Barth's theological claims and political commitments is hard to pin down, not least because of the radicality of his christocentrism. But for those of us who engage Barth's theology from the perspective of the Black struggle, in South Africa, it is a drastic mistake to depoliticize the "Red Pastor," and it is important to reckon seriously with the fact that the young Barth, as well as the Barth of the *Kirchenkampf*, can serve as a genuine theopolitical inspiration. Indeed, reading Barth as a *resource* for engaging with politics from the underside of history, and particularly as a voice that challenged Apartheid, should be a crucial dimension of the South African reformed church tradition, even as the issue of how Black

---

20. Cited in Dirk J. Smit, "'…The Doing of the Little Righteousness'—On Justice in Barth's View of the Christian Life," in *Essays in Public Theology: Collected Essays 1*, ed. Dirk J. Smit (Stellenbosch: SunPress, 2007), 361.

21. Dirk J. Smit, "On Adventures and Misfortunes: More Stories about Reformed Theology in South Africa," in *Vicissitudes of Reformed Theology in the Twentieth Century*, ed. George Harnack and D. van Keulen (Leiden: Brill, 2004), 208–35.

theologians might apply his work (and that of any other European and/or North American thinker) to our context remains an open question.

Black Theology of Liberation as a Guerrilla Enterprise

Black theologies of liberation found resonance in South Africa because white racism permeated South Africa. The lived experiences of Black people in the United States, more particularly, proved significant for those wrestling with the idea of a God who was just and merciful.

While Black theology in the United States owes much to the civil rights movement, the Black Power movement, and Black clergy, as well as to those who refined it as an academic discipline, it landed in South Africa in the early 1970s under the auspices of the University Christian Movement. Those who spearheaded it included Sabelo Ntwasa, Manas Buthelezi, Bonganjalo Goba, Desmond Tutu, Allan Boesak, Barney Pityana, and others. Given the political climate at that time, it was propagated through student-run seminars: university teachers were largely uninterested in tying questions about God with the material conditions of Black people. And it was at such seminars that a Black theology of liberation found an ally in the Black Consciousness Movement. The name of Steve Biko comes to mind here, for he engaged with students of Black theology of liberation on multiple occasions.[22]

Reflecting on the emergence of Black theologies of liberation in South Africa, Sabelo Ntwasa and Basil Moore wrote poignantly: "too many blacks have been beaten in every conceivable way until they have come to see themselves through the white man's eyes. Black is evil, dark, secret, and reeking of 'witchcraft.' Black culture and religion are heathen and immoral. Black people are inferior, stupid, untrustworthy, cowardly, cringing."[23] They go on to say that

> In this situation, black theologians have to be iconoclasts of the "white" God. They must tear down every image and symbol which, by presenting God as "white," reinforces this sense of human inferiority and worthlessness. This means not only removing "white God" pictures, but more important, the white men who seem to believe that it is their whiteness that places them closer to God and thus to the source of truth and ability.[24]

Indeed, the gradual recasting of "black" as a positive, affirmative term must be seen in the light of what blackness had come to represent—not only to the whites

---

22. On all this, see Mokgethi Motlhabi, *African Theology/Black Theology in South Africa: Looking Back, Moving On* (Pretoria: UNISA Press, 2008).
23. Sabelo Ntwasa and Basil Moore, "The Concept of God in Black Theology," in *Black Theology: The South African Voice*, 24–5.
24. Ibid., 25.

who propagated injurious ideas but to Black people themselves. It was an attempt to support self-love and self-affirmation. It sought to help Blacks to reject the idea that God committed a mistake by creating them, and to challenge the belief that economic exclusion, squalor, and alienation were a result of divine ordination.

Even so, Manaz Buthelezi was correct in claiming that the word "Black" captures the brokenness of many living in South Africa and across the globe. It is a "category that embraces the totality of my daily existence. It determined the circumstances of my growth as a child and the life possibilities open to me. It now determines where I live, worship, minister and a range of my closest life associates."[25] And nearly a half-century after these words found their way into print, it is important that we reckon directly with the myth that the notion that "Black," at least as the term is used by liberation theologians, signifies militancy. It is because of this myth that the rhetoric of the Black theology of liberation has increasingly been displaced by more neutral terms and discourses, ranging from "constructive theology" in the 1990s and, more recently, "public theology." This displacement is obviously troubling, for it serves only to exacerbate the marginalization of theologies of liberation in democratic South Africa.[26]

Let me make the point more fully. Taking as its point of departure the concrete experiences of oppression and suffering in a white-dominated society, where Christian faith was consistently (but not exclusively) used as an oppressive instrument to legitimize the socioeconomic and political dominance of whites, Black theology is rightly critical, not only of situations of injustice and oppression, but also of colonial theologies that lend tacit support to the privileged status of white people. "Color-blind" theology is nothing of the sort; it continues to function as a tool of the racist status quo. Given this situation, it is entirely legitimate for there to be a forthright affirmation of Black consciousness—an existential and political counterpart of Black theologies of liberation. It is entirely legitimate for there to be a *Black* theology of liberation.

To be sure, contemporary critics of Black theology are right to point out its flaws. In South Africa, it has been tepid on issues of gender-based violence and on issues that affect LGBTQIA+ communities. It is also worth noting that, after the end of legal Apartheid, many of its former proponents have come to head strategically significant sectors in the academy and government, thus losing interest in Black theologies of liberation as a critical hermeneutical tool.[27] I would add, further, that

---

25. Manas Buthelezi, "An African Theology or a Black Theology," in *Black Theology: The South African Voice*, 33.

26. See E. de Villiers, "Editorial: Special Issue—Responsible South African Public Theology in a Global Era," *International Journal of Public Theology* 5 (2011): 1–4. See also Tinyiko Maluleke, "Why I am Not a Public Theologian," *The Ecumenical Review* 73, no. 2 (2021): 297–315.

27. Rothney S. Tshaka, "The Black Church as the Womb of Black Liberation Theology? Why the Uniting Reformed Church in Southern Africa (URCSA) Is Not a Genuine Black Church?" *HTS Teologiese Studies/Theological Studies* 71, no. 3 (2015): Art. #2800.

Black theologies of liberation have been overeager to be recognized by detractors as engaged in "proper" theological reflection—this being the same eagerness that has led scholars to disregard African theology and philosophy as a serious conversation partner in the struggle to affirm the full humanity of Blacks in South Africa and the wider world.[28]

But these shortcomings ought not to obscure the ways that Black activism—often Black Christian activism, fired by Black liberation theology—played a crucial role in propelling South Africa beyond legal Apartheid. The dominant Dutch Reformed Church affirmed biblical and theological support for Apartheid. Those who voiced opposition and insisted that politics could not be avoided were labeled unserious theologians. It is for this reason, too, that Barth's reticence toward the integration of political theory into Christian theology is something of a problem for Black theology in South Africa today.

Consider again Barth's Tambach lecture, "The Christian in Society," which made it clear that any fusion of socialism and Christianity must be challenged. While that made sense as Barth sought to release himself from the legacy of Hermann Kutter and Leonhard Ragaz, socialist and Marxist modes of analysis have proven invaluable in South Africa: they have provided a hermeneutical tool with the ability to debunk a hegemonic ideology that imagines racial hierarchy can be scripturally justified. Consider, also, Barth's resistance to the suggestion of "determination by situation" and his claim that the human being

> intended by God and addressed in His Gospel may be quite unavoidably a child or an adult, a man or a woman, healthy or sick, Eastern or Western, European or African, ancient, mediaeval or modern, uncivilised, half-civilised, or highly civilised, riveted to this or that economic and political context; but always and everywhere, however determined, he is man himself who as such is immediate to God, and therefore to his neighbour. (CD IV/1: 804)

While Barth's concern to disaggregate the human being from their context makes a good deal of sense in the context of a critique of bourgeois European religion, it functions differently when one deals with those on the underside of history. There is a risk of reinforcing patterns of marginalization, trivialization, and discrimination; there is a risk of non-visibility being perpetuated in theological discourse. It is for this reason, in fact, that it can appear unhelpful to compare Barth's work with Black liberation theology in South Africa, which operated at a distance from the mainstream and disposed itself as a guerrilla enterprise. (The reasons for this status are varied. Suffice it here to say that, beyond the fact that South Africa universities have struggled to take seriously the lived experiences of Blacks—and, for a long time, the teachers of Black people were largely white—

---

28. Rothney S. Tshaka, "Do Our Theological Methodologies Help Us to Deal with Situations of Violence in Black Communities, Specifically Afrophobia," *Journal of Theology for Southern Africa* 138 (2010): 124–35.

most Black students of theology were essentially trained to be ministers of the Word, and the white Dutch Reformed Church determined what would be taught. Anyone who challenged this state of affairs would imperil the economic support given to a local Black congregation.[29])

A Black theology of liberation is a theological hermeneutic practiced from the underside of history. And it is a means toward an end. There would have been no need for Black theology, were it not for racist theology that used scripture to justify white supremacism. Black theology, more generally, emerged in light of the realization that Black people across the globe are subjected to oppression. Not as a result of a divine "ordering" of society, which decreed that Blacks should be subservient to whites, but because of the unjust conquest of Africa and her people. That the Christian faith played a crucial role in this conquest is no exaggeration. Black theology in South Africa is thus a crucial step toward resistance. It is an indication of the emergence of a decolonial theology and, as such, stands in an ambiguous relationship to Barth's theology—and, for that matter, any theology of produced by white Europeans.

I must again note that Black theology in South Africa has been weakened by its concern to be recognized as "proper" theology, according to the standards of hegemonic white theology. And in its attempt to explain itself to its detractors, it has lost the opportunity of becoming a meaningful interlocutor with non-Christian African theology. On one level, because Black theology has focused greatly on the inclusion of Black people into political life, distinctly African worldviews have largely been left on the margins (an issue to which I will return). On another level, Black theology has mostly been done along ecclesiastical lines, with authors viewing themselves as first and foremost Anglican, Lutheran, Reformed, Methodist, and so on, and only secondarily as Black South Africans. As I have argued elsewhere:

> Although Black theology propagated itself chiefly by means of seminars and ministers' caucuses . . . [many] of the first-generation Black theologians endeavoured to develop Black theology in relation to their confessional traditions. Among these theologians were Manas Buthelezi, Desmond Tutu and Allan Boesak. This project was carried on by theologians such as Buti

---

29. South Africa has four racial categories: white, Indian, Colored, and Black. In the context of the reformed tradition, this church is divided along racial lines and the white Dutch Reformed Church is considered the "mother church," while these other three missionary churches are considered the daughter churches. So, one has the Dutch Reformed Church—white; the Reformed Church in Africa—Indian; the Dutch Reformed Mission Church—Colored; and the Dutch Reformed Church in Africa—Black. The Dutch Reformed Mission Church united with a huge section of the Dutch Reformed Church in Africa to form the Uniting Reformed Church in Southern Africa. This is also the church that produced the Belhar Confession. For more on this subject, see Rothney S. Tshaka, "The Black Church as the Womb of Black Liberation Theology?"

Tlhagale, Takatso Mofokeng, Bongajalo Goba and Itumeleng Mosala, to mention but a few.[30]

Ecclesiastical traditions, of course, form part of what is often called South African's "mainline church traditions," which insist on the immersion of their students into academic theology. But historic African worldviews have always been looked down upon—not just by the "system" but also, sadly, by Black students associated with the mainline church traditions. This fact has itself sowed division. It is precisely why Vuyani Vellem discerns a bifurcated reality, with those associated with mission stations, on the one hand, and those who remained "unschooled," on the other (in isiXhosa, categorized as "Amakholwa" and "Amaghqoboka").[31] As well as moving beyond Barth, then, we also need a Black theology of liberation that will start a conversation with African theology, and that looks toward resolving the problems brought about by the arrival of Western Christianity to our shores.

African Conceptions of the Divine

The dominant assumption that God is white is not innocuous. As Kofi Asare Opoku notes, it is "a direct result of an understanding of the notion of religion in the West." He goes on to argue that "what scholars call religion is not a separate category in African societies, but part and parcel of their culture which, in addition to their social structure, is infused with a spirituality that cannot be separated from life in community." In Africa, "the Supreme Being is essentially a spirit and since spirit has no form or shape, there are no visual representations in the form of sculptures or paintings." And the absence of visual representations "reflects the lack of limitation placed by humans on the Great Spirit, as well as an expression of inexpressible reverence. God is believed to be wholly other and no stretch of the human imagination can capture God's being in visual form."[32]

The portrayal of Jesus in paintings that missionaries brought to Africa, by contrast, was an idealized image of European origin—and thus hardly an image of the historical, human Jesus. As Opoku notes, Susannah Herschel has identified the thinking behind "Aryan" images of Jesus. "[They] were crucial to racism in establishing the primary criterion of whiteness: Christ himself. For the European male to define himself as a 'white man' he had to fantasize himself as Christ, a

---

30. Rothney S. Tshaka, "Malcolm X's the Ballot or the Bullet Speech? Its Implications for Black Liberation Theology in Present-day South Africa," *HTS Teologiese Studies/Theological Studies* 71, no. 3 (2015): Article 1420L.

31. Vuyani S. Vellem "Unshackling the Church," *HTS Teologiese Studies/Theological Studies* 71, no. 3 (2015): Art. #3119.

32. Kofi Asare Opoku, "The Baobab Tree of Truth: Response to Two Papers on Barth and Comparative Theologies," Unpublished paper, 3 and 11.

Christ ... imaged not as a Jew but Aryan."[33] Granted Barth's insistence upon Jesus' Jewishness, the *Church Dogmatics* risks leaving in place the assumption of Christ's whiteness. That is to say: it risks letting the ideology of whiteness go unchallenged, with Jesus as "elected human" viewed through a racialized ideology—one that might well make space for ancient Israel, at least in principle, but does little to complicate the presumption of Eurocentrism.

As noted earlier, the problem of Eurocentrism has been intensified by Black theologies of liberation seeking "acceptance" in the South African academy. These theologies have become complicit in perpetuating falsehoods against African cultures and African worldviews—most obviously, when they decline to treat African religious and philosophical viewpoints as a genuine conversation partner. It is for this very reason that there continue to be tensions between the Black theology of liberation and African theology.[34] And, again, these tensions are exacerbated by the fact that Black theologians in South Africa who have engaged with Black theology of liberation have done so along lines laid down by their ecclesiastical traditions.[35] In most cases, they view themselves as Reformed, Lutheran, Anglican, Catholic, or Methodist before they see themselves as African. The outcome is noteworthy: the concerns raised by African theology are left unattended.

Opoku worries that the problem is perpetuated by Africans ourselves as we continue to draw our cultural framework from external sources and perpetuate missionary attitudes. Quite rightly, he argues that

> the continued use of European imagery in the church, such as paintings of a white Jesus and other biblical figures, that adorn many sanctuaries in Africa, and the rarity of any African religious symbols, together with the unhesitating condemnation and even demonization of African culture, even in churches founded by Africans, suggest that Africans have internalized the European missionary idealization of European values and have immersed themselves in an irredeemable self-hatred that has paralyzed Africans and stands in the way of recovery and regeneration in the new millennium.[36]

---

33. Susannah Herschel, *The Aryan Jesus: Christian Theologians and the Bible in Nazi Germany* (Princeton: Princeton University Press, 2010), 28.

34. See John Mbiti, "An African Views American Black Theology," in *Black Theology: A Documentary History*, vol. 1, *1966–1979*, ed. James H. Cone and Gayraud S. Wilmore (Maryknoll: Orbis, 1993), 379–84.

35. Rothney S. Tshaka, *Confessional Theology? A Critical Analysis of the Theology of Karl Barth and its Significance for the Belhar Confession* (Cambridge: Cambridge University Press, 2010), 232.

36. Kofi Asare Opoku, "Standing on a Stone: Nkrumah and the African Genius," Unpublished paper, 4.

Even when engaging with Barth as a "giant" of Reformed theology, it is vital that Africans support the recovery and regeneration of the richness of who we are as a people. That will only come about only when we refuse to forget our own cultural background, which has itself enabled the reception of Christianity and other faiths. Correspondingly, as we honor our openness to the "other," we must admit that there has subsequently developed a tendency to embrace what is foreign and to ridicule what is our own. We continue to nurture an unhealthy kind of xenophilia.

If there is indeed one lesson that a Black theology of liberation should learn from African theology, it is that our struggles are not confined to a history of oppression. We have, after all, not always been oppressed. It is time to recover a holistic history, one that was not completely obliterated through the West's conquest of Africa. The courage needed for this task will unfortunately *not* be found in Karl Barth, but in the example of how our ancestors engaged the divine and each other.

Conclusion

The absence of Black narratives in mainstream discourses is what Bonaventura De Souza Santos calls "societal fascism."[37] Societal fascism is a process by which specific populations are kept outside or expelled from a social contract. In the age of fallist movements[38] and in a context in which there are urgent calls for the Africanization and decolonization of the university curriculum in South Africa, it is vital to reconsider what it means to exist in community, to consider how involvement in the community bears on our understanding of the divine, and to think how best to go about doing theology.[39] Further, as suggested earlier, reflection on these matters

---

37. Boaventura de Sousa Santos, "Public Sphere and Epistemologies of the South," *Africa Development* 37, no. 1 (2012): 43–67.

38. The Fallist movement refers to grassroots movements that sprung up across South Africa between 2013 and 2015. These movements called for the total shutdown of institutions that remained unreformed. While there are a number of such institutions, the most notable were #RhodesMustFall and #FeesMustFall. #RhodesMustFall had to do with the removal of statues that continue to remind Blacks of their exploitation; #FeesMustFall was a call for tertiary education to be made free, compulsory, and decolonial. For a concise overview of some of these matters, see Francis B. Nyamnjoh, *#RhodesMustFall: Nibbling at Resilient Colonialism in South Africa* (Mankom: Langaa Research & Publishing Common Initiative Group, 2016).

39. For an insightful assessment of public theology in South Africa and some of its shortcomings, see Jakub Urbaniak, "Elitist, Populist or Prophetic? A Critique of Public Theologizing in Democratic South Africa," *International Journal of Public Theology* 12, no. 3–4 (2018): 332–52. This article also deals decisively with the challenge that the Fallist movement has brought to theological reflection in South Africa.

must be accompanied by an acknowledgment that distorted accounts of African cultures and worldviews have proven hugely damaging.[40]

African theology, while having the potential to uplift the self-understanding of marginalized communities, has struggled to achieve a footing in Christian theological circles. It has not been treated as a serious conversation partner. Even those of us who have found a way into the castles of empire have often succumbed to the expectations associated with being a university professor, neglecting the vitality of alternative modes of reflection.[41] It can seem convenient to continue with a familiar theological diet—one that does not require the lived material conditions of marginalized Blacks to frame theological questions. And, without concerted engagement with African theology, undertaken in academic journals, change will not happen.

Ali Mazrui speaks to this issue when engaging the subject of "educated Africans" in politics and society. He argues that most of the foremost African rulers were products of the colonial process of intellectualization. Some, such as Kwame Nkrumah and Milton Obote, were in fact distinguished by a capacity to handle colonial ideas effectively.[42] But there are alternatives, as demonstrated in challenges to distorted views about Africa and her people. Consider the impact that Kwame Nkrumah had on the re-Africanization of Ghana, which occurred at exactly the time when Apartheid was being consolidated in South Africa, with the banning of Black political organizations and the imprisonment of Black leaders opposed to Apartheid. At that time, no serious talk about re-Africanization was possible in South Africa; it was viewed as "backward."[43] And such views have persisted, even after the end of legal Apartheid, because of the impact of Western Christianity on Africans' self-perception. Opoku makes the point lucidly:

> Black theology ignored . . . [African theology] to its own detriment. If we are going to come up with a theology that reflects who we are, it must be based on our world view, and not on our experience of oppression. We have not always

---

40. The Eritrean philosopher Tsenay Serequeberhan argues that "Eurocentrism is a pervasive bias located in modernity's self-consciousness . . . It is grounded at its core in the metaphysical belief or Idea (*Idee*) that European existence is qualitatively superior to other forms of human life." See Tsenay Serequeberhan, "The Critique of Eurocentrism and the practice of African philosophy," in *The African Philosophy Reader*, ed. P. H. Coetzee and A. P. J. Roux (London: Routledge, 2003), 64.

41. Dwight Hopkins writes succinctly on this issue, and in ways to which Black South Africans can intimately relate. See Dwight Hopkins, *Heart and Head: Black Theology, Past, Present and Future* (New York: Palgrave, 2002).

42. Ali A. Mazrui, *Political Values and the Educated Class in Africa* (Berkeley: University of California Press, 1987), 17.

43. Re-Africanization for me simply means the enthusiastic debunking of the perceptions of Africa as made popular by Joseph Conrad in *Heart of Darkness* (London: Strauss Publishing, 2013).

been an oppressed people; our theology must be based on the totality of our experience on the planet.⁴⁴

It is crucial, then, that a Black theology of liberation overcome its neglect of African cultures and worldviews, and that it understand that colonialism is not only a political but also a cultural experience.⁴⁵ We need to move beyond the "templates" inherited from the past—templates that continue to be used, albeit with modifications. (Stanley Booth-Clibborn's review of Kwesi Dickson's *Theology in Africa*, titled "Decolonising Theology," speaks to my frustration. He writes in his introduction to that review, "on Sunday mornings at my local church in what was then known as the African estates, the services proceeded in stately Anglican fashion, 'decently and in order.' Although the language was in an African tongue, Swahili, the style was English, following the prayer book and with the familiar hymn tunes which I had sung since childhood."⁴⁶)

The production of knowledge in universities is also a factor. Consider Ali Mazrui's argument that the university in Africa is merely a "transmission belt" for Western epistemology.⁴⁷ The process of re-Africanization, then, calls for a theological mindset that embraces and promotes the rich tapestry of African people and beliefs. It calls for a mindset that is open for dialogue with the world, that refuses to limit God's own revelation to the Bible, that insists that we drink from our own wells (and refuse to be branded as "uncivilized" for so doing). It requires an unapologetic acknowledgment that God was active in Africa before the arrival of Western Christianity.

I end, then, with ambiguity. While I am drawn to Barth, I continue to believe that Barth cannot contribute much to Black and African theologies. The contexts are vastly different, and the issues needing attention are similarly vast. To force Barth to speak a "good word" for Black liberation theologies is to make a mockery of a situation that requires both local context and lived experience to be honored. What is needed are Black theologies of liberation that engage African theology, and make it clear that there was a divine presence in Africa before the arrival of Western forms of Christianity. To make this claim is not to suggest that Barth is unwelcome; it is to suggest that we need to avoid repeating the mistakes of the past.

---

44. Kofi Asare Opoku in a private email, March 26, 2019.
45. Mazrui, *Political Values*, 23.
46. Stanley Booth-Clibborn, "Decolonising Theology," *Third World Book Review* 1, no. 4 and 5 (1985): 64.
47. Mazrui, *Political Values*, 366.

Chapter 8

LIBERATION THEOLOGY IN A SOUTH AFRICAN CONTEXT

DOES KARL BARTH HAVE ANYTHING TO OFFER HERE?

Graham Ward

My title is deliberately provocative—perhaps as provocative as putting "Karl Barth" and "liberation theology" in the same headline for a conference or an edited book. But it can be, I hope, a productive provocation. Part of what is provocative stems from what is increasingly seen and critiqued as a colonial, Enlightenment heritage that established the academic teaching of theology in universities in terms of distinctive subject areas: philosophical theology, systematic theology, scriptural exegesis, and practical theology (covering homiletics, ethics, liturgy, and pastoral theology). There was nothing innocent about this intellectual carve-up of the field. Even in my own early training in theology at Cambridge, divinity was as class-ridden as the education more generally. Bright and ambitious thinkers were encouraged to specialize in philosophical and systematic theology; the linguistic high-flyers were encouraged to specialize in patristics and biblical studies; and practical theology (which now has other labels like "contextual theology" and "public theology") was the domain for less skilled ministerial development. The divide between the academic and nonacademic modeled in university curricula predominated, expanding the divide in earlier, secondary education between "grammar" schools and "technical" schools (although, in the UK, we had moved to "comprehensive" schools with "mixed ability" learning by that time). Even today, in some universities, a class division remains between straight theology and "applied" theology.

All this is beginning slowly to change, and the part played by liberation theology cannot be underestimated (at least in beginning to rethink theological method). Although it is significant to note that important figures in early liberation theology (Jon Sobrino, Leonardo Boff, and Gustavo Gutiérrez) all did their doctorates in Europe in either West Germany or Belgium. As did David J. Bosch, an important figure in South African liberation theology. More about South Africa later. At any rate, Barth's education, as well as his work in the German and Swiss university systems, was shaped by many of the aforementioned divisions within theology, a field of study that understood itself as a *science*. The system had been set down since the redesigning of the new university in early-nineteenth-century Berlin.[1] As such, there is little attention in Barth's theology to the impact of cultural history and context, and the way these will necessarily fashion, if unreflected upon, a mid-twentieth-century Swiss/German theology that is distinctively white, male, and Western. The dominant keys in which liberation theology is composed, which involve close attention to praxis and sociocultural location, are relatively absent. Indeed, in modern dogmatic theology, praxis and context are often viewed at odds with the pursuit of the theo-logic determining the interconnections between the propositional loci of Christian doctrine and its clarification. But this dominant mode of thinking theologically became increasingly seen as inadequate to the situations theologians found themselves in and the questions being asked about, for example, white colonial paternalism. Under the pressure of social and historical circumstances, the way of thinking theologically had to change. And in the wake of the changes brought about by liberation theology, it was increasingly recognized that theological discourse is, like all other forms of discourse, a cultural production. Hence the question mark in my title: Does Barth's theology offer anything in a contemporary theological context? To what extent is Barth's theology now part of a past dogmatic tradition, to be treated more as a historical *archive*, important (and no one is casting any doubt about its importance) to the Reformed tradition? And to what extent is Barth's theology relevant for addressing the constructive challenges of the present?

While keeping these questions hanging in the background, three concepts will be central to this essay: context, culture, and experience—and, thus, the human experience of living in a certain context and inhabiting a certain culture. I want to approach all three concepts not in their abstraction, which tends to reduce complexity to monolithic hypostases, but rather in and through the very particular and located situation in which they become relevant. So, I will proceed to answer the questions posed above in three stages.

First, I will determine, somewhat sketchily, a particular social context and culture. Second, I will say something about the reception of Karl Barth's theology in that context. Third, I will attempt to outline a possible modulation of Barth's theology in response to the liberation theology articulated within that context on the basis of social conditions found within it. This modulation will confront some questions concerning the polemical and "crisis" nature of liberation theology. Questions such as: Is the prophetic voice occasional or an abiding aspect of doing theology? Can the adversarial nature of liberation theology handle complex social, cultural, economic, and historical situations? Does it oversimplify them? And, perhaps more broadly, what is the relation of theology to human flourishing?

---

1. See Johannes Zachhuber, *Theology as Science in the Nineteenth Century: From F. C. Baur to Ernst Troeltsch* (Oxford: Oxford University Press, 2013).

Context and Culture

I am going to be talking about liberation theology in its South African context, rather than its Latin American context. I live and work part of the year in South Africa, so I have some experience of the particularity of its context.[2] The word "context" immediately presents itself here and can be understood broadly as comprising social, political, economic, and cultural dynamics. These dynamics never exist in isolation. They issue from land, peoples, and languages; and with land, South African land, we are dealing with complex histories—of colonization and decolonization, of rock, soil, climate, vegetation, animal life, and even rainfall. Context is ever expansive.

Liberation theology in South Africa grew from two interrelated roots: white theologians aware of their privilege and the unjust oppressions of Apartheid, on the one side, and the Black Consciousness movement, on the other.[3] It consciously understood itself as prophetic, and as politically engaged in the struggle for social and political transformation. Although, in propaganda by the Apartheid regime, such a theology was often allied with Marxism (in the way Latin American liberation theology drew upon notions of capital, labor and worker alienation, and poverty from Marx), there was actually little explicit referral to Marx—or even, to begin with, to poverty. Race and justice were central. Black Consciousness in South Africa owed much more to the various movements, some revolutionary and some more conciliatory, in North America.[4] Being white was explicitly associated with Eurocentrism, colonialism, and exploitative oppression. Indeed, there was and still is very little consciousness of "whiteness" in South Africa, even though several white South African churches and theologians supported and developed a theology of liberation (while maintaining in general, it must be admitted, their privileged position). Whiteness the world over seems to be very much like the bureaucratic ideal of transparency: it has limited scope for reflecting upon its own

---

2. For a more expansive account of "context" and the production of theological discourse within it, see my *Ethical Life I: How the Light Gets In* (Oxford: Oxford University Press, 2016), 115–44.

3. With respect to white theologians, I am thinking here of the work, among others, of Beyers Naudé, Albert Nolan (a Dominican priest), David J. Bosch, John de Grucy (Congregationalist), and Charles Villa-Vicencio. With respect to Black theologians, I am thinking here of the work, among others, of Simon Maimela, Takatso Mofokeng, and Allan A. Boesak. The best book I know on these two roots, which develops the most sustained and critical genealogy of liberation theology in South Africa, is George Jacobus van Wyngaard, *In Search of Repair: Critical White Responses to Whiteness as a Theological Problem—a South African Contribution* (Amsterdam: Vrie Universiteit Press, 2019).

4. The influence of James Cone cannot be underestimated. Cone's own early thinking, of course, emerged in dialogue with Karl Barth. On which, see the chapter by Tyler B. Davis and Ry O. Siggelkow in this volume.

conditions and mediations. Apartheid may have been enshrined in segregation laws and states of emergency legislation, but its binary logics operated socially, culturally and psychologically. As Desmond Tutu recalls, while the Anglican church spoke of resistance to Apartheid (unlike the Dutch Reformed Church, at least until 1985),[5] "[m]any white congregations were opposed to receiving Holy Communion alongside their domestic workers" and paid a lower stipend "to clergy according to race."[6]

This is Allan Boesak's definition of "Black Consciousness":

> an awareness of black people that their humanity is constituted by their blackness . . . that black people are no longer ashamed that they are black, that they have a black history and a black culture distinct from the history and culture of white people . . . that blacks are determined to be judged no longer by, and adhere no longer to, white values. It is an attitude, a way of life.[7]

Boesak made that statement in his major work from 1976, *Farewell to Innocence*. As such, it is somewhat dated and marked by the dualistic ideology of Apartheid. Who is Black, after all, is not just a matter of skin color, as Franz Fanon realized.[8] It is not, either, a theological statement. At least not explicitly, although Black Consciousness in South Africa emerged in the University Christian Movement of the late 1960s and returns again and again to the one book that most South Africans, whatever their social status, have read or know well: the Bible. At this

---

5. It is well attested that there were several white theologians of the Dutch Reformed tradition who not only supported Apartheid but also actively sought theological support for its position. All of the white Dutch Reformed theologians who actively worked for radical systemic change—like Naudé and Bosch—were sidelined, criticized, tipped with the poison "Marxist," and threatened. It is interesting to note one strong similarity among theologians resistant to South African and Latin American liberation theology: the appeal to a radical separation between theology and politics, spirituality and social justice. This handing over the soul to the churches and the body to the state in Latin America was central to William T. Cavanaugh's first book, *Torture and the Eucharist: Theology, Politics, and the Body of Christ* (Oxford: Blackwell, 1998).

6. Desmond Tutu, *No Future without Forgiveness* (London: Rider Books, 1999), 146.

7. Allan A. Boesak, *Farewell to Innocence: A Socio-Ethical Study on Black Theology and Black Power* (Maryknoll: Orbis, 1976), 1. Again, it is interesting to note the Barthian substructure of Boesak's theology: his Black theology issues from an insistence on "a genuine encounter between God's Word and his world" (14). Yet Boesak insists that for this encounter to be "genuine," human "experience" has to be taken seriously—that is, theologically. Faith and faithfulness cannot be separated from social experience and the ideological practices that shape it.

8. See, inter alia, Franz Fanon, *Black Skin, White Masks*, trans. Charles Lam Markmann (London: Pluto Press, 2008).

point in his writing, Boesak frequently blurs any lines that might divide Black Consciousness from Black theology; and "Black" is too much of a catchall.[9]

But I want to draw attention to aspects of Boesak's definition that any theological examination of Black Consciousness would need to take on board. First, in tackling questions of race (and, more broadly, ethnicity), theology would have to be concerned with how humanity is constituted, and concerned also then with complex variations in color, gender, class, and levels of physical ability. These complex variations are not static, nor are they easily universalized. Racism, while continually associated with colonialism, is nationally inflected: being Black in South Africa is not the same as being Black in the United States. Second, such a theology would also have to be concerned with affect, in particular the constitution and transformation of emotional cultures in the direction of human flourishing. Shame rings loud here. That is, the internalization of certain cultural values or vilifications, and the social practices that install and ingrain them, such that persons are supported in or denied ways to live. We need a theological anthropology that will wrestle with questions of experience and human flourishing, while able also to examine the practices and systems that perpetuate oppression and facilitate well-being. Third, such a theology would need to articulate its relation to protest, to speaking prophetically about faith as it seeks understanding and Spirit-led direction in the circumstances in which believers find themselves. It would have to be conscious of what it, in itself and as theology, was and is trying to do. That is, what *in* the situation (systemic victimization and impoverishment) raises a theological (rather than an economic or a political or even a human rights) problem. What is its theological purpose with respect to those it is speaking to and speaking for? For Black Consciousness, as Boesak defines it here, it is about judgment and being judged; about the polemical insistence on justice and the exposure of injustice. And this brings sin into focus. Not sin as moral lapse or even flagrant disobedience, but sin as systemic violence in which the human ability to choose itself is violated, and reconciliation between peoples made impossible. The biblical basis for Black Consciousness also called into question white interests and ideologies informing biblical hermeneutics—again something that "whiteness" and "being Western" had not, and maybe still has not, reflected upon adequately.

For liberation theology, the practice of theology itself has a social and formative role with respect to reshaping a cultural ethos and sets of relational values. Apartheid was not only countenanced theologically; it was informed throughout with Western colonial values and mentalities based in white supremacy that had prescribed the ways in which sin, salvation, obedience, and authority were

---

9. There were other oppressed ethnic groups in South Africa (so-called "Colored," "Indian," and migrants from other African countries), and the early Black theology was both male and straight. The problem, theologically, is that an unnuanced confrontation between monolithic blocks—white and Black—persistently reinforces the binary logics of Apartheid. And in doing so, it fosters political resistance but not necessarily a theology of reconciliation.

to be understood. But it shamed and dehumanized Black and "Colored" South Africans. It installed not just a Reformed, colonial, missionizing Christianity; it inscribed white, male regimes and habits of mind on Black bodies *in the name of Christ*. A Christian theology that spoke of healing, liberation, and reconciliation with respect to a covenant with God harvested, then, emotional damage, systemic slavery, and violent social fracturing to a very high percentage of the population. The white man thought he was Moses when in fact he was Pharaoh laying down a law through a political theology exploitation in the name of both divine truth and economic Mammon. (Incidentally, later Black theology, having understood poverty as a key concern in liberation theologies from Latin America, allowed Marxist analyses of class and economic injustice to come to the fore.)[10]

To broaden the view, one might say the following. Being prophetic and polemical, liberation theology is *affect*-driven—by shame, humiliation, dispossession, fear, and outrage—just as religious conviction is always affect-driven. And it is fueled both by context and the Bible. But there are tensions here: the Bible and the Protestant orthodoxy that informed both its reading and its status in the lives of the majority of South African people are the importation of white men, mainly Dutch, German, and British. Biblical theologies thus have to find new consonances with contextual situations, and with the overwhelming human, Black, and "Colored" experience of alienation and oppression.

Liberation theology is not a second-order, rational science, reflecting upon justification by God and the two natures of Christ. It is a first-order affective practice employing rhetorical strategies. Without the fostering of love or mercy, healing or setting free, then any secondary reflection is not only otiose; it is ideological. But when a theology participates in redemption, it does not just talk about it forensically. Its task is directly related to a vision of human flourishing. It lifts Marx's call for transformation rather than just the interpretation of the world to levels where doxology might be possible in being liberated from oppression, poverty, and institutional violence. This is important because it counters some criticisms from Christian theologians wary of using Marx on the grounds that his brand of revolutionary socialism is coextensive with critical tools that make the relationship between class and capitalism visible. The critical tool is, of course, valuable. It also counters the criticism that liberation theology is liberal humanism before it is theology—what Barth called "Prometheanism."[11] Black liberation

---

10. For example, Takatso Mofokeng, *The Crucified Among the Crossbearers: Towards a Black Christology* (Kampen: J. H. Kok, 1983). In this book, Mofokeng takes up Jon Sobrino's attention to the theological importance of economic oppression, with the poor as the crucified. Interestingly, in this book (researched and published as a doctorate in Kampen, the Netherlands), Barth plays an important role in the construction of a Black Christology. Mofokeng finds a resource in Barth's theology for the creation of a new active subject, truly human, who emerges from encountering Christ.

11. Karl Barth, *Protestant Theology in the Nineteen Century*, trans. Brian Cozens and John Bowden (London: SCM, 2001), esp. 19–65.

theology was Bible-based, Spirit-led, and Christ-centered. If it did not go in for the niceties of theo-logic concerning Trinitarian relations, it did not collapse the Trinity into social relations on the ground that that would not be biblical. (And, for what it is worth, the Bible does not go in for the niceties of Trinitarian exposition either.) The focus of this liberation theology was God ad extra—God as liberator and redeemer. This is clearly evident in Takatso Mofokeng's writing, for while he accepts an ideological critique of the Bible along Marxist lines (pointing to the way in which some biblical texts are written from the perspective of the ruling class, not the subjected and "crucified" people), his christocentrism remains founded upon the way Black people read the Bible. *This* is the key resource, not any kind of "ideological storehouse."[12]

Modulating Barth

As liberation theology was gathering pace in Apartheid South Africa, the theology of Karl Barth played second violin to Bonhoeffer's lead, and it is important to understand why. It was not simply that Bonhoeffer's active involvement in resistance to National Socialism offered a model for Christian activism (although it certainly did). Nor was it that Bonhoeffer's theological reflections throughout his time of imprisonment offered an inspirational resource for theologians, Black and white, who had either themselves been imprisoned, knew people who were imprisoned, or lived under the continual threat of being imprisoned (although they certainly were). It was also that Bonhoeffer's theology provided for a much more explicit understanding of the relationship between theological dogmatics and social ethics. The relationship between dogmatics and ethics in Barth's theology was much more contested, and always has been, despite the work of scholars such as Friedrich-Wilhelm Marquardt, Helmut Gollwitzer, George Hunsinger, and Timothy Gorringe.[13]

This is, of course, not to say that Barth was uninterested in the social and political conditions under which he lived. He certainly was, and explicitly so in his early work (to which many South African theologians referred). But his theology was also used by the conservative wing of the Reformed church in South Africa, not to validate Apartheid but to validate a certain political pietism that

---

12. Takatso Mofokeng, "Black Christians, The Bible and Liberation," *Journal of Black Theology in South Africa* 2, no. 1 (1988): 40.

13. See here Friedrich-Wilhelm Marquardt, *Theologie und Sozialismus: Das Beispiel Karl Barths*, 3rd edn (Munich: Chr. Kaiser Verlag, 1985); W. Travis McMaken, *Our God Loves Justice: An Introduction to Helmut Gollwitzer* (Minneapolis: Fortress, 2017), as well as Helmut Gollwitzer's essay "Kingdom of God and Socialism in the Theology of Karl Barth," in *Karl Barth and Radical Politics*, ed. George Hunsinger (Philadelphia: Westminster, 1976), 47–76; and Timothy J. Gorringe, *Karl Barth: Against Hegemony* (Oxford: Oxford University Press, 1999).

strengthened the status quo and viewed activism as revolutionary socialism, as far too "Promethean." Barth himself, having rejected any belief in liberal immanentism, from his 1919 Tambach lecture onward, could embrace his socialist tendencies even in the final part of *Church Dogmatics,* but always under the aegis of God's preferential option for the poor in Jesus Christ.[14] All action had to be divinely governed, divinely ordered, and divinely inspired. Human beings should recognize and respond obediently to God; this was the basis for ethical life, not activism. So, one might say (and I will return to this issue) that Barth certainly had a theology of action, but unlike someone like Maurice Blondel, it was only a theology of *divine* action. A Christology in which human beings might be recipients, but not co-respondents of grace governed all reflection on human action. The miracles were paradigms of God's grace. They happened *to* us in our various poverties and subjections.

Nevertheless, eight years prior to the capitulation of the Apartheid regime and sixteen years after the Sharpeville massacre that became the clarion call for political change, a book appeared in 1988, edited by Charles Villa-Vicencio: *On Reading Karl Barth in South Africa.* The book did not change much; as it stands, Bonhoeffer remains the most widely regarded white theologian in South Africa. But the book's appearance drew attention to the way that Barth's theology operated as an undercurrent, helping theologians in South Africa to think theologically about questions of reconciliation and justice.[15] It attempted to provide Protestant theologians in South Africa with a resource for reflection that, while working with liberation theology, attempted to ground its humanitarian agenda within a christological framework. It was an effort to reclaim the Christian heritage for the oppressed.

---

14. This was at the forefront of Mofokeng's critique of Barth in *The Crucified Among the Crossbearers:* Barth moved too quickly to resurrection life in Christ and could not appreciate "'the long Good Friday' existence of Black people" (226).

15. There is an often-cited story of a seminar presided over by Professor Jaap Durand in 1978 in which students asked why Apartheid raised theological question. In the words of one of the students at that seminar: "Together we revisited Karl Barth's theology. Eventually, our class arrived at the idea that apartheid takes its point of departure in the irreconcilability of people. That represented the theological centre of the problem of Apartheid" (see H. Russel Botman, "Barmen to Belhar: A Contemporary Confessing Journey," *Ned Gerek Teologiese Tydskrif* 47, no. 1&2 [2006]: 240). Even so, Charles Villa-Vicencio can state in 1988 that Barth's theology "never reached either the English-speaking or Afrikaans communities in South Africa, and . . . has made little or no impact in the black community" (Charles Villa-Vicencio, "Introduction: Reclaiming the Christian Heritage," in his edited volume, *On Reading Karl Barth in South Africa* [Grand Rapids: Eerdmans, 1988], 12). Villa-Vicencio does not raise the question of why this white, European theological voice might not be heard within Black communities. I raise this question, because Barth's theology provided a white man's bridge, in South Africa, for conversation in which shared issues of justice and reconciliation across the Black–white divide (an Apartheid mentality) were made possible.

Whatever the secret deals that made the transition from Apartheid tyranny to republican democracy in South Africa possible—and there were secret deals—the anticipated bloodbath of revolution did not occur. Rather, theologically, the transit marked what Martin Luther King, Jr., defined as a "revolution of values." And the key concept in this revolution was "reconciliation." It is exactly at this point that a political situation touches upon an axiomatic concern in Barth's theology, given that the doctrine of reconciliation bears all the weight of redemption and, indeed, the gospel for Barth. If, then, we are to offer some answer to what Barth's theology might offer South African liberation theology, then it is here that the investigation must begin.

The Truth and Reconciliation Commission (TRC) was set up immediately following Nelson Mandela becoming president of the new South Africa, with Desmond Tutu heading it. Not only does the name and mandate of the committee reflect key concerns in the Christian gospel; a former Anglican Archbishop and a Christian theologian was charged with overseeing its proceedings. And, of course, the TRC from beginning to end was both lauded and critiqued, with some liberation theologians like Allan Boesak convinced that it betrayed its roots in the Christian tradition. What is of particular interest to me was that the word "reconciliation," in being pulled in several directions—religiously, with respect to the other faiths practiced in South Africa; politically, with respect to a liberal secular agenda—became a highly contested term, freighted with different expectations and hopes from a multitude of perspectives. A theological understanding of redemption, construed in terms of liberation from oppression, floundered as the TRC progressed in its work. It became increasingly clear that the TRC operated on a belief (vindicated in part) in the therapeutics of storytelling, with some but very limited reparations for violation of human rights and the granting of amnesties to certain perpetrators of those violations who, to use a theological language, confessed their sins.

Nevertheless, if the TRC is taken as a case-study, then it highlights a fundamental theological tension at the heart of liberation theology and a question about the task of theology itself with respect to the salvation upon which it reflects. If the aim of liberation theology is social justice and the enfranchisement of all from the forces of dehumanization, then it has to look beyond the oppressive situation to the restitution of order. Justice is not established by reconciliation; rather, justice has to emerge from reconciliation. But *civic* reconciliation, like civic justice, is not the same, and cannot be the same as Christian reconciliation and justice. If it were, then one form of political hegemony would simply be replaced by another. In South Africa's case: Apartheid racist tyranny would be transposed into a Christian political theology—and both hegemonies are not simply cultural but institutional, or at least have to be or have to become institutionalized if they are to be established. It is not that Christian orthopraxis and Christian orthodoxy are antithetical. As we will see, in my modulated Barthian theology, they are not. But in a religiously pluralist nation state (in which agnosticism, secular humanism, and atheism have also to be respected), Christian orthopraxis and Christian orthodoxy cannot be imposed. They must position themselves alongside other perspectives that do not share or accept the gospel and the notions of redemption in and through Christ on which they are based.

To make this tension in liberation theology more apparent, I want to venture into Barth's doctrine of *Versöhnung* (reconciliation), which treats Christ's atoning work as the basis of reconciliation. The discussion in §§57 and 58 of *Church Dogmatics* IV/1, where Barth establishes the theological axioms of his exposition are particularly relevant. Fundamental in reconciliation, of course, is the sovereign act of God in Christ and as Christ. This is worked out in brief through a commentary on Jn 3:16: "God so loved the world, that he gave his only begotten Son, that whosoever believeth in him should not perish, but have everlasting life" (KJV). Toward the end of Barth's reflections, he links that verse to the Pauline text of 2 Cor. 5:19: "God was in Christ, reconciling the world unto himself, not imputing their trespasses unto them; and hath committed unto us the word of reconciliation" (KJV). Barth's emphasis is characteristic: All is grace; we can only be recipients.

On this basis, there is a tension between systematic and liberation theology. How do we develop a theology of liberation, in both senses of that genitive, that is also a systematic theology or a systematic theology that is also and determinatively a theology of liberation? I say "determinatively," because we can deduce from any systematic theology certain assumptions or even statements that are political or have political ramifications. Like Barth's reflections on work, for example, in *Church Dogmatics* III/4, §55 ("The Active Life"). But, in a systematic theology that is *determinatively* a theology of liberation, the politics of discipleship need fleshing out in terms of examinations of the relationship between ecclesiology, missiology, pneumatology, and context. We might make this point another way. Liberation theology is rooted in the discernment of crisis, and it is the poor and destitute in their grieving and oppression who reveal and announce that crisis. The crisis is recognized as a *kairos* moment of inbreaking divine judgment, and the church, to be the church in this moment, must be prophetic in joining protest with resistance to civil society as it has been constructed. It receives, in the crisis, the understanding that the times are out of joint, for the inbreaking of *kairos*, God's time, reveals what should be beyond what is. What *is*, is apocalyptic; what *should* be is eschatological. And in South Africa, this eschatological vision is represented as a community, a nation, a democratic *sizwe* (in Xhosa) that is nonracial, nonsexist, and participatory. But how can this prophetic church, in its active involvement in overthrowing oppression and exposing systemic violence, also be the church of the atonement, ministers of *Versöhnung* and the "word of reconciliation"? How can this church resist the placations and opiates of theological placebos? These cannot be ecclesiologies, missiologies, and pneumatologies *in abstracto*, because theological doctrine is lived. That means taking human experience as it is and, in that articulation, attempting to perform a revolution of values in and through the name of Christ. Systematic theology has to be one with a political theology. The theology required must be not just christocentric, but christomorphic. The political lies not in inferences drawn from doctrine, but rather in doctrine that is itself transformative in the way it is articulated, promulgated, and practiced.

The prophetic is a call to repentance; an entering into the crisis that liberation theology proclaims; a repentance that some, including Desmond Tutu, saw absent or at least not self-evident in the amnesties offered and given in the procedures of the TRC. But—and here is my central point—the prophetic is not then *a moment* in Christian theology, not a discrete a mode of polemical engagement. It is not a locus in systematic theology. The transformations involved in *metanoia*, rather, are perennial and ongoing. For Gregory of Nyssa, they are eternal, because they are caught up in a divine operation going from glory to glory in an endless doxology.[16] Conversion to Christ is the work of the Word, the Logos, within us, as we are caught up in the dynamics of providence and formation, pedagogy and sanctification. Sanctification is the endless imputation and work of justification; it is the eternal operation of grace, not an event. There is only one event: salvation as union with the Godhead. Each moment in our redemption has to be understood eternally. We are time-bound creatures employing time-bound language tied to specific cultures, lands, and civilizations. If we conceive conversion as a beginning and origin, we have to understand grace is without beginning and origin (of faith and participation); it is God in Godself given in an eternal Trinitarian condition as love and mercy and justice as and in the flourishing of right and true relations. The call to liberation, then, is written into creation itself as the call not just to receive passively (that is, to bear witness), but to receive actively (that is, to testify as a doxological response). The biology of emotion and the organics of sentience are relevant here: reception and response are not dialectical opposites but rather two integrated aspects of the interdependent relations whereby all biotic things flourish. Cause and effect are not temporally distinct but rather part of feedback and feed-forward loops in the teleonomy of life; circular not linear. I throw out this claim, aware of its generality: Barth's attention is on the *gift* of grace and, granted his recognition that this constitutes Christian experience, he is less detailed in his account of the *reception* of grace. Perhaps because the reception of grace for Christianity has to begin with an examination of Marian theology—something Barth conceives as deeply "Roman" and therefore problematic. And while I agree with him that the Roman account of grace issuing from the Marian theology articulated in Pius XII's encyclical *Munificentissimus Deus* is over-schematic and scholastic, I think it is fair to say that Barth cannot listen beyond the polemics of his Protestantism versus Catholicism. Maybe, more generously, in the Catholic distinctions between *gratia externa, praeveniens, operans, sufficiens, interna, habitualis, efficax*, and so on, what is being registered is the different tonalities of grace; tonalities registered in its reception. To consider the role of Mary, on this reckoning, is to engage in a theological account of reception.

---

16. See Gregory of Nyssa, *The Life of Moses*, trans. Abraham J. Malherbe and Everett Ferguson (New York: Paulist, 1978): "It is not in the nature of what is unclosed to be grasped. But every desire for the Good which is attracted to that ascent constantly expands as one progresses in pressing on to the Good. This truly is the vision of God: never to be satisfied in the desire to see him" (116).

The Archimedean point, at any rate, is justification by faith, and it is here that I find an irresolvable crux in Barth's theology between the christological imputation of such faith and the *analogia fidei* that this imputation enables. As I see it, the *analogia* is not sufficiently analogical. For however radical the difference between analogate and analogans, between the uncreated creator and created kind, there is a smidgen of similarity upon which a theology of participation must rest. There is a divine accommodation to our creaturely reality just as there is an accommodation to our human flesh in Jesus Christ. So faith is not, for me, only imputed, extrinsic, and therefore a passive surrender; it is also intrinsic and therefore an active entrustment. We walk in the invisibility of God's grace, into the cloud of unknowing, but that grace is not in opposition to nature, but rather an entry into seeing the natural differently—the natural as it is given, as it is created, as an act of liberal and liberating generosity given active testimony in doxological response. Sanctification lies in the transfiguration of perception. Faith as relinquishment is lived, actively; lived in Christ for our lives are hidden in Christ—creaturely lives, whether saint or sinner. It works a vulnerability that makes suffering and injustice stand out as painful and intolerable. The gravel in the heart is turned to sentient flesh. Only then can there be identification and solidarity that exposes cheap, self-rewarding charity and all the masquerades of paternalism. We suffer *with*—and that is active, not passive. What the relinquishment of faith reveals to us is the depths of our own poverties and the embarrassment of our riches. We discover, maybe, something of a *common* fragility. Then reconciliation is possible, as restitution is possible. They are then lived as social justice and healing. Action and activism have necessarily to follow while we abide in the continual sense of inadequacy. Such activity is a demanded practice of hope in that face of this inadequacy.

As noted earlier, Barth's christological reading of reconciliation moves from an exegesis of Jn 3:16 to an exegesis of 2 Cor. 5:19: "God was in Christ reconciling the world to himself, not imputing their trespasses unto them; and hath committed unto us the word of reconciliation" (KJV). But in his exegesis, something is not observed, something that I think crucial to ensure that dogmatics *is also* social ethics. It is that last phrase: "and hath committed unto us the word of reconciliation." Barth rightly understands the evangelical commission here, but he fails to hear the scriptural text beyond his own Protestantism. Two points are salient for a more comprehensive reading. First: God was in Christ reconciling the world to Godself, but what is translated as "not imputing" is the present participle *mē logizomenos*, which is balanced in the next clause by the present participle *themenos* ("hath committed"). The deponent verb *logizomai* is from *logos*, and the subject acting here is God in Christ, the Logos. There is a phonetic and semantic play in this text in which the work of Christ is countering the reasonings and calculations of sin that we might be *themenos*—that is, placed or set elsewhere. *Themenos* is an action with respect to taking up or occupying a position under certain conditions; in this case, a new position and a new condition. It's the participle of a complex irregular verb *tithēmi* (to place, to put, to render). Second, what this new condition or situation brings about in us is our involvement in *logos tēs katallagēs*, the christic work of reconciliation. The work of the *Logos* with respect to the reconciliation of the world, then, operates in and through *we* who are placed within that operation; that *we* who are in Christ might work in Him for that self-same reconciliation. *We* who are reconciled, in other words, must now reconcile.

What I am doing here is drawing out the affective pedagogy of faith as grace is received and experienced. Without that reception there can be no account of grace or faith at all; God would simply give to God in and through God. God could not be God *for us*—a point that is so fundamental for Barth. What I am also drawing out is that the new human being in Christ is the human being created in and through the Logos. Creation, not just a Christology founded upon the historical incarnation, pertains to salvation as reconciliation. Christ is written into creation (not "nature" as we have conceived it since the seventeenth century). All creation, and ourselves as created, as "his own [*ta idia*]" (Jn 1:11). The point between what Barth is saying and what I am modifying is both christological and ontological. Barth states boldly, "Christians exist in Him" (CD IV/1: 92), but I would want to say all creaturely reality exists in and through Him. Setting aside questions about the extent to which other creatures possess their own forms of consciousness, human beings as rational creatures think, plan, and give an account of ourselves—*logizomenos*. But the Logos is the key to salvific thinking, planning, and giving an account of ourselves. God's giving of God's self in the triune redemptive work of Christ and the Spirit turns our created ability to rationalize—and to rationalize is not just a cognitive but an affective and corporeal activity—into a conscious participation in the Logos. We are always in Christ, as all created things exist in Christ. That is why not just human but cosmic reconciliation is possible. To wit: Paul's redemption of the body of creation itself (Rom. 8:22–23). Barth's inadequate attention to the Greek in 2 Cor. 5:19, brought about by a certain theological closure in terms of justification by faith, misses something fundamental about *how* grace can be received and what that sanctifying reception enables not just *for us* but also *in us*.

Or does it? Because this point that I have drawn attention to is ambivalent in Barth. Having emphasized that only Christians exist in Christ, he then goes on to add: "It is not that they"—that is, non-Christians—"lack (*fehlt*) Jesus Christ and in Him the being of man reconciled to God. What they lack is the obedience to His Holy Spirit" (CD IV/1: 93). I find this complex to think through theologically. Maybe it is the separation of the ontological from the noetic that the distinction between Jesus Christ and the Holy Spirit seems to point to, and that Barth develops later in *Church Dogmatics* IV. There is something speculative, even modalist, about such a distinction. Existentially it has no purchase at all. Maybe it is just the imprecision of that negative *nicht . . . fehlt*. But whatever the ambiguities, they do not need addressing as such for the theology I wish to pursue. I note them, because I want to try and be balanced.

What this means is that our redemption in Christ is and always will be partial until all things are reconciled; until the work of divine grace brings all things to rest at the feet of Christ and situates them (*themenos* again) with respect to Himself. Until, that is, all things are liberated. And, in the affective pedagogy of

God's grace, the liberty we are brought into works with God's own freedom to act to bring about that liberation of all creation.

Conclusion

A final note: There are some theologians in South Africa who feel they need to return to their 1985 Kairos document, because they believe liberation theology stalled there in the quiet revolution that took place in the aftermath of the end of Apartheid.[17] We might view this as a hiatus rather than a lapse; a refocusing in the light of dramatic and significant changes to the governance of the country. For liberation theology can never come to an end. What Allan Boesak called "faithful resistance" must continue while any single person remains unliberated, while any single person still suffers under oppressive deprivations, and until Christ and His Kingdom are fully established.[18] Whatever that might mean, and howsoever that might look; for none of us knows. For that, we all need a theological vision in which the determinations of Christian doctrine inform (in the strong sense of that word), and are informed by, the social and political ethics that are lived and are to be lived. And in South Africa, I wonder whether Christian theology needs to step back. It has been so infused with colonialism, and mission as colonialism, that there is a need to decolonialize Christian theology; to seek the triune God who has always been there in Africa and a Christ who, as incarnate God, is both transhistorical and transnational. They do not need more westernized depictions of the Mediterranean Jesus. I am not saying the theology of Karl Barth cannot help as an inspiration, but his theology (like mine) is white and Western, rooted in context, culture, and experience that are not South African except by importation. It needs a gospel that is not freighted with a "heathenism" that needs converting to Western civilized ideals. South Africa needs to continue nurturing its own theologians, rooted in their land, their languages, their histories, and their cultures (magnificently plural) in the way Barth was within his. Only *their* theology can do this.

---

17. Kairos Theologians, *Challenge to the Church: A Theological Comment on the Political Crisis in South Africa*, 2nd edn (Braamfontein: Skotaville Publishers, 1986).

18. See Allan A. Boesak, *Pharaohs on Both Sides of the Blood-Red Waters: Prophetic Critique on Empire: Resistance, Justice, and the Power of the Hopeful Sizwe—A Transatlantic Conversation* (Eugene: Cascade, 2017).

Chapter 9

USING BARTH "TO JUSTIFY DOING NOTHING"

JAMES CONE'S UNANSWERED CHALLENGE TO THE WHITENESS OF BARTH STUDIES

David L. Clough

James H. Cone died in April 2018, almost exactly fifty years after he sat down to write *Black Theology and Black Power* in the early summer of 1968. It was an eventful year. Cone wrote the book in the aftermath of the assassination of Martin Luther King, Jr., angry at white ministers who condemned Black violence in the riots that followed in major US cities while remaining silent about the white violence inflicted on Black people. Later that summer, the Conference of Latin American Bishops met in Medellín, Columbia, and adopted the "preferential option for the poor." Karl Barth died that December.

In 1968, having completed a PhD on Barth, Cone was angry with European and North American Barthian theologians in particular, "who used [Barth] to justify doing nothing about the struggle for justice" and "confused white-talk with God-talk."[1] Fifty years on, it is striking that little has changed. With a few minor exceptions, white scholars of Barth have ignored Cone's critique. When I first drafted this essay, in May 2020, Black people were still being killed on American streets, with global protests following the killing of George Floyd by a Minneapolis police officer.[2] Floyd was only the latest in a long series of police killings of Black people in the United States. The cases that have made headlines have been caught on video; many similar killings go unreported.

Cone later described his project as a Black theology of liberation, but he was deeply critical about the comparative reception of liberation theology and Black theology by white male theologians, complaining that white male North American theologians preferred to talk about solidarity with the poor of Latin America than

---

1. James H. Cone, *My Soul Looks Back* (Maryknoll: Orbis, 1985), 45; and idem, *A Black Theology of Liberation* (Maryknoll: Orbis, 2010), 88.
2. Joanna Walters and Jackie Renzetti, "George Floyd Killing: Sister Says Officers Should Face Murder Charge as Protests Grow," *The Guardian*, May 28, 2020.

their Black neighbors at home.³ In taking up the theme of Karl Barth and liberation theology today, it would be irresponsible to fail to attend to Cone's critique of the white reception of Black theology, especially among Barthians.

The problems Cone identified are clearly not unique to the United States. Nor is the racism that results in the lethal police discrimination against Black people particular to the United States. In the UK, where I live, Black people are killed in disproportionate numbers by police as well.⁴ The Black British theologian Robert Beckford points out that the vast majority of white British theologians have failed to take seriously the imperial context of British theology and, as a result, "white theology in Britain has not decolonized itself and is therefore still very much anti-black." Beckford thus calls for white British theologians "to produce exorcized white theologies that have the categories of thought and action to embrace their black and brown brothers and sisters and strive towards a new inclusive British Christian theology and church life."⁵ I count myself among the white British theologians who need urgently to respond to Beckford's call.

This chapter rehearses and digests the implications of Cone's critique, while considering how the work of Barth may be brought to bear on the field of liberation theology. It also offers a short, "worked" example of what it might mean to take seriously a critical theology of race for Barth studies at the intersection of Barth, race, and animals.

Cone on Barth and Barthians

The relationship between James Cone and Karl Barth starts with a particularly acute irony. Cone was put off studying Christian ethics by the fact that the professor of Christian ethics was "one of the most blatantly racist professors" at Garrett Biblical Institute (now Garrett-Evangelical Theological Seminary).⁶ Garrett had never had a Black PhD student, and the professor told Cone not to apply because they had their pick of straight-A white students from Yale and Harvard—a claim that turned out to be a lie. Cone found William Hordern, who taught systematic theology, much more supportive; but Cone decided that he would not get a PhD from Garrett if he wrote on theology and race. His choice to focus on Barth for his dissertation was therefore a defensive move in the context of a racist academy. Cone was later criticized by Black theologians, including his brother, for an overdependence on Barth and other white European theologians in his early work.

---

3. James H. Cone, *Risks of Faith: The Emergence of a Black Theology of Liberation, 1968–1998* (Boston: Beacon, 1999), 133.

4. Nazir Afzal, "Black People Dying in Police Custody Should Surprise No One," *The Guardian*, June 11, 2020.

5. Robert Beckford, *Documentary as Exorcism: Resisting the Bewitchment of Colonial Christianity* (London: Bloomsbury, 2014), 202.

6. Cone, *My Soul Looks Back*, 37.

He acknowledged and responded to this critique by drawing increasingly on Black authors and church traditions.

With that said, there were also positive reasons for Cone's choice of Barth, for Cone recognized common ground between Barth's theological approach and the Black church experience. Cone saw in Barth an example of how to relate theology to life, valued Barth's christological starting point, and found laudable Barth's emphasis on the Word of God in scripture and preaching.[7] He felt a spiritual kinship with Barth, especially the Barth of *The Epistle to the Romans*, and he took inspiration from the way Barth was prepared to challenge received norms. As he said, later in life: "I purposely intended to be provocative in much the same way that Barth was when he rebelled against liberal theology."[8]

Most of Cone's critiques of Barthian thought are not of Barth himself, but of the use Barthians made of him:

> I was angry not with Barth but only with European and North American Barthians who used him to justify doing nothing about the struggle for justice. I have always thought that Barth was closer to me than to them. But whether I was right or wrong about where Barth would stand on the matter, the truth was that I no longer was going to allow privileged white theologians tell me how to do theology.[9]

Cone was disappointed by the lack of response to his *Black Theology and Black Power* (1969) from white theologians, commenting in 2010 that

> Not many white theologians accepted my challenge to them to speak. They just kept writing about their favorite academic themes as America's cities burned. They are still silent or only make marginal reference to the role of white supremacy in America and its theology.[10]

Cone's analysis of this white silence was clear and direct:

> Because white theologians live in a society that is racist, the oppression of black people does not occupy an important item on their theological agenda. Again, as Karl Marx put it: "It is not consciousness that determines life, but life that determines consciousness." Because white theologians are well fed and speak for a people who control the means of production, the problem of hunger is not a theological issue for them. That is why they spend more time debating the

---

7. James H. Cone, *Black Theology and Black Power* (Maryknoll: Orbis, 1997), 87; *My Soul Looks Back*, 88–91 and 87.
8. Cone, *Risks of Faith*, xxii; Cone, *My Soul Looks Back*, 45.
9. Cone, *My Soul Looks Back*, 45.
10. Cone, *A Black Theology of Liberation*, 154.

relation between the Jesus of history and the Christ of faith than probing the depths of Jesus' command to feed the poor.[11]

As then, so today: Cone provides good reason for well-fed white theologians to reconsider how their relative comfort bears on their theological concerns.

Cone points out that being descendants of slave masters rather than slaves—or, one might add, in a British context, the heirs of those who accumulated wealth through the trade in slaves—affects the mental grid of theologians: "not only what books they read when doing their research, but also which aspects of personal experience will shape theological style and methodology."[12] This problem is amplified when white theologians "claim objectivity for their theological discourse."[13] As Cone stated in *A Black Theology of Liberation* in 1970, "American theology is racist" in that "it identifies theology as dispassionate analysis of 'the tradition,' unrelated to the sufferings of the oppressed."[14] Twenty years on, in *Risks of Faith*, he asked: "Is racism so deeply embedded in Euro-American history and culture that it is impossible to do theology without being antiblack?"[15] In the same work, he complained that despite the blatant use of Christianity "to justify slavery, colonialism, and segregation for nearly five hundred years . . . white theologians in the seminaries, university departments of religion and divinity schools, and professional societies refused to acknowledge white supremacy as a theological problem and continued their business as usual, as if the lived experience of blacks was theologically vacuous."[16] Indeed, he commented: "Their silence on race is so conspicuous that I sometimes wonder why they are not greatly embarrassed by it."[17]

Finally, as I noted in my opening remarks, Cone criticized the hypocrisy of white North American theologians who expressed solidarity with the poor of Latin America while ignoring their Black neighbors:

> It was not until Orbis Books published the translated works of Latin American liberation theologians that white North American male theologians cautiously began to talk and write about liberation theology and God's solidarity with the poor. But they still ignored the black poor in the United States, Africa, and Latin America. Our struggle to make sense out of the fight for racial justice was dismissed as too narrow and divisive. White U.S. theologians used the Latin American focus on class to minimize and even dismiss the black focus on race. African-Americans wondered how U.S. whites could takes sides with the poor out there in Latin America without first siding with the poor here in

---

11. James H. Cone, *God of the Oppressed* (Maryknoll: Orbis, 1997), 47–8.
12. Ibid., 48.
13. Cone, *A Black Theology of Liberation*, xv.
14. Ibid., 19.
15. Cone, *Risks of Faith*, 131.
16. Ibid., 131 and 134.
17. Ibid., 131.

North America. It was as if they had forgotten about their own complicity in the suffering of the black poor, who often were only a stone's throw from the seminaries and universities where they taught theology.[18]

Cone seems generous in characterizing the neglect of North American white theologians to the suffering of Black near neighbors as forgetfulness; we might instead diagnose a failure of Barthians to appreciate that this context was relevant to the task of theology.

Responding to Cone's Critique

I hope it is clear that the problem is not just in the past. The role of Christian voters in electing Donald Trump as president of the United States and enabling, among other atrocities, the tearing of children from parents at the Mexican border to be placed in cages is but one indicator of the enduring relevance of Cone's critique. We need to acknowledge many factors in understanding the remarkable phenomenon of how Trump came to occupy the White House, of course, but among them we must number the association between white churches and white supremacy. But the problem is also still closer to home. Follow #SeminaryWhileBlack on Facebook or Twitter for firsthand accounts of what it is like to be a Black seminarian in the United States today. A 2018 post from a student at Fuller Theological Seminary noted that James Cone appeared on just *three* pages in the systematic theology textbook used in four of her MDiv modules. She observes that this is the same number of references to Bach (as in J. S.), whereas there are *forty* references to Barth (as in Karl). Cone's concern that white North American theologians prioritize European theologians like Barth over theologies attentive to those disadvantaged in the context of the United States, such as Black and womanist theologies, is obviously still relevant fifty years on. (The problem obtains in the UK, also: a Black ordinand recently made public his rejection for a curacy on the basis that he would not be a "good fit" for a majority white parish.[19]) Thus it is that white scholars of Barth studies, both in North America and in other contexts, such as mine, where racism remains powerfully operative within theology and beyond, have a particular responsibility to reflect on the unexamined whiteness of their discipline. It is not hard to locate thoughtful engagements with Cone's critique of Barth and its legacy from Black theologians: Josiah Young, Raymond Carr, Vincent Lloyd, J. Kameron Carter, Willie Jennings, and Beverly Eileen Mitchell, among others, have done important work on this very issue.[20] These

---

18. Ibid., 133.
19. Gabriella Swerling, "Church of England Embroiled in Racism Row for Turning Down Black Trainee Vicar," *The Telegraph*, June 16, 2020.
20. Raymond C. Carr, "Barth and Cone in Dialogue on Revelation and Freedom: An Analysis of James Cone's Critical Appropriation of 'Barthian' Theology" (PhD diss.,

accounts reflect interesting disagreements about the implications of Barth and Cone for theological accounts of race today. But when I searched, I found only two white theologians who discuss Cone's critique of Barth even briefly.[21] My literature search may be incomplete, but it is very unlikely that any supplement will demonstrate that white theologians have given sufficient time to digesting and responding to the challenge Cone presents.

I recognize the discomfort of being a white male theologian attempting to engage issues of race and whiteness. As I write this chapter, I am very aware that I am speaking from a position of guilt. The system of white male privilege operates to my benefit and I play a role in perpetuating it. This feeling of guilt is accompanied by an acute sense of an inexcusable belatedness in addressing the issue of race now, when it has not previously been the focus of my academic work, and the consequent embarrassment in publicly acknowledging this inadequacy. My theological education at Cambridge, Oxford, and Yale not only failed to address issues of race, but also left me with prejudices about theological methodology, which meant that I thought I had reasons for being inattentive to the work of theologians using sources and methodologies such as those of Cone.

I am persevering in raising the issue of the problematic whiteness of Barth studies, despite this discomfort, because it now seems to me that it is academically, theologically, and morally indefensible to fail to do so. I have been helped to this realization by reading and hearing the scholarship of Robert Beckford and Anthony Reddie in the UK, and Emilie Townes, Willie Jennings, and J. Kameron Carter in the United States, among others.[22] But I have also been helped to see things differently by the conversation I had at the American Academy of Religion a few years back with a young Black male pastor who was completing a PhD but

---

Graduate Theological Union, Berkeley, 2011); J. Kameron Carter, *Race: A Theological Account* (Oxford: Oxford University Press, 2008); Willie James Jennings, *The Christian Imagination: Theology and the Origins of Race* (New Haven: Yale University Press, 2010); Vincent Lloyd, "Black Secularism and Black Theology," *Theology Today* 68, no. 1 (2011): 58–62; Beverly E. Mitchell, "Karl Barth and James Cone: The Question of Liberative Faith and Ideology" (PhD diss., Boston College Graduate School, 1999); Josiah U. Young III, "'Betwixt and Between' Afrocentrism and Neoorthodoxy: A Simple Call to Freedom," *The Journal of Religious Thought* 50, no. 1–2 (1993–1994): 72–80.

21. See D. Stephen Long, *Divine Economy: Theology and the Market* (London: Routledge, 2000), 165–6; Paul Dafydd Jones, "Liberation Theology and 'Democratic Futures' (By Way of Karl Barth and Friedrich Schleiermacher)," *Political Theology* 10, no. 2 (2009): 270–1 and 277.

22. See, for example, Robert Beckford, *Dread and Pentecostal: A Political Theology for the Black Church in Britain* (London: SPCK, 2000); Anthony G. Reddie, *Is God Colour-Blind? Insights From Black Theology for Christian Ministry* (London: SPCK, 2009); Emilie M. Townes, *Womanist Ethics and the Cultural Production of Evil* (Basingstoke: Palgrave Macmillan, 2006); Jennings, *The Christian Imagination*; and Carter, *Race*.

considering leaving the United States because, in the neighborhoods where he felt called to pastor, the risk of being killed by police, even when wearing a clerical collar, was becoming too great for him and his family to tolerate. And by another recent conversation I had at the conference with a young Black female prospective PhD student who had been told that womanist ethics were not an appropriate topic for doctoral study. And by a challenge brought to a conference session of the Animals and Religion Group by a Black woman who challenged the whiteness of the group's preoccupations. I am grateful for the help I have received from all these quarters to recognize the need to do theology differently.

A few years ago, I participated as an external representative on a PhD review of a young white male North American student. He wanted to write a project at the interface of theology and politics. He presented to me and the white male internal reviewer a project outline in which he would look at the work of two white male theologians on a number of ethical topics. "Why those ethical topics," I asked, "when there are others so pressing, such as Black Lives Matter, immigration, wealth inequality, famine, gender relations, or ecological crisis?" He replied that he had picked the topics because they were important in the work of both of the authors he had identified. And why those authors? The answer was that they seemed to be recognized as important in the discipline. I suddenly had a dizzying sense of the conservative mechanics of reproduction within the theological academy: the inevitably blinkered preoccupations of one generation setting the agenda for the next, valorizing and perpetuating a strange subset of interests with very little relation to what issues in our world stand in need of theological attention.

I agree with Cone's statement that Barth was more on *his* side than on the side of the European and North American Barthians, whom he characterized as seeking to justify doing nothing in relation to the struggle for racial justice.[23] The chapter I originally planned to contribute to this volume would have noted Barth's observation in the second edition of the commentary on *Romans*, that "it is our pondering over the question 'What shall we do?' which compels us to undertake so much seemingly idle conversation about God" (RII: 438). In other words, it is the pressing practical duties with which the world is filled and the wickedness in the streets and the daily papers that drive us to the Bible and to theology, where we find that the ethical question is nowhere left out of account in Paul's letter to the Romans. Indeed, Barth was himself engaged in the most urgent political issues of his day: Wilhelm II's war policy, the rights of workers in Safenwil, the rise of Nazism, the plight of the Jews, the need to maintain good relations with Germany and Russia after the Second World War, nuclear disarmament, and so on. So there seems to be grounds here for recognizing a congruence with the liberationist identification of praxis as the starting and ending point of theology. But in advance of debates about whether Barth's thought *could be* a useful basis for liberationist theologies, white theologians who work in Barth studies in North America, Britain, and elsewhere need to address the question of why, for the

---

23. Cone, *Risks of Faith*, xxii.

most part, Barth studies *has in fact not* stimulated or been hospitable to critical reflections on race, whiteness, and liberationist concerns.

Cone's critique is that white male theologians take up studying Barth and other white male theologians in place of engaging substantively with race and other pressing social issues that are proximate to their own contexts. If he is wrong about that, it could be because we can now demonstrate that Barth studies is proactively engaging race and other social issues. This volume is a positive sign in that regard, but I think we have to conclude that Barth studies generally is not characterized by sustained attention to pressing social questions. Or Cone could be wrong, because we reject the connection between studying Barth or other white male theologians and being inattentive to social issues. Again, while we could cite examples of where studying white male theologians has been a provocation to engage social issues, in the main, I think we would have to concede that Cone is right that there is an unsurprising correlation between choosing white male theological sources and being insufficiently attentive to patterns of oppression on grounds, such as race, that have a relatively slight impact on white males.

If the connection Cone draws between selecting white male sources and being inattentive to pressing social issues is valid, perhaps we are tempted to accept the connection but reject the critique. We could do so on the grounds that the abstraction of theology from social issues is not necessarily a weakness, that there are many abstract theological issues that merit academic attention. A search for the articles in recent years published in the *International Journal of Systematic Theology* referencing Karl Barth in the title, for example—which all appear to be by white men—treat his doctrine of creation, the relationship between his thought and that of Kierkegaard, his doctrine of redemption, and his theology of mission. Many theologians would recognize the interest of these inquiries and would defend the value of such academic work. Certainly Barth's deliberations about such abstract questions prove stimulating. But it is important to recognize that Barth was attentive to the relevance and practical implications of such theological abstractions for the political and social world in which he found himself. Cone was not critical about the balance Barth struck between addressing abstract theological themes and the social issues that confronted him; he was critical of the European and North American Barthians who took up abstract themes from Barth's work without attending to pressing social questions such as the oppression of Black people. White theologians in Barth studies should take heed. We must acknowledge the validity of Cone's critique that to do theology without paying attention to our pressing practical duties and the wickedness in the streets, as Barth put it, is both irresponsible and, one might say, un-Barthian.

To respond to Cone's challenge does not, therefore, mean that white theologians may write of race and nothing else, but it seems to me that it requires at least three things of us.

First, we must attend to what it means to pursue our work—on Barth's doctrine of creation, or redemption, or mission, or his relationship with Kierkegaard, or whatever—and become acutely alert as to how our enquiries are informed by theological and philosophical traditions that have promoted and enabled white supremacy and the oppression of people of color. If you are not yet convinced by this, I would suggest reading J. Kameron Carter's *Race: A Theological Account*, Emilie Townes's *Womanist Ethics and the Cultural Production of Evil*, and Willie Jennings's *The Christian Imagination: Theology and the Origins of Race*. It is hard to come away from these books unconvinced that serious theological work is required to contest and dismantle the racist foundations that have been core elements in most theological education.

Second, white theologians must attend to what it means to pursue their work in the social context in which they are located. Famously, Barth advised theologians to read both the Bible and the newspaper.[24] Theologians need to do theology alert to the events of our own day—attentive to the lenses of different sources of news, including structurally racist filters that reinforce white normativity and supremacy—and to the ways in which the theology we undertake might bear on the most urgent issues of the day. That does not mean everyone must become theological ethicists (although as an ethicist, I think we could do with more of them!), but everyone should be aware of how their work pertains to the most pressing questions that confront us. Key among these questions, as Cone helped us to see, is the continuing force of white supremacy and the racism that leads so many Black, Latinx, Asian, and Native peoples to experience attacks, abuse, and discrimination. We should note that the modern academy does not always encourage the pursuit of academic research in the light of social context, which heightens the need to recognize this as important, personally and corporately.

Third, white theologians must attend in particular to how their theological pursuits intersect with issues of race and whiteness. If we do not realize how our studies—of Barth's doctrine of creation, or redemption, or mission, or his relationship with Kierkegaard, or whatever—bear upon white privilege and the enduring power of racism, it is very likely that our scholarship will perpetuate these patterns of injustice. One initial remedy is to read authors in our fields who are alert to this linkage and intersection, who are currently most likely to be people of color. The next section of this chapter is a "worked" example of this in relation to my own concern with the place of other-than-human animals in Christian theology and ethics.

A "Worked" Example: Barth, Race, and Animals

One of the most important tasks in my book *On Animals*, volume 1, *Systematic Theology*, was to challenge poorly grounded and ill-thought out theological assertions of anthropocentrism within the doctrinal headings—taken up by Barth, of course—of creation, reconciliation, and redemption.[25] Along the way,

---

24. "Barth in Retirement," *Time Magazine* 81, no. 22, May 31, 1963.
25. David Clough, *On Animals: Vol. 1. Systematic Theology* (London: T&T Clark, 2012).

I developed a strong antipathy to human/nonhuman binaries. I came to see that theological anthropologies, alongside others, often tended to be based on the othering of the nonhuman animal, in the form that "unlike any other animal, humans are X, have X, or can X." We seem to have inherited from ancient Greek philosophers an irresistible trope for understanding what it means to be human, very largely in contradistinction to other animals.

I became concerned to interrogate and deconstruct this oppositional understanding of human identity because it seemed to encourage and be supported by bad Christian theology and result in bad Christian ethics, particularly in relation to other than animals. It runs counter to a basic theological understanding of ourselves as creatures of God, a status that affirms human commonality and solidarity with all God's creatures—that is, everything that God has made, and everything that exists apart from Godself. Biblical texts recognize humans in common with other animal creatures as fleshy creatures with the breath of life, recipients in common of God's grace in creation and providence, subjects in common of blessing and judgment, participants in common in the praise of God, beneficiaries in common of the work of Christ reconciling all things in heaven and earth, enduring in common the labor pains of a groaning creation, and looking forward in common to their liberation into the freedom of the children of God. This theological vision subverts the human-separatist logic that motivates our obsession to differentiate ourselves from other animals and justifies our use of them as mere material to exploit for our own ends. And, contrastingly, it celebrates our position among God's creatures, part of the magnificently diverse and incomprehensibly immense creaturely order celebrated in Ps. 104 and the closing chapters of Job, and encourages us to seek to enable the flourishing of our fellow creatures and their glorification of God.

For a long time, I naïvely supposed that while the erection and patrolling of this human/nonhuman barrier had been negative for nonhuman animals, it had been positive for many humans, on the basis that the recognition that all humans were entitled to the recognition of basic rights was a moral advance. I had in mind a magical circle encompassing and offering protection to all humans. I was concerned for the nonhumans left outside of the circle, but I did not want to improve their lot at the cost of humans losing rights to protections (as Peter Singer's preference utilitarian theory explicitly does in relation, say, to newborn infants). But then I read Giorgio Agamben's *The Open*, which tells of the "anthropological machines" that divide human and inhuman or "man" and animal, but inevitably produce a "zone of indeterminacy," the result of which is Jews being classified as "non-man" and vulnerable to extermination in death camps.[26] And then I read J. Kameron Carter's *Race: A Theological Account*, which unmasks Immanuel Kant's typology of human races, whereby "the American people" (by which Kant means Native Americans) are judged incapable of education; "the Negro Race"

---

26. Giorgio Agamben, *The Open: Man and Animal*, trans. Kevin Attell (Stanford: Stanford University Press, 2004).

only capable of being educated as servants; "the Hindus" capable of training in the arts but not the sciences; and *all* to be stamped out by the "Race of Whites" that uniquely "contains within itself all motivations and talents."[27] Carter demonstrates that Kant's moral universalism, the foundation of so much progressive moral philosophy and theological ethics, involves the universalizing of whiteness, a project of eradicating inferior humans in favor of his fellow whites. (In other work, incidentally, Carter critiques Agamben and notes the need to extend our understanding of the anthropological machine to recognize "how the Jews were pushed towards a blackened, indeed a colonized position, shall we say, closer to the slave and therefore closer to killable flesh."[28]) And then I read *The Christian Imagination: Theology and the Origins of Race*, in which Willie Jennings recounts key episodes from Christianity's colonial history, illuminating the exuberant way in which white colonizers saw themselves as co-creators with God of the new world and made whiteness, and the racial oppression it enabled, central among their creations. Most striking for me from Jennings's analysis is his critique of the Anglican bishop John William Colenso's nineteenth-century theology arising from his experience of colonial South Africa. Concerned to find a place for the evident faith of his Black South African theological conversation partners William Ngidi and Magema Magwaza Fuze, Colenso proposed that "God has simply provided a righteousness to the whole human race in Jesus Christ."[29] Despite his good intentions, however, Jennings shows how this theological move, repeated by many later Christian theologians—among which we might number Barth—turns away from and refuses to recognize the South African cultural logic that Colenso encountered, and results in "a universalism that undermines all forms of identity except that of the colonialist."[30]

After reading Agamben, Carter, and Jennings, I have abandoned my previous naïve belief that establishing and patrolling a human/nonhuman barrier fence is positive for humans. It now looks to me that the creating and policing of this border is bad for vulnerable humans, and disproportionately bad for those racialized as nonwhite, whose humanity may be placed in question by the existence of the barrier, as well as bad for the nonhuman animals who are kept outside our moral concern. And here is one of many sites of convergence I have encountered where critical attention to race and to animals in a theological context turns out not to be in competition or contradiction, but as complementary critiques of the same structural issue.

I am increasingly convinced that the complementarity of thinking critically about race and animals is anything but coincidental. It is instructive that many cultural and religious traditions do not begin with a human/nonhuman opposition

---

27. Carter, *Race*, 91.

28. J. Kameron Carter, "The Inglorious: With and Beyond Giorgio Agamben," *Political Theology* 14 (2013): 85.

29. Quoted in Jennings, *Christian Imagination*, 218.

30. Ibid., 220 and 234.

to establish human identity, and it is especially instructive that this difference has been generated by white colonial thinkers, in order to label indigenous and nonwhite peoples as "primitive." Indeed, anthropological studies have enabled us to recognize that other traditions of religion and culture begin with *affirming* commonality with nonhuman creatures, perhaps captured most dramatically in the statement by members of the Brazilian Bororo tribe to the German anthropologist Karl von den Steinen that they were red parrots, as discussed in Jonathan Z. Smith's famous article from 1972. Smith notes the pattern of similar reports by anthropologists of indigenous peoples identifying with nonhuman creatures—"the Trumai of North Brazil say that they are aquatic animals, the natives of Mabuiag think of themselves as cassowaries, the headman of the Dieri tribe was thought to be a seed-bearing plant," and that such examples are used by anthropologists as characterizing a "primitive mentality."[31] Aaron Gross has recently gone further, in his book *The Question of the Animal and Religion*, arguing that the human/nonhuman distinction is foundational for the discipline of religious studies.[32] The key reason critical perspectives on race and animals are often complementary, one might say, is that whiteness as a human universal ideal is constructed in opposition *both* to humans racialized as not white *and* animals identified as nonhuman. The intersection with feminist animal studies, such as in the work of Carol Adams, adds gender to the mix, unmasking the depiction of a normative white male humanity in contradistinction from Black, brown, and female humans, and nonhuman animals.[33] It follows, then, that we can recognize a core theological task at this intersectional nexus: the deconstruction of white male human supremacy. And of course, the complexity multiplies, as we attend to Latin American liberation theologies attending to socioeconomic status and political power, queer theologies challenging normative sexualities, disability theology challenging ableist norms, and so on.

This intersection between theology, race, and animals has implications for interpreting Barth's theology. In the first volume of *On Animals*, I critiqued the radical anthropocentricity of Barth's account of creation as the "external" basis of the covenant between God and humanity.[34] The idea that the whole of creation other than the human was brought into being to enable God's relationship with humanity runs counter to much of the theology of creation and redemption in the Bible, and is profoundly problematic for Christian animal ethics. As a remedy to Barth's problematic commitment, I explored the path Barth identified but did

---

31. Jonathan Z. Smith, "I Am a Parrot (Red)," *History of Religions* 11, no. 4 (1972): 392–3.

32. Aaron Gross, *The Question of the Animal and Religion: Theoretical Stakes, Practical Implications* (New York: Columbia University Press, 2014).

33. See, for example, Carol J. Adams, *The Sexual Politics of Meat: A Feminist-Vegetarian Critical Theory* (Cambridge: Polity, 1990); and idem, *Neither Man Nor Beast: Feminism and the Defense of Animals* (London: Bloomsbury, 2018).

34. Clough, *On Animals*, vol. 1, 3–25.

not take in the Preface of *Church Dogmatics* III/2: that "the limits of the term 'creature' may with the necessary boldness and sobriety be more widely drawn than I have dared attempt" (CD III/2: x).[35] In the light of the critiques of Agamben, Carter, and Jennings, however, Barth's focus on the universal human as the object of God's covenant looks problematic for some humans, as well as for animals. The anthropocentricity of Barth's unreconstructed position is structurally similar to a white supremacist position that judges the interests of nonwhite humans and all nonhumans as subordinate to those of white humans. Here it seems to me that a synergy between critical theologies of race and of animals point to the need for reworking Barth's doctrine of creation, with implications for other areas of his thought, such as election, too.

Conclusion

I have argued in this chapter that most white scholars of Barth, including me, have reason to be red-faced when confronting the uncomfortable truth that fifty years have passed since James Cone wrote *Black Theology and Black Power*, critiquing the un-Barthian ways in which Barth was being appropriated in Europe and North America. In that half-century, during which Cone developed and refined his critique, white Barth scholars have almost completely ignored it, and as a result, we find that Cone's strong and persuasive critique of Barthian theological studies remains valid fifty years on. Without overestimating the influence of Barth studies, this culpable inattention must be understood as part of the complex in which the president of the United States can order the seizing and caging of immigrant children and, much more directly, contributes to educational cultures where the hashtag #SeminaryWhileBlack is needed.

If theology is to be in good faith, it seems to me that white scholars of Barth need to attend to Cone's worry that it seems easier for European and North American theologians to engage with Latin American liberation theologies in solidarity with the poor far away, than it is for them to address the challenge of near neighbors at home who are discriminated against on the grounds of race.

After recognizing the culpable neglect of Cone's critique of Barthians, I have argued that white scholars in Barth studies need, first, to become alert to the ways in which the theological traditions passed on to them are shaped by racist colonial attitudes; second, to attend to the theological work demanded by wickedness in the streets and the practical duties that press upon them; and, third, to be attentive to the connections between their particular theological passions and critical liberationist perspectives, including those focused on race and whiteness. A necessary step in undertaking these tasks will be learning not only from Cone's corpus, but also from the broad and diverse literature engaging and going beyond Cone at the interface between theology and race, especially in Black, womanist,

---

35. I have used this quotation elsewhere; See Clough, *On Animals*, vol. 1, 92–3.

Latinx, African, and Asian theologies. All scholars of Barth have reason to value and celebrate these contributions, and to encourage and foster a continuing widening of the diversity of theological scholarship on Barth and within theology as a whole. Fellow authors within this volume provide some useful starting points.

Practically, and immediately, academics who do not yet engage these perspectives and critiques in their courses on Barth and other white male figures should do so, doctoral proposals that show no awareness of these challenges to the white theological status quo should be judged inadequate, and scholarship sent for peer review that is inattentive to these concerns should be returned for revision. These are not new or original suggestions. They are already in place in other contexts, and they need to be supplemented by many others in order to effect the change of scholarly culture that is now required. However, I think them worth stating, because they are not yet common neither in Barth studies nor in wider theological scholarship. Only through such conscious, deliberate, and practical action can white scholars of Barth be confident that their successors fifty years from now will be in a different position to the embarrassing one in which they find themselves today when rereading Cone's critique of the whiteness of Barth studies.

Chapter 10

CLOTHED IN FLESH

THE ARTIST, LIBERATION, AND THE FUTURE OF BARTHIAN THEOLOGY

Brian Bantum

It had been a few years since I read Karl Barth. In graduate school, I took a seminar on Barth as a master's student, was a teaching assistant for another as a doctoral student, and I worked with Barth an extensive amount in my dissertation. I have also taught Barth's theology in courses for undergraduates and seminarians. And then Trayvon Martin was murdered, then Eric Garner, then Ferguson, then the acquittals, and repeat. And Barth did not seem to be enough for this historic moment. Instead of reading Barth, I read Claudia Rankine's *Citizen: An American Lyric*, Kelly Brown Douglas's *Stand Your Ground*, Gloria Anzaldúa's *Borderlands/La Frontera*, and more recently, Patrisse Khan-Cullors's *When They Call You a Terrorist*.[1] Barth seemed far down the list.

And then I received the invitation to be a part of the 2018 Karl Barth conference on the theme of "Barth and the Future of Liberation Theology." The book that came to mind immediately was Barth's commentary on the book of Romans. I pulled this book from my shelf and sat in my torn faux leather chair, began on page one, and read those first descriptions of Paul: "Paul is no genius rejoicing in his creative ability" (RII: 27). For Barth, Paul's mode of theological inquiry is entwined with encounter and creation. And a juxtaposition of encounter and creativity offers us a way of imagining Barth's theological project, if not as liberation theology in a strict sense, then as a theology deeply concerned with our bondage and our freedom in this world and in this moment.

In this essay, I want to consider how Barth points to the possibility of a liberative theological method and argue that, intertwined with its obvious theological concerns, his Romans commentary can be read as an aesthetic or artistic project, a

---

1. Claudia Rankine, *Citizen: An American Lyric* (Minneapolis: Graywolf, 2014); Kelly Brown Douglas, *Stand Your Ground: Black Bodies and the Justice of God* (Maryknoll: Orbis, 2015); Gloria Anzaldúa, *Borderlands: The New Mestiza/La Frontera*, 3rd edn (San Francisco: Aunt Lute Books, 2007); and Patrisse Khan-Cullors, *When They Call You a Terrorist: A Black Lives Matter Memoir* (New York: St. Martin's, 2018).

"word clothed in flesh." Indeed, the future of Barthian theology, if it is to realize its liberative possibilities in our current world, will need to find its deepest resources in the reciprocity of argument and form that Barth (perhaps unwittingly) displays in *Romans*—a disruption that is a disruption through form, and that continues throughout his work and especially in his *Church Dogmatics*. However, while Barth's project gestures toward liberative possibilities, we must also go beyond Barth in order to realize those possibilities. We must move toward what I call a *literary theology*.

In *Church Dogmatics*, Barth offers a confession that arises out of a confrontation, an encounter. This encounter is not singularly his, but in Romans, we come to see that it is a shared encounter. By grace, we experience something alongside the Apostle Paul. Out of this encounter, we come to discover a common condition, a situation that oppresses us, and within which God seeks to meet us. As we consider the relationship between liberation theology and Barth, we need to ask, quite specifically, what this common condition is. Paul is caught between internal recognition and external encounter. He is not a thinker or a theologian. Paul is found, held, and struck, and he must navigate this finding, holding, and striking that propels him into a life not his own.

Barth's claims concerning the human situation before God, one might say, are fairly clear. But Barth's discursive forms and rhetorical urgency draws us into Paul's condition and into his situation. In doing so, Barth shifts the reader's point of view from an "objective" analysis of a text to that of a subject who exists *within* the text. His commentary, in other words, only partially involves an exegesis of passages or the unfolding of an argument. Paul is not simply a writer of a letter. For Barth, he is the co-subject of a text that participates in a story unfolding the world within which we find ourselves. In confronting this world, Barth's commentary is a stripping or a tearing away at the objectivity of our condition or the possibility of "scientific inquiry."

Barth famously refers to John the Baptist pointing to the crucified Christ in Grünewald's painting of the crucifixion as a gesture of pointing toward Christ. This is the task of the theologian: to point and witness to God. In what follows, my claim is that Barth's approach to exegesis in *Romans* displays the character of John in Grünewald's Isenheim Altarpiece—not just theologically, but also aesthetically—in his pointing to God. Moreover, while this gesture suggests a differentiation between the theologian and Christ, John himself is in the picture and is himself part of the narrative. This point has tremendous significance. More than dialectical method or infinite qualitative difference, more than even the question of epistemology and revelation, the significance and hope in Barth's thought and writing reside in an aesthetic and artistic sensibility he offers—one that is crucial for the realization of the theological task. And while music is undoubtedly one possible frame of reference to engage this point—Barth's love of Mozart is well known, but it is also significant that the first and second editions of Romans were written in the aftermath of Stravinsky's "Rite of Spring" (1913)—I would suggest that we can also read and interpret his work through two additional artistic metaphors: sculpture and painting.

Der Römerbrief *as Sculpture*

The underlying character of encounter that permeates Barth's theological assertions and his style includes the following: we are always in the world, we are indicted, or promised to, or seen, even as we see. We are and exist *in* the image, pointing to a Word beyond ourselves who is present. Barth's preface to the second edition of *Romans* frames the task of theological scholarship thus:

> When an investigation is rightly conducted, boulders composed of fortuitous or incidental or merely historical conceptions ought to disappear almost entirely. The Word ought to be exposed in the words. Intelligent comment means that I am driven on till I stand with nothing before me but the enigma of the matter; till the document seems hardly to exist as a document; till I have almost forgotten that I am not its author; till I know the author so well that I allow him to speak in my name and even be able to speak in his name myself. (RII: 8)

Barth's critique of certain "scientific" approaches to scripture and his analogy of removal and excavation bring to mind conversations of paragone among Renaissance artists: debates about which art form can better express the true (and, by extension, which artist can better express truth). While this is perhaps a somewhat odd reference to make in a discussion of Barth's theology, paragone debates exemplified the European fascination with knowledge, truth, and classification, and most importantly, with the ways that truth is expressed, mastered, or discovered in the material world. The artists of the Renaissance were not simply craftspeople; they sought to understand themselves as intellectuals, and they strove to view their works as exercises in knowledge and discovery. Indeed, in comparisons between sculpture and painting, sculptors would claim themselves and their methods to be the ideal, since a deeper truth lay in creating a three-dimensional object—in a work of art that one could walk around. But in order to create such an object, you have to shape, remove, and shave off material. In order to discover the truth that an object holds, you have to take away something.[2]

Barth's project in *Romans* has a sculptural quality since he seeks knowledge of God through excision and violent depressions. The negations, "the night," the refusals of what can be known, page by page—all of this chips, sands, and splits the text of Romans (and, ultimately, the reader). Every negation, every slab of stone cleaved from the whole, is freeing and revealing. We see something of this cleaving in Barth's preface to the second edition of *Romans*:

> Can scientific investigation ever really triumph so long as men refuse to busy themselves with this question, or so long as they are content to engage themselves

---

2. On which, see Helen Langdon, "Paragone," in *The Oxford Companion to Western Art*, ed. Hugh Brigstocke (Oxford: Oxford University Press, 2001). See https://www.oxfordreference.com/view/10.1093/acref/9780198662037.001.0001/acref-9780198662037-e-1961.

with amazing energy upon the work of interpretation with the most superficial understanding of what interpretation really is? For me, at any rate, the question of the true nature of interpretation is the supreme question.—Or is it that these learned men, for whose learning and erudition I have such genuine respect, fail to recognize the existence of any real substance at all, of any underlying problem, of any Word in the words? Do they not perceive that there are documents such as the books of the New Testament, which compel men to speak at whatever cost, because they find in them that which urgently and finally concerns the very marrow of human civilization? (RII: 9)

Far from abstraction, in every strike of the hammer upon the chisel, Barth has in mind a material moment: an occasion in which the no-god has coiled itself around us to the point that we mistake stank air for life, and quell or kill any semblance of truth that disrupts our illusion of freedom and knowledge. The stripping away of falsehood and presuppositions, then, is an act of liberation, one that discloses a central concern of who we are and who God is. To say what we are *not* is the first moment of recognizing reality, and the first step toward a true inhabitation of Christ's life and mission.

But where sculpture remains an object grounded in one place, Barth's literary excavation works upon us in multiple spaces. The "we" of his work is not incidental. In this regard, a second aspect of Barth's commentary is his use of the literary tropes—character, point of view, metaphor, narrative arc, and so on—that feature in his explication of Paul's text. The slippage of first person, second person plural, and third person throughout *Romans*, coupled with their negation, places the reader within the paradox of Barth's argument. We do not know, but we are nonetheless encountered. There is mystery and presence; an accounting of existence that cannot be negated completely because it experiences *something*. Again: we are John, in the painting, at the cross.

Barth's Romans text mirrors Kierkegaard's in thought and form, both in its resistance to epistemological and cultural hubris and also in the use of metaphor and character to unfold a theological or philosophical question. Paul, one might say, is not simply a writer in Barth's commentary; he is a character whose identity seems to unfold over the course of the letter.

Recall some of the claims made in the opening pages. Paul begins as a "servant, not a master"; as an "impossibility" who "belongs to them—indeed he belongs to many!" until, finally: "In him a void becomes visible" (RII: 27, 28, 32, and 33). In these first few pages, which exegete Paul's simple greeting, Barth ascribes to him character and action, and with that a story of encounter and crisis. Paul is not simply a writer or a thinker for Barth. Paul is both a person whom God encounters and a metaphor for the theologian and the human being encountered by God. And, again, as Barth's exegesis unfolds, we are caught within this story. We too are implicated in the conditions of refusal where "[s]ubmerged and hidden is the true ground of our existence; unrecognized is the Unknown God, fruitless the traces of His faithfulness, unused His promises and gifts" (RII: 79). Barth makes plain the interrelationship between artistic and theological claims in his exegesis of Romans 4:17b by suggesting the following:

> Here is the impossibility of knowing, the impossibility of resurrection, the impossibility of God, Creator and Redeemer, in whom "here" and "there" are both one. Abraham is brought within the scope of the impossibility by faith, itself the non-historical and impossible factor, which makes possible and by which history is established. A similar faith appears on the borderland of philosophy of Plato, of the art of Grünewald and Dostoevsky, and of the religion of Luther. And yet, it must not be supposed that knowledge is a fortuitous thing, that resurrection is a contingent happening, and that God is bound to the contradiction between "here" and "there." God is pure negation. He is both "here" and "there." (RII: 141–2)

When I have taught passages like this, students come away forlorn. "What do you mean there is nothing that we can know? God is negation?" But here Barth's gesture toward artists is especially helpful, for it returns us to the analogy of sculpture. Whether carving or casting, form emerges from removal, via that which creates gaps and evokes shallowness and depth. Similarly, at certain points in *Romans*, Barth refers to the crater left by God's acts. This cratering is not the destruction but rather the indentation of God's presence upon us and in us. The negation is an assertion of what we are, and an assertion and promise of presence. It is not an endless plane without depth or height; it is that which shapes and forms us anew.

By the end of *Romans*, Barth suggests to us that "Here we have opened out before us a little world" (RII: 535). With this end, we have an epistle that is both an exhortation against Paulinism and a warning against ourselves. We have a spiritual and literary contestation of a world whose words have failed, even though Barth displays that failure of language in and through human words. History, time, and point of view are all reconfigured in a treatise that refuses to clarify what we are or to capture the perfection of form and reason and insight. Barth's commentary is a story, akin to Kierkegaard's *Fear and Trembling* or Dostoevsky's *The Brothers Karamozov*, that immerses us in a presence that confounds. We want to say that we cannot know, but we cannot say that we are not encountered, that there is no presence, and that we do not exist in this moment. Therefore, we must account for something. We, too, are excavated, chipped away, and sanded down until a new shape begins to emerge, until we begin to see that what constitutes our lives is more than what we imagined as singular individuals.

Dogmatics as Painting

If Barth's *Romans* was sculptural, communicating through excision and removal, perhaps we might consider his work in the *Dogmatics* as the other side of the paragone—that is, as painting. Renaissance artists who considered painting the higher art suggested that painting allowed the artist to display whole scenes, whether a landscape or a vast array of characters. This required deeper intellectual work and skill, because perspective, shade, light, and dark in a painting were not by-products of a physical process. The artist had to create these pieces of art and bring them into being through their skill and craft.

Although I have often wondered why a man so sure of what we could not know would go on to write so much, the painting analogy seems to highlight what Barth is doing in the *Dogmatics*. Through a painstaking process of mixing, creating basic layers, and outlining shapes, Barth slowly builds an image, layer by layer, with each facet of the argument seeming to draw us off the ground to survey the land around us—or, conversely, submerging us into the shadows of the cliffs that tower over us.

With respect to the progression of *Church Dogmatics*, the doctrine of the Word of God (CD I) forms a basis upon which diverse structures will be formed. The christological centering of the prolegomena (CD I/2, §15), specifically, can be read as the infusion of a hue into the blues and blacks, with highlights added in subsequent volumes. Understood in an artistic mode, the epistemological questions that Barth addresses in earlier paragraphs cannot be understood as primary or foundational, as a statement of "first principles"; they are rather a way of providing depth, the creation of a frame, and the establishing of textures that inform what will come.

Consider, for instance, what it means for Barth to write, in §15, "The Word became." As he sees it,

> that points to the centre, to the mystery of revelation, the happening of the inconceivable fact that God is among us and with us . . . "The Word became"—if that is true, and true in such a way that a real becoming is thereby expressed without the slightest surrender of the divinity of the Word, its truth is that of a miraculous act, an act of mercy on the part of God. (CD I/2: 159)

Read conceptually, of course, Barth focuses theological inquiry on the Word of God in Christ. But if we read these lines aesthetically, as *hue*, where the orange Barth paints with is made of burnt umber and deep yellow, the color of the entire painting moves in and out of those tones. The process of mixing and forming colors goes in and out of the colors that made up the orange and draw from the orange itself. Where a painting leaves us with a cohesive image, with various the layers hidden beneath others, made visible because of the effect they offer, Barth's "painting" gives us the impression of progressive ideas built upon one another, with the weight of volumes as the reflective of a process of layering, re-layering, and re-layering again.

Indeed, while Barth claims not to be a musicologist, one cannot help but wonder if the *Dogmatics* displays some of the qualities he admired in his most beloved artist, Wolfgang Amadeus Mozart. For Barth, "What occurs in Mozart is rather a glorious upsetting of the balance, a turning in which the light rises and the shadows fall, though without disappearing, in which joy overtakes sorrow without extinguishing it, in which the Yea rings louder than the ever-present Nay. Note the reversal of the great dark and the small light episodes in Mozart's life!"[3] When we turn to the *Dogmatics*, we see several of the same literary tropes employed in *Romans* unfolding again.

---

3. Karl Barth, *Wolfgang Amadeus Mozart* (Grand Rapids: Eerdmans, 1986), 55.

But whereas Romans began with the character, Paul—one was put into question, one who was encountered and was bound to the one calling him—the main character of the *Dogmatics* is the *church*. "The Church confesses God as it talks about God. . . . But as it confesses God the church also confesses both the humanity and responsibility of its action" (CD I/1: 3). Throughout the opening pages of *Church Dogmatics* I/1, we see the church as possessing character and agency, while also called to a kind of self-examination, undertaken in a mood of *hope*. Put differently: we see the negation of certainty and knowledge as the central mark of the church's hope, and yet in the unknowing, in the gap, we are also confronted with the reality that the church is not left without God. This negation is not an erasure of personhood but rather an elaboration of who we are and of who God is. Each volume of the *Dogmatics* builds upon this central claim, weaving the "we," the "I," and the "they" in and out of one another, unfolding doctrine within the all-encompassing and narrowing arc of God's decision to be with us, and culminating in the doctrine of reconciliation explicated in *Church Dogmatics* IV.

Read in the context of Barth's pastoral work in Safenweil and the tortuous conditions of workers in burgeoning industrial towns, the nationalistic and anti-Semitic aggression of Germany in the First and Second World Wars, and the complicity of theology in the reception and participation in these dramas, *Romans* and the *Church Dogmatics* challenged the Enlightenment's lionization of "objectivity," immersing our world within God's world and God's world within ours. God's transcendence and God's immanence makes our very existence possible, and it is, of course, the case that God's "objectivity" is lauded in Barth's works. But God's presence with us also means that mystery and unknowing are identified as fundamental marks of our life with God. For Barth, the most violent and egregious acts of human and theological violence occur when we fail to see the totality of our lives as being marked by God's presence. Both *Romans* and the *Dogmatics*, in fact, are extended pleas for us to see ourselves inside of God's life and participants in God's presence—and to understand that mystery and unknowing are ingredient to the Christian condition. In *Romans*, God's presence meant a recognition of what we were not before God; in the *Dogmatics*, God's presence meant seeing the unfathomable depths and layers of what God does as God forms the Christian community. In both texts, there is mystery and there is presence.

And yet there is also continuity, spanning the individual and communal. Much like John the Baptist in Grünewald's Isenheim Alterpiece, Barth wrote in ways that helped readers to view themselves as confronted by God in a way that forbids looking away, even as we are forbidden from looking "within." Perhaps one could say that Barth wanted us to be free, while insisting that liberation requires encountering and embracing what we do not know, so that we no longer try to dominate what we think we know.

Liberation

While Martin Luther King, Jr., might have thought Barth's account of God overplayed transcendence and distance, when examined through the lens of form, we begin to see the texture of Barth's thought, and we begin to see how God's difference is not equivalent to distance. The opposite is the case: God's difference is rather an assertion of proximity and a presence that animates the entirety of our context. For Barth, in other words, there is no place without God. God is the plane of our being and the agent with whom we act and move. God is the setting, the character, and the plot. This confusion of literary devices is particularly evident in Barth's claim that "atonement is history." As he writes: "But the atonement is the very special history of God with man, the very special history of man with God" (CD IV/1: 157). To put it very starkly: claims about God can never be made apart from the materiality of our world and the materiality of God's work in the world and with us.

In this way, Barth might be understood as a liberation theologian of a sort, one who supposes that the material conditions that oppress and enslave communities and individuals are always manifestations of a refusal of existence within God's life. History is never an unfolding idea; it is the intersection of real lives and the interpretation of those same lives. These real lives, in fact, are always presumed for Barth, just as God's presence in those lives is understood to be the substance of God's activity. This radical presumption of a divine presence that acts in history and for those oppressed by humanity's "no" to God's presence might thus be seen as a consonant tone between liberation theologies and Barth's work—God's radical movement for and identification with those who are oppressed.

The task for the future of Barth scholarship, to my mind, is to rediscover its liberative hope and its constructive, performative modality and edge. In this way, I wonder if we could say that James Cone, Gustavo Gutiérrez, and Willie Jennings are Barth's most faithful interpreters—not because any of them would identify as a "Barthian," but rather because they knew that the future of his work did not reside in parsing dialectics, debating the problem of knowledge, or sharpening doctrinal formulations. Cone, in particular, deepens the significance of Barth's observation regarding the "way of the son of God into the far country." He describes what is classically viewed as the communication of idioms as the movement of the divine word into human flesh in terms of a redemption that includes political transformation:

> According to the New Testament, Jesus is the man for others who views his existence as inextricably tied to other men to the degree that his own Person is inexplicable apart from others. The others, of course, refer to all men, especially the oppressed, the unwanted of society, the "sinners." He is God himself coming into the very depths of human existence for the sole purpose of striking off the chains of slavery, thereby freeing man from ungodly principalities and powers that hinder his relationship with God.[4]

Notice Cone's invocation of the hypostatic union. It is God's movement toward humanity that is redemptive—God's act of taking up human existence and life into

---

4. James H. Cone, *Black Theology and Black Power* (Maryknoll: Orbis, 1997), 39.

God's own life, and thus imparting to it a redemptive reality that sets captives free. Cone then radicalizes this movement even further, suggesting that

> Jesus' work is essentially one of liberation. Becoming a slave himself, he opens realities of human existence formerly closed to man. Through an encounter with Jesus, man now knows the full meaning of God's action in history and man's place within it.... It is a message about the ghetto, and all other injustices done in the name of democracy and religion to further the social, political, and economic interests of the oppressor. In Christ, God enters human affairs and takes sides with the oppressed. Their suffering becomes his, their despair, divine despair. Through Christ the poor man is offered freedom now to rebel against that which makes him other than human.[5]

If the invocation of the *communicatio idiomatum* in a political register was not explicit enough, Cone finally delivers the punchline: "This is 'Black Power!' They"—that is, civil rights groups and Black Power advocates—"want the grip of white power removed." That is "what black people have in mind when they cry, 'Freedom Now!' now and forever.... Is this not why God became man in Jesus Christ so that man might become what he is?"[6] This is the groundwork, in fact, which leads Cone to claim that "Jesus is Black." Cone is not engaging the cultural question that occupied Howard Thurman; he is deploying the theological intuitions of the creeds to suggest that not only did Christ take up human nature but also a human situation, and, in this very moment, that Christ brings God's freedom to those for whom freedom has been systematically deprived. To live "in Christ," for Cone, is to live into the situation of the oppressed and the possibility of their redemption in the political realities of the world.

Reading through Cone's use and critique of Barth, then, we can begin to see that Barth's epistemological questions were not universal but contextual—albeit in a way that Barth himself did not always make explicit. Even so, I return to Barth's work, still, because I see in his writing fundamental questions and possible answers to the query: "How do we become free? How do we apprehend the fullness of what God has done and bear witness to those truths in our lives and work?"

Toward a Literary and Liberating Theology

In this final section, moving with and beyond Barth and Cone, I want to suggest that a *literary* theology is a liberating theology—a theology that allows us to see the particularities of our lives with clarity, and a theology that instills in us the courage to not turn away. Literary theology, of course, is not new. The literary and the poetic are constants in Christian reflection. But I want to suggest here that

---

5. Ibid., 35–6.
6. Ibid., 39.

even theology in its most scholarly instantiations requires what Emilie Townes describes as the "dancing mind" of womanist theologians (she takes the term from Toni Morrison). Townes writes, "This womanist dancing mind is more than my attempt to make sense of the worlds surrounding us—sometimes enveloping us, sometimes smothering us, sometimes holding us, sometimes birthing us." She continues: "the womanist mind is one that comes from a particular community of communities yearning for a common fire banked by the billows of justice and hope."[7] It is entirely appropriate, then, that Townes's work is punctuated by her own poetry. Both the poetic and the scholarly circulate around the particulars of a moment, an experience, and a history. By refusing the universal, Townes marks out the possibilities of freedom within the textures of the present. She engages in literary as well as theological work.

What is at stake here for me is the question of what theology could gain from writers and critics. Here I am adapting a distinction made by Anne Dillard in *Living by Fiction*. She writes,

> a work of fiction is indeed interpretive in the special sense that it is, by intention, an object to be interpreted. Unlike the critic, who intends his interpretation to be near the level of a "final say," and who does not, at any rate, expect the world to devote much energy to analyzing his interpretation, the fiction writer intends his work to be a primary object. He intends it to be interpreted.[8]

Dillard goes on to suggest that the

> writer is certainly interested in the art of fiction, but perhaps less so than the critic is. The critic is interested in the novel; the novelist is interested in his neighbors. Perhaps even more than in his own techniques, then, the writer is interested in knowing the world in order to make real and honest sense of it. He worries the world and probes it; he collects the world and collates it. No part of it is outside his field.[9]

To stumble toward a *literary* theology, then, is to stop and ask, "who is writing? Who is creating?" A literary theology is the invocation of a writer, one whose life is attuned and attuning to those around them and the world they live in. Literary theology is therefore constantly emerging from the questions and observations

---

7. Emilie M. Townes, *Womanist Ethics and the Cultural Production of Evil* (New York: Palgrave Macmillan, 2006), 2. For more on the "dancing mind," see Toni Morrison, *The Dancing Mind: Speech Upon Acceptance of the National Book Foundation Medal for Distinguished Contribution to American Letters on the Sixth of November, Nineteen Hundred and Ninety-Six* (New York: Alfred A. Knopf, 1996).

8. Annie Dillard, *Living by Fiction* (New York: Harper & Row, 1982), 150.

9. Ibid., 151.

that writers see among them. To do literary theology is to see the world in a particular way and hone the craft of drawing others into that vision.

After my oldest son came home from an art lesson, I asked him what he learned to draw. He told me, "Dad, we do not learn to draw things, we learn how to see." He told me how he sees shade instead of lines, light instead of colors. He told me that art was translating all of this through various media in order to convey and reconfigure those media. The literary theologian, by the same token, cannot write of God without writing of the world, and cannot write of ideas without discerning light and shade. But literary theology also suggests that what is created is to be interpreted. It presumes interpretation—nay, demands it. It asks to be entered into, but it does not (and cannot) dictate what will be gleaned by the reader while they occupy the space created.

Like Bonaventure's reflection on the incarnation, then, a literary theology invites the reader into the room. And, in this regard, the writer does not try to exorcise the unknown, turning on every lamp in the house to ensure there is no corner without shadow; or, conversely, shutting off every lamp so that only the corner you want people to see is revealed. Some might wander in and become fixated on the frayed orange leather chair in the corner that still smells like the cigarettes and sherry that your grandmother enjoyed religiously every day at four in the afternoon. Others may hover around the ceramic elephants your partner insists on bringing back from every trip they take.

The writer does not get to decide. In this way, a literary theology *subjects itself to the world*, offering that world to readers in ways that are at once discomforting and holy, even as it remains attentive to God as subject. It is a theology that offers itself to its readers. To be sure, knowledge or a lack of knowledge is still wielded. I am not suggesting a lazy vagueness or lack of clarity of insight or skill. The writer puts you in this room, with these people. Unknowing is eased out with craft and intention. Drops of light come through underneath doors or through gaps in curtains that the writer has set just far enough apart. And is this not what makes the presence of artists and writers lasting, not simply what they said about the human condition, but their ability to draw us into the situation of that truth?

There are novelists and poets who do this theological work in profound and meaningful ways. I do not mean to suggest, of course, that this kind of work, broadly speaking, is *not* being done by artists or that artists cannot be theologians. My question is, what happens when theology begins to refuse the differentiation or the dichotomy of the literary and the doctrinal? What qualifies a person to be a theologian, after all? What happens when theology is not simply a knowledge of what artists have produced or the interrelationship between them and their social location, but an attempt to see the world as artists do? What if the theologian is called to create and hone their craft in a way that does not require the accumulation of knowledge, or at least knowledge in the way the Western academy has conceived it? Does not a literary theologian have something unique to contribute?

I wonder, in other words, how theological thought and writing can be reimagined when theologians take up their work as *art*. In my view, the artistic process helps theological work to overcome a number of problematic dichotomies: flesh/spirit, beauty/ugliness, sacred/profane. The artistic process does not leave these dichotomies to themselves; it tries to make sense of them through a material process. Whether one is dealing with a story, a painting, a song, or a rock sculpted to create a new form, there are no neat, easily delineated distinctions, laid out in discrete sections and paragraphs; there is no process of dissection and analysis. No, colors must be mixed and layered upon a canvas, the strings of the guitar must be struck and pressed, and sometimes even slapped to draw sounds from its body that are loud and quiet, smooth and sharp. The paradoxes and contrasts are bound up together through the manipulation and relationship of the materials in front of you, their limits, and their possibilities, and they are intended to be received and interpreted by the totality of our senses.

In this process, the dualities and dichotomies are not collapsed into one another into a muddy cacophony. They are woven on top of and under one another, and the whole process can be called beautiful. It can be called beautiful because it causes us to see in new ways, because it captures the best of us in the world. It can be called beautiful because it names our pain so truthfully, allowing us to find a modicum of control when the suffering makes us feel like we have none. Indeed, the ability to *name* affliction can give us hope. It is beautiful, because it names our pain and reminds us that in our living and survival in the face of it, we too are more beautiful than we had first imagined possible.

My hope in beginning to articulate a shape of literary theology is to make sense of my own work, and also to begin to chart a path or tender an invitation for theologies that can speak to violence, marginalization, and the world in general in ways that are not simply "accessible" or simplified, but *incarnate*. This new path would seek to speak and teach by how one enters into the world and through the worlds into which a theologian invites their readers. I do not think this is the sole arena of artists. Rather, in many ways, it is the fundamental task of a faithful theology: to reflect on the nature of the One who animates existence *in the world*.

But this posture does make our relationship to ideas difficult. In a writing class that I took, my professor would often chide me for starting with a concept. "Brian," she would say, "you are trying to make a claim about being human here, aren't you? We don't start with a concept, we start with the character, the person's life, where they sat and ate." The story, plot, and character: those are primary. If a novel is about an idea it will read like polemic, because it is not art. This is the greatest difficulty in conceiving of a literary theology. Theology is a discipline of ideas above all. Or at least that is how it has held its place in the academy and the church, erecting a scaffolding of doctrine, histories, and rationales.

Is it even possible, then, to return to the bodied offering that literature often provides? I think so. In an introduction to a collection of photographer Robert Bergman's portraits, Toni Morrison wrote, "[i]n all its burnished majesty his gallery refuses us unearned solace and one by one each photograph unveils us, asserting a beauty, a kind of rapture that is as close as can be to a master template of the singularity, the community, the unextinguishable sacredness of the human race."[10] For all of Dillard's (and my teachers') pressing against the presence of ideas—of writers' structures and what they want to say being burned off—when I read Morrison I see an opposite movement. Morrison seems to press so deep into an idea that she brings it into being on the page as flesh and blood. It is material and every word oozes with it until the narrative is propelled along, and, before the reader realizes it, they are drowned or quenched by its truthfulness in their lives.

Like Dillard, Morrison's neighbors and people are her concern, but perhaps differently to Dillard, Morrison understands how ideas have cleaved stories into people's bodies. The idea of language is made plain in the first lines of Morrison's *The Bluest Eye*: "Here is the house. It is green and white. It has a red door."[11] By the end of the paragraph, the lines have disappeared and the words have collapsed into one another. And by the end of the book this same phrase is repeated but has lost even its capitalization and the reader is disoriented even further. *The Bluest Eye* is the story of a little girl, Pecola, who fantasizes about having blue eyes. She is the child of parents, and parent's parents, navigating and trying to survive the violent specters of white supremacy and anti-Blackness. In the end those streams ultimately flow into Pecola's life and the tragic and painful ways she tries to find some semblance of meaning. Morrison opens her narrative with a searing idea that "there is really nothing more to say—except why. But since why is difficult to handle, one must take refuge in how."[12] Morrison has given us the idea of language and race, and she made them both manifest in the character of Pecola, while also displaying the impossibility of this little girl's life and her neighbor's life being told truthfully with an essay.

While Barth's work does not take up this literary task completely, I think that, in his own way, he is stumbling toward it, and he is trying to voice theology in a new timbre. I think it could also be said that those of us who have experienced the underside of modernity's epistemological and colonial violence already inhabit what this theology looks like.

To be more explicit: Black bodies, like art, are the material convergence of colonial dissection. It was out of our bodies that colonizers sought to draw light from dark, flesh from spirit, and beauty from ugliness. The Black body is created by and placed in a world imagined through dichotomies. And yet, Black bodies contest dichotomization in the creative act of living, creating, and making visible our being in the midst of the assertion of our non-being. This contestation comes through the creative acts of singing, painting, playing, and speaking wholeness out of our supposed incompleteness.

The materiality or bodiliness of human existence is a theological phenomenon that shows, perhaps, that only art can help us to fathom if our theology is to be true. Perhaps even more, if theology is to be true, it might require the beauty of

---

10. Toni Morrison, *What Moves at the Margin: Selected Nonfiction* (Jackson: University of Mississippi Press, 2008), 142.
11. Toni Morrison, *The Bluest Eye* (New York: Plume, 1994), 1.
12. Ibid., 6.

the dark body that defiantly creates wholeness in the face of a world bent on the denial of its humanity. But even in this moment, art cannot become a panacea or an illustration that falls into yet another dichotomy of art versus theology. Rather, the artistic process ushers us, time and again, into the difficult truth of our bodied lives. We are both need and mystery. We need others, and we are saturated with mystery. And theology is a discovery of the possibilities of our lives together and ourselves.

This brings me, finally, to a more explicitly theological center of a literary theology. It is in Christ that we see the beautiful mystery of wholeness, of Word and materiality, of far and near, of knowing and unknowing. His body is the site which exposes the dichotomies that are knit into the world, and a life that displays to us what we have done to one another, what we have done to ourselves. At the same time, his body represents a wholeness and beauty that is both present and perpetually possible. Morrison and literatures of the margins understand something of this. They highlight the power of language. The conditions that generated the material life of Morrison are incarnations of language—fictions about bodies. And, if nothing else, christological reflection shows us that descriptions of Jesus are always also descriptions of the human condition. Narratives about who he is and what he saves are stories of what is off-balance, skewed, or evil in our midst. Correspondingly, the language we weave around these questions of who we are, of who Christ is, of what we might become are themselves political acts of world-making. Lifting out seemingly mundane acts—forms of community, dances, food, hashtags, shifting pronouns, reconfiguring names, or redeploying epithets—language and personhood are symbiotic. The Word becomes flesh and flesh becomes Word.

That is what is so important about *The Bluest Eye*. It discerns the place where the idea and the body meet, then traces that thread to where the idea shaped the body or the body resisted. What Morrison and other writers from the margins make visible is the illusion of the dichotomy, the notion that there could be an idea without a body or a body without an idea. A literary theology asks us to struggle with these possibilities in our theological writing, and in our vocations as people who write about who God is and what this world is.

A literary theology is not simply a creative theology or an artful theology. It is a liberative theology that asks us to see the world, to speak, and to write in ways that breaks apart hegemony, evokes silence, and destabilizes our notions of God, the self, and the world.

Conclusion

I want to close by returning to the image Barth returned to so often, which he encountered at the Isenheim Altar. For Barth, theology always points toward God. But I have also suggested that we are nonetheless in the picture, a part of the story, somehow bound to the One who is bound on the cross. And which God is John pointing to? I ask this, because when we open the altarpiece, we are again confronted with Christ. We see the hunched back of a Roman soldier stunned or humbled. We see the face of Christ transfigured, recognizable but obscured in glory and light. We see him hovering above death, skin healed of its sores, the wounds of subjection now pouring out Spirit, hope, the truth of what all wounds might become.

But where is John? Or Mary? Or Jesus' mother?

They are present in color. Christ is clothed in them, in their red, orange, and white; and we are with him, risen whole. To put this image in Barth's own words, "He does not will to be God without us" (CD IV/1: 7). Grünewald itself, then, points toward a liberation theology with images that disclose a God who identifies with our affliction, takes upon himself our isolation and pain, and offers himself (and us) up to God for restoration. In the risen Christ, we see the one healed, liberated from bondage, and the fullness of his identity revealed. We are with him and in him in this freedom.

As we begin to imagine the future of Barthian theology, I hope it is not simply Barth's ideas that we seek to explicate. Is it possible that the future of Barthian theology resides in a risk, the kind of risk that arises when the theologian becomes visible in his or her writing, as he or she unveils the limitations and contextuality of the words written, spoken, or taught? Is it possible that liberation is not possible as long as we stand apart, pointing toward? Is it possible that liberation comes only when we allow the presence of the resurrected one to draw us into a transfiguration of our person, where our words might be clothed in flesh?

> She heard a voice. So Mary stepped away from the fire and as the dirt fell dim she got the cool falling down. Like rain slipping off the branches, until the ground was black and the air was cool and damp. She heard it again, her name. But maybe not, she didn't really hear as much as felt the tone of her name, the way she hears her mother when she calls, never really registering her own name, but knowing who it was that called her before the sound ceased, she was already on her way.

> But her mother was not there that night. Mary. Now she prayed, she fell to her knees and ran her fingers through the dirt as she whispered, her breath coming quicker now. And she felt her robes cling to her side as her name became a song.

> Favored?

> Child?

> How can this be? What about days that came and went with the fruit of their work, filling other men's baskets? Even as she thought of the promises to Abraham and Sarah, that word mingled with the memory of soldiers marching, and swords and spears, and the bloodied bellies of her people on their tips.

> She heard her name and saw it tilted towards marriage and children and a decent man's wife. She sat, quiet, even as promise was already knitting into

muscle and bone, a word pulling and sowing, saying "I want you to teach me to pray, your life to be the one I follow with my eyes as the world becomes known to me. I want to feel the tremor of your voice when we walk among the throngs who hunger and thirst."

She sat just a bit longer, then began to whisper, "How can this be? To see my beginning and my end conceived within me?"

"Yes," she says, a bit more loudly now. Yes, as she sits up and steps back towards the fire, hemming in the holy of holies tightly behind the curtains of her robes.

Chapter 11

THELONIOUS MONK, ICON OF THE ESCHATON
KARL BARTH, JAMES CONE, AND THE "IMPOSSIBLE-POSSIBILITY" OF A THEOLOGY OF FREEDOM[1]

Raymond Carr

> Ring the bells that still can ring
> Forget your perfect offering
> There is a crack, a crack in everything
> That's how the light gets in
>
> —Leonard Cohen

The discipline of theology mirrors the relativity of human experience. It refracts truth from our various standpoints, leading some theological music, to paraphrase Karl Barth, to have a more or less pure sound.[2] And it is in this light, in view of this peculiar kind of relativity, brokenness, or ambiguity, that I invite the reader to contemplate the relationship between Karl Barth and liberation theology, the theme that runs throughout this book. Indeed, the title I am giving this chapter envisages a new kind of relationship between Barth, James Cone, and liberation theology. In view of Barth's audacious proposal that North American theologians develop a

---

1. This chapter was first prepared in public gratitude for the life, friendship, and theological contributions of James Hal Cone. What he contributed to my development as a theologian cannot be quantified. As mentioned to attendees at the Karl Barth Conference in 2018, I discovered Karl Barth in the stacks at Lubbock Christian University in 1995, and because of my biblical formation, I had a profound appreciation for his theology almost immediately. I was introduced to Cone's theology, however, about three years later and came to know the man personally. These two separate experiences sum up why I view Cone in light of the profound concrete nature of his theology and Barth more abstractly, although I believe Barth's theology is anything but abstract. Cone's embodiment nevertheless witnesses to something beyond the somewhat discursive presentation here. He encouraged me, not without critique, to go my own way theologically and expressed interest in my interpretation of Barth.

2. Karl Barth, *Letters, 1961–1968*, ed. Jürgen Fangmeier and Hinrich Stoevesandt, trans. Geoffrey W. Bromiley (Grand Rapids: Eerdmans, 1981), 105.

theology of freedom, I intend to use the music of the jazz great, Thelonious Sphere Monk, to explore the interconnections between Barth and Cone and to transpose their provocative insights into a new key.

Monk is known for rethinking the jazz tradition, embracing the legacy of African American music with his left hand but improvising in a way described as "completely 'free' with his right hand."[3] To invoke Monk with respect to liberation theology signals that I do not want simply to repristinate the paths blazed by Barth and Cone. Rather, I aim to tease out the continuities between them, while celebrating their differences and expanding the theological imagination through a constructive dialogue. I begin by explaining why I choose Monk as the iconic symbol or medium for a constructive conversation between Barth and Cone, highlighting Monk's celebration of tradition, Monk's individuation, and, most importantly, Monk's adoption of a holistic perspective that allowed him to transcend his differences with other bebop artists. This same holistic perspective, I go on to suggest, helps one to transcend the theological differences between Barth and Cone. Next, I sound a dissonant note in the chapter's bridge, which "brings problems" to Barth by analyzing his encounter with Charles H. Long, the historian of religions who questioned Barth during his visit to the United States in 1962. Finally, I close by deploying Monk's music to frame what I will coin as a *spiritual secular,* a variation on Barth's "secular parables" and Cone's "secular spirituals." This deployment enables me to articulate an eschatological vision of theology, animated by a pneumatological emphasis, that indicates how the discipline of theology can be musically informed.[4] Overall, I hope to develop a proposal wherein the disparate parts sound in relation to the whole, silences speak relative to sound, and sacred witnesses arise in the midst of the secular and profane. And I hope to show how this proposal points toward to God's freedom in the midst of human relativity—for that, I believe, is "how the light gets in."[5]

A final introductory note on the issue of freedom: in response to Barth's exhortations, there were several attempts to develop "theologies of freedom" in the context of the United States.[6] With this chapter, I am therefore contributing to what I perceive as an ongoing conversation, knowing that any reorientation

---

3. Laurent de Wilde, *Monk,* trans. Jonathan Dickinson (New York: Marlowe & Company, 1997), 20.

4. "Theomusicology," a term coined by Jon Michael Spencer, is apposite: it refers to "musicology as a theologically informed discipline" (see here Jon Michael Spencer, *Theological Music: Introduction to Theomusicology* [Westport: Greenwood Press, 1991], xi). But I am after something different: a musically informed theology.

5. Cohen, "Anthem," AZLyrics, accessed August 1, 2021; see www.azlyrics.com/lyrics/leonardcohen/anthem.html.

6. Three immediately come to mind: Charles H. Long, "The Black Reality: Toward a Theology of Freedom," which forms part of "Interpretations of Black Religion in America," in *Significations: Signs, Symbols, and Images in the Interpretation of Religion* (Aurora: The Davies Group, 1995), 145–53; Alexander McKelway, *The Freedom of God and Human*

of theological inquiry means first acknowledging, as Amos Wilder writes, that "God is doing a new thing in our time."[7] Indeed, an implication of this chapter is that human freedom, undertaken in correspondence to God, is often manifest in *resistance* to the possible inertia of our traditions—in a willingness to examine ourselves fully and audaciously to cross the threshold into a future that (re)imagines and realizes new possibilities with God. With courageous gestures of faith and ears attentive to the past, figures like Barth and Cone can (re)sound and help us to (re)assess and (re)cast our traditions, institutions, and conventions in light of the strange new world of the Bible—if only we have ears to hear. This need to hear things afresh in light of God's ongoing freedom to act ever anew in the present, in fact, explains why Monk's rethinking of the jazz tradition is so important for the field of Christian theology. Monk does not simply forget the past; always, "he was playing around with it, off it, and through it," demanding that other musicians, listeners, and critics come to terms with the legacy he embraces, even as he creates something new.[8]

Why Thelonious Monk?

The first question I am often asked in conversations about Monk, whose birth centenary was celebrated in 2017, is: "Why Thelonious Monk?" That is, what does theology have to do with Monk, and what does Monk have to do with theology? The question of how his music can prove itself an apt icon for thinking about the future of theology—and, more specifically, nourish an eschatological approach to a theology of freedom—is not typically on the minds of the questioners. Moreover, among jazz aficionados (and, for that matter, even those with a rudimentary knowledge of jazz), a follow-up question is: "Why not Bud Powell or John Coltrane, who gave the jazz world 'Love Supreme,' or even one of the other beboppers like Charlie Parker or Dizzy Gillespie?" Sometimes, questioners even go on to suggest that jazz itself may be passé, an artifact meant only for certain cultural elites today.

In response to such questions, I respond with several reasons (and will only note a few for the purposes of this chapter). First, to set the scene, I note that no musician's stylistics in the early bebop tradition are as distinctive as Monk's. He translates the styles of earlier artists, including blues, swing, and stride piano, into riffs and inversions borrowed from jazz greats such as James P. Johnson, Art Tatum, Fats Waller, Duke Ellington, Willy "The Lion" Smith, Mary-Lou Williams (who later was a champion of the new bebop music), and others. A key to understanding

---

Liberation (London: SCM, 1990); and, in the sphere of Christian ethics, William Stringfellow, *Free in Obedience* (New York: Seabury, 1964).

7. Amos Wilder, *Theopoetic: Theology and the Religious Imagination* (Philadelphia: Fortress, 1976), 55.

8. Stanley Crouch, *Considering Genius: Writings on Jazz* (New York: Basic Civitas, 2006), 88.

Monk, further, is to recognize that in the process of composing and improvising he constantly honored his own subjectivity when modifying received patterns—exactly what justifies thinking of him as an "icon of the eschaton."[9] Hugh Roberts describes this "individuation" in Monk as part of a spiritual journey that evinces the "immanence of God" in Monk's life and music. Monk's "subjective" feature, moreover, according to Billy Taylor (the dean of modern jazz), marks him as the quintessential jazz musician. And subjectivity or individuation as an act of self-expression may have something important to offer theological inquiry on the threshold of a "new arche" in the twenty-first century.

Second, I would argue that Monk's bebop (and perhaps even jazz in general) combines two tendencies in a way that commends a new theological paradigm: theology in the mode of Monk. Monk's composing provides an iconic *Aufhebung*, one that encompasses something of Barth's emphasis on the "objective" content of God's work in Christ and Cone's "subjective" articulation of Black experience through the spirituals and blues—"objectivity" naming a style of theology that fixates on the basic shape of God's self-revelation, "subjectivity" naming a style of theology that takes heed of the historical contexts, cultural systems, and struggles for justice that mark communities who receive and respond to God's self-revelation.[10] And this way of connecting Barth, Cone, and Monk opens the door to what Zora Neale Hurston called an "exchange and re-exchange of ideas among groups."[11] When Cone is interpreted in relation to Barth, one moves historically from European classical music to spirituals and blues legacies, and then onward to the modalities of jazz, a genre often designated as "African American classical music."[12] Monk as an icon, one might say, negotiates the tension between contextual "individuation" and the larger traditions that a theologian inhabits and masters.

The third and most important response to the question, "Why Monk?" brings me to Barth's distinctive interpretation of Mozart, and shifts reflection toward an wide-angled account of creation. In his inspired book on the eighteenth-century

---

9. I first came across this phrase in the concluding sentence of Hugh J. Roberts' brief discussion, "Improvisation, Individuation, and Immanence: Thelonius [sic] Monk," *Black Sacred Music* 3, no. 2 (1989): 50–6. Roberts conceives of Monk as an icon pointing to the "golden city of jazz."

10. According to Barth, "theological objectivity" is grounded in the incarnation; see Karl Barth, *Göttingen Dogmatics: Instruction in the Christian Religion*, vol. 1, ed. Hannelotte Reiffen, trans. Geoffrey W. Bromiley (Grand Rapids: Eerdmans, 1991), 192. For an insightful account of the motif of objectivism in Barth's theology, see George Hunsinger, *How to Read Karl Barth: The Shape of His Theology* (New York: Oxford University Press, 1991), 35–42.

11. Zora Neale Hurston, "Characteristics of Negro Expression," in *The Jazz Cadence of American Culture*, ed. Robert G. O'Meally (New York: Columbia University Press, 1998), 304.

12. See Lewis R. Gordon, *Her Majesty's Other Children: Sketches of Racism from a Neocolonial Age* (Lanham: Rowman & Littlefield, 1997), 215.

composer, Barth argues that Mozart composed in light of a strong center that opens out to a complex periphery, such that parts and whole relate in elaborate ways. He claimed to hear "an intuitive, childlike awareness of the essence or center—as also the beginning and end—of all things."[13] (Hans Urs von Balthasar, incidentally, advances a similar interpretation, stating that Mozart "had this whole sound in his ear to such an extent that, on occasion, he could write down the single instrumental line of an entire movement because he 'heard' it within the sym-phony of all the parts."[14]) This emphasis on a strong center echoes Barth's christological concentration, with Christ being the objective center around which revolves everything that exists in time and space. George Hunsinger puts it well: "by relating the periphery to the center . . . Barth claims to 'prove' or substantiate the dogma of creation. Jesus Christ is taken to be the known quantity and creation the unknown quantity."[15] The parts and the whole cohere, and in this coherence, indirectly witnessed throughout Mozart's music, there is also implied the analogy noted earlier: one that holds together the objective reality of God in the revelation of Christ and the subjectivity of the human being.

In his amplification of Calvin's catechism, for example, Barth puts it thus: "When we grasp each position simply within the movement of the whole, it can also be rightly remarked that we grasp the whole in each position (even as each note of a melody contains the entire melody)."[16] And this centering melody did more than enable Mozart to impose limits on the discord of life. It provided the latitude for him to be "at play"[17] amid this discord, such that Mozart could move through life with a "free objectivity" wherein "life served his art, not the other way around."[18] It is no wonder, too, that in hearing Mozart, Barth could hear a guiding keynote for his own life and theology and joyfully confront the political problems he faced.[19]

But let us turn back to Monk. Like Mozart, Monk approached music improvisationally from the vantage point of holistic shapes and designs, thereby ensuring that the discord of the periphery was honored, but never to such a degree that it overtook the principal melody (or melodies) in play.[20] Gunther Schuller

---

13. Karl Barth, *Wolfgang Amadeus Mozart*, trans. Clarence K. Pott (Eugene: Wipf & Stock, 2003), 16.

14. Hans Urs von Balthasar, *Symphony: Aspects of Christian Pluralism*, trans. Graham Harrison (San Francisco: Ignatius, 1987), 7–9.

15. Hunsinger, *How to Read Karl Barth*, 60.

16. Karl Barth, *The Faith of the Church: A Commentary on the Apostle's Creed According to Calvin's Catechism*, trans. Gabriel Vahanian (New York: Living Age Books, 1958), 57.

17. Barth, *Wolfgang Amadeus Mozart*, 33–5.

18. Ibid., 48–9.

19. Karl Barth, *Final Testimonies*, ed. Eberhard Busch, trans. Geoffrey W. Bromiley (Grand Rapids: Eerdmans, 1977), 24–5.

20. Nat Hentoff, *The Jazz Life* (New York: Dial Press, 1961), 183. For an extensive discussion of the way Monk based music on a centering melody, see my book *Theology in*

explains this approach as follows: "Where many pianists less original than Monk are exclusively concerned with playing the 'right' (or acceptable) notes, Monk, at his most inspired, thinks of *over-all* shapes and designs or ideas . . . and, because he is a man of great talent, or perhaps even genius, he does play the *right* notes, almost as a matter of course."[21] So rather than thinking of Monk as being determined by variations heard in rhythmic displacement, harmonic discordance, or melodic innovations, I prefer to think of Monk creating holistically within a framework that has its anchor in a strong center—that is, composing in view of a central melody, much in the same way that Barth thought of dogmatics as being anchored in the history of Jesus of Nazareth. And just as Monk could combine parts and whole in diverse ways, so Barth could toggle between and integrate different genres of theological reflection. One might say that Barth's "regular" theology is made up of "irregular" parts in much the same way that a strong center or centering melody provided Monk with the freedom to revel in the dissonances on the periphery.

Monk's way of composing also resembles James Cone's claims in *The Spirituals and the Blues*.[22] It is the history of Black Americans, which is itself the history of blues people, that orients Cone's work in this text. Throughout, Cone demonstrates concern with much more than mere identifications, categories, or ethnographic techniques aimed at retrieving critical memories. He is primarily concerned with Black religious experience and the world emerging from the cataclysm of the Middle Passage and the brutal enslavement of men, women, and children.[23] He describes the issue thus:

> Black history . . . is the stuff out of which the black spirituals were created. But the "stuff" of black history includes more than the bare historical facts of slavery. Black history is an experience, a soulful event. And to understand it is to know the being of a people who had to "feel their way along the course of American slavery," enduring the stresses and strains of human servitude but not without a song, *Black history is a spiritual!*[24]

As Cone elaborates elsewhere, his own work was not a matter of "a European theologian, not even Barth, control[ling] what I said about the gospel and the black struggle for freedom. It was the other way around. Jesus as defined by the black experience and the Bible decided how I used European theology."[25] This

---

the Mode of Monk: An Aesthetics of Barth and Cone on Revelation and Freedom (Eugene: Cascade, forthcoming).

21. See Hentoff, *The Jazz Life*, 183–4. Emphases in the original.

22. See James H. Cone, *The Spirituals and the Blues: An Interpretation* (Maryknoll: Orbis, 1972).

23. See Dwight N. Hopkins, *Down, Up, and Over: Slave Religion and Black Theology* (Minneapolis: Fortress, 2000).

24. Cone, *Spirituals and the Blues*, 31. Emphases in the original.

25. James H. Cone, *My Soul Looks Back* (Maryknoll: Orbis, 1986), 83.

accent on Christ, interpreted through the lens of Black experience and song, correlates with Barth's emphasis on the Word of God. But when routed through Cone's christological concentration, it is anchored in the fact that "Jesus Christ occupies the center of the gospel message in the black church": in sermons, songs, prayers, experiences, and testimonies that are the "stuff," the aesthetics, the aural vehicles that Black people employ to "tell the story," often amid a racist discord and racialized periphery. Jesus is so central for Blacks that "Jesusology," a troublesome term for Cone, was nevertheless the way the Black community referred to this important christological center, thus articulating and improvising on its own "subjectivity."[26]

Monk, I would argue, signifies stylistically upon the musical heritage of the Black church that was so central for Cone. Black spirituals and other tunes, including "This is my Story, This is my Song" (sometimes called "Blessed Assurance"), are expanded harmonically and rhythmically in his musical catalogue, and the dissonance in the songs echoes the dissonance of life as Monk encountered it. Indeed, thinking from Monk's vantage point, we witness one who is not at a distance from Cone's spirituals and blues, and we move toward what I am calling theology in the mode of Monk—a new variation on the expansive movement of Black liberation theology. "Blues is jazz and jazz is Blues," as an article from the early twentieth century noted.[27] And with these continuities between Monk, Barth, and Cone in mind, the third reason for choosing Monk as an interlocutor returns to view. Monk, as a parable of the kingdom, can be proposed as a mediating icon: one who captures the "objective" concern with God's eternity and constancy found in Barth's work *and* Cone's fascination with the "subjectivity" of diverse historical affirmations of Black faith, thereby providing us with a way to play in the space between Barth and Cone and forge a more comprehensive way forward.

Playing between the Theological Cracks

An example of how Monk allows one to mediate between and, in some sense, to *integrate* Barth and Cone is nicely clarified by Randy Weston, a brilliant pianist and interpreter of Monk's jazz. In *African Rhythms*, Weston mentions his friend Ahmed Abul Malik, a jazz bassist with exposure to African instruments, and he describes their common experience of searching for new ways to play music. They were seeking to innovate and eventually, through Malik's engagement with instruments such as the kanoon and the oud, they experimented with the idea

---

26. Ibid., 80–1. For more on Cone's christological norm, see also James H. Cone, *God of the Oppressed*, rev. edn (Maryknoll: Orbis, 1997), 116–26.

27. See Gordon Seagrove, "Blues Is Jazz And Jazz Is Blues," *Chicago Tribune* (July 11, 1915): 54.

of "trying to play the notes between the cracks."[28] Playing the notes between the cracks means playing the standard notes on the Western musical scale, while also playing between them, thereby expanding and enhancing that very scale. At some point, Weston and Malik discovered that Thelonious Monk was already playing in the new mode they were seeking. And the contribution of such musical thinking to theology is not inconsequential.

When hearing Monk as an anticipation of the kingdom, as well as a hermeneutical key for combining Barth and Cone, we arrive at the threshold of new theological possibilities. What would it mean to articulate a Christology, universal in scope, while expanding the concepts of theology in relation to the experiences of Black people in America? The all-too-common impasse between these sites of inquiry—Christian faith and Black religious experience—represents the heretical situation in the United States that Cone sought to correct.[29] Monk enables an additional step, with an emphasis on Barth's "objective" christological concentration, understood in terms of the more inclusive emphasis on revelation in the left-wing Barthian tradition,[30] paired with Cone's attention to the diverse concretizations of Black experience. His music can function, in fact, as something akin to a "parable of the kingdom." While honoring Barth's emphasis on the priority of revelation, allowance is made for myths, symbols, parables, or signs, all of which emerge within the Black religious tradition, to bear new witness to the light of Christ. Barth's phenomenon of the "little light" that witnesses, of course, is established *within* the parameters of faith; but once this occurs, *Monk* as a "little light" becomes a "true word" or icon for thought.

Because Monk is not a "saint" in the classical sense of the word, much less an icon in a religious sense, the selection of his music prevents us from thinking of the icon narrowly—as some kind of fixed, representative image. Moreover, given his way of "improvising on the melody," Monk suggests a way to think from the "inner material content" of faith in Christ, while allowing for improvisational choices between various additional voices ("saints" in religious terms). Monk becomes a way to think correlationally: thinking of various parts, sounds and silences, and

---

28. Randy Weston, *African Rhythms: The Autobiography of Randy Weston*, ed. Willard Jenkins (Durham: Duke University Press, 2010), 60.

29. James H. Cone, "Christian Faith and Political Praxis," in *The Challenge of Liberation Theology: A First World Response*, ed. Brian Mahan and L. Dale Richesin (Maryknoll: Orbis, 1981), 62.

30. Initiated by Friedrich-Wilhelm Marquardt's 1972 work on Barth and socialism, the tradition often identified as left-wing Barthianism or "the Berliner's Barth" has historically emphasized the sociopolitical dimensions of Barth's thought, his potential for supporting interreligious dialogue, an openness to religious pluralism, and radical inclusivity. See, inter alia, Friedrich-Wilhelm Marquardt, *Theologie und Sozialismus: Das Beispiel Karl Barths*, 3rd edn (Munich: Chr. Kaiser Verlag, 1985); *Karl Barth and Radical Politics*, ed. George Hunsinger, 2nd edn (Eugene: Cascade, 2017); and Paul S. Chung, *Karl Barth: God's Word in Action* (Eugene: Cascade, 2008).

voices in relation to the centered whole; thinking in light of subjectivity, that is, that which is the subjectively concrete in relation to the objectivity of the thing itself; thinking with the subject matter, *die Sache*, even as one celebrates various modes of being within the world.

Put differently: as a parable of the eschaton, Monk provides a new mode for the constructive theologian to engage tradition, understood in the broadest sense of the word. Through his mode of composing and improvising, the whole and the parts cohere and relate in novel and surprising ways, enabling a theological stylistics or hermeneutic that fires the imagination to reckon with the multidimensional nature of humankind (and, of course, of "otherkind": what Andrew Greeley calls the "otherness in everything," including mountains, oceans, lakes, rivers, and human productions).[31] One can hereby think *from the end*, not merely from the beginning, encompassing the diverse aesthetics and temporalities that participate in the polyphony of creation. Monk nudges us to imagine the reality of a new creation, a world whose multiplicities, in the words of Gerard Manley Hopkins, have become "charged with the grandeur of God."[32] He makes audible the *whole* of creation, with even the rhythmic displacements, dissonances, and silences of life related to the glory of the subject matter, the cantus firmus that resounds in freedom. And just as the cantus firmus does not simply "control" the harmonics of Monk's imaginative improvisations, so a theologian's apprehension of Christ allows for a widened imagination.

Free and imaginative ways of thinking are significant in the context of the United States. As Barth notes, North American Christianity has been "marked by the somewhat superficial reasoning of the Enlightenment movement," being more wedded to discursive modes and often lacking interest in imaginative thinking in terms of a nonreligious icons (or, again, what I want to call "spiritual seculars").[33] Barth, on the other hand, is also adamant that "we can and must be prepared to encounter 'parables of the kingdom' in the full biblical sense, not merely in the witness of the Bible and the various arrangements, works, and words of the Christian Church, but also in the secular sphere, i.e., in the strange interruption of the secularism of life in the world" (CD IV/3: 117). These strange interruptions can be heard in Barth's Mozart, in the plaintive blues of Cone's Black experience, *and* in the interstices heard in the soaring affirmations of life in the jazz modalities that I am championing.

31. Andrew M. Greeley, *Religion: A Secular Theory* (New York: The Free Press, 1982), 72. See also my essay, "Wade in the Water Children: Charles Long, Karl Barth, and the (Re)Imagination of Matter," *American Religion* 2, no. 2 (2021): 61–86.

32. Gerard Manley Hopkins, *Poems and Prose* (London: Penguin, 1953), 27.

33. See Karl Barth, "The 'Un-Mozartean' Swiss," in *Fragments Grave and Gay*, ed. Martin Rumscheidt, trans. Eric Mosbacher (London: Collins, 1971), 49.

Karl Barth and an American Theology of Freedom: A Bridge to Understanding America as a Hermeneutical Situation

To shorten the distance between Barth and Cone, however, is not possible without a slight detour—without a "bridge." For the same "strange interruptions" to which Barth draws attention in the secular sphere were in fact *not* engaged by Barth when he visited the United States in 1962. Barth's theological categories, intended to honor God's radical objectivity, supplanted his sensitivity to Black experience, perhaps because of his long interest in the white history of the United States. Put more fully: although Barth was typically wary of commenting on political situations in other nations, knowing that different problems require Christians to interpret situations in different ways,[34] he could not really avoid those problems as he encountered the "swarms of individuals of all lands, races, occupations, and endeavors" ongoing in this nation. America, he noted, was "fascinating" and possessed a "strange unity as well as contrast of humanity in the East, West, and South of the continent."[35] This continent, with all of its strange unity and contrasts, continuities and discontinuities, sounds and silences, and harmonies and dissonances, was where Barth encouraged theologians to develop a theology of freedom. An audacious proposal! But this continent was also where Barth failed to reckon with one of the most intractable challenges in world history: white supremacy. And perhaps nowhere is Barth's failure more on display than in his encounter with Charles H. Long, a history of religions scholar, who is sometimes described as the "bringer of problems."[36]

In a verbal exchange with Long, who collaborated academically with Mircea Eliade, Joseph Kittagawa, and Jonathan Smith, Barth was confronted with a question: "How do you like this *strange place* called the United States?" Barth noted in correspondence that the question was posed by a "literally black colleague"

---

34. Barth displays such wariness in his dialogue with a pastor in *How to Serve God in a Marxist Land*, ed. and trans. H. Clark, J. D. Smart, and T. Wieser (New York: Association Press, 1959). He wrote that "one would need to have spent all these years with you, to have experienced in one's own life the growing pressure under which you stand. One would need to have tried out personally the various possibilities of withstanding it, in order to avoid coming up with some kind of wisdom which, because of deficient knowledge of the facts, situations, and persons, might be totally irrelevant to your questions" (47).

35. Karl Barth, *Evangelical Theology: An Introduction*, trans. Grover Foley (Grand Rapids: Eerdmans, 1963), vi.

36. See Chris Cameron, "'Bringer of Problems': Charles H. Long and the Basic Question of Humanity," *Black Perspectives*, December 9, 2015: https://www.aaihs.org/bringer-of-problems-charles-h-long-and-the-basic-question-of-humanity/. Although I will limit my comments here to Barth's immediate encounter with Long, I offer a longer discussion of Barth's fascination with the "Lost Cause" in "Wade in the Water Children."

and that he answered cautiously.³⁷ Even after returning to Basel, Barth refused to publish his "American impressions in articles, lectures, etc.," limiting himself to conversations about those impressions in the Basel prison.³⁸ Nevertheless, in his description of Long as a "literally black colleague," he inadvertently placed his finger directly on the site of "strangeness," as Long understood it. The Black experience was in fact the basic reason Long described the United States as "a hermeneutical situation."³⁹ But when coming to the United States, Barth's emphasis on God's objective self-involvement in Jesus Christ and his subsequent criticisms of the relationship between Christianity and religion served, by and large, to trivialize Black experience and to thwart the possibility of discerning any continuity between his own interest in "secular parables" and Cone's identification of "secular spirituals." This speaks to what Cone himself identified as a weakness in Barth's theology: a reluctance to "set forth the political and social implications of the divine-human encounter with sufficient clarity."⁴⁰ And, in an North American context, this reluctance played into "the heresy of substituting faith for action."⁴¹ It is worth asking, too, if this reluctance marks a basic shortcoming of Barth's own theology, or instead a failure of those who sought to promote Barth's "revelational objectivism" in the United States.⁴²

At any rate, Long's work problematizes the tendency to oppose dogmatic *categories* and human *experiences*—a tendency that serves often to hold the experience of Black life at a distance from theological inquiry. A primary concern is the interpretation of Black cultural symbols and religious ways of being, often rendered invisible or subservient to systematic conventions. Indeed, if Barth's emphasis on revelation functions primarily as a way to distinguish God's Word from worldviews (*Weltanschauungen*), religions, politics, and signs (including any natural phenomena interpreted as a sign of faith), a lack of attention to the context in which theological inquiry is undertaken, as well as an overemphasis on established conventions, can actually serve to narrow the theological imagination.⁴³

---

37. Barth writes, "Yesterday a black professor asked me: *Which is your impression of that strange place, called the United States?* I gave a very restrained answer both to him and to others who put the same question—yes, the blacks too." See Barth, *Letters*, 44 (asterisks in original).

38. Ibid., 49.

39. Long, "The Black Reality," in *Significations*, 153.

40. Cone, *God of the Oppressed*, 133.

41. Cone, "Christian Faith and Political Praxis," 61.

42. Hunsinger writes on the general and particular aspects of "revelational objectivism" in *How to Read Karl Barth*, 76–92.

43. See Barth's terse statements in response to Ben Marais's questions in *Colour: Unsolved Problem of the West* (Cape Town: Howard Timmins, 1952), 300–19. Also, note Barth's sharp criticism of Georges Casalis who, in Barth's estimation, was teaching Cameroonian scholars "a theory according to which the fact of religions is a sign to faith that man is made for fellowship with God" (Barth, *Letters*, 119). What is clear and unsurprising in Barth's

Dogmatic categories and human experiences begin to function as polar opposites, with the result that new political and religious possibilities, particularly the polyphony of meanings in signs, symbols, secular parables, or secular spirituals, remain unconsidered.

Although Long does not respond directly to Barth's theological program, Long always attends to concrete, contextual realities and endeavors to avoid harmonizing or synthesizing differences.[44] There is a constant concern to expand the scope of reflection, particularly as it relates to symbolic, religious experience. And what Long brings into view with respect to the differences between Barth and Cone, specifically in his declaration of America as a hermeneutical situation, he defines as a tertium quid or third way: a hermeneutical orientation that attends to what is often overlooked.[45] Central here is the awareness that Black bodies were consistently the site of the ideologies that justified enslavement according to a logic of transactionality.[46] And Christian theology, at least as it has emerged in the West, has consistently failed to take Black embodiment into account. It has simultaneously "fixed" the location of Black people and obscured Black modes of being. This problem led Long to describe Black theologies and Native American theologies (and empirical "Others") as "theologies opaque."[47]

Just as Long challenges scholars to reckon seriously with Black modes of being, so Monk's way of composing proves generative for theological reflection. His penchant for expanding the normal Western scale and playing notes "between the cracks" models a mode of thinking in which theologians uphold, but nonetheless work in between, Barth's "objective" conceptuality and Cone's "subjective" emphasis on Black experience.[48] There emerges a way of reimagining the continuities

---

answers to South African questions on race is his implicit dependence to his own situation, that is, his background in Switzerland and Germany.

44. Of course, Barth himself believed in "speaking by way of juxtaposition." For an excellent summary of Barth's recognition of "antithetical modes of thought . . . built into church doctrines," which can be interpreted as a hermeneutical strategy, see George Hunsinger, "The Wit and Wisdom of Karl Barth," in *Conversational Theology: Essays on Ecumenical, Postliberal and Political Themes, with Special Reference to Karl Barth* (London: T&T Clark, 2015), 3–18 (quotation from 11). What I am writing about here, however, has to do with a dialecticism that extends to the *concrete* life of Black Americans—something that Barth did not engage.

45. In conversation, Long often used this term to refer to an irreducible framework within his mode of thinking. Monk as a medium would be an aural analog of revelation that prevents a kind of irreducibility to church, doctrine, and various religious symbols—something akin to Barth's view of words spoken *extra muros ecclesia*.

46. Long, *Significations*, 211.

47. Ibid., 204–8.

48. Concepts for Barth, of course, do not capture the essence of revelation. Marquardt demonstrates awareness of this problem, noting that the ultimate concept of theology, the concept of God, is framed "not as a positive, technical definition, but as the intellectual

and discontinuities between Barth and Cone that echoes the concerns of Black scholars of religion who, on one hand, have often reprised Long's complaints about theological categories, and Black theologians, on the other hand, who question the categories Cone supposedly adopted, "drawn ready-made from Barth."[49] While the way Cone appropriates Barth's categories certainly merits debate, God-talk in "the mode of Monk" represents a form of continuity with Barth's way of theologizing. It enables the voicing of a counterpoint, a welcome corrective and expansion of Barth's project: one that ensures that enduring violations of human rights are not ignored, trivialized, or exploited; one that ensures that the meanings secreted in the material aspects of Black experience are not obscured, but cherished as nonbiblical witnesses to revelation—even as "secular parables" (CD IV/3: 115–17).[50] Perhaps Barth was wise to speak of America only to individuals in the Basel prison after his return. But the exchange between Long and Barth nevertheless reveals a primary reason why Cone, Long, and Barth, when reinterpreted together, may contribute to a twenty-first-century theology of freedom that expands the harmonics of our religious self-understanding.

Thelonious Monk and "Spiritual Seculars"

If uncritically adopted in the United States, the weakness in Barth's theology is an unwillingness, or at the least a marked reluctance, to proffer a true word in face of white supremacism. So while we may argue Barth exercises humility or "sensitivity to danger" in relation to revelation and the larger Christian tradition, his cautious tone fails to honor the meaning of Black religious experiences and expressions in *this* context.[51] Am I expecting too much of Barth here? I would say not. James Noel's assessment of European theology applies to any theologian whose understanding of religion "fails to do justice to the depth, diversity, complexity and richness of the actuality of black religion." And Noel is right to argue that it matters little whether the theologian is Black or white, given that the problem resides in

---

ground of open-ended experience, a ground that opens up new experience. In his concept of God, Barth did not abandon the dialectic between theory and praxis—he explicated it." See Hunsinger, ed., *Karl Barth and Radical Politics*, 40–1.

49. J. Deotis Roberts, Sr., *A Black Political Theology* (Louisville: WJKP, 1974), 20. Roberts sharply and persistently criticized James Cone for his adoption of Barth's christocentric, "metaphysical" viewpoint.

50. See Long's reflections which address what he described as one-hundred-year cycles where he links the nation's founding to the Civil War and Civil Rights Movement in *Significations*, 165.

51. See Eberhard Busch, "Deciding Moments in the Life and Work of Karl Barth," *Grail* 2, no. 4 (1986): 55.

the very categories that render Blacks "empirical others."[52] The bottom line is this: Black subjectivity and self-understanding is absent from Barth's theological vision. So there is no challenge to the way that African American and other colonized and enslaved people are configured in the Western *epistēmē*, formed as it is through missionary discourse and the new human sciences promoted by the Enlightenment and Romantic thinkers.[53] Black people remain victimized by the trope of the "civilized" or the "objective"; they are defined as racialized "others."

The problem of uncritically adopting Barth for the American situation becomes more acute as we return to Barth's description of Mozart. Barth describes Mozart's music as "unburdened, effortless, and light," moving "freely within the musical laws"—a description that discloses something of Barth's relationship to orthodoxy and the tenor of his "theo-anthopology," at least when the term is properly understood.[54] Read as a secular parable, Mozart reflects the objectivity of God like a mirror and echoes the beauty of God's "yes" to creation. Barth revels in this "free Mozartean 'objectivity,'" sometimes becoming quite rhapsodical:

> With God, the world, himself, heaven and earth, life—and, above all, death—ever present before his eyes, in his hearing, and in his heart he was a profoundly unproblematical and thus a free man: a freedom, so it seems, *given* to him—indeed *commanded* and therefore exemplary for him. . . . This implies that to an extraordinary degree his music is free of all exaggeration, of all sharp breaks and contradictions. The sun shines but does not blind, does not burn or consume. Heaven arches over the earth, but it does not weigh it down, it does not crush or devour it. Hence earth remains earth and does not need to maintain itself in a titanic revolt against heaven.[55]

Mozart, according to Barth, transcends Bach's religion, Beethoven's confessions, and in fact all other composers.[56] But his rhapsodical assessment lacks anything akin to the plaintive laments, courageous acts of self-affirmation, and emphases of a will to freedom that Cone found in the spirituals and blues.[57] According to Barth, one might even say that Mozart is not actually trying to communicate anything

---

52. James A. Noel, "Charles H. Long Tribute" (paper read at the American Academy of Religion annual meeting held in San Diego, 2015).

53. Long uses the term *epistēmē* to refer to an organized body of knowledge that functions as a normative mode of interpretation for American religio-cultural psychic reality while, correlatively, repressing and concealing the reality of minoritized others. See Charles Long, "A New Look at American Religion," *Anglican Theological Review* 1 (1973): 124.

54. Barth, *Evangelical Theology*, 12.

55. Barth, *Mozart,* 51 and 53. Emphases in the original.

56. Ibid., 37.

57. For an account that addresses black affirmation through song, see Jon Michael Spencer, *Protest and Praise: Sacred Music of Black Religion* (Minneapolis: Fortress, 1990).

of his own time and space, never mind his own life. What Barth finds here is a reflection of God's objective reality; and while this reflection allows Barth to live in the midst of the polyphony of life with a joy that transcends suffering, it seems exclusive of anything akin to the Black experience in the United States. And while an account of the objectivity of God, echoed in Mozart's compositions, may have constituted a strength in a European context, wearied and traumatized by war, this strength becomes a weakness in the United States, obscuring the importance of a wide variety of human and nonhuman responses to God—lamentful, protesting, and playful in their free and obedient responses to God's commands.[58]

So while Mozart can be heard as a "secular parable," an uncritical adoption of Barth's aesthetics at this juncture is risky in the United States. His silence with respect to Black life compounds the problem. And one way to correct this problem in Barth's theological "music" is to engage in an audacious countermovement, discerning and describing "secular parables" in a manner akin to Cone's extraordinary use of the blues as "secular spirituals." At exactly this point, Cone's theology provides a powerful counterpoint: it attends to the "stuff" of Black religion, especially the spirituals, blues, and other folk narratives, and it prepares the way for the deeper development of Black subjectivity before God. Most valuably, Cone is wholly unapologetic about his connection to Black people, arguing with Aunt Molly Jackson that "the blues are made by working people . . . when they have a lot of problems to solve about their work, when their wages are low and they don't have no way to exist hardly and they don't know which way to turn and what to do."[59] And this same feeling, according to Cone, is expressed by Blind Lemon Jefferson in song:

> I stood on the corner, and I almost bust my head,
> I stood on the corner, almost bust my head,
> I couldn't earn me enough money to buy me a loaf of bread.[60]

Blues, as "secular spirituals," represent an existential encounter with the trials of life, modulated into the melody and rhythm of song.[61] There arises the possibility of a Black theological aesthetic: one that discerns "true words," "extraordinary witnesses," and "free communications" that receive Black experience as a "lesser light," kindled by Christ as the "light of the world." To draw now on Barth:

---

58. Here I am reminded of Raymond Anderson's recounting of Barth's "Word-Study for Americans," in which terms like "commandment" and "obedience" are colored by the German verb, *gehorchen*, a term that escapes mechanistic notions of duty-bound subservience and highlights a kind of spontaneous response to grace. See Raymond K. Anderson, *An American Scholar Recalls Karl Barth's Golden Years as a Teacher (1958–1964): The Mature Theologian* (Lewiston: Edwin Mellen Press, 2013), 109–14.
59. Cone, *Spirituals and Blues*, 103–4.
60. Ibid., 104.
61. Ibid.

No Prometheanism can be effectively maintained against Jesus Christ. As the One who suffered and conquered on the cross, He has destroyed it once and for all and in all its forms. But this means that in the world reconciled by God in Jesus Christ there is *no secular sphere* abandoned by Him or withdrawn from His control, even where from the human standpoint it seems to approximate most dangerously to the pure and absolute form of utter godlessness. If we say that there is, we are not thinking and speaking in light of the resurrection of Jesus Christ. But if we refrain from this inflexible attitude, we will certainly be prepared at any time for *true words* even from what seem to *be the darkest places*. (CD IV/3: 119; emphasis added)

Keeping both Barth's "objectivity" and Cone's "subjectivity" in mind, I would argue that Cone and Barth should be heard as expressing an "organismic" or "harmonious" relationship. Both theologians bear witness to the words of the living God, but from different vantage-points.[62] Further, I would argue that what we should hear in terms of the theological aesthetics I am proposing is not only a teaching of "lights," but rather a *Melodielehre*—a doctrine or teaching of melodies. Using Monk as a hermeneutical criterion, and with a little effort to bend our ear, a doctrine of melodies can ring in the spirituals, in the harmonies of liberty of the Black National Anthem, and, to my mind most tellingly, in the harmonic dissonances of Monk's jazz. "There is no secular sphere abandoned" by Christ, and Black dissonance can mean more than sounding brass and tinkling symbols. If like a jazz artist we "stretch the form" and hear Barth and Cone together, the surplus between category and experience can be grasped and explored, and silences, shadows, and ambient sounds can be included in our apprehension of the flourishing of creation. Those who would hear Monk's *Melodie*, of course, will have to cultivate ears attuned to the acoustics of the darkness—an acoustic that reaches *beyond* Mozart. But in so doing they may hear an icon of the eschaton.

To hear the music of Thelonious Monk as a "spiritual secular," we have to be open to the fact that the Spirit of Christ blows where it wills. This openness requires attending to the ambiguities in our experiences—or, as Adrio König, the systematic theologian and Bushveld farmer insists, acknowledging that theological thinking *follows* rather than leads.[63] I would only add that such

---

62. I derive the language of organismic or harmonious thinking from Max Kadushin, a purveyor of rabbinic thought, who argues that organic thinking transcends "strict logical consistency." See Rabbi Max Kadushin, *The Theology of Seder Eliahu: A Study in Organic Thinking* (New York: Bloch Publishing Co., 1932), 24–9; and Peter Ochs, *Understanding the Rabbinic Mind: Essays on the Hermeneutic of Max Kadushin* (Atlanta: Scholars Press, 1990), 27–31.

63. The full quotation: "it is a mistake to lay down as a condition, as is sometimes done, that the church must first attain theoretical clarity about the many problems.... Theological reflection is essentially a follower, not a leader." See Adrio König, *Here Am I! A Christian Reflection on God* (Grand Rapids: Eerdmans, 1982), 53.

thinking does not only entail following God (Barth's *nachdenken*) but also involves following human experience, coming to terms with our transactions, exchanges, relativities, and ambiguities. It is in the pairing of God's revelation in Christ and the materiality of Black experience in America that possibilities emerge, and that theologians do well to acknowledge.

Conclusion

Theology in the mode of Monk does not represent a danger to Barth's way of theologizing; it represents a needed corrective of Barth's thought to the North American context. And because Monk signifies a turn, a joyful turn, in and beyond the bebop tradition, it does not represent a danger to Cone's way of theologizing either. We can joyfully engage in solidarity with Barth and Cone through the musical witness of Monk.

Embracing Monk as an icon of the eschaton means reveling in the surplus of meaning that transcends the false binary of "objective" (systematic) theology and "subjective" (contextual) theology. It becomes possible to honor both the freedom of God *and* the spontaneous human responses to God located within the cultural matrix of the United States. To be sure, Monk's music, with all of its silences, spaces, and brilliant corners, provides no finalized vision. It does not commend a religious piety that celebrates moral achievement; it does not romanticize a communal ethics or politics in which human persons achieve the kingdom through the enactment of the social gospel; it does not idealize doctrinal purity. Such outcomes would limit the universal scope of the gospel, reducing the polyphony of the speech of God "to the narrower and smaller sphere of the Bible and the Church" (CD IV/3: 117). Theology in the mode of Monk, instead, affirms a "coming of age," a realistic and playful self-awareness. It bespeaks what Jon Michael Spencer calls a "rhythmic confidence," evidenced in the willingness to improvise in the midst of established—and sometimes restrictive—categories and conventions.[64] It looks toward a time in which a white aesthetic regime is no longer determinative for all peoples and their creative products—a time in which Monk is embraced as an icon of the eschaton.

---

64. Jon Michael Spencer, *The Rhythms of Black Folk: Race, Religion, and Pan-Africanism* (Trenton: Africa World Press, 1995).

Chapter 12

TURNING BARTH RIGHT-SIDE-UP

JAMES CONE AND THE RISK OF A CONTEXTUAL THEOLOGY OF REVELATION

Tyler B. Davis and Ry O. Siggelkow

Characterizing his rebellion against the North American and European theological establishment in *My Soul Looks Back*, James Cone comments on his relationship to Karl Barth:

> As Barth had turned liberal theology up-side-down, I wanted to turn him right-side-up with a focus on the black struggle in particular and oppressed people generally. No longer would I allow an appeal to divine revelation to camouflage God's identification with the fight for justice. I was not angry with Barth but only with European and North American Barthians who used him to justify doing nothing about about the struggle for justice. I have always thought that Barth was closer to me than to them.[1]

The image of Cone turning Barth "right-side-up" recalls Karl Marx's efforts to invert dialectical thought, turning right-side-up that which G. W. F. Hegel had stood on its head to the glorification of the existing order.[2] Far from a passing reference, Cone's use of this image is key to understanding his contextual theology of divine revelation. Just as Marx aimed to demystify dialectics by wresting it from idealism and returning it to the earth, so Cone aimed to turn Barth "right-side-up" by challenging the way Barthian theologians had mystified divine revelation by stranding it in the heavens and ignoring the essential meaning of revelation as good news for the crucified people of the earth.

Seeking to appreciate the significance of this intervention, this chapter identifies and tracks Cone's efforts to demystify revelation by construing the

---

1. James H. Cone, *My Soul Looks Back* (Maryknoll: Orbis, 1986), 45.
2. See the afterword to the second edition of the first volume of *Capital*, where Marx writes: "With [Hegel], [dialectical thought] is standing on its head. It must be inverted, in order to discover the rational kernel within the mystical shell." See Karl Marx, *Capital: A Critique of Political Economy*, trans. Ben Fowkes, vol. 1 (New York: Penguin, 1976), 103.

critique of natural theology in terms of a risk of faith that demands "doing something" in the struggle for justice. While Cone's relationship to Barth is central to the concerns of this chapter, our interest is not to enter into conversations concerning the extent or limits of Barth's influence.[3] Moving beyond the question of influence, our interest is to elaborate Cone's articulation of a contextual theology of revelation—indeed, it is this theological vision which makes sense of Cone's conviction that Barth was closer to himself than to European and North American Barthians.

To this end, the chapter proceeds by highlighting four "conjunctural" moments in Cone's articulation of a contextual theology of divine revelation.[4] The first conjuncture is Cone's deep engagement with Barth's theology in his dissertation, specifically with the "Copernican Revolution" of the critique of natural theology, an insight which resonated with theological traditions Cone received from the Black church. Second, the chapter attends to how the 1967 Detroit uprising, an event which struck Cone as "a sudden bolt from the blue," led to the radical concretization of the problem of natural theology in Cone's account of Black liberation theology.[5]

The significance of this concretization, which amounts to a reimagining of the work of theology, has been largely overlooked in contemporary scholarship. In an effort to understand why, we turn to a third conjuncture in which Cone's theology was met by strong criticisms from otherwise sympathetic "left-wing" Barthians. Reconstructing these criticisms brings into focus how accounts of divine revelation in modern and contemporary theology have been structured in a way to avoid the risks which accompany the concrete discernment of divine revelation. Finally, we turn to *The Cross and the Lynching Tree* as a deepening of Cone's commitment to reimagine of the work of theology in terms of the context-specific discernment of Jesus Christ's presence and activity in the world—a call to prophetic struggle against unjust orders and to the action of building a new heaven and earth.

Karl Barth's "Copernican Revolution": The Critique of Natural Theology

Trained in modern European theological and philosophical traditions during graduate school, James Cone was particularly shaped by his study of the theology

---

3. For an in-depth study on this question, see Raymond Carr, "Barth and Cone in Dialogue on Revelation and Freedom: An Analysis of James Cone's Critical Appropriation of 'Barthian' Theology" (PhD diss., Graduate Theological Union, 2011).

4. Following Stuart Hall, the "conjunctural" indicates the necessity of analytic intervention into complex transitions within specific configurations of power. Such analysis requires a methodology oriented by a radical contextualism. See especially Les Back and Stuart Hall, "At Home and Not at Home: Stuart Hall in Conversation with Les Back," in *Essential Essays*, vol. 2, *Identity and Diaspora*, ed. David Morley (Durham: Duke University Press, 2019), 263–300.

5. James H. Cone, *Said I Wasn't Gonna Tell Nobody* (Maryknoll: Orbis, 2018), 9.

of Karl Barth. The appeal of Barth's theology was the doctrine of revelation, formulated in *Church Dogmatics* I/1 as the threefold Word of God: the Word of God revealed in Jesus Christ, the Word of God as witnessed to in scripture, and the Word of God proclaimed in preaching (see CD I/1: 120–1).[6] Cone saw in Barth's treatment of revelation striking resonances with his experiences growing up in the Macedonia AME church in Bearden, Arkansas. Jesus Christ as "the one to whom the people turn in times of trouble and distress, because they believe that he can heal their wounded hearts and broken spirits," occupied the beating heart of Black preaching, song, prayer, and testimony.[7] And the Bible, the first text that most enslaved people learned to read, had endured throughout many generations as the "good Book," being the primary source for knowledge about God and Jesus and a guide for how to live.[8]

The central contention of Cone's 1965 dissertation, "The Doctrine of Man in the Theology of Karl Barth," is that Barth's theology marked a "Copernican Revolution" in twentieth-century Protestant Christianity comparable to that effected by Martin Luther in the sixteenth century.[9] As Cone puts it, "Just as Luther was once a monk in a monastery, trying to make himself worthy before God, Barth was once a liberal who was endeavoring to establish the Kingdom of God on earth."[10] For Cone, the driving question for both Luther and Barth centered on the relationship between God and humanity, and whether divine revelation and divine agency would play the determining role in that relationship—or whether God would play "second fiddle" to humanity. A critical issue in this question was the place of natural theology in theological reflection. While the focus of Cone's dissertation is on the doctrine of the human person as it is systematically articulated in *Church Dogmatics* III/2, Cone's interpretation is consistently guided by a concern to determine humanity's capacity not only to *know* God, but to *relate* to God on the grounds of that which is "given." Cone argues that Barth's polemic against natural theology is "an integral part of his whole theological position."[11] The critique of natural theology, which Cone traces primarily to the influence of Kierkegaard's

---

6. Cone, *My Soul Looks Back*, 80–2.
7. Ibid., 80–1.
8. Ibid., 81. It is important to recognize that Cone's study of Barth's thought was not simply the outcome of unconstrained intellectual exploration. His early focus on Barth reflected the European preoccupations of the North American theological academy. His command of Barth's theology also functioned as a "mask," helping Cone gain academic legitimacy and navigate a system of higher education defined by the protocols of white supremacy. On the "masks" Cone was forced to wear growing up in the Jim Crow South and studying at Garrett-Evangelical Theological Seminary and Northwestern University, see Cone, *Said I Wasn't Gonna Tell Nobody*, 1–30.
9. James H. Cone, "The Doctrine of Man in the Theology of Karl Barth," (PhD diss., Northwestern University, 1965), 1.
10. Ibid.
11. Ibid., 8.

insistence on maintaining an "infinite qualitative distinction" between God and humanity, thus shapes Barth's entire theological project.

Given its importance in midcentury theological discussions, the debate between Barth and Emil Brunner provides Cone with the occasion to analyze Barth's polemic against natural theology.[12] Against Brunner, Barth famously maintained that human beings have neither the capacity nor any naturally given "point of contact" (*Anknüpfungspunkt*) to relate to God or to receive the gospel. Humanity is in fundamental rebellion against God, and this rebellion is not merely a problem of the individual but "affects the whole cosmos."[13] Cone reads Barth as affirming that it is only through divine revelation that humanity is given to hear and heed the truth of the gospel. Barth was thus, according to Cone, misunderstood by early interpreters as a "theologian of pessimism." Rather, for Barth, it is God's grace, not humanity's sin, that stands at the center of theological reflection. "There is no fundamental distinction," Cone notes, "between [Barth's] *Epistle to the Romans* and his later writings." Any modifications that Barth makes in his later work do not stand in contradiction to this "one *central* theme" that "controls the development of his theological outlook."[14] Cone does not believe, in other words, that Barth turns from dialectical or crisis theology to "analogical thinking" in his development of a theological anthropology.[15] Instead, Barth's resounding "Nein!" to Brunner and his provocative denunciation of the *analogia entis* as "the invention of the anti-Christ" remain the touchstone of Barth's entire theological framework.[16] Cone's

---

12. See the famous exchange in Karl Barth and Emil Brunner, *Natural Theology: Comprising "Nature and Grace" by Professor Dr. Emil Brunner and the reply "No!" by Dr. Karl Barth*, trans. Peter Fraenkel (Eugene: Wipf & Stock, 2002).

13. Cone, "The Doctrine of Man in the Theology of Karl Barth," 13.

14. Ibid., 20.

15. Contra Hans Urs von Balthasar, *The Theology of Karl Barth*, trans. Edward T. Oakes (San Francisco: Ignatius, 1992 [1951]) and anticipating Bruce McCormack's critique by twenty-five years. See Bruce L. McCormack, *Karl Barth's Critically Realistic Dialectical Theology: Its Genesis and Development 1909–1936* (New York: Oxford, 1995).

16. For Barth's famous comments on the *analogia entis*, see CD I/1: xiii. There is, of course, an enormous amount of literature on the subject of Barth's critique of the *analogia entis*, most of which centers on the relationship between Barth's theology and Roman Catholicism. The debate between Barth and Erich Przywara between 1929 and 1932 led to what one recent Roman Catholic interpreter identified as "the single most important ecumenical controversy of the twentieth century" (See Thomas Joseph White, "The *Analogia Entis* Controversy and Its Contemporary Significance," in *The Analogy of Being: Invention of the Anti-Christ or the Wisdom of God?* ed. Thomas Joseph White [Grand Rapids: Eerdmans, 2011], 1). It is worth noting that Cone does not view the significance of Barth's critique of the *analogia entis* as a matter of distinguishing Protestant theology from Catholic theology. The problem of the *analogia entis* is, rather, a matter of the need to distinguish Christ from antichrist in a concrete and historically specific context. In other words, the distinction

dissertation thus homed in on the epistemological and doctrinal significance of Barth's critique of natural theology.

"A Sudden Bolt from the Blue": The Apocalypse of the Detroit Rebellion

Things changed during Cone's time as a professor at Adrian College in Michigan. In late July 1967, the Detroit Rebellion erupted. Precipitated by a police raid on a "blind pig" (an after-hours bar) in the commercial center of one of the largest Black neighborhoods on Twelfth Street in Detroit, the Black rebellion was a massive uprising emerging in opposition to the postwar racial nomos that naturalized police repression, racist discrimination, and structural impoverishment.[17] Alongside Newark, the Detroit Rebellion accounted for the largest uprising during the tumultuous summer of 1967.[18] When the smoke cleared after five days of upheaval, thousands of people had been injured, over 7,200 people had been arrested, and hundreds of buildings had been destroyed. Forty-three people died during the rebellion, the majority of whom were Black residents and protesters killed by the police or members of the National Guard and the army.[19]

An editorial in *The Washington Post* expressed a dominant narrative of the Rebellion as a tragedy, perhaps "the greatest tragedy" in the history of Black "outbursts."[20] Cone, on the other hand, saw something beyond tragedy in the Black uprising. Inspired by Black protesters who painted the face of a white statue of Jesus black on the campus of Sacred Heart Major Seminary—a creative iconoclasm that

---

between Christ and antichrist is not a matter of ecclesiastical allegiance, but ingredient to the theological task as a "worldly risk" of discerning who God is and what opposes God.

17. We borrow the language of racial nomos for this explication from Paul Gilroy. For one elaboration among many, see Gilroy's symposium response to Robert J. Sampson; "A Response," *The British Journal of Sociology* 60, no. 1 (2009): 33–8.

18. For a recent study chronicling in detail the real scope of Black uprisings from the late 1960s through the early 1970s, see Elizabeth Hinton, *America on Fire: The Untold History of Police Violence and Black Rebellion Since the 1960s* (New York: Liveright, 2021). Following Cone and Hinton, we characterize Detroit as a "rebellion" rather than a "riot" to indicate that Detroit, like other uprisings of the era, "did not represent a wave of criminality, but a sustained insurgency" of people struggling "against a broader system that had entrenched unequal conditions and anti-Black violence over generations" (Hinton, *America on Fire*, 7).

19. *Report of the National Advisory Commission on Civil Disorders* (Washington, DC: U.S. Government Printing Office, 1968), 60–1; Thomas J. Sugrue, *The Origins of the Urban Crisis: Race and Inequality in Postwar Detroit* (Princeton: Princeton University Press, 2005), 259–61; Hinton, *America on Fire*, 4. See also Hubert G. Locke, *The Detroit Riot of 1967* (Detroit: Wayne State University Press, 2017) and Sidney Fine, *Violence in the Model City: The Cavanaugh Administration, Race Relations, and the Detroit Riot of 1967* (East Lansing: Michigan State University Press, 2007).

20. As quoted in Fine, *Violence in the Model City*, 1.

literally realized James Baldwin's call to give Christ a new face after the bombing of the 16th Street Baptist Church in Birmingham, Alabama—Cone described Detroit as an apocalypse, a decisive and revelatory event.[21] "Detroit exploded and so did I," he wrote. It "was like a revelation, a sudden bolt from the blue, a fire burning inside me."[22]

Catalyzed by the apocalypse of Detroit, Cone realized that he could no longer teach and write theology the same way but had to speak concretely of the gospel of freedom as he witnessed it in the people's uprising.[23] Cone sought "a *new* way of talking about God that was accountable to black people and their fight for justice."[24] Thus, while the US government was developing policy in response to the Kerner Commission's report on the urban crises of the late 1960s, much of which reproduced conditions for predatory exploitation,[25] Cone was developing new language for what would become a planetary theology of freedom attentive to the concrete dynamics of divine revelation.

Sensitive to early criticisms of his work,[26] Cone also knew that becoming a "*black radical* theologian" guided by the "black fire" that Detroit had ignited in

---

21. On the Jesus statue at Sacred Heart Major Seminary, see Nicquel Terry, "Black Jesus Statue One of Most Iconic '67 Landmarks," *The Detroit News*, July 21, 2017. https://www.detroitnews.com/story/news/religion/2017/07/21/black-jesus-statue-landmark/103908276/. See also Baldwin's opening remarks in conversation with Reinhold Niebuhr in "The Meaning of the Birmingham Tragedy, 1963," *Presbyterian Historical Society*, https://digital.history.pcusa.org/islandora/object/islandora%3A71692.

22. Cone, *Said I Wasn't Gonna Tell Nobody*, 6 and 9.

23. Ibid., 1.

24. Ibid., 2. Emphasis original.

25. On the pernicious way that housing policy in the late 1960s and early 1970s created conditions for new forms of predatory inclusion in concert with the real estate industry, see Keeanga-Yamahtta Taylor, *Race for Profit: How Banks and the Real Estate Industry Undermined Black Homeownership* (Chapel Hill: University of North Carolina Press, 2019).

26. Reflecting on his "inordinate methodological dependence upon the neo-orthodox theology of Karl Barth" in the preface to the 1986 edition of *A Black Theology of Liberation*, Cone acknowledges the legitimacy of such criticism: "Many of my critics (black and white) have emphasized this point. It is a legitimate criticism, and I can offer no explanation except to say that neo-orthodoxy was to me what liberal theology was to Martin Luther King, Jr.—the only theological system with which I was intellectually comfortable and which seemed compatible with the centrality of Jesus Christ in the black church community" (James H. Cone, *A Black Theology of Liberation, Fortieth Anniversary Edition* [Maryknoll: Orbis, 2016], xxiii). See also the preface to the 1989 edition of James H. Cone, *Black Theology and Black Power* (Maryknoll: Orbis, 2019) where Cone remarks that these criticisms were "totally unexpected" and "shook [him] as nothing else had" (xxix–xxx). For Cone's reflections on these early criticisms, see Cone, *Said I Wasn't Gonna Tell Nobody*, 85–97. Elsewhere Cone notes that Barth, like Tillich, was "merely instrumental in giving conceptual structure to a

him would require removing the mask of European theology.²⁷ Yet removing the mask did not amount to a wholesale rejection of Barth. As Cone writes in *My Soul Looks Back*, what was needed instead was to turn Barth "right-side-up," to focus on "the black struggle in particular and oppressed people generally" as the irruptive site of divine revelation.²⁸

To be sure, Cone understood the "ideological dangers" of identifying the gospel of Jesus Christ with a political movement.²⁹ And yet, Cone resolved after Detroit: "No longer would I allow an appeal to divine revelation to camouflage God's identification with the human fight for justice."³⁰ Cone knew that his bold thesis would provoke "the theological hairs on the heads of white theologians and preachers to stand up straight," particularly among the Barthians, but he nonetheless maintained that "Barth was closer to me than to them."³¹

Removing the Mask: Black Power Is the Gospel!

Detroit set Cone on a new trajectory. Driven by the *"black fire* burning [and] demanding expression," Cone moved beyond a merely academic interpretation of

---

primary commitment determined by the black church community" (James H. Cone, "Martin Luther King, Jr., Black Theology—Black Church," *Theology Today* 40, no. 4 [1984]: 415).

27. See esp. Cone, *Black Theology and Black Power*, xix. Emphasis original. Cone, *Said I Wasn't Gonna Tell Nobody*, 7. Works such as James H. Cone, *The Spirituals and the Blues* (Maryknoll: Orbis, 1991); idem, *For My People: Black Theology and the Black Church* (Maryknoll: Orbis, 1984); idem, *Martin & Malcolm & America: A Dream or a Nightmare* (Maryknoll: Orbis, 2012); and idem, *The Cross and the Lynching Tree* (Maryknoll: Orbis, 2013), as well as his extended involvement with the Ecumenical Association of Third World Theologians (EATWOT), all exemplify Cone's effort to remove the mask of Europe in defining Black liberation theology.

28. Cone, *My Soul Looks Back*, 45.

29. "Identifying the gospel with historico-political movements was anathema," Cone wrote, "to anyone who bases his theology on divine revelation" (Cone, *My Soul Looks Back*, 45).

30. Ibid.

31. Ibid. Few interpreters of Barth have seriously wrestled with Cone's contribution to Barth scholarship. Raymond Carr has powerfully made this point: "Cone's clear embrace of Barth as seen in his master's thesis, dissertation, two seminal texts, i.e., *Black Theology and Black Power* and *A Black Theology of Liberation*, and several articles, which were all deeply influenced by Barth's theology, makes the oversight of Cone that much more egregious when one considers the varied interpretations of the reception of Barth in America." Moreover, Carr contends that "Cone's relationship to Barth is arguably the first time Karl Barth's theology has been used in any sustained systematic treatment of theology in America" (Carr, "Barth and Cone in Dialogue on Revelation and Freedom," 26 and 115). See also Beverly Eileen Mitchell, "Karl Barth and James Cone: The Question of Liberative Faith and Ideology" (PhD diss., Boston College, 1999).

Barth's critique of natural theology.[32] The real heart of this critique, he came to see, was not essentially a doctrinal point about revelation as key to discerning God's wholly otherness from the world. Confronted by the uncompromising gospel in the apocalypse of Detroit, Cone recast the critique of natural theology as a call to *praxis*. At stake was the urgency of discerning the difference between the presence of Christ and the antichrist in the world, a difference that was being enunciated in Black freedom struggles.[33]

In February of 1968, Cone wrote an essay titled "Christianity and Black Power," which quickly grew into the manifesto *Black Theology and Black Power*, which was first published in 1969. The arrival of *Black Theology and Black Power* represents Cone's linking of the problem of natural theology to the racial nomos that the Black uprising sought to overturn. "The problem of color," Cone argues, persists in white theology and in the white church because of the natural identification of God with the world, the gospel with ruling power, and Christian ethics with law and order. Within the context of the United States, to conceive of God's relationship to the world in terms of a creaturely "given" is to accommodate the gospel to the racial nomos of the land. It is now time, Cone argues, for a *catalytic theology* that makes "a radical break with its identity with the world by seeking to bring to the problem of color the revolutionary implications of the gospel of Christ."[34] Yet this disidentification of God and the world does not amount to simply extracting God from the world, as though the gospel could find refuge in an abstract assertion of divine transcendence. Theologians must undertake something far more concrete than natural theology. The work of theology must be reimagined as a "worldly risk" that creatively identifies the gospel "with the problems of the disinherited and unwanted in society" and in contradiction with oppressive power.[35]

In *Black Theology and Black Power*, Cone understood the concretization of the critique of natural theology as authentic to Barth's own insight. Barth's theological

---

32. Cone, *Said I Wasn't Gonna Tell Nobody*, 13. Emphasis original. Recalling the racism of his early life in Bearden, Arkansas, Cone understands white supremacy to be a problem of identifying the social and political arrangements "as part of the natural orders of creation" (Cone, *My Soul Looks Back*, 18).

33. Cone on this point: "It didn't matter whether Barth or Harnack was right in their debate about the meaning of revelation. I wasn't ready to risk my life for that. Now with Black Power, everything was at stake—the affirmation of black humanity in a white supremacist world. I was ready to die for black dignity" (Cone, *Said I Wasn't Gonna Tell Nobody*, 8).

34. Cone, *Black Theology and Black Power*, 83. We credit James Kay for introducing the concept of "catalytic theology" to characterize this precipitating dimension of Cone's theology. Moreover, this concept was essential to Paul Lehmann's understanding of contextual theology. Lehmann maintained that a catalytic theology is "a prophetic theology whose function is and remains that of a *creative iconoclasm*. A creative iconoclasm in the doing of theology is always prepared for the collapse of its own idols as it exhibits the idolatry in other perspectives" (Paul Lehmann, "Contextual Theology," *Theology Today* 29, no. 1 [1972]: 7–8).

35. Cone, *Black Theology and Black Power*, 84–5.

perspective, he supposed, has nothing to do with an abstract account of grace over against nature, as though the critique of Brunner's "point of contact" could be idealistically isolated from the social situation of interwar Germany. Cone writes,

> It was the rise of a new political order that caused Barth to launch a devastating and relentless attack on natural theology. . . . When Barth said "Nein!"—no natural theology, no blending of the Word of God and the word of man—the *political* implication was clear: Hitler is the Antichrist; God has set his face against the Third Reich.[36]

The real power of Barth's critique of natural theology, for Cone, lies in its radical contextualism, that is, as a mode of relating theology to life and praxis.[37]

Cone would later summarize his position: "Any theology in America that fails to engage white supremacy and God's liberation of Black people from that evil is not Christian theology but a theology of the Antichrist."[38] For Cone, turning Barth right-side-up meant discerning the movement of God in the Detroit uprising, a theological task that followed from the recognition that a demystified understanding of divine revelation must speak to urgent situations of life and death. Barth's critique of natural theology provided Cone with theological material to critique accommodating the gospel to the racial nomos of white supremacy. But critique was only a first step. To relate theology to life required a second step—namely, that of engaging in the *worldly risk* of discerning where the good news of Jesus Christ is being proclaimed and enacted as the liberation of the oppressed. The declaration that "Black Power is the gospel of Jesus in America today!" followed from this conviction.[39] In the aftermath of the Detroit Rebellion, the conjunction of critique and discernment became essential to Cone's contextual theology of revelation. However, as we detail herein, this articulation of revelation was met with significant resistance from the white theological establishment.

The Barthians Respond to Black Theology

Responses to Cone ranged from white reactionary defensiveness to implicit repudiation by way of silence and nonengagement.[40] Still, some seriously engaged

---

36. Ibid., 87. Emphasis original.

37. Cone, *A Black Theology of Liberation*, 52. See Cone's remark that European theologians like "Barth and Bonhoeffer" can serve as "examples of how to relate theology to life," while not "defining *our* major issues" (Cone, *Black Theology and Black Power*, 88. Emphasis original).

38. Cone, *Said I Wasn't Gonna Tell Nobody*, 18.

39. Ibid., 9.

40. See, for example, Paul L. Holmer, "About Black Theology," in the first edition of *Black Theology: A Documentary History, 1966–1979*, ed. Gayraud S. Wilmore and James H. Cone (Maryknoll: Orbis, 1979), 184 and 189–90. See also Cone's "Introduction" to

Cone's challenge, particularly those who comprised the "left wing" of Barthian theology. In a 1975 issue of the *Union Seminary Quarterly Review*, Frederick Herzog,[41] Helmut Gollwitzer,[42] and Paul Lehmann[43] were all tasked with writing responses to Cone's provocative essay, "Black Theology on Revolution, Violence, and Reconciliation," which appeared in the opening pages of that same issue.[44] Cone was only thirty-seven years old in 1975. Lehmann and Gollwitzer, however, were nearly seventy by the time they engaged Cone, having over several decades undertaken significant work that drew out the prophetic dimension of a "Barthian" theology in revolutionary situations against European and US imperialism, racism, and fascism. If Cone's theology was going to gain a hearing among *any* white theologians, one would expect it to occur among these Barthians.

While all three theologians expressed their general affirmation of Cone's challenge to white theology, they also articulated sharp criticisms. Their criticisms were, in fact, deeply informed by their shared "Barthianism," affirming with Cone the liberative core of the gospel, while also offering a series of cautionary remarks about the dangers of the ideological captivity of the gospel. Formulated in the

---

part 3, "Black Theology and the Responses of White Theologians," in *Black Theology: A Documentary History, 1966–1979*, 141. Cone recalls another example of white defensiveness in *Said I Wasn't Gonna Tell Nobody*, when at a meeting at the Society of Christian Ethics, Waldo Beach dismissed Black theology as so much "tribal theology" (78).

41. Herzog had studied with both Barth and Lehmann and, by 1975, had already been significantly affected by Cone's challenge to white theology. See Frederick Herzog, *Liberation Theology: Liberation in Light of the Fourth Gospel* (Eugene: Wipf & Stock, 2013). Cone commended Herzog's book as "concrete evidence that white theologians do not have to remain enclosed in their little white boxes" (James H. Cone, *God of the Oppressed* [Maryknoll: Orbis, 2013], 46).

42. Gollwitzer had studied under Barth in Basel in the 1930s and had been a prisoner of war in the Soviet Union from 1945 to 1949. Later, Gollwitzer played a significant role in mobilizing students in Berlin during the German student movement of 1967 and 1968.

43. Lehmann, too, had been deeply shaped by the theology of Barth and especially Dietrich Bonhoeffer, who numbered among Lehmann's closest friends and confidants. By 1975, Lehmann had long been a significant figure in the formation of a "theology of revolution." See, for example, Paul Lehmann, "A Theological Defense of Revolutions," *Africa Today* 15, no. 3 (June–July 1968): 18–21. Lehmann's work had a wide influence, helping to shape not only a generation of North American theologians but also emergent liberation theologies in places like Brazil, Cuba, Argentina, and South Africa. For an important history of these connections, see Beatriz Melano, "The Influence of Dietrich Bonhoeffer, Paul Lehmann, and Richard Shaull in Latin America," *The Princeton Seminary Bulletin* 22, no. 1 (2001): 64–84. Lehmann's contributions were not lost on Cone, who observed that "no white theologian took black theology more seriously than [Lehmann] did" (see Cone, *Said I Wasn't Gonna Tell Nobody*, 79).

44. James H. Cone, "Black Theology on Revolution, Violence, and Reconciliation," *Union Seminary Quarterly Review* 31, no. 1 (Fall 1975): 5–14.

spirit of Barth, each scholar felt the need to insist on God's transcendence—God's "wholly otherness"—from human reality, and so also the need to distance God from an identification with the historical struggle for Black freedom from white domination.

We briefly examine essays by Gollwitzer and Lehmann because they clarify the limits of a Barthian theology that depends upon a critique of ideology, grounded in a notion of divine transcendence, that formally prioritizes divine agency and revelation in contrast to "mere" human agency. Gollwitzer's remarks, while doing more than the others to name the history of white theology's pernicious justification of the global devastation wrought by centuries of European colonialism, imperialism, and racial slavery, explicitly invoked Barth to raise the question as to whether Cone's "language about God" fell prey to the Feuerbachian critique of theology as merely a matter of "religious projection."[45] As Gollwitzer writes,

> One is entitled to call [Cone's] attention to the negative examples from the history of theology. We might often turn to the Gospel on the existential level of our needs, and our believing affirmation of the Gospel may find its initial motive often enough in the fact that we discover our needs affirmed in the Gospel. But theology has no right to make this route her law.[46]

Instead, if it is to follow the "biblical route," theology must move not from "our needs to God" but from "God's revelation to our needs."[47] It must begin not with human experience but with the "promise of grace," the movement of the "eternal God" who "makes the condition of us temporal human beings his condition" and thereby "sends us to our brethren in prison, to participate in their struggle for the discovery of new impulses and new criteria in the struggle."[48]

Gollwitzer affirms that "God is black" on the basis that God's grace is revealed in God's action to choose "what is weak in the world to shame the strong" (1 Cor. 1:27), but he urges Cone to understand that this is not because "the weak and the black were better in his eyes," for "all have sinned and fall short of the glory of God" (Rom. 3:23). For Gollwitzer, a theology that begins with God's revelation and promise of grace is first of all oriented by the call to *metanoia* directed at both white and Black people, even if the "concrete form" of such conversion may be different. Gollwitzer elaborates this point in his discussion of Cone's treatment of reconciliation and revolution. While he agrees with Cone that theology needs

---

45. Helmut Gollwitzer, "Why Black Theology?" *Union Seminary Quarterly Review* 31, no. 1 (Fall 1975): 52. The essay was reprinted in the first edition of *Black Theology: A Documentary History, 1966–1979*, ed. Gayraud S. Wilmore and James H. Cone (Maryknoll: Orbis, 1979), 152–73.
46. Gollwitzer, "Why Black Theology?" 52.
47. Ibid.
48. Ibid.

to reject forms of what he calls "reconcilism" (here, he is explicitly drawing on Lenin) that would "demobilize" revolutionary struggle, he worries that Cone's identification of God's revelation with the Black freedom struggle leads to an uncritical adoption of reactionary violence. Gollwitzer illustrates his concerns in the following way: "When Nat Turner with his band rose up—empowered by the reading of the Bible and divine visions—in order to kill whichever white person got in their way, it was a sheer reaction to white crimes, not a struggle which would take into account the white wrongdoers as sinners reconciled to God."[49]

The example of Nat Turner is revealing for what it says about the nature of Gollwitzer's fears about the ideological risks of Cone's theology—fears, we might note, that resonate with a much deeper history of white reactionary racial politics in the United States. For Gollwitzer, one of the central problems of Cone's theology is that it leads inevitably to a kind of theological hubris such that "we" would come to "think of ourselves as the righteous against the unrighteous, the guiltless against the guilty," tempting Black people to adopt a new form of "Pharisaism." But, in light of God's reconciling act in Jesus Christ, Gollwitzer maintains that "self-justification and condemnation are no longer possible."[50] This does not mean that theologians can remain neutral in the struggle for justice, but that taking sides in the struggle must be oriented toward "peace with the enemy and not his destruction or oppression." The conflictual dimension of the struggle for justice must resist the temptation to seek vengeance, for even the enemy in a conflict is to be viewed as one who is "already loved and sought by God." Ultimately Gollwitzer's contention is that Black theology may avoid such hubris by remembering the *cross*—that reality which leads one to "respect the difference between God's liberation struggles and our liberation struggles."[51]

Lehmann's essay rehearses similar concerns, while giving way to a greater sensitivity than Gollwitzer in its appreciation for the necessity of a theology that is open to the socio-theological concreteness and contextuality of the "truth" to which Black theology seeks to bear witness. Lehmann draws on Frantz Fanon to express the need to define "the destiny and task of black people in broader terms than those confined to black Americans," so that it might be possible to call "Europeans and Americans, including theologians, to break out of their social, cultural, and ideological parochialisms, and join black people in *their* present calling to 'work out new concepts, and to try to set afoot a new man.'"[52] Lehmann thinks that the "Black" in Cone's Black theology might be better clarified if it was understood as primarily a "socio-theological" reality rather than a merely "chromatic" one.[53]

---

49. Ibid., 53.
50. Ibid.
51. Ibid., 57.
52. Paul L. Lehmann, "Black Theology and 'Christian' Theology," *Union Seminary Quarterly Review* 31, no. 1 (Fall 1975): 31. The latter citation is drawn from Cone, "Black Theology on Revolution, Violence, and Reconciliation," 12.
53. Lehmann, "Black Theology and 'Christian' Theology," 32.

While the "chromatic sense" matters as it pertains to the "color factor" in Black theology, it must be understood as "only the point of entry into the primary socio-theological reality of blackness in America required by the concreteness towards which all 'Christian theology' must strive."[54]

Despite Lehmann's attentiveness to contextuality and the concreteness of the "truth" to which Cone's Black theology seeks to bear witness, he too displays a concern to "underline the *distance* between any given theology and 'the truth' to which every theology is bound." Hence the title of Lehmann's essay "Black Theology and 'Christian' Theology" is meant to indicate not that Black theology is *not* Christian theology, but to insist that every theology must be aware of "the *tentativeness* with which the self-disclosure of God . . . lends itself to theological description and conceptualization." Just as Gollwitzer cautions against the ideological risks of Cone's Black theology by appealing to the cross as check against overconfidence in discerning God concretely in the world, so too Lehmann underlines the "distance" between the general truth of the transcendence of the divine subject to which every theology seeks to bear witness and any particular mode of theologizing by humans, which must necessarily be tentative as a function of the "listeningness" of a theology that seeks to make room for the "freedom and priority of the 'the truth.'"[55] As Lehmann puts it, "In short, 'Christian' theology is a compound of transcendence and humility. The transcendence for which such theology makes room signals the freedom of God in and over every theology."[56]

The Moving Charge of Ideology

Gollwitzer's concern with hubris and Lehmann's prudential insistence on balancing transcendence and humility both disclose a worry that Cone risks collapsing theology into ideology.[57] If Cone's early insight involved both (a) the recognition of the racial nomos as a problem of natural theology and (b) the discernment of God's liberation in and through Black Power, it is the second which is at issue for Gollwitzer and Lehmann. The question is: how can Cone affirm the need to disarticulate God from the world and, in the next breath, insist upon the necessity of concretely identifying God's action in particular sites and movements? Does the second dimension of turning Barth right-side-up contradict the first? For Gollwitzer and Lehmann, the latter appears to be the case, as Cone's identification

---

54. Ibid., 33.
55. Ibid.
56. Ibid.
57. There is a certain irony in the cautionary and prudential nature of Lehmann's response to Cone, particularly when juxtaposed to his critique of Paul Ramsey: "Those who begin with prudence never get to prophecy." See Christopher Morse, "Paul Lehmann as Nurturer of Theological Discernment," in *Explorations in Christian Theology and Ethics*, ed. Michelle J. Bartel and Philip G. Ziegler (Burlington: Ashgate, 2009), 26.

of the gospel with Black Power operates similarly to what Barth perceived as the basic logic of natural theology: it identifies divine revelation with a merely human arrangement. Cone's failure properly to qualify the otherness of divine transcendence, then, renders his theology vulnerable to the charge of natural theology and ideological distortion.

In Cone's opening words in response to his interlocutors, printed in the same issue of *Union Seminary Quarterly Review*, he clearly discerns the stakes:

> The penetrating critiques of my essay . . . coalesce at the point of the problem of ideology and thus force me to re-examine it in the light of my perspective on black theology. My critics think that, in my zeal to unmask the ideological thinking of white theologians, I tend to overlook that my view on black theology is open to a similar critique.[58]

His response to the problem is to suggest that the distinct task of the theologian is to "accept the burden and the risk laid upon him [sic] by both social existence and divine revelation."[59] To accept this burden and this risk is to recognize that social existence and revelation must be approached "dialectically" and that the precise relationship cannot "be solved once and for all time." In other words, the theological task is inextricably contextual, conjunctural, and so risky; its fundamental tentativeness and openness to revision and "listeningness," as Lehmann had put it, is not grounded in an abstract notion of transcendence and humility, but in relation to God's revelatory activity within particular social contexts. "By becoming human in Christ in a particular social setting," Cone argues, "God makes plain that he has chosen to bind himself to our situation."[60] The social context of divine revelation matters, then, because it discloses what is "wholly other" and what is "like" God. It is precisely by taking seriously this disclosure in God's revelation that we come to know "that we have a way of cutting through the maze of political and social confusions."[61]

An alternative perspective on the question of ideology is offered in Theo Witvliet's study, *The Way of the Black Messiah*.[62] According to Witvliet, theologians

---

58. Cone, "Black Theology and Ideology: A Response to My Respondents," *Union Seminary Quarterly Review* 23, no. 1 (Fall 1975): 71. While we do not examine the criticisms of Black theologians in this issue (Herbert Edwards and C. Eric Lincoln) because they do not emerge from the same "Barthian" perspective, Cone registers their criticisms as coalescing on the same point.

59. Ibid., 76.

60. Ibid.

61. Ibid. See also Cone, *God of the Oppressed*, 92.

62. See Theo Witvliet, *The Way of the Black Messiah: The Hermeneutical Challenge of Black Theology as a Theology of Liberation*, trans. John Bowden (Oak Park: Meyer Stone, 1987). Though often overlooked in the North American context, Witvliet's book represents one of the most in-depth treatments of Cone's early thought.

often make "things too easy when it comes to distinguishing between theology and ideology." Cone, Lehmann, and Gollwitzer share a negative and narrow account of ideology that reflects a deficient conceptualization, which is better understood in wider and not necessarily pernicious terms. Witvliet contends ideology is better grasped "as the way in which people envisage their reality, as the imaginary relation of human beings to the conditions in which they really live." Ideology is thus "not a false awareness of power relationships (though it can be that), but that which precedes and determines consciousness."[63]

Christian faith, Witvliet writes, "lives in ideology and not outside of it." What follows once we grasp that theology is ideological in the wider sense of the term is the recognition that "the struggles between the idols of death and the God of life … is not the struggle between ideology and faith but that between 'faith' and 'faith.'"[64] If all theology is ideology, the question of discerning the difference between the reality of God and the antichrist—the question at the heart of the critique of natural theology after Detroit—must be adjudicated not by means of appeals to the objectivity of divine revelation but through the power of storytelling. Witvliet thus highlights the importance of Cone's account of Black storytelling in *God of the Oppressed*.[65] The appeal to storytelling is, in part, a way of recognizing that theologians do "not have more means than anyone else for showing that this story is more than a subjective, situationally determined vision of reality."[66] Still, it is also part of an affirmation of the power of narrative—both personal and biblical—through which listeners may be enlivened to the power of the Holy Spirit.

Witvliet's sympathetic account of Cone emphasizes that the Word of God, who through the incarnation has subjected himself to the human world of ideology, is encountered through the power of storytelling. However, for Cone, the task of the theologian is not only to tell a story. Storytelling is only one way for the people of God to bear witness to their experience of the revelation of God in history. Just as there are many witnesses, so too there are many expressions of life in the Spirit, including Black music, arts, dance, poetry, and folk traditions. While Witvliet is right to claim that stories are ideological in that they reflect the way people envisage their reality, for Cone, neither stories nor other multivalent cultural forms can be grasped as merely ideological. Theologically, they must also be seen as potential Spirit-filled signs of a *community*, engaged in struggle and beloved by

---

63. Ibid., 255–6. The theological debate regarding ideology is further explicated by Beverly Eileen Mitchell through the representative work of Juan Luis Segundo and Allan Boesak. See Beverly Eileen Mitchell, *Plantations and Death Camps: Religion, Ideology, and Human Dignity* (Minneapolis: Fortress, 2009), 86–94.

64. Witvliet, *The Way of the Black Messiah*, 256.

65. See Cone, *God of the Oppressed*, 93–8.

66. Witvliet, *The Way of the Black Messiah*, 256. So Witvliet: "Theologians must become aware that however indispensable the formation of concepts and analysis, argumentation and abstract summary may be, the story is the basic material and basic structure of theological reflection" (ibid., 258).

God. For Cone, theologians must risk speaking here-and-now of divine liberation as qualitatively distinct from the idols of death and structures of sin. As "critical reflection on Christian praxis in light of the Word," to use Gustavo Gutiérrez's famous phrase, theology is a worldly risk to discern the liberating activity and concrete presence of God in history.[67] In the final assessment, it is the cross as it relates to the material conditions of the least and the last that grounds Cone's insistence on the distinction between the reality of God's liberating presence among the "scourged Christs" of the earth and ideological projections of God.[68]

Discerning Jesus Christ in Context Today: The Cross and the Lynching Tree

At the age of seventy-five, Cone published *The Cross and the Lynching Tree*, marking a "continuation and culmination" of his previous work, which is motivated by the central question: "how to reconcile the gospel message of liberation with the reality of black oppression."[69] This is not a question of theodicy for Cone. It is rather the question of the *skandolon* of the cross, which, in the words of Jon Sobrino, finally "renders all natural theology impossible."[70] Unlike Gollwitzer, then, who interpreted the cross as a *skandolon* to the universal human pretense to claim knowledge of God, Cone interprets the cross in the light of the lynching tree. In doing so, he makes a decisive break from the Barthians by taking on the worldly risk of concretely naming the ongoing activity and presence of God in history, just as Barth had done in naming God as standing unequivocally against the natural-theological fascism of the Third Reich: "The cross places God in the midst of crucified people."[71]

For the cross to place God in the midst of crucified people means that testimonies to the Black experience in America, including diverse stories, poems, and music—expressed profoundly in the spirituals and the blues—are to be seen as bearing witness to the ongoing power of the liberating presence of the Black

---

67. Gustavo Gutiérrez, *A Theology of Liberation: History, Politics, and Salvation*, trans. and ed. Sister Caridad Inda and John Eagleson (Maryknoll: Orbis, 1988), 11.

68. On the "scourged Christs" of the earth, see Gustavo Gutiérrez, *Las Casas: In Search of the Poor of Jesus Christ*, trans. Robert R. Barr (Eugene: Wipf & Stock, 2003 [1995]), 45–66.

69. Cone, *The Cross and the Lynching Tree*, xv and xv–xvi.

70. Jon Sobrino, *Christology at the Crossroads: A Latin American Approach*, trans. John Drury (Maryknoll: Orbis, 1978), 222.

71. Cone, *The Cross and the Lynching Tree*, 26. Cone's invocation of "the crucified people" is a direct reference to the concept developed by the martyred Jesuit theologian Ignacio Ellacuría. See especially, Ignacio Ellacuría, "The Crucified People: An Essay in Historical Soteriology (1978)," in *Ignacio Ellacuría: Essays on History, Liberation, and Salvation*, ed. Michael E. Lee (Maryknoll: Orbis, 2013), 195–224. See also M. Shawn Copeland, *Knowing Christ Crucified: The Witness of African American Religious Experience* (Maryknoll: Orbis 2018), 133–6.

Christ. But to place God in the midst of the crucified people also means that one must come to recognize the *skandolon* as an unmasking of crucifiers and their world. In the context of the United States, the truth is plain for those with eyes to see and ears to hear "the cry of black blood" that comes from the ground at the foot of the lynching trees.[72] That whites could lynch Black people and still claim to follow a crucified Lord meant that they and their whole world, along with all of its claims to knowledge, especially its claims to "natural" knowledge of God, must be rejected in no uncertain terms. In remembering their lives and confronting the brutality of white supremacy, we come face to face with the cross and so also a hope beyond tragedy. "The theology of the resurrection is . . . a chapter in the theology of the cross," Ernst Käsemann has said; it is "the signature of the one who is risen."[73] "Just as the Germans should never forget the Holocaust," Cone remarks, "Americans should never forget slavery, segregation, and the lynching tree."[74]

The cross and the lynching tree are symbols, for Cone, of the "spiritual meaning" of Jesus that has bound Black and white life inextricably together in "Christian America."[75] The historical reality of lynching means that the *skandolon* of the cross in the United States is thus also a reckoning with the reality that in lynching Black people, whites were "literally and symbolically lynching themselves—their sons, daughters, cousins, mothers and fathers, and a host of other relatives."[76] Yet, for Cone, the acts of concrete solidarity expressed in the love that "empowered blacks to open their arms to receive the many whites who were also empowered by the same love to risk their lives in the black struggle for freedom" bear witness to the reality that "[w]hat God joined together, no one can tear apart."[77]

The concerns that preoccupied Cone from his time growing up in Jim Crow Arkansas, to writing his dissertation on the theology of Karl Barth, to witnessing the Detroit Rebellion coalesce in *The Cross and the Lynching Tree*. Cone elaborates a theology of the cross that disavows the crucifying racial nomos of the land and concretely discerns God's radical availability to the crucified people of history. To *discern* God along these lines in the context of the regimes of plantations and lynchings means speaking of God's presence to lynching victims and God's activity among those who oppose such regimes through the power of the Spirit. For Cone, Barth's "Nein!" to natural theology must ultimately be heard as a great *No* to the

---

72. James H. Cone, "The Cry of Black Blood: The Rise of Black Liberation Theology" (lecture), February 23, 2016, https://utsnyc.edu/james-cone-live/.

73. Ernst Käsemann, "The Pauline Theology of the Cross," *Interpretation* 24, no. 2 (April 1970): 177; and idem, "The Saving Significance of the Death of Jesus in Paul," in *Perspectives on Paul*, trans. Margaret Kohl (Philadelphia: Fortress, 1971), 56. Cited in Cone, *The Cross and the Lynching Tree*, 26.

74. Ibid., 165.

75. Ibid.

76. Ibid.

77. Ibid., 165–6.

crucifying world. Conversely, a *Yes* must be discerned in the life of those who struggle with God in the making of a new heaven and earth.[78]

The task of theology is fraught. It involves not merely speaking against the crucifying forces of the world but speaking of the liberating power of God in mundane and miraculous ways in the midst of that world.[79] To name God in the midst of the world, then, can never be an exercise in doctrinal abstraction. Cone believed that Barth had grasped this insight most forcefully and decisively in his critique of natural theology within the context of the Third Reich. But Cone perceived that to read Barth faithfully on this point in the context of the racial nomos of the United States must mean risking anew the challenge of theology's relation to life. White theologians had turned Barth upside-down; Cone turned him right-side-up again. In doing so, Cone connected Barth with a much wider and, indeed, planetary tradition of liberation, expressed in many times and places—a tradition of creating new forms of life in spite of havoc-wreaking forces that the powerful conceal beneath the cover of the "natural" and the "divine." Cone engages in this same task, a theological and worldly one, by insisting that in the context of the twenty-first century, we must learn to speak of God at the foot of today's lynching trees. This is where we can begin to hear the promise of the gospel in context: "God took the evil of the cross and the lynching tree and transformed them both into the triumphant beauty of the divine."[80]

---

78. "God in Christ did not make an absolute distinction between divine revelation and the black experience but rather took that experience as God's own reality" (Cone, *Said I Wasn't Gonna Tell Nobody*, 80).

79. Lehmann described contextual theology as a *confessional* theology that risks a certain kind of "theological positivism"; that is, it risks a commitment to "the truth and life-giving power of the referent to which its context points. Such theology confesses what it knows; it does not confess where it does not know" (Lehmann, "Contextual Theology," 6–7).

80. Cone, *The Cross and the Lynching Tree*, 166.

Chapter 13

LIBERATION THEOLOGY AND KARL BARTH IN THE SHADOW OF THE ALT-RIGHT

WHITE SUPREMACISM, POLITICAL PROTEST, AND ECCLESIOLOGY AFTER CHARLOTTESVILLE

Paul Dafydd Jones

... nicht "zur Lage," sondern "zur Sache."

—Karl Barth, *Theologische Existenz Heute!*

Black Lives Matter!
Whose streets? Our streets!

—Antiracist/antifascist slogans

Theology in Context: Charlottesville's "Summer of Hate"

Throughout 2017, the city of Charlottesville, Virginia, was subjected to a series of brutal assaults. On May 13, sympathizers of the Alt-Right—a toxic muddle of white nationalists, anti-Semites, neo-Nazis, and far-right activists—marched between two parks and held a torchlit rally.[1] Their immediate purpose was to

---

1. In this essay, "Alt-Right" serves as a canopy under which a number of cognate ideologies can be placed. Distinctive features include an espousal of white nationalism, often paired with support for the formation of a white ethno-state in North America; an amorphous online presence, centered around racist "news" sites, conspiracy theories, clandestine social media groups, and a penchant for trolling; a core of supporters who are young, male, and largely antipathetic to religious commitment; and an idolization of Donald Trump. It is also important to note that, while the Alt-Right stands in continuity with twentieth-century racist movements in the United States, it owes particular debts to the "European New Right." For more details, see George Hawley, *Making Sense of the Alt-Right* (New York: Columbia University Press, 2017). For valuable background, see also Michael Barkun, *Religion and the Racist Right: The Origins of the Christian Identity Movement*, revised edn (Chapel Hill: The University of North Carolina Press, 1997) and

protest the proposed removal of a statue of a Confederate general; their broader goal, to contest the "war on whites" that is supposedly being orchestrated by coastal elites, Jewish saboteurs, and people of color, and thus to remind any and all that the project of white supremacism is alive and kicking. There was plenty of chanting. In addition to the infamous pairing of "blood and soil," participants used a slogan favored by many racist groups: "You will not replace us." Then, on July 8, having secured an official permit, a Ku Klux Klan group rallied near a statue of another Confederate general. Although the city arranged community events and discouraged counterprotests, the Klan were met with resistance on the part of local faith-leaders, the Charlottesville chapters of Black Lives Matter and SURJ ("Showing Up for Racial Justice"), and hundreds of incensed residents. The Klan were decisively outnumbered and roundly outshouted. After their departure, a small number of counterprotesters (who, again, were *challenging* the Klan) disregarded the police's call to disperse; scuffles, arrests, and the deployment of tear gas followed.

Worse was to come. On the evening of August 11, a procession of torch-bearing Alt-Right activists marched through the grounds of the University of Virginia. University officials knew about the event before it occurred but made little effort to hinder it, and neither university nor city police were present when a clutch of student counterprotesters engaged—at considerable cost to their physical and mental well-being—the Alt-Right beneath a statue of Thomas Jefferson.[2] There was more racist chanting: "Blood and soil," "White Lives Matter," "Hail Trump," and "You will not replace us," with the final phrase sometimes modulated to "*Jews* will not replace us." At 8:31 am of the next day, August 12, about thirty armed members of the Pennsylvania and New York Lightfoot Militia appeared at Emancipation Park in downtown Charlottesville, ostensibly to provide "security" for a highly publicized Alt-Right rally (which, as with the Klan, was permitted by the city, albeit with squabbles over location). About ninety minutes later, affiliates of multiple groups—the same nasty mishmash of white nationalists, anti-Semites, neo-Nazis, and far-right extremists that had previously terrorized the city—began to arrive. While city officials again discouraged engagement, local activists had presciently grasped the need for a more direct response. Following a sunrise service and march, a number of (mostly) local clergy and faith-leaders positioned themselves on the edge of a street in front of the park. Their goal was to protest against and peacefully to disrupt the rally, thereby giving religious witness to

---

Damon T. Berry, *Blood and Faith: Christianity in American White Nationalism* (New York: Syracuse University Press, 2017).

2. A fact that surprised at least one demonstrator, who remarked: "'If you notify law enforcement that white nationalists were going to march on a public university with torches, you would think they would take an interest.'" See Timothy J. Heaphy et al., "Final Report: Independent Review of the 2017 Protest Events in Charlottesville, Virginia" (Hunton & Williams LLP), 117 (hereafter "Final Report"). A good deal of information in this chapter about the events of 2017 is drawn from this report.

antiracist, antisexist, and antifascist values. They joined arms, sang hymns, and prayed. Meanwhile, another crowd of counterprotesters, ostensibly nonreligious in bearing, gathered nearby.

Fights between Alt-Right activists and members of this other crowd soon broke out. Shortly before 11am, "a massive column of hundreds of Unite the Right demonstrators marched west down Market Street towards the southeast entrance of Emancipation Park. Led by members of the League of the South and the Traditionalist Workers Party"—a secessionist/white nationalist organization and a neo-Nazi group, respectively—the demonstrators "wore helmets and carried shields, flagpoles, and pepper spray." In response, a "crowd of counter-protestors . . . rushed east to form their own blockade in front of the clergy. They locked arms and blocked Market Street."[3] This split-second intervention was hugely consequential: eyewitnesses and participants believe that the blockade, established and held by an ostensibly *non*religious crowd, which actively absorbed and responded to far-right violence, protected the peaceful religious counterprotesters from grave physical harm. Even so, events continued to spiral out of hand. Subsequent to racist taunts and threats, an aerosol was lit and directed at a rallygoer. A Klansman fired a round from a handgun at the ground. When the police declared a state of unlawful assembly, people swarmed onto the downtown mall and nearby streets. After a struggle over a flag, a counterprotester named DeAndre Harris was beaten by a "mob of angry Alt-Right demonstrators . . . with flagsticks, shields, and pieces of wood."[4] Then, in the early afternoon, an Alt-Right rally participant purposefully drove his car into a crowd of counterprotesters. Dozens of individuals were physically injured; many more were severely traumatized. A local activist, Heather Heyer, was killed. Horror upon horrors.

It need hardly be said that the political situation in Charlottesville and the United States more broadly has changed dramatically since 2017. The Covid-19 pandemic has ravaged the nation and contributed, at least at the time of writing, to the death of nearly a million residents. Various reprehensible actions during his presidency and an unserious, bungled handling of the pandemic led to Donald Trump's decisive defeat in the election of 2020, and while Trump has yet to suffer meaningful legal and economic penalties, his moral inadequacies and political failures—the instigation of an assault on Congress and the prodigious dissemination of misinformation being particularly appalling—have likely secured him an ignominious place in US history. The Biden administration, meanwhile, has striven to act in ways that (sometimes) heartens those of us who number ourselves among the secular and "religious left," while restoring a measure of transparency, reasonableness, and dignity to government.[5] What has *not* changed, however, is the need for theologians to reckon seriously with the events of 2017.

---

3. "Final Report," 130.
4. Ibid., 138.
5. I use the phrase "religious left" reluctantly: it risks underplaying differences between centrists, liberals, progressives, and democratic socialists (terms which are themselves fairly

This reckoning, of course, must include political analysis, and political analysis must acknowledge squarely the continuing threat posed by the Alt-Right.[6] Hard questions loom at this juncture. Was what has come to be called the "summer of hate" the result of the mainstreaming of already-potent racist and anti-Semitic ideologies, facilitated by internet activism and media conglomerates that peddle false narratives? A resurgence of what Richard Hofstadter once described as the "paranoid style" in US politics, whereby a sizeable portion of the citizenry imagines a grand conspiracy orchestrated by Jewish financiers (personified now by George Soros), traitorous presidents and shady bureaucrats (Barack Obama and the "Deep State"), and leftist academics who peddle "cultural Marxism"?[7] A side effect of increased economic inequity, demographic change, and a widening urban/rural divide?[8] Or should the events of 2017 be viewed more simply, as one more nadir in the racist tragedy that has played out across the United States for the last 500 years—Charlottesville being a city with a track record in maintaining and promoting racial and religious hierarchies, the University of Virginia being an institution founded by an advocate of white supremacism that has often endorsed and bolstered a racist status quo?[9] If these angles of vision are not mutually exclusive, each has the distinction of being clear-eyed about the depth of the problem, and each obliges a theologian to engage the quotidian with due seriousness—even as that theologian continues pursue the age-old task of faith seeking understanding. There might be times, at least in principle, in which theologians are entitled to focus narrowly on doctrine, in past and present; and there might be times, at least in principle, in which theologians opt to hold themselves at a distance from the political sphere, in order to attend exclusively to ecclesial matters (proclamation, baptism, the Eucharist, etc.). But those times have rarely, if ever, existed, and those

---

baggy), while also obscuring the different concerns of Roman Catholics, Orthodox, and various kinds of Protestants.

6. See, for example, the summary of data in a *Washington Post* investigation of domestic terrorism by Robert O'Harrow Jr., Andrew Ba Tran, and Derek Hawkins, "The Rise of Domestic Extremism in America," *Washington Post*, April 12, 2021. https://www.washingtonpost.com/investigations/interactive/2021/domestic-terrorism-data/.

7. Richard Hofstadter, *The Paranoid Style in American Politics* (New York: Vintage, 2008).

8. This perspective might be associated with Robert Wuthnow, *The Left Behind: Decline and Rage in Rural America* (Princeton: Princeton University Press, 2018) and Arlie Russell Hochschild, *Strangers in Their Own Land: Anger and Mourning on the American Right* (New York: New Press, 2016).

9. As the poet Karl Shapiro put it in "University": "To hurt the Negro and avoid the Jew/ Is the Curriculum"; see *Poems, 1940–1953* (New York: Random House, 1953), 152. Two instructive texts on race and racism in Virginia are *Educated in Tyranny: Slavery at Thomas Jefferson's University*, ed. Maurie D. McInnis and Louis P. Nelson (Charlottesville: University of Virginia Press, 2019) and Gregory Michael Dorr, *Segregation's Science: Eugenics and Society in Virginia* (Charlottesville: University of Virginia Press, 2019).

times are certainly not now. Even if the immediate dangers posed by Trump, his enablers, and his supporters have subsided, at least for a while, the last decade or so has laid the groundwork for the continuation and intensification of far-right activity in the United States—activity that puts already-marginalized communities under new pressure and imperils a host of democratic practices and processes. Karl Barth's counsel regarding Nazism, offered during the Second World War, is thus worryingly apropos. If this menace was initially viewed with "a certain superficial sensational interest . . . the most delightful complacency, the strongest possible determination not to see the danger, not to have to meet it under any circumstances," then *we* can hardly afford to make the same mistake when it comes to the Alt-Right.[10]

Yet political analysis is hardly enough—and, Barth would surely add, political analysis must never bulk so large that a theologian starts to lose sight of her ultimate concerns. While moral outrage, a tough-minded scrutiny of the quotidian, and situational vigilance have their place, Christian theology must not become reactive to current events. It must continue to be "determined by the impetus which it receives from within its own domain and from its own *object*"; it must focus on the divine *Sache* and not become overly absorbed by the "situation" at hand.[11] In formal terms, that means a single-minded focus on the event of divine self-revelation, to which scripture and proclamation bear preeminent witness. In material terms, that means attending constantly to God's election of Israel, the incarnation of the Word, and the sending of the Spirit—free and loving acts that empower creatures to become "good and faithful servant[s]" of the Kingdom (Matt. 25:21, KJV). Or, to use a slightly different idiom, developed in outline by the late John Webster: the Christian theologian must ensure that a degraded kind of curiosity, that "movement of mind that terminates on corporeal properties of things newly known, without completing its full course by coming to rest in the divine reality which is their principle," is always being outbid by *studiousness*—a disposition that trains its attention on God's ways and works, the sum of which comprise the "domain of the Word," and strives to make them determinative of thinking, writing, and acting.[12]

---

10. Karl Barth, "The Role of the Church in War-time (A Letter to American Christians)," in *The Church and the War*, trans. Antonia H. Froendt (Eugene: Wipf & Stock, 2008), 20. This piece was originally written in 1943. When considering the relationship between the United States today and Germany in the 1930s, a provocative starting point is the short text by Timothy Snyder, *On Tyranny: Twenty Lessons from the Twentieth Century* (New York: Tim Duggan, 2017).

11. Karl Barth, *Evangelical Theology*, trans. Grover Foley (Grand Rapids: Eerdmans, 1963), 16; and GA III.49: 311. The epigraph to this chapter is a direct quotation from the same page.

12. John Webster, *The Domain of the Word: Scripture and Theological Reason* (London: T&T Clark, 2012), 196.

So we are left with a difficult but familiar tension. On one hand, there is a disquieting sociopolitical situation that Christians must not ignore—a situation that appears to be just as perilously poised as in multiple decades of the twentieth century. For a theologian to imagine that a responsibility to elaborate the understanding ingredient to faith licenses disregard for this situation would be a huge mistake. It would amount to a disavowal of responsibility for the patch of creation in which she or he has been placed; it would also require that she or he suppose, in advance, that reflection limit itself to an analysis of matters conventionally associated with the church. On the other hand, theologians must continue to heed a basic *evangelische* imperative: reckon constantly with God's communicative action, centered as it is on the incarnation of God in Christ, and consider how this action provokes, sustains, and animates various kinds of Christian community, known and unknown.

The question, then, is how to inhabit this tension, so that resistance to far-right extremism goes hand in hand with a grateful and responsible residency in the "domain of the Word."

Doing Theology "As if Nothing Had Happened"?

This question, of course, was one that Barth wrestled with in his final years in Germany, not least in a famous treatise from 1933: *Theological Existence Today!* Writing in response to Adolf Hitler's seizure of power and his plans for the Protestant churches, Barth announced that he was "endeavoring to do theology, and only theology . . . going on as before, as if nothing had happened—perhaps in a quietly raised tone, but without direct references" (GA III.49, 302). Now these words represent a relatively small part of Barth's response to Nazism, and one should not suppose that the part stands in for the whole. *Theological Existence Today!* has a delimited, propaedeutic function: closing off the possibility that there could ever be a "coordination" (*Gleichschaltung*) of Christian theology and Nazi ideology, and thus establishing a space in which readers could begin to think anew about the connection between evangelical witness and political resistance. (Friedrich-Wilhelm Marquardt's counsel is worth recalling at this point: to read Barth well, one must engage his "'pure' theological texts with . . . an eye to their non-theological implications . . . as palimpsests, as it were."[13]) Even so, in what

---

13. Friedrich-Wilhelm Marquardt, *Theological Audacities: Selected Essays*, ed. Andreas Pangritz and Paul S. Chung (Eugene: Pickwick, 2010), 217. The essay from which this quotation is drawn is an important development of an argument laid out in Friedrich-Wilhelm Marquardt, *Theologie und Sozialismus: Das Beispiel Karl Barths*, 3rd edn (Munich: Chr. Kaiser Verlag, 1985). One of Marquardt's intriguing suggestions, which unfortunately cannot be considered here, is that Barth's opposition to Nazism sometimes stumbled because the idiom in which he worked was better suited to disrupting liberal capitalist ideology than challenging the threat of fascism.

follows I want to take Barth's words seriously and use them as a starting point for my own reflections.

On one hand, I want to try to continue doing "theology, and only theology." The foundation on which this chapter rests is in fact very similar to that of *Church Dogmatics*: I treat God's self-communicative, saving activity as the precondition of theological reflection and view human activity as occurring within (and, ideally, bearing witness to) a covenant fulfilled by Christ and overarched by the Spirit. On the other hand—and here I break somewhat with Barth—I do not intend to proceed "as if nothing had happened," and I make no effort to avoid "direct references." In an experimental key, I attempt to develop a positive theological commentary on nonreligious and religious activists' response to the far-right's assault on Charlottesville, expanding Barth's claim that "church proclamation" comprises "the material of dogmatics" (CD I/1: §3). Specifically, I suggest that antifascist activity, both Christian and non-Christian, ought to factor into reflection on ecclesiology and Christian life in the present. Now this does not mean—for I am acutely aware that readers immersed in Barth may immediately flinch at this move—that Christian theology suddenly ceases to be "a function of the Church" (CD I/1: 3). Nor, for that matter, does this chapter take leave of the belief that the *ratio* ingredient to faith is the principal medium for understanding God's creative, providential, reconciliatory, and redemptive activity. My contention is simply that *ratio* can be stretched in ways that allow one to approach ecclesiology as a dogmatic locus whose (apparently) self-evident subdivisions are patient of addition and expansion, not least when Christ's headship of his body is viewed in terms of Christ's continuing action as one who lives as the "light of the world" (Jn 8:12 and 9:5). And my goal is to use a vivid sense of Christ's ongoing headship as a warrant for inhabiting the tension between the *evangelische* imperative and a responsibility for the quotidian, thereby showing how Barth's work can nourish theological projects that are not just orthodox and modern, but—to return to a phrase used in this book's introduction—orthodox, modern, *and liberative*.[14]

To this end, the next section offers programmatic remarks about Barth's thought and liberation theology. It establishes some provisional shared ground, indicating how Barth's understanding of "religion" and liberationist analyses of sin can be combined to shed light on the ideology of the Alt-Right and suggesting that the category of experience, so crucial for many liberationist thinkers, can be construed in a manner that connects with Barth's distinctive brand of theocentrism. The subsequent section argues that the efforts of ostensibly secular counterprotesters on August 12, which protected multifaith protesters from extremist violence, ought to factor into ecclesiological reflection. Judith Butler comes into play at this juncture: I use her understanding of "assembly" to consider the possibility of ad hoc irruptions of the Kingdom, as Christ's body gains new modes of historical

---

14. The phrase "orthodox and modern," of course, is not my own. See Bruce L. McCormack, *Orthodox and Modern: Studies in the Theology of Karl Barth* (Grand Rapids: Baker, 2008).

realization. Finally, a brief coda draws on Hugo Assmann's work to present the church as an open-ended, ongoing event—a modality of association and assembly that is provoked, made, and, one hopes, remade by the Word and the Spirit.

Barth and North American Liberation Theology: Building a Coalition

On Idolatry, Ideology, and "Religion" in the United States

If one were to look for scholarship that illustrates Calvin's belief that human "nature is, so to speak, a perpetual factory of idols," and that the sinful mind "dares to imagine a god according to its own capacity," the liberationist tradition is an excellent place to start.[15] Landmark works by scholars such as Mary Daly, James Cone, Ada María Isasi-Díaz, Elizabeth Johnson, and George "Tink" Tinker, as well as recent texts by Marcella Althaus-Reid, Kelly Brown Douglas, and M. Shawn Copeland, do much more than track and delineate patterns of discrimination. They expose a range of feedback loops, showing how theological discourse is both shaped by structures of domination and lends ideological support to structures of domination. When paired with select social-scientific and historical studies (some of which have recently noted deep connections between white evangelicalism and white supremacism in the United States),[16] such works support a capacious account of sin in the here-and-now. They ensure that an analysis of the malformed intentions that give rise to sin (an invaluable dimension of the classical tradition) is paired with concrete accounts of the devaluation and mistreatment of communities and individuals on the basis of class, caste, dis/ability, ethnicity, gender, race, sex, sexuality, and so on.

It is customary, at least in many circles, to treat Barth's work as hailing from a quite different time and place. His account of religion is understood—not incorrectly—as a development of Protestant criticisms of works-righteousness, updated via an appropriation of Feuerbach and applied newly to the ethos of liberal Protestantism. But one can also view Barth's construal of religion as a mode of critique that anticipates contemporary diagnoses of various social, political, and cultural ills. The essays collected in *Das Wort Gottes und die Theologie*, after all, do not limit themselves to the theological missteps of Barth's former teachers; they also take direct aim at European Christians' uncritical embrace of bourgeois and militaristic mores. The second edition of *Romans* follows suit, with an added polemic against romanticism and a slightly sharper Marxian edge (thus the association of religion

---

15. John Calvin, *Institutes of the Christian Religion*, ed. John T. McNeil, trans. Ford Lewis Battles (Louisville: WJKP, 2006), 108 (I.xi.8).

16. See, recently, Robert P. Jones, *White Too Long: The Legacy of White Supremacy in American Christianity* (New York: Simon & Schuster, 2020) and Anthea Butler, *White Evangelical Racism: The Politics of Morality in America* (Chapel Hill: The University of North Carolina Press, 2021).

and "passion" with the claim that religion "acts . . . like a drug which has been extremely skillfully administered" [RII: 236]). And if CD I/2 reprises key elements of *Romans*, albeit with a slightly stronger sense that God might bring about an *Aufhebung* of distorted practices and beliefs, *The Christian Life* extends the reach of Barth's critique still farther. Earlier analyses of bourgeois self-accreditation, inside and beyond the church, are now married to a critique of "lordless powers" that anticipates the post-socialism of Ernst LaClau, Chantal Mouffe, and others, as well as contemporary studies of intersectionality.[17] Might one not say, in fact, that liberationist thinkers pick up where Barth left off? If Barth's writing concludes with warnings against political absolutism, capitalism, ideology, and chthonic forces (as well as intriguing remarks on fashion, sport, hedonism, and transportation), do not more recent projects begin with exposés of the ways that theological claims give sanction to comparably sinful ideologies? Reading Barth and liberationist projects together, arguably, engenders a highly textured account of "religion" as a hydra-like phenomenon that supports numerous structures of domination and injustice—sometimes through the medium of putatively "respectable" discursive conventions and norms; sometimes by justifying diverse valuations of class, race, ethnicity, sex, gender, dis/ability, and the like; and sometimes via the apparently "respectable" rhetoric of progressive politics, past and present, as it extols "internationalism," "multiculturalism," "love," and "inclusivity," but baulks at a meaningful redistribution of access, wealth, and opportunity.[18]

With this convergence in view, it is worth considering how Barth and liberationist thinkers might together help scholars reckon with the threat posed by the Alt-Right. On one level, looking "back" to Barth has obvious pertinence for those who worry about a number of old idols (race, nation, "manhood," heterosexuality, and the like) whose stock has risen noticeably in recent years. An address given after Hitler's seizure of power, "The First Commandment as an Axiom of Theology," is particularly instructive. As is typical in his theological work, Barth does not immediately name his opponents or strike an explicitly political tone. He opts for what might be described as a "decolonized" discourse: a rhetorical performance that purposefully ignores *völkisch* habits of mind, so as to underscore their utter invalidity.[19] It is only once Barth has secured his claim that the "first axiom" of

---

17. See here Ernesto LaClau and Chantal Mouffe, *Hegemony and Socialist Strategy: Toward a Radical Democratic Politics*, 2nd edn (London: Verso, 2001); and, inter alia, *Intersections of Gender, Race, and Class*, ed. Marcia Texler Segal and Theresa A. Martinez (Los Angeles: Roxbury, 2007).

18. On which, see Vincent W. Lloyd, *Religion of the Field Negro: On Black Secularism and Black Theology* (New York: Fordham University Press, 2018).

19. Some of Barth's dogmatic work, on this reckoning, bears comparison to Sylvia Wynter's famous juxtaposition of the "human" with "Man." Thus Wynter: "one cannot 'unsettle' the 'coloniality of power' without a redescription of the human outside the terms of our present descriptive statement of the human, Man, and its overrepresentation." See Sylvia Wynter, "Unsettling the Coloniality of Being/Power/Truth/Freedom: Towards the

theology is the event of divine self-disclosure, authenticated by way of its own "reality and validity in the moment" (and thus "*not* abstractly discernible in creation"), then, that he inveighs against those who would offer an "apology for nationhood, morality, and the state."[20] And while this is a largely indirect critique of those who tolerated or favored far-right extremism, it is no less powerful for that. By the end of the address, it is clear that any move to accredit Nazi ideology as a "live option" amounts to a contravention of the first commandment and a betrayal of the gospel. There must always be "opposition in theology so that nowhere is there peace with the 'other gods'"; there must always be *conflict* with those who attempt to usurp or qualify the lordship of Christ.[21] Or, to make the same point in contemporary language: when it comes to Christian thought in face of far-right extremism, do not imagine that engagement (or, perhaps, "dialogue," undertaken "civilly" and "respectfully") will get you anywhere. It will not. Understand that there can be no common ground; there can only be constant vigilance and unsparing critique, undertaken in clear view of God's absolute primacy.

On another level, it is possible to tie Barth's early critique of North European fascism to recent analyses of race and racism in the United States, especially those developed in a liberationist key. It is possible, that is, to ensure that theological statements that opt not to trade in "direct references"—a live option today, albeit one rarely taken up—are flanked by theopolitical projects that expose, in a ruthless and quite explicit way, the roots and workings of contemporary iterations of idolatry.

Consider the integration of anti-Jewish/anti-Semitic and anti-Black/anti-Brown habits of mind that proved so important to those who attacked Charlottesville in 2017. Absorbing the pseudo-history underpinning the "Christian Identity" movement and neo-Nazi groups like Aryan Nations and fired up by extremist screeds on websites like the *Daily Stormer* and *The Right Stuff Blog*, many who flocked to Charlottesville in 2017 had embraced the idea that the combined conspiratorial potency of Jews and people of color is such that white Americans teeter on the brink of extinction. This is the reason why "*You* will not replace us" so easily morphed into "*Jews* will not replace us," and vice versa; this is the reason why both phrases amounted to a positioning of racism and anti-Semitism under the broad canopy of "whiteness."

Now the temptation here—and it is one to which some white liberals, progressives, and leftists have succumbed—is to scoff at such claims, to suppose that their vacuity portends their imminent demise, and to disengage. But that will not do. The very fact that there is no "there, there" does not count against the

---

Human, After Man, Its Overrepresentation—An Argument," *CR: The New Centennial Review* 3, no. 3 (2003): 268.

20. Karl Barth, "The First Commandment as an Axiom of Theology," in *The Way of Theology in Karl Barth: Essays and Comments*, ed. H. Martin Rumscheidt (Eugene: Pickwick, 1986), 66, 69, and 73.

21. Ibid., 78.

force and efficacy of this ideological formation. A lack of substance is precisely what makes the Alt-Right as a contemporary "lordless power," one that contrives to convert a (supposedly) threatened racial identity into a warrant for "defensive" (read: racist) actions against minoritized communities. And this lordless power draws on a host of precedents with deep roots in the broader Western philosophical and theological tradition, tied as it has often been to the project of colonialization and conquest. As J. Kameron Carter, Willie Jennings, and others have shown, a key reason why the *Juden-* and *Rassenfragen* comprise two sides of the same coin is that the Western philosophical and theological tradition has consistently failed to take seriously ancient Israel's ineliminable place in the scriptural witness, and thus failed to reckon with the fact that the Word "became *Jewish* flesh" (CD IV/1: 166, my emphasis)—a flesh that is markedly *other* than that which is borne by white gentiles.[22] This failure is the opening for visions of racial hierarchy to wheedle their way into the Christian imagination, with the result that Christianity (and, by extension, the modern West) comes to be defined in terms of whiteness, whiteness comes to be defined in terms of Christianity (and, by extension, the modern West), and Christian faith is frequently thought to require the reassertion of white supremacism. The theological task, accordingly, is to tackle the problem at its root while also exposing its influence in the present. And both Barth and liberationist thinkers can help with this. If the New Testament bears witness to "the Spirit of God who was driving Israel toward the Gentiles in the space constituted by Jesus' body"[23]—a claim that stands in obvious continuity with the reading of the Hebrew Bible in later volumes of *Church Dogmatics*—then Christian theologians today are obliged to honor the path on which the Spirit urges us to travel, framing the present and future theological battle against anti-Judaism and anti-Semitism as a battle against anti-Black and anti-Brown racism, and the present and future battle against anti-Black and anti-Brown racism as a battle against anti-Judaism and anti-Semitism. Put more bluntly: theologians who are advantaged by the idol of whiteness in North America must set about elaborating intellectual, practical, and political pathways for Christians to become *race traitors*, individuals and communities whose refusal of a demonic ideology is a hallmark of our commitment to the gospel of Jesus Christ, one who "exists in direct and unlimited solidarity" (CD IV/1: 172) with the people of ancient Israel.

---

22. J. Kameron Carter, *Race: A Theological Account* (Oxford: Oxford University Press, 2008); and Willie James Jennings, *The Christian Imagination: Theology and the Origins of Race* (New Haven: Yale University Press, 2010). It is worth noting that Carter's and Jennings's insistence on integrating an analysis of anti-Black and anti-Brown racism with an analysis of anti-Judaism and anti-Semitism is a step beyond some earlier theological pioneers; see, for instance, Cornel West, *Prophesy Deliverance! An Afro-American Revolutionary Christianity* (Philadelphia: Westminster, 1982), 47–65.

23. Jennings, *The Christian Imagination*, 270.

On Experience

A second claim moves thought beyond critique, while also enabling the dissolution of a (apparent) point of disagreement between Barth and many liberationist thinkers. It has to do with the vexed category of experience and its place in theological reflection.

Barth's wariness toward experience as a source of insight is rarely reprised in liberationist thinking. That is unsurprising. Whether it be a positive appraisal of Black experience, an insistence that the everyday lives of women should factor into theological work, or queer delight in the interplay of divine and human desire, liberationist appeals to experience do not involve what Barth consistently feared: the divine being converted into "an attainable and entirely useful tool for life," and to such a degree that the resurrection of Christ falls from view—and with it a belief "in the absolutely otherworldly reconstruction of all that is creaturely" (WGT 83 and 46). Instead of serving as a pretext for upholding the status quo, analyses of experience in liberationist scholarship typically reflect a concern to track God's action among minoritized persons, so as to attend to the transformative possibilities that God makes ingredient to creaturely life.[24] One must remember, to make the same point a bit differently, that the kind of experience that Barth challenged did not have to do with communities and individuals disvalued on the basis of class, race, ethnicity, sex, sexuality, etc. His principal concern was "bourgeois mythologizing":[25] a late modern exemplification of works-righteousness, anchored in a "noxious assurance" of civilizational progress and the "existing order," the force of which ensured that the "Great Disturbance" of the gospel was summarily pushed aside. Liberationist appeals to experience, by contrast, are anything but that. There is no desire to invert the relationship of God and world; at issue is the recovery of subjugated knowledges and, more particularly, the belief that God's ways and works might be discerned by those who have been consistently excluded from the "glories of marriage . . . family life . . . Church and State . . . and Society" (RII: 462).

Failure to grasp this point has done much to drive an unnecessary wedge between Barth's thinking and liberative projects. Consider the claim that Elizabeth Johnson's commendation of a "creative 'naming toward God' . . . from the matrix of [women's] experience" amounts to an attempt to "exchange the revelation of God

---

24. A point that Barth himself might grant, given a comment in CD I/1: "There can be no objection in principle to describing this event as 'experience' and even as 'religious experience.' The quarrel is not with the term nor with the true and important thing the term might finally denote, namely, the supremely real and determinative entry of the Word of God into the reality of man. But the term is burdened—this is why we avoid it—with the underlying idea that man generally is capable of religious experience or that this capability has the critical significance of a norm" (193).

25. Marquardt, *Theological Audacities*, 180.

for the experience of women and thus collapse theology into anthropology."[26] One finds here a grievous closure of thought, justified by a too-hasty appeal to Barth's early work. While the early chapters of *She Who Is* certainly do reckon often with women's experience, later chapters make it clear that what authorizes this focus— or, better, what serves as the prior condition of the experiences that Johnson considers—is nothing other than God's activity, routed through (and appropriable to) the unified efforts of the God's three persons: Spirit-Sophia, Christ-Sophia, and Mother-Sophia. The account of women's experience that Johnson offers, in other words, is not presented as a *source* for dogmatic work that stands apart from and over against the God who reveals Godself in scripture; it is presented as the *consequence* of God's gracious, revelatory advance—something underscored by Johnson's deft exegetical labors as they move from the Spirit, to Christ, and to God in God's first way of being in order to establish a theological framework that does justice to women's involvement in the divine economy. James Cone thinks along similar lines, albeit with a shift from Johnson's interest in Trinitarian doctrine (which compares with *Church Dogmatics* I) to a far-reaching acclamation of the risen Christ (which compares with *Church Dogmatics* IV). Cone does not present the Black experience of challenging white supremacism as a human undertaking that garners religious amplification; he treats that experience as the manifestation of One who is "not dead but resurrected and alive"—one whose risen life is so expansive, so sovereign, so *free*, that solidarity with the oppressed of the ancient world continues in a new mode, and "the black revolution" can be understood as "God's kingdom becoming a reality in America."[27] Cone's identification of Christ as the animating force of revolution and Cone's assertion that Christ's church is found whenever and wherever "wounds are being healed and chains are being struck off," accordingly, have little to do with religion as an ideological construct. These claims lack meaning apart from Cone's understanding of God's election of Israel and God's action in Christ, crucified and risen, as a past and present event.[28] Once again, there is no departure from the determination to proceed *von Gott aus*; there is only a startling sense of the expansive reach of grace, with God's saving action identified as the precondition for liberative activity, inside and beyond the church.

While I am, of course, looking past some significant points of contrast with Barth—in Johnson, a particular kind of apophaticism and a distinctive understanding of analogy, both of which bespeak a certain reading of Aquinas; in Cone, a deft appropriation of Tillich's understanding of revelation as a (prior)

---

26. Elizabeth Johnson, *She Who Is: The Mystery of God in Feminist Discourse* (New York: Crossroad, 2002), 5; Paul D. Molnar, *Divine Freedom and the Doctrine of the Immanent Trinity: In Dialogue with Karl Barth and Contemporary Theology* (London: T&T Clark, 2002), 10.

27. James H. Cone, *A Black Theology of Liberation* (Maryknoll: Orbis, 1990), 124 and 125.

28. Ibid., 134.

"answer" that can be correlated with situational "questions," and a rather more synergistic understanding of salvation than Barth would allow—the basic point should now be clear. When Barth's critique of religion is broadened to include additional sociopolitical concerns and when liberationist appeals to experience are nested within an expansive account of God's creative, reconciliatory, and redemptive work, the possibility of discerning common ground comes into view. Barth scholars, in particular, are freed up to dispense with our collective neuralgia about the category of experience, and to appreciate anew the theological framework within which many liberationist theologians operate. It becomes possible, in fact, to offer a new account of the history of twentieth-century European and North American theology—one in which Barth is not simply read as a repudiation of nineteenth-century neo-protestant theology (then used, uncritically, as a club to bludgeon contemporary thinkers) but as a forerunner and ally of liberationist voices.

Taking on the Alt-Right: A Barthian-Liberationist Thought Experiment

Thus far, I have identified two points at which Barth and liberationist discourses converge. The first has to do with a diagnosis of the Alt-Right's old-yet-new bundling of discriminatory trajectories—a bundling that Barth and liberationist thinkers, together, are well placed to diagnose and challenge. The second bears on liberationist appeals to experience. While those indebted to Barth might be inclined to discern here a hypostatization of values immanent to the quotidian, there is a better option: treating "experience" as an event that happens downstream of divine activity, and, accordingly, accepting that Barth and (some) liberationist thinkers offer a theocentric—and, in fact, Trinitarian and Christocentric—vision of human life.

Building on these claims, while returning to the events described at the beginning of this chapter, this section takes a constructive turn. It attempts to stretch Barth's ecclesiology, in a tentative and experimental way, in order to make sense of the brave witness of those who challenged the Alt-Right in Charlottesville in 2017.

With and beyond Barth on the Church

The starting point for this line of reflection is the actualistic and open-ended ecclesiological statement of *Church Dogmatics* IV/1. The actualism stands in plain view, and will come as no surprise to readers familiar with Barth's work: Barth describes the "that" and "what" of the church as the "earthly-historical form of Jesus Christ. . . . His body, created and continually renewed by the awakening power of the Holy Spirit" (CD IV/1: 661). While the open-endedness of Barth's ecclesiology has perhaps received less attention, it adds an important twist. Put in terms of a dogmatic rule: understand that the church's "where" and "when" cannot be taken for granted, for it depends entirely on God's initiative as it elicits fitting human responses; understand, accordingly, that Christ's earthly-historical body is as much a mobile event as an empirically circumscribable institution, and to such a degree that it becomes necessary to "abandon the usual distinctions between being and act, status and dynamic, essence and existence" (CD IV/1: 650) when thinking about the church.

To be sure, Barth's ecclesiological statement does not terminate here. Talk of God's "gathering" of the Christian community in *Church Dogmatics* IV/1 is soon complemented by statements about God's "upbuilding" and "sending" of that community (CD IV/2 and IV/3, respectively). And it is only as Barth's ecclesiology unfolds, over hundreds of pages, that one gains sight of its other important features: the prioritization of community over individual; the insistence that the church's self-understanding include an acclamation of its ineliminable relationship with Israel; the expansion of a (already-rich) pneumatology that identifies the Spirit as the divine person who presents Christ to believers; the suggestion that churches, rather than existing for themselves, ought to serve the world through their witness to God.[29] But in the course of this unfolding, it is regrettable that Barth does not really linger over an intriguing possibility: namely, that his actualistic and open-ended ecclesiology might include, or at least be informed by, specific forms of political activity—say, ad hoc acts of resistance to far-right extremists—that occur on the fringes of, or adjacent to, communities whose lifeblood is the reading of scripture, the work of proclamation, and the distribution of the sacraments. Neglect of this possibility amounts, in fact, to a missed opportunity. For might not "works of love amongst the sick, the weak, and those in jeopardy" (CD I/1: 3), works sometimes undertaken *without* acknowledgement of the lordship of Christ, become germane to an analysis of what the church is and does? Could not the church's in/visibility be grasped anew, in light of the spiritual and political turbulence wrought by the Spirit, as it manifests itself in protest against the Alt-Right? Might not Barth, alongside thinkers such as James Cone, also be able to say that Christ's "earthly-historical body" is instantiated wherever and whenever "wounds are being healed and chains struck off"?

A reflexive answer to such question is *no*. It might be elaborated as follows. Yes, theologians should honor those who contested the cruelty and stupidity of the Alt-Right in Charlottesville: an ad hoc cluster of faith-leaders and political groups, as well as an array of individuals and groups gathered under the loose banner of Antifa. And yes, contestations of racist cruelty and stupidity might well serve as occasions in which the coming of the Kingdom is indirectly glimpsed, as well as a reminder that theologians should sit lightly on pairings that can sometimes rigidify into inflexible binaries (church/world, sacred/secular, spiritual/political, etc.). But one cannot leverage any of this for ecclesiological purposes if one wishes to remain within Barth's orbit. While it is important to remind ourselves that "it can never

---

29. On all this, see the excellent essay by Paul T. Nimmo, "Church," in *The Oxford Handbook of Karl Barth*, ed. Paul Dafydd Jones and Paul T. Nimmo (Oxford: Oxford University Press, 2019), 435–50.

be the case that the Word of God is confined to the proclamation of the existing Church, or to the proclamation of the Church as known to us" (CD I/1: 54), that does not justify expanding the meaning of "proclamation" to activities that lack direct reference to God's ways and works, to which scripture bears preeminent witness. Put differently: while one can legitimately ask if antifascist activity might number among the "parables of the Kingdom"—events that happen beyond the church, yet nevertheless perhaps point to Christ's ongoing, sovereign reign over history—one ought not to forget that proclamation, baptism, the distribution of the sacraments, Christian education, and so on remain integral to what they mean for the church to exist and happen as a "visible" manifestation of Christ's body.[30] At issue here is not a foreclosure of the ecclesiological imagination, much less an unwillingness to experiment. At issue is a right ordering of thought, so that the clarity with which one approaches the doctrine of God is replicated, in a different way, in one's approach to a dogmatic analysis of Christian communities. Indeed, doesn't the proposal to stretch Barth's ecclesiology risk thinking *von* Welt *aus*? Are we not on the cusp of a refurbished kind of *Kulturprotestantismus*?

I do not want to dismiss this answer to the questions above, much less to make light of the demand that Christian theology remain grounded in the scriptural witness to God's ways and works and stay connected with the life of Christian communities. But I would also recall my earlier claim that theologians are called to inhabit the sociopolitical context in which we live *and* the domain of the Word, and I would reiterate that there may be ways "to do with theology, and only theology" *without* "going on as before"—all the while continuing to train one's attention on the activity of the risen Christ and his Spirit. That is especially the case when "going on as before" could lead to a disquieting inarticulacy about occasions in which instances of Christian witness and secular protest run together, with the latter being proximate to, congruent with, and directly supportive of the former. Yes, of course: words like "proximity," "congruence," and "supportive" risk a troublesome kind of fuzziness, a refusal to differentiate cleanly between the visible church and political activity. But it is at exactly this point that liberationist appeals to "experience" encourage one to press on, to check the temptation to foreclose, in advance, a theological account of how God might be gathering God's people, and to consider how it is that God animates the struggle for liberation in the United States. Put differently: if one is compelled by the claim that "Black Power *is* the gospel in American today," that "God in Christ did not make an absolute distinction between divine revelation and the black experience but rather took that experience as God's own reality," and that the spirituals and the blues complicate

---

30. On such parables, see George Hunsinger, *How to Read Karl Barth: The Shape of His Theology* (Oxford: Oxford University Press, 1991), 234–80 and, in a different vein, Tim Hartman, *Theology after Colonization: Kwame Bediako, Karl Barth, and the Future of Theological Reflection* (Notre Dame: University of Notre Dame Press, 2020).

the differentiation of the sacred and the secular;[31] and if one is persuaded of the claim that, since "Jesus inserted his body into the tension between resistance and desire," so freedom can be "enfleshed" in surprising ways today[32]—well, there is good reason to keep thought moving, and to see what *else* might be said about how it is that God gathers God's people for the sake of the Kingdom.

A first step is to understand Christians' knowledge of God in Christ does not have as a necessary correlate detailed knowledge about how Christ, in the Spirit, forms and animates his body in the here-and-now. Some words from Paul Lehmann, himself obviously indebted to Barth, prove instructive on this front:

> There is ... one marginal possibility which must always also be kept in mind. ... The marginal possibility is that God himself is free to transcend—*ubi et quando visum est Deo* ("where and when it pleaseth him")—what he has done and continues to do in and through the church. ... Of course, God is bound *to* what he does and has done. But he is not bound *by* what he has done. It may therefore always be possible that the distinguishable, though inseparable, relation between the *koinonia* [the invisible fellowship of those united with Christ] and the [visible, empirical] church may be strengthened, or corrected, or even set upon an entirely fresh track, by the unexpected eruption into visibility of the invisibility of God's purposed fellowship in Christ. If and when such a marginal possibility occurs, it can only be welcomed by those who belong to the *koinonia* anywhere.[33]

Although Lehmann's suggestion of God being bound "to" or "by" what God has done is a touch ambiguous, his basic point is compatible with Barth's ecclesiological outlook. God's freedom for the church might also entail freedom *from* the church—or, more precisely, freedom to make and remake the church, and in ways that outrun expectation and overturn convention. The invisible *koinonia* that God establishes and animates might irrupt upon the quotidian in new ways, thus compelling a reconsideration of what theologians say about the gathering, upbuilding, and sustaining of Christian community. Again, such irruption does not undermine the conviction that Christian theology involves reflection on church proclamation, bound as it is to God's revelatory activity and the witness of scripture. That remains a *conditio sine qua non* of dogmatic work. But that conviction can now go hand in hand with an awareness that the shockwaves of the Word ramify, in an unsystematic and surprising manner, in the world at large, and one can toy with the possibility that such shockwaves, rather than being treated as "little lights," enkindled by Christ's ongoing prophetic work, have material

---

31. James H. Cone, *Said I Wasn't Gonna Tell Nobody* (Maryknoll: Orbis, 2018), 36 and 80.

32. M. Shawn Copeland, *Enfleshing Freedom: Body, Race, and Being* (Minneapolis: Fortress, 2010), 59.

33. Paul Lehmann, *Ethics in a Christian Context* (New York: Harper & Row, 1963), 72–3.

relevance for reflection on what Christian community is and could be, now and in the future.

From Assembly to Ekklesia and Back Again

One of Judith Butler's recent books, *Notes Toward a Performative Theory of Assembly*, helps me clarify and develop this point. Butler's principal object in this work is to develop a framework that renders popular demonstrations philosophically and politically intelligible. She considers how an "alliance" or "assembly" (words whose meanings bear the imprint of Gilles Deleuze and Jasbir Puar) comes to be, with diverse bodies acting in concert, "taking up space and obdurately living" to protest injustice.[34] If Butler's career began with an interest in local performances of gender, then, her concern now is localized performances of political agency: how it is that a discrete "we" emerges in the quotidian, laying claim to the right of recognition and agitating for material change. And while Butler's book opens with remarks on Tahrir Square, an important location in the Egyptian uprising of 2011, it is no stretch to say that the Black Lives Matter movement in the United States supplies a nice illustration of her basic position, especially when she argues that the convocation of a dissenting assembly proves the meaning of the constitution's acclamation of "we the people"—a "way of making evident that very truth ... truth enacted or exercised through a particular kind of plural action."[35] Democratic life, on this reckoning, is not reducible to run-of-the-mill procedures (elections, voting, legislation, etc.). It is something that *happens* at specific moments in time, especially whenever there are collective and purposeful demonstrations against conditions that impede the pursuit of life, liberty, and flourishing. Such moments of opposition "open ... up time and space outside and against the established architecture and temporality of the regime."[36] They set in motion attempts to reconstitute the body politic.

This perspective also provides an instructive gloss on the efforts of Christians, Jews, and non-Christians who challenged the Klan on June 7 and disrupted the Alt-Right on August 11 and 12. The counterprotest of August 12, particularly, serves as a case-study in what Butler calls "Bodily Vulnerability" and "Coalitional Politics." "Bodily vulnerability" can refer to the witness of religious actors (the group of clergy and faith-leaders who stood against the rallygoers) and others who put themselves "on the line," taking the risk of occupying space and projecting sound to deny space to and contest the voices of those espousing white supremacism. "Coalitional politics" identifies an adjacent action, undertaken by an amorphous, chaotic, apparently nonreligious crowd—one that made a spontaneous decision to protect vulnerable faith-leaders through the absorption of offensive far-right

---

34. Judith Butler, *Notes Toward a Performative Theory of Assembly* (Cambridge: Harvard University Press, 2015), 18.
35. Ibid., 177.
36. Ibid., 75.

violence and through a tactical use of defensive violence.[37] Both, in their own way, amount to an enactment of "we the people," and both sought to strike a blow against a reinvigorated far-right.

Now when Butler chose the title, *Notes Toward a Performative Theory of Assembly*, she was likely not thinking about the charged Greek word, ἐκκλησία: a term of art appropriated and reworked by Christian communities in the first and second centuries. But Butler supplies a useful way to think about how the sum-total of counterprotesters in Charlottesville, both "sacred" and (ostensibly) "secular" in bearing, manifest ἐκκλησία in a new key. One might view the peaceful, prayerful witness of clergy and faith-leaders as something of a proclamatory "center," while identifying the crowd who protected them as a "margin" that needs to be thought in conjunction with that center. The starting point for thought, to be sure, is two discrete modes of gathering—one ecclesial and political, the other, purely political. But that differentiation is soon sublated, overwritten by what seems to be the growing of *one* ἐκκλησία, *one* assembly, *one* body. In the blink of an eye, the clergy and faith-activists who raised their voices against the Alt-Right were deemed so precious, so worthy, so sacred, that their witness had to be protected at all costs. A secular mass that sought to challenge the Alt-Right discerned an imperative to *move* and support a cluster of religious agents, and it was the heeding of this imperative that ensured that the peaceful witness of Christians and others was not drowned out—or, more chillingly, stamped out—by the clamor of extremist violence. And the consequence of this movement was a surprising kind of integration. The proclamatory center suddenly gained a new margin; both the clergy and faith-leaders who encircled the park *and* the crowd of counterprotesters who rushed to their defense were rendered—in a mysterious, fleeting, and somewhat chaotic way—a coherent whole. A margin that was initially "outside" the church became a margin *for* the church; and a margin for the church became a margin *of* the church.

But does not this identification of church imperiously assimilate a diverse clutch of people into the body of Christ, riding roughshod over their own religious (or irreligious, areligious, antireligious) convictions? Does it not seem, also, to imply that some portion of Christ's body does not now actually *know* its head, thus extending the Pauline claim that Christ's body has "many members" (1 Cor. 12:12–31) beyond what is reasonable? With respect to the first concern: I would not deny a measure of presumption, but I do not judge it to be disqualifying. Christian theologians regularly make claims about "what's going on" in the world, and those claims frequently stand at odds with non-Christian paradigms and outlooks. That is not an indication that non-Christian paradigms and outlooks are misguided, much less needing to be dismissed out of hand; it is simply a function of an epistemological standpoint that, cognizant of the provisionality and revisability of its judgments, supposes itself competent to assess and redescribe events in the quotidian. The second concern is a bit harder to answer, especially given Paul's

---

37. Although Butler, arguably, worries about *any* kind of violence. See *Notes*, 187–92.

claim that "in the one Spirit we were all baptized into one body . . . and we were all made to drink of one Spirit" (1 Cor. 12:13). But the concern is mitigated if one allows that baptism into one body and drinking of one Spirit need not be construed narrowly, and if one qualifies Barth's assumption that a "stabilized" knowledge of God in Christ distinguishes those who belong to the Christian community. James Cone's claim that the church of Christ is realized in liberative *action* is useful here. It enables one to interpret the efforts of (putatively) secular protesters on August 12 in terms of a response to a discrete call, wherein God's Word "comes as a summons," even as the claim that "the hearing it finds in [a human being]" (CD I/1: 200–1) is unhooked from a distinctively defined, manifestly Christian *ratio*. Indeed, the "summons" that convenes the church might well be judged—provisionally, of course—as encompassing *both* the premeditated decision of a self-aware faith community to assemble, putting its collective body on the line and rendering itself vulnerable for the sake of the gospel, *and* the spontaneous, split-second action of a crowd moved to defend those who would bear witness to God's peace through an absorption of violence. If the obedience of the "center" *and* the obedience of the "margin" occur in different modalities and take different forms, both amount to a divine "determination of human existence" (CD I/1: 201) and both result in a discrete vector of theopolitical activity. And if neither margin nor center exhausts the meaning of church, both prove instructive when it comes to thinking what the church might be and is.

One can keep going, too, looking beyond the defensive action undertaken by the crowd for the sake of the line of clergy and faith-leaders and considering the more general quality of this spontaneous, hybridized assembly. Specifically, one might view this moment of opposition to the Alt-Right as an expansion of the political assertion of "we, the people." In the same moment in which there was an enactment of sinful assembly on the part of the Alt-Right—an assembly that was apparently intended to demonstrate unity-in-diversity, yet which resulted in nothing more than a disclosure of dull homogeneity, since what was "united" seemed to be nothing more than a bunch of non-Jewish, Caucasian, cis-gendered, shouty wannabes, brought to a boil by low-grade political pretenders and a hapless, racist president—there was *also* a performance of an alternative mode of human sociality. A new kind of "time and space outside the established architecture of the regime" of white supremacism became evident: a declaration of unapologetic heterogeneity, a convergence of diverse genders, races, sexualities, ethnic identities, and religious and nonreligious identities.[38] And with this unapologetic heterogeneity in view, one espies another indication as to what "church" might mean, envisaged now as a Christ and Spirit-led recapitulation of creation's beginning: a lively jumble of creaturely differences that lampoons the flat, identitarian ideology of the Alt-Right and that presages what the future could entail.[39] At this moment, "You will not replace us" is given striking rebuttal and a

---

38. Ibid., 171 and 75.
39. On Alt-Right identitarianism, see Hawley, *Making Sense of the Alt-Right*, 61–3.

familiar slogan, "This is what democracy looks like!" gains a vital complement: "This is what *creation* looks like!"

Once again, I venture these claims tentatively. It is obviously wrong to assume that a combination of proclamation and social protest constitutes the growing edge of Christian community, just as it is wrong to assume that holiness is the predicate of any given instance of preaching (or, for that matter, any particular distribution and receipt of the sacraments). But assumption is not the order of business here. My concern is simply to suggest that God might gather God's people in surprising ways, and to consider how theological reflection might keep pace with what God may be doing in the here-and-now. If Rowan Williams is right to say that "where the Church is itself, finite action is conformed to and woven into the eternal initiative of the Word through union with Jesus Christ," with such finite action being "irregular and episodic," there are compelling reasons to position this claim within a widened ecclesiological imagination—one that Barth and liberationist thinkers are well placed to help us develop.[40]

Conclusion

I am aware that this chapter has covered a good deal of ground. After a description of Charlottesville's "summer of hate," paired with an affirmation of the importance of theologians fixing their attention on the divine *Sache* and the political context of the United States, I attempted to show points of connection between Barth's thought and that of liberationist thinkers. I then argued that Barth's ecclesiology might be expanded to take account of a discrete "secularreligious" moment, when an assemblage of secular and faithful protesters confronted the Alt-Right.[41] That is a good deal, perhaps too much, for a brief essay, and it may well have engendered a number of vexing questions. But the dual obligation with which I began—to keep on doing theology in view of God's self-revelation, to which the scriptural witness bears preeminent witness, *and* to address the context in which we find ourselves in a more direct way than Barth typically favored—is one that cries out for an expansive, sometimes experimental mode of inquiry. Both the sociopolitical situation (*die Lage*) *and* the lively sovereignty of the divine subject (*die Sache*) ask this of us; our task is to work out how best to respond.

A final note. While the previous sections have drawn frequently on the *Dogmatics*, some words from Hugo Assmann's *Theology for a Nomad Church*, a text written a few years after Barth's death in 1968, supply a useful—and aptly eschatological—coda to this essay as a whole:

---

40. Rowan Williams, *Christ: The Heart of Creation* (London: Bloomsbury, 2018), 78.
41. I borrow "secularreligious" from Catherine Keller. See her *Political Theology of the Earth: Our Planetary Emergency and the Struggle for a New Public* (New York: Columbia University Press, 2018), 18 and passim.

The transcendence of God consists in the fact that he stands before us on the frontier of the historical future. God is *pro*-vocative—he calls us forwards, and is only to be found as one who goes forward with his people in a constant process of uprooting . . . [T]he language of "God's action in history" . . . actually means the opposite of what it is taken so often to mean: the fixing of God at certain points in history. Its aim is . . . to put before us a *pro*-voking God, one who calls us forward, one working on the frontier of the future foreseen in challenges to the existing social order.[42]

While Assmann's comments relate intriguingly to the theopolitical agenda of Barth's *The Christian Life*, they also fit with the claims of this chapter. On one level, there is here a frank awareness that God seeks to transform the world, and that God does so through the Word that "not only sheds new light on, but materially changes, all things and everything in all things" (CD II/1: 258).[43] Liberationist thinkers maintain this momentum: they insist, from various angles, that salvation ramifies across history, generating and sustaining a peculiar kind of "restlessness" regarding "the imperfections of the present."[44] The theological task, accordingly, is to try to keep pace with God: to find ways to describe and honor what God is doing and where God is acting, with and for us, in the here-and-now. On another level, Assmann suggests also that the forms of Christian community toward which we are being called are not self-evident but, rather, are indexed in the surprising fact of a future Kingdom that is encroaching upon the present. We do not know in advance what "church" is; we must be ready to learn and relearn how it is that God acts to assemble God's people.

Quite what forms of Christian community will be forged in years to come, of course, is not given to us to know. It may be that the meaning of church will continue to expand, given the sociopolitical (and ecological) travails ahead. It may be that the meaning of church will narrow, perhaps for salutary reasons, perhaps for reactive reasons, and surely for reasons that we cannot yet anticipate. Even so, it seems fair to say that trenchant opposition to white supremacism might serve as an occasion, as Vincent Lloyd has recently suggested, in which "something like the church invisible manifests" itself, and in which we find ourselves "continuously reborn."[45] If that rebirth is not itself in our power—it certainly is not—we can at least hope that it will become a possibility that we are enabled, by grace, to realize; and we can at least hope that such a rebirth plays its part in checking the rising tide of far-right extremism, in the United States and farther afield, before it is too late.

---

42. Hugo Assmann, *Theology for a Nomad Church*, trans. Paul Burns (Maryknoll: Orbis, 1976), 35 and 89.

43. These words, of course, were pivotal for Friedrich-Wilhelm Marquardt's reading of Barth.

44. Cone, *A Black Theology of Liberation*, 149.

45. Lloyd, *Religion of the Field Negro*, 157 and 238.

Bibliography

Abu Zayd, Nasr. *Reformation of Islamic Thought: A Critical Historical Analysis*. Amsterdam: Amsterdam University Press, 2006.
Adams, Carol J. *Neither Man Nor Beast: Feminism and the Defense of Animals*. London: Bloomsbury, 2018.
Adams, Carol J. *The Sexual Politics of Meat: A Feminist-Vegetarian Critical Theory*. Cambridge: Polity, 1990.
Adams, Nicholas. "Barth and Hegel." In *Wiley Blackwell Companion to Karl Barth*, edited by George Hunsinger and Keith L. Johnson, vol. 2, *Major Figures and Themes*, 519–34. Oxford: Wiley Blackwell, 2019.
Afzal, Nazir. "Black People Dying in Police Custody Should Surprise No One." *The Guardian*, June 11, 2020.
Agamben, Giorgio. *The Open: Man and Animal*. Translated by Kevin Attell. Stanford: Stanford University Press, 2004.
Althaus-Reid, Marcella. *Indecent Theology*. London: Routledge, 2002.
Anderson, Raymond K. *An American Scholar Recalls Karl Barth's Golden Years as a Teacher (1958–1964): The Mature Theologian*. Lewiston: Edwin Mellen Press, 2013.
Anzaldúa, Gloria. *Borderlands: The New Mestiza/La Frontera*. 3rd edn. San Francisco: Aunt Lute Books, 2007.
Aquinas, Thomas. *Summa Theologiae*. Translated by the Fathers of the English Dominican Province. 5 vols. New York: Benziger, 1948.
Arce, Sergio Martínez. "Cristo y la liberación social." In *Teología en revolución. Volumen I*, 45–56. Matanzas: Centro de Información y Estudio "Augusto Cotto," 1988.
Arce, Sergio Martínez. *Karl Barth y su Doctrina de Palabra de Dios*. Mantanzas: Seminario Evangelico de Teologia, 1957.
Arce, Sergio Martínez. *La doctrina de justificación según Karl Barth*. Matanzas: Seminario Evangelico de Teologia, 1964.
Assmann, Hugo. *Opresión-Liberación: Desafío a los cristianos*. Montevideo: Tierra Nueva, 1971.
Assmann, Hugo. *Theology for a Nomad Church*. Translated by Paul Burns. Maryknoll: Orbis, 1976.
Atkinson, James. "Atonement." In *A Dictionary of Christian Theology*, edited by Alan Richardson, 18–24. London: SCM, 1969.
Baark, Sigurd. *The Affirmations of Reason: On Karl Barth's Speculative Theology*. London: Palgrave Macmillan, 2018.
Back, Les and Stuart Hall. "At Home and Not at Home: Stuart Hall in Conversation with Les Back." In *Essential Essays*, vol. 2, *Identity and Diaspora*, edited by David Morley, 263–300. Durham: Duke University Press, 2019.
Balboa, Jaime Ronaldo. "*Church Dogmatics*, Natural Theology, and the Slippery Slope of *Geschlecht*: A Constructivist-Gay Liberationist Reading of Barth." *Journal of the American Academy of Religion* 66 (1998): 771–90.

Baldwin, James. "The Meaning of the Birmingham Tragedy, 1963." *Presbyterian Historical Society*. https://digital.history.pcusa.org/islandora/object/islandora%3A71692.
von Balthasar, Hans Urs. *Symphony: Aspects of Christian Pluralism*. Translated by Graham Harrison. San Francisco: Ignatius, 1987.
von Balthasar, Hans Urs. *The Theology of Karl Barth*. Translated by Edward T. Oakes. San Francisco: Ignatius, 1992.
Barkun, Michael. *Religion and the Racist Right: The Origins of the Christian Identity Movement*. Rev. edn. Chapel Hill: University of North Carolina Press, 1997.
"Barth in Retirement." *Time Magazine* 81, no. 22, May 31, 1963.
Barth, Karl. *Against the Stream: Shorter Post-War Writings, 1946–1952*. New York: Philosophical Library, 1954.
Barth, Karl. *Christ and Adam: Man and Humanity in Romans 5*. Translated by Thomas Allan Smail. New York: Macmillan, 1968.
Barth, Karl. *Church Dogmatics*. Translated by G. W. Bromiley, T. F. Torrance, and others. Edinburgh: T&T Clark, 1936–1977.
Barth, Karl. *"Der Götze wackelt": Zeitkritische Aufsätze, Reden und Briefe von 1930 bis 1960*. Berlin: Vogt, 1961.
Barth, Karl. *The Epistle to the Romans*. Translated by Edwyn C. Hoskyns. Oxford: Oxford University Press, 1968.
Barth, Karl. *Evangelical Theology*. Translated by Grover Foley. Grand Rapids: Eerdmans, 1963.
Barth, Karl. *The Faith of the Church: A Commentary on the Apostle's Creed According to Calvin's Catechism*. Translated by Gabriel Vahanian. New York: Living Age Books, 1958.
Barth, Karl. *Final Testimonies*. Edited by Eberhard Busch. Translated by Geoffrey W. Bromiley. Grand Rapids: Eerdmans, 1977.
Barth, Karl. "Die These 5 der Barmer Erklärung und das Problem des gerechten Krieges." In *Texte zur Barmer Theologischen Erklärung*, edited by Martin Rohkrämer, 185–211. Zürich: TVZ, 1984.
Barth, Karl. "The First Commandment as an Axiom of Theology." In *The Way of Theology in Karl Barth: Essays and Comments*, edited by Martin Rumscheidt, 63–78. Eugene: Pickwick, 1986.
Barth, Karl. *Fragments Grave and Gay*. Edited by Martin Rumscheidt. Translated by Eric Mosbacher. London: Collins, 1971.
Barth, Karl. *Gespräche 1964–1968*. Edited by Eberhard Busch. Zurich: TVZ, 1995.
Barth, Karl. *Göttingen Dogmatics*. Vol. 1. Edited by Hannelotte Reiffen. Translated by Geoffrey W. Bromiley. Grand Rapids: Eerdmans, 1991.
Barth, Karl. *The Great Promise*. Translated by Hans Freund. New York: Philosophical Library, 1963.
Barth, Karl. *How to Serve God in a Marxist Land*. Edited and translated by H. Clark, J. D. Smart, and T. Wieser. New York: Association Press, 1959.
Barth, Karl. *The Humanity of God*. Translated by John N. Thomas and Thomas Wieser. London: Collins, 1961.
Barth, Karl. *Karl Barth Gesamtausgabe*. Zürich: TVZ, 1971–2022.
Barth, Karl. *Letters, 1961–1968*. Edited by Jürgen Fangmeier and Hinrich Stoevesandt. Translated by Geoffrey W. Bromiley. Grand Rapids: Eerdmans, 1981.
Barth, Karl. "Ludwig Feuerbach. Mit einem polemischen Nachwort." *Zwischen den Zeiten* 5 (1927): 10–40.
Barth, Karl. "Politische Entscheidung in der Einheit des Glaubens." *Theologische Existenz heute* 34 (1952): 1–19.

Barth, Karl. *Protestant Theology in the Nineteen Century*. Translated by Brian Cozens and John Bowden. London: SCM, 2001.
Barth, Karl. *Theological Existence To-Day! (A Plea for Theological Freedom)*. Translated by R. Birch Hoyle. London: Hodder and Stoughton, 1933.
Barth, Karl. "The Role of the Church in War-time (A Letter to American Christians)." In *The Church and the War*, translated by Antonia H. Froendt, 19–34. Eugene: Wipf & Stock, 2008.
Barth, Karl. *Wolfgang Amadeus Mozart*. Translated by Clarence K. Pott. Eugene: Wipf & Stock, 1986.
Barth, Karl. *The Word of God and Theology*. Translated by Amy Marga. New York: T&T Clark, 2011.
Barth, Karl and Emil Brunner. *Natural Theology: Comprising "Nature and Grace" by Professor Dr. Emil Brunner and the reply "No!" by Dr. Karl Barth*. Translated by Peter Fraenkel. Eugene: Wipf & Stock, 2002.
Bayat, Asef. *Revolution Without Revolutionaries: Making Sense of the Arab Spring*. Stanford: Stanford University Press, 2017.
de Beauvoir, Simone. *The Second Sex*. Translated by Constance Borde and Sheila Malovany-Chevallier. London: Vintage, 2015.
Beckford, Robert. *Documentary as Exorcism: Resisting the Bewitchment of Colonial Christianity*. London: Bloomsbury, 2014.
Beckford, Robert. *Dread and Pentecostal: A Political Theology for the Black Church in Britain*. London: SPCK, 2000.
Berry, Damon T. *Blood and Faith: Christianity in American White Nationalism*. New York: Syracuse University Press, 2017.
Bodley-Dangelo, Faye. *Sexual Difference, Gender, and Agency in Karl Barth's Church Dogmatics*. London: T&T Clark, 2020.
Boesak, Allan A. *Farewell to Innocence: A Socio-Ethical Study on Black Theology and Black Power*. Maryknoll: Orbis, 1976.
Boesak, Allan A. *Pharaohs on Both Sides of the Blood-Red Waters: Prophetic Critique on Empire: Resistance, Justice, and the Power of the Hopeful Sizwe—A Transatlantic Conversation*. Eugene: Cascade, 2017.
Boesak, Allan A. "Poverty, Wealth, and Ecology: A Theological Perspective." In *Living Theology: Essays Presented to Dirk J. Smit on his Sixtieth Birthday*, edited by Len Hansen, Nico Koopman, and Robert Vosloo, 569–84. Wellington: Bible Media, 2011.
Boff, Leonardo. *Igreja, carisma e poder: ensaios de eclesiologia militante*. Petrópolis: Vozes, 1981.
Boff, Leonardo. *Jesus Cristo libertador; ensaio de cristologia crítica para o nosso tempo*. Petrópolis: Editôra Vozes, 1972.
Bonhoeffer, Dietrich. *Letters and Papers from Prison*. Edited by Eberhard Bethge. London: Folio Society, 2000.
Bonino, José Míguez. "Introducción" to Karl Barth, *Introducción a la teologí evangélica*, 11–25. Buenos Aires: Ediciones La Aurora, 1986.
Booth-Clibborn, Stanley. "Decolonising Theology." *Third World Book Review* 1, nos. 4 and 5 (1985): 64.
Botman, H. Russel. "Barmen to Belhar: A Contemporary Confessing Journey." *Ned Gerek Teologiese Tydskrif* 47 (1&2): 240–9.
Bromiley, Geoffrey W. *An Introduction to the Theology of Karl Barth*. Grand Rapids: Eerdmans, 1979.
Busch, Eberhard, ed. *Barth in Conversation*, vol. 1, *1959–1962*. Louisville: WJKP, 2017.

Busch, Eberhard. "Deciding Moments in the Life and Work of Karl Barth." *Grail* 2, no. 4 (1986): 51–67.
Busch, Eberhard. *The Great Passion: An Introduction to Karl Barth's Theology*. Translated by Darrell L. Guder and Judith J. Guder. Grand Rapids: Eerdmans, 2004.
Busch, Eberhard. *Karl Barth: His Life from Letters and Autobiographical Texts*. London: SCM, 1976.
Butler, Anthea. *White Evangelical Racism: The Politics of Morality in America*. Chapel Hill: University of North Carolina Press, 2021.
Butler, Judith. *Notes Toward a Performative Theory of Assembly*. Cambridge: Harvard University Press, 2015.
Calvin, John. *Institutes of the Christian Religion*. Edited by John T. McNeil. Translated by Ford Lewis Battles. Louisville: WJKP, 2006.
Cameron, Chris. "'Bringer of Problems': Charles H. Long and the Basic Question of Humanity." *Black Perspectives*, December 9, 2015; https://www.aaihs.org/bringer-of-problems-charles-h-long-and-the-basic-question-of-humanity/.
Carr, Raymond C. "Barth and Cone in Dialogue on Revelation and Freedom: An Analysis of James Cone's Critical Appropriation of 'Barthian' Theology." PhD diss. Graduate Theological Union, 2011.
Carr, Raymond C. *Theology in the Mode of Monk: An Aesthetics of Barth and Cone on Revelation and Freedom*. Eugene: Cascade, forthcoming.
Carr, Raymond C. "Wade in the Water Children: Charles Long, Karl Barth, and the (Re)Imagination of Matter." *American Religion* 2, no. 2 (2021): 61–86.
Carter, J. Kameron. "An Unlikely Convergence: W. E. B. Du Bois, Karl Barth, and the Problem of the Imperial God-Man." *New Centennial Review* 11, no. 3 (2012): 167–224.
Carter, J. Kameron. "The Inglorious: With and Beyond Giorgio Agamben." *Political Theology* 14 (2013): 77–87.
Carter, J. Kameron. *Race: A Theological Account*. Oxford: Oxford University Press, 2008.
Cavanaugh, William T. *Torture and the Eucharist: Theology, Politics, and the Body of Christ*. Oxford: Blackwell, 1998.
Chacón, Jonathan Pimentel. *Modelos de Dios en las teologías latinoamericanas*. Heredia: Universidad Nacional de Costa Rica, 2008.
Chalamet, Christophe. "Barth and Liberal Protestantism." In *The Oxford Handbook of Karl Barth*, edited by Paul Dafydd Jones and Paul T. Nimmo, 132–46. Oxford: Oxford University Press, 2019.
Chung, Meehyun. "Barth's Theology for Peace." *Korean Journal of Systematic Theology* 8 (2003): 54–73.
Chung, Meehyun. *Karl Barth, Josef Lukl Hromádka, Korea. Das Verständnis von Offenbarung und Geschichte im Denken Karl Barths: ein Vergleich mit dem Offenbarungs- und Geschichtsverständnis Josef Lukl Hromádkas in bezug auf ihre theologische und politische Tätigkeit*. Berlin: Alektor Verlag, 1995.
Chung, Meehyun. "Letter of Barth to Hromádka." *Korean Journal of Systematic Theology* 2 (1996): 155–76.
Chung, Meehyun. "The Problem of the Natural Theology in Connection with the First Article of Barmen's Confession." *Korean Journal of Systematic Theology* 1 (1995): 85–101.
Chung, Meehyun. "Revisiting the Issue of US Military Prostitution and Culture of Militarism in Post Korean War." *Madang* 27 (2017): 43–69.
Chung, Meehyun and Lisa Sedlmayr. "Soon Kyung Parks feministische Theologie als koreanisches Beispiel reformierter Theologie im 20. Jahrhundert." In *Reformierte*

Identität, edited by Marco Hofheinz and Matthias Zeindler, 191–210. Zürich: TVZ, 2013.

Chung, Paul S. *Karl Barth: God's Word in Action*. Eugene: Cascade, 2008.

Chung, Sookja and Marlene Perera, ed. *Sustaining Spiritualities with Living Faiths in Asia in the Context of Globalization: Proceedings of the 5. Asian Theological Conference of the Ecumenical Association of Third World Theologians (EATWOT), January 9–16, 2000, Lewella, Kandy, Sri Lanka*. Colombo: Centre for Society and Religion, 2002.

Clough, David. *On Animals*, vol. 1, *Systematic Theology*. London: T&T Clark, 2012.

Coakley, Sarah. *Powers and Submissions: Spirituality, Philosophy and Gender*. Oxford: Blackwell, 2002.

Cobban, Helena. *The Palestinian Liberation Organisation: People, Power and Politics*. Cambridge: Cambridge University Press, 1984

Coetzee, P. H. and A. P. J. Roux, ed. *The African Philosophy Reader*. London: Routledge, 2003.

Cone, James H. *Black Theology and Black Power*. Maryknoll: Orbis, 1989 and 1997.

Cone, James H. "Black Theology and Ideology: A Response to My Respondents." *Union Seminary Quarterly Review* 23, no. 1 (Fall 1975): 71–86.

Cone, James H. *A Black Theology of Liberation*, Fortieth Anniversary edition. Maryknoll: Orbis, 1990, 1997, 2010, and 2016.

Cone, James H. "Black Theology on Revolution, Violence, and Reconciliation." *Union Seminary Quarterly Review* 31, no. 1 (Fall 1975): 5–14.

Cone, James H. "Christian Faith and Political Praxis." In *The Challenge of Liberation Theology: A First World Response*, edited by Brian Mahan and L. Dale Richesin, 52–64. Maryknoll: Orbis, 1981.

Cone, James H. *The Cross and the Lynching Tree*. Maryknoll: Orbis, 2019.

Cone, James H. "The Cry of Black Blood: The Rise of Black Liberation Theology." Lecture, February 23, 2016. https://utsnyc.edu/james-cone-live/.

Cone, James H. "The Doctrine of Man in the Theology of Karl Barth." PhD diss. Northwestern University, 1965.

Cone, James H. *For My People: Black Theology and the Black Church*. Maryknoll: Orbis, 1984.

Cone, James H. "Foreword" to *Church Conflicts: The Cross, Apocalyptic, and Political Resistance*, by Ernst Käsemann, vii–viii. Translated by Roy A. Harrisville. Edited by Ry O. Siggelkow. Grand Rapids: Baker, 2021.

Cone, James H. *God of the Oppressed*. Maryknoll: Orbis, 1975, 1997, and 2013.

Cone, James H. "Introduction" to part 3, "Black Theology and the Responses of White Theologians." In *Black Theology: A Documentary History, 1966–1979*, edited by Gayraud S. Wilmore and James H. Cone. Maryknoll: Orbis, 1979.

Cone, James H. *Martin and Malcolm and America: A Dream or a Nightmare*. Maryknoll: Orbis, 2012.

Cone, James H. "Martin Luther King, Jr., Black Theology—Black Church." *Theology Today* 40, no. 4 (1984): 409–15.

Cone, James H. *My Soul Looks Back*. Maryknoll: Orbis, 1985.

Cone, James H. *Risks of Faith: The Emergence of a Black Theology of Liberation, 1968–1998*. Boston: Beacon, 1999.

Cone, James H. *Said I Wasn't Gonna Tell Nobody*. Maryknoll: Orbis, 2018.

Cone, James H. *Speaking the Truth: Ecumenism, Liberation, and Black Theology*. Grand Rapids: Eerdmans, 1986.

Cone, James H. *The Spirituals and the Blues: An Interpretation*. New York: Seabury, 1972.

Copeland, M. Shawn. *Enfleshing Freedom: Body, Race, and the Human Being*. Minneapolis: Fortress, 2010.
Copeland, M. Shawn. *Knowing Christ Crucified: The Witness of African American Religious Experience*. Maryknoll: Orbis, 2018.
Creamer, Debra. *Disability and Christian Theology: Embodied Limits and Constructive Possibilities*. New York: Oxford University Press, 2009.
Creamer, Debra. "Theological Accessibility: The Contribution of Disability." *Disability Studies Quarterly* 26, no. 4 (2006), https://dsq-sds.org/article/view/812/987.
Crouch, Stanley. *Considering Genius: Writings on Jazz*. New York: Basic Civitas, 2006.
Daly, Mary. *Beyond God the Father: Toward a Philosophy of Women's Liberation*. Boston: Beacon, 1985.
Daniélou, Jean, Reinhold Niebuhr, and Karl Barth eds. *Gespräche nach Amsterdam*. Zollikon-Zürich: Evangelischer Verlag, 1949.
Dempsey, Michael T., ed. *Trinity and Election in Contemporary Theology*. Grand Rapids: Eerdmans, 2011.
Dickson, Kwesi A. *Theology in Africa*. Maryknoll: Orbis, 1984.
Dillard, Annie. *Living by Fiction*. New York: Harper & Row, 1982.
Dolamo, Ramathate Tseka Hosea. "The Relevance of Karl Barth's Theology for Church and State for South Africa." PhD diss., University of South Africa, 1992.
Dorr, Gregory Michael. *Segregation's Science: Eugenics and Society in Virginia*. Charlottesville: University of Virginia Press, 2019.
Dorrien, Gary. *Social Democracy in the Making: Political and Religious Roots of European Socialism*. New Haven: Yale University Press, 2019.
Douglas, Kelly Brown. *Stand Your Ground: Black Bodies and the Justice of God*. Maryknoll: Orbis, 2015.
Duff, Nancy J., Ry O. Siggelkow, and Brandon Watson, eds. *The Revolutionary Gospel: Paul Lehmann and the Direction of Theology Today*. Minneapolis: Fortress, forthcoming.
Dussel, Enrique. *Filosofía Ética Latinoamericana*. Vol. 5. México: Editorial Edicol, 1977.
Dussel, Enrique. *The Invention of the Americas: Eclipse of "the Other" and the Myth of Modernity*. Translated by Michael D. Barber. New York: Continuum, 1995.
Dussel, Enrique. *Philosophy of Liberation*. Translated by Aquilina Martinez and Christine Morkovsky. Maryknoll: Orbis, 1985.
Dussel, Enrique and Daniel Guillot, ed. *Liberacion latinoamericana y Emmanuel Levinas*. Buenos Aires: Editorial Bonum, 1975.
Edelman, Lee. *No Future: Queer Theory and the Death Drive*. Durham: Duke University Press, 2007.
Eiesland, Nancy. *The Disabled God: Toward a Liberatory Theology of Disability*. Nashville: Abingdon, 1994.
Ellacuría, Ignacio. "The Crucified People." In *Mysterium Liberationis: Fundamental Concepts of Liberation Theology*, edited by Ignacio Ellacuría and Jon Sobrino, 580–603. Maryknoll: Orbis, 1994.
Ellacuría, Ignacio. "The Crucified People: An Essay in Historical Soteriology (1978)." In *Ignacio Ellacuría: Essays on History, Liberation, and Salvation*, edited by Michael E. Lee, 195–224. Maryknoll: Orbis, 2013.
Fanon, Franz. *Black Skin, White Masks*. Translated by Charles Lam Markmann. London: Pluto Press, 2008.
Feldman, Noah. *The Arab Winter: A Tragedy*. Princeton: Princeton University Press, 2020.

Feuerbach, Ludwig. *The Essence of Christianity*. Translated by George Eliot. Amherst: Prometheus Books, 1989.

Fiddes, Paul S. "Mary in the Theology of Karl Barth." In *Mary in Doctrine and Devotion: Papers of the Liverpool Congress, 1989, of the Ecumenical Society of the Blessed Virgin Mary*, edited by Alberic Stacpoole, 111–27. Collegeville: Liturgical Press, 1990.

Fine, Sidney. *Violence in the Model City: The Cavanaugh Administration, Race Relations, and the Detroit Riot of 1967*. East Lansing: Michigan State University Press, 2007.

Flannery, Austin P., ed. *Vatican Council II. The Basic Sixteen Documents: Constitutions, Decrees, Declarations*. Northport: Costello Publishing, 1996.

Fletcher, Karen Baker. *Dancing with God: The Trinity from a Womanist Perspective*. St. Louis: Chalice Press, 2007.

Freire, Paolo. *Pedagogy of the Oppressed*. Translated by Myra Bergman Ramos. London: Continuum, 2005.

Gebara, Ivone. *Longing for Running Water: Ecofeminism and Liberation*. Minneapolis: Fortress, 1999.

Gilroy, Paul. "A Response." *The British Journal of Sociology* 60, no. 1 (2009): 33–8.

Girma, Mohammed and Cristian Romocea, ed. *Christian Citizenship in the Middle East: Divided Allegiance or Dual Belonging?* London: Jessica Kingsley, 2017.

Gockel, Matthias. *Barth and Schleiermacher on the Doctrine of Election: A Systematic-Theological Comparison*. Oxford: Oxford University Press, 2006.

Goizueta, Roberto. *Liberation, Method, and Dialogue: Enrique Dussel and North American Theological Discourse*. Atlanta: Scholars Press, 1988.

Goizueta, Roberto. "Toward a Transmodern Christianity." In *Thinking from the Underside of History: Enrique Dussel's Philosophy of Liberation*, edited by Linda Alcoff and Eduardo Mendieta, 181–93. Lanham: Rowman & Littlefield, 2000.

Gollwitzer, Helmut. "Kingdom of God and Socialism in the Theology of Karl Barth." In *Karl Barth and Radical Politics*, edited by George Hunsinger, 47–76. Philadelphia: Westminster, 1976.

Gollwitzer, Helmut. "Why Black Theology?" *Union Seminary Quarterly Review* 31, no. 1 (Fall 1975): 38–58. Reprinted in *Black Theology: A Documentary History, 1966–1979*, edited by Gayraud S. Wilmore and James H. Cone, 152–73. Maryknoll: Orbis, 1979.

Gordon, Lewis R. *Her Majesty's Other Children: Sketches of Racism from a Neocolonial Age*. Lanham: Rowman & Littlefield, 1997.

Gorringe, Timothy J. *Karl Barth: Against Hegemony*. Oxford: Oxford University Press, 1999.

Gotay, Samuel Silva. *El pensamiento cristiano revolucionario en América Latina y El Caribe: Implicaciones de la teología de la liberación para la sociología de la religion*. Salamanca: Ediciones Sígueme, 1981.

Gotay, Samuel Silva. *O pensamento cristão revolucionário na América Latina e no Caribe (1960–1973)*. São Paulo: Edições Paulinas, 1985.

Greeley, Andrew M. *Religion: A Secular Theory*. New York: The Free Press, 1982.

Gregersen, Niels Henrik. "Deep Incarnation: Why Evolutionary Continuity Matters in Christology." *Toronto Journal of Theology* 26, no. 2 (2010): 173–87.

Gregersen, Niels Henrik, ed. *Incarnation: On the Scope and Depth of Christology*. Minneapolis: Fortress, 2015.

Greggs, Tom. *Barth, Origen, and Universal Salvation: Restoring Particularity*. Oxford: Oxford University Press, 2009.

Gregory of Nyssa. *The Life of Moses*. Translated by Abraham J. Malherbe and Everett Ferguson. New York: Paulist, 1978.

Gross, Aaron. *The Question of the Animal and Religion: Theoretical Stakes, Practical Implications*. New York: Columbia University Press, 2014.

de Gruchy, John W. "The Reception and Relevance of Karl Barth in South Africa: Reflections on 'Doing Theology' in South Africa After Sixty Years in Conversation with Barth." *Stellenbosch Theological Journal* 5, no. 1 (2019): 11–28.

de Gruchy, John W. "Toward a Reformed Theology of Liberation: A Retrieval of Reformed Symbols in the Struggle for Justice." In *Toward the Future of Reformed Theology*, edited by David Willis and Michael Welker, 103–19. Grand Rapids: Eerdmans, 1999.

Gutiérrez, Gustavo. *A Theology of Liberation: History, Politics, and Salvation*. Translated and edited by Sister Caridad Inda and John Eagleson. Maryknoll: Orbis, 1988.

Gutiérrez, Gustavo. *Las Casas: In Search of the Poor of Jesus Christ*. Translated by Robert R. Barr. Eugene: Wipf & Stock, 2003.

Gutiérrez, Gustavo. "The Meaning and Scope of Medellín." In *The Density of the Present: Selected Writings*, 59–101. Maryknoll: Orbis, 1999.

Gutiérrez, Gustavo. *Teología de la liberación: perspectivas*. Salamanca: Sígueme, 1973.

Hancock, Angela Dienhart. *Karl Barth's Emergency Homiletic, 1932–1933: A Summons to Prophetic Witness at the Dawn of the Third Reich*. Grand Rapids: Eerdmans, 2013.

Hanna, Hani. *The Christology of Karl Barth and Matta Al-Miskīn*. Lanham: Lexington Books/Fortress Academic, 2019.

Haraway, Donna. *Staying with the Trouble: Making Kin in the Cthulucene*. Durham: Duke University Press, 2016.

Hartman, Tim. *Theology after Colonization: Kwame Bediako, Karl Barth, and the Future of Theological Reflection*. Notre Dame: University of Notre Dame Press, 2020.

Hassan, S. S. *Christians Versus Muslims in Modern Egypt: The Century-Long Struggle for Coptic Equality*. Oxford: Oxford University Press, 2003.

Havenga, Marthinus. "Worship as Primary Ethical Act: Barth on Romans 12." *HTS Teologiese Studies/Theological Studies* (2020): a5824.

Havenga, Marthinus and Robert Vosloo. "On Knowing the Time: Temporality, Love and Confession in Barth's *Der Römerbrief*." *Pistis & Praxis* 14, no. 1 (2022): 115–32.

Hawley, George. *Making Sense of the Alt-Right*. New York: Columbia University Press, 2017.

Heaphy, Timothy J. et al., "Final Report: Independent Review of the 2017 Protest Events in Charlottesville, Virginia." Hunton & Williams LLP, 2017.

Heidegger, Martin. "Only a God Can Save Us." In *Heidegger: The Man and the Thinker*, edited by Thomas Sheehan, 45–67. Chicago: Precedent, 1981.

Hennelly, Alfred T., ed. *Liberation Theology: A Documentary History*. Maryknoll: Orbis, 1992.

Hentoff, Nat. *The Jazz Life*. New York: Dial Press, 1961.

Herschel, Susannah. *The Aryan Jesus: Christian Theologians and the Bible in Nazi Germany*. Princeton: Princeton University Press, 2010.

Herzog, Frederick. *Liberation Theology: Liberation in Light of the Fourth Gospel*. Eugene: Wipf & Stock, 2013.

Hinton, Elizabeth. *America on Fire: The Untold History of Police Violence and Black Rebellion Since the 1960s*. New York: Liveright, 2021.

Hobbes, Thomas. *De Cive: The Latin Version Entitled in the First Edition Elementorum Philosophiae Sectio Tertia de Cive, and in Later Editions Elementa Philosophica de Cive*. Edited and translated by Howard Warrender. Oxford: Clarendon, 1983.

Hochschild, Arlie Russell. *Strangers in Their Own Land: Anger and Mourning on the American Right*. New York: New Press, 2016.

Höfner, Markus. *Theo-Politics? Conversing with Barth in Western and Asian Contexts*. Lanham: Lexington Books/Fortress Academic, 2022.

Hofstadter, Richard. *The Paranoid Style in American Politics*. New York: Vintage, 2008.

Holmer, Paul L. "About Black Theology." In *Black Theology: A Documentary History, 1966-1979*, edited by Gayraud S. Wilmore and James H. Cone, 183-92. Maryknoll: Orbis, 1979.

Hopkins, Dwight N. *Down, Up, and Over: Slave Religion and Black Theology*. Minneapolis: Fortress, 2000.

Hopkins, Dwight N. *Heart and Head: Black Theology, Past, Present, and Future*. New York: Palgrave, 2002.

Hopkins, Gerard Manley. *Poems and Prose*. London: Penguin, 1953.

Horne, Alistair. *A Savage War of Peace: Algeria 1954-1962*. New York: Penguin, 1987.

Houston, Walter J. *Contending for Justice: Ideologies and Theologies of Social Justice in the Old Testament*. London: T&T Clark, 2006.

Hunsinger, George. *Conversational Theology: Essays on Ecumenical, Postliberal and Political Themes, with Special Reference to Karl Barth*. London: T&T Clark, 2015.

Hunsinger, George. *Disruptive Grace: Studies in the Theology of Karl Barth*. Grand Rapids: Eerdmans, 2000.

Hunsinger, George. *How to Read Karl Barth: The Shape of his Theology*. Oxford: Oxford University Press, 1991.

Hunsinger, George. "Karl Barth and Liberation Theology." *The Journal of Religion* 63, no. 2 (1983): 247-63.

Hunsinger, George, ed. *Karl Barth and Radical Politics*. Philadelphia: Westminster, 1976.

Hunsinger, George, ed. *Karl Barth and Radical Politics*. 2nd edn. Eugene: Cascade, 2017.

Hunsinger, George. "Karl Barth's Christology: Its Basic Chalcedonian Character." In *The Cambridge Companion to Karl Barth*, edited by John Webster, 127-42. Cambridge: Cambridge University Press, 2000.

Hurston, Zora Neale. "Characteristics of Negro Expression." In *The Jazz Cadence of American Culture*, edited by Robert G. O'Meally, 298-310. New York: Columbia University Press, 1998.

Jehle, Frank. *Ever Against the Stream: The Politics of Karl Barth, 1906-1968*. Eugene: Wipf & Stock, 2002.

Jenkins, Willis. *Ecologies of Grace: Environmental Ethics and Christian Theology*. Oxford: Oxford University Press, 2008.

Jennings, Willie James. "Barth and the Racial Imaginary." In *The Oxford Handbook of Karl Barth*, edited by Paul Dafydd Jones and Paul T. Nimmo, 497-516. Oxford: Oxford University Press, 2019.

Jennings, Willie James. *The Christian Imagination: Theology and the Origins of Race*. New Haven: Yale University Press, 2010.

Jenson, Matt. *The Gravity of Sin: Augustine, Luther, and Barth on Homo Incurvatus Se*. London: T&T Clark, 2006.

Johnson, Elizabeth. *Quest for the Living God: Mapping Frontiers in the Theology of God*. New York: Continuum, 2007.

Johnson, Elizabeth. *She Who Is: The Mystery of God in Feminist Discourse*. New York: Crossroad, 2002.

Jones, Paul Dafydd. "Barth and Anselm." In *Wiley Blackwell Companion to Karl Barth*, edited by George Hunsinger and Keith Johnson, vol. 2, *Major Figures and Themes*, 435–48. Malden: Blackwell, 2020.

Jones, Paul Dafydd. "Barth and Anselm: God, Christ, and the Atonement." *International Journal of Systematic Theology* 12, no. 3 (2010): 257–82.

Jones, Paul Dafydd. *The Humanity of Christ: Christology in Karl Barth's Church Dogmatics*. New York: T&T Clark, 2011.

Jones, Paul Dafydd. "Karl Barth." In *The Oxford Handbook of Political Theology*, edited by Shaun Casey and Michael Kessler. Oxford: Oxford University Press, forthcoming.

Jones, Paul Dafydd. "Karl Barth's *The Christian Life* and the Task of Political Theology." In *Theo-Politics? Conversing with Barth in Western and Asian Contexts*, edited by Markus Höfner, 337–55. Lanham: Lexington Books/Fortress Academic, 2022.

Jones, Paul Dafydd. "Liberation Theology and 'Democratic Futures.'" *Political Theology* 10, no. 2 (2009): 261–85.

Jones, Paul Dafydd. "Schleiermacher, Neo-Orthodoxy, and Dialectical Theology." In *The Oxford Handbook of Friedrich Schleiermacher*, edited by Andrew Dole, Shelli M. Poe, and Kevin Vander Schel. Oxford: Oxford University Press, forthcoming.

Jones, Richard P. *White Too Long: The Legacy of White Supremacy in American Christianity*. New York: Simon & Schuster, 2020.

Kadushin, Rabbi Max. *The Theology of Seder Eliahu: A Study in Organic Thinking*. New York: Bloch Publishing Co., 1932.

The Kairos Document: Challenge to the Church: A Theological Comment on the Political Crisis in South Africa. 2nd edn. Braamfontein: Skotaville Publishers, 1986.

Karl Barth—Rudolf Bultmann, Letters 1922–1966. Translated by Geoffrey W. Bromiley. Grand Rapids: Eerdmans, 1981.

Käsemann, Ernst. "The Pauline Theology of the Cross." *Interpretation* 24, no. 2 (1970): 151–77.

Käsemann, Ernst. "The Saving Significance of the Death of Jesus in Paul." In *Perspectives on Paul*, 32–59. Philadelphia: Fortress, 1969.

Keller, Catherine. *Face of the Deep: A Theology of Becoming*. New York: Routledge, 2003.

Keller, Catherine. *Political Theology of the Earth: Our Planetary Emergency and the Struggle for a New Public*. New York: Columbia University Press, 2018.

Khan-Cullors, Patrisse. *When They Call You a Terrorist: A Black Lives Matter Memoir*. New York: St. Martin's, 2018.

Kheir-El-Din, Hanaa, ed. *The Egyptian Economy: Current Challenges and Future Prospects*. Cairo: The American University in Cairo Press, 2008.

Kim, Sung-Sup. *Deus Providebit: Calvin, Schleiermacher, and Barth on the Providence of God*. Minneapolis: Fortress, 2014.

König, Adrio. *Here Am I! A Christian Reflection on God*. Grand Rapids: Eerdmans, 1982.

van der Kooi, Cornelis. *As in a Mirror: John Calvin and Karl Barth on Knowing God: A Diptych*. Translated by Donald Mader. Leiden: Brill, 2005.

Kupisch, Karl, ed. *Der Götze wackelt. Zeitkritische Aufsätze, Reden und Briefe von 1930–1960*. Berlin: Käthe Vogt, 1961.

LaClau, Ernesto and Chantal Mouffe. *Hegemony and Socialist Strategy: Toward a Radical Democratic Politics*. 2nd edn. London: Verso, 2001.

Langdon, Helen. "Paragone." In *The Oxford Companion to Western Art*. Edited by Hugh Brigstocke. Oxford University Press, 2001. https://www.oxfordreference.com/view/10.1093/acref/9780198662037.001.0001/acref-9780198662037-e-1961.

Laubscher, Martin. "Reforming Our Barth?" *Stellenbosch Theological Journal* 3, no. 2 (2017): 181–98.
Lee, Daniel D. *Double Particularity: Karl Barth, Contextuality, and Asian American Theology*. Minneapolis: Fortress, 2017.
Lehmann, Paul L. "A Theological Defense of Revolutions." *Africa Today* 15, no. 3 (1968): 18–21.
Lehmann, Paul L. "Black Theology and 'Christian' Theology." *Union Seminary Quarterly* 31, no. 1 (1975): 31–7.
Lehmann, Paul L. "Contextual Theology." *Theology Today* 29, no. 1 (1972): 3–8.
Lehmann, Paul L. *Ethics in a Christian Context*. New York: Harper & Row, 1963.
Lehmann, Paul L. "Karl Barth, Theologian of Permanent Revolution." *Union Seminary Quarterly Review* 28 (1972/1973): 67–81.
Lehmann, Paul L. *The Transfiguration of Politics*. New York: Harper & Row, 1975.
Lindbeck, George A. *Dialogue on the Way: Protestants Report from Rome on the Vatican Council*. Minneapolis: Augsburg, 1965.
Lloyd, Vincent W. "Black Secularism and Black Theology." *Theology Today* 68, no. 1 (2011): 58–62.
Lloyd, Vincent W. *Religion of the Field Negro: On Black Secularism and Black Theology*. New York: Fordham University Press, 2018.
Locke, Hubert G. *The Detroit Riot of 1967*. Detroit: Wayne State University Press, 2017.
Long, Charles H. "A New Look at American Religion." *Anglican Theological Review* 1 (1973): 117–25.
Long, Charles H. *Significations: Signs, Symbols, and Images in the Interpretation of Religion*. Aurora: The Davies Group, 1995.
Long, D. Stephen. *Divine Economy: Theology and the Market*. London, New York: Routledge, 2000.
Louth, Andrew. *Mary and the Mystery of the Incarnation: An Essay on the Mother of God in the Theology of Karl Barth*. Fairacres: SLG, 1977.
Machovec, Milan. *Marxismus und die dialektische Theologie*. Zürich: EVZ-Verlag, 1965.
Maluleke, Tinyiko. "Why I am Not a Public Theologian." *The Ecumenical Review* 73, no. 2 (2021): 297–315.
Marais, Ben. *Colour: Unsolved Problem of the West*. Cape Town: Howard Timmins, 1952.
Marga, Amy. *Karl Barth's Dialogue with Catholicism in Göttingen and Münster: Its Significance for His Doctrine of God*. Tübingen: Mohr Siebeck, 2010.
Marquardt, Friedrich-Wilhelm. "Socialism in the Theology of Karl Barth." In *Karl Barth and Radical Politics*, edited by George Hunsinger, 24–49. Eugene: Cascade, 2017.
Marquardt, Friedrich-Wilhelm. *Theological Audacities: Selected Essays*. Translated by Don McCord, H. Martin Rumscheidt and Paul S. Chung. Edited by Andreas Pangritz and Paul S. Chung. Eugene: Pickwick, 2010.
Marquardt, Friedrich-Wilhelm. *Theologie und Sozialismus: Das Beispiel Karl Barths*. 3rd edn. Munich: Chr. Kaiser Verlag, 1985.
Martínez-Olivieri, Jules. *A Visible Witness: Christology, Liberation, and Participation*. Minneapolis: Fortress, 2016.
Marx, Karl. *Capital: A Critique of Political Economy*. Vol. 1. Translated by Ben Fowkes. New York: Penguin, 1976.
Marx, Karl. "Theses on Feuerbach." In *The Marx-Engels Reader*, 2nd edn, edited by Robert C. Tucker, 143–5. New York: W. W. Norton & Co., 1978.

McCormack, Bruce L. "Grace and Being: The Role of God's Gracious Election in Karl Barth's Theological Ontology." In *The Cambridge Companion to Karl Barth*, edited by John Webster, 92–110. Cambridge: Cambridge University Press, 2000.
McCormack, Bruce L. *The Humility of the Eternal Son: Reformed Kenoticism and the Repair of Chalcedon*. Cambridge: Cambridge University Press, 2021.
McCormack, Bruce L. "The Identity of the Son: Karl Barth's Exegesis of Hebrews 1:1–4 (And Similar Passages)." In *Christology, Hermeneutics, and Hebrews: Profiles from the History of Interpretation*, edited by Jon C. Laansma and Daniel J. Treier, 155–72. New York: T&T Clark, 2012.
McCormack, Bruce L. *Karl Barth's Critically Realistic Dialectical Theology: Its Genesis and Development 1909–1936*. Oxford: Clarendon, 1995.
McCormack, Bruce L. "Kenoticism in Modern Christology." In *Oxford Handbook of Christology*, edited by Francesca Aran Murphy, 444–57. Oxford: Oxford University Press, 2015.
McCormack, Bruce L. "The Lord and Giver of Life: A Barthian Defense of the Filioque." In *Rethinking Trinitarian Theology: Disputed Questions and Contemporary Issues in Trinitarian Theology*, edited by Guilio Maspero and Robert Wozniak, 230–53. New York: T&T Clark, 2012.
McCormack, Bruce L. *Orthodox and Modern: Studies in the Theology of Karl Barth*. Grand Rapids: Baker, 2008.
McCormack, Bruce L. "Seek God Where He May be Found: A Response to Edwin van Driel." *Scottish Journal of Theology* 60, no. 1 (2007): 62–79.
McCormack, Bruce L. and Thomas White, ed. *Thomas Aquinas and Karl Barth: An Unofficial Catholic-Protestant Dialogue*. Grand Rapids: Eerdmans, 2013.
McInnis, Maurie D. and Louis P. Nelson, ed. *Educated in Tyranny: Slavery at Thomas Jefferson's University*. Charlottesville: University of Virginia Press, 2019.
McKelway, Alexander. *The Freedom of God and Human Liberation*. London: SCM, 1990.
McMaken, W. Travis. *Our God Loves Justice: An Introduction to Helmut Gollwitzer*. Minneapolis: Fortress, 2017.
Melano, Beatriz. "The Influence of Dietrich Bonhoeffer, Paul Lehmann, and Richard Shaull in Latin America." *The Princeton Seminary Bulletin* 22, no. 1 (2001): 64–84.
Mercedes, Anna. *Power For: Feminism and Christ's Self-Giving*. New York: T&T Clark, 2011.
Migliore, Daniel. "Jesus Christ, the Reconciling Liberator: The Confession of 1967 and Theologies of Liberation." *Journal of Presbyterian History* 61, no. 1 (1983): 33–42.
Mitchell, Beverly E. "Karl Barth and James Cone: The Question of Liberative Faith and Ideology." PhD diss. Boston College, 1999.
Mitchell, Beverly E. *Plantations and Death Camps: Religion, Ideology, and Human Dignity*. Minneapolis: Fortress, 2009.
Mofokeng, Takatso. "Black Christians, The Bible and Liberation." *Journal of Black Theology in South Africa* 2, no. 1 (1988): 34–42.
Mofokeng, Takatso. *The Crucified Among the Crossbearers: Towards a Black Christology*. Kampen: J. H. Kok, 1983.
Molnar, Paul D. *Divine Freedom and the Doctrine of the Immanent Trinity: In Dialogue with Karl Barth and Contemporary Theology*. London: T&T Clark, 2002.
Moltmann, Jürgen. *The Crucified God*. Translated by R. A. Wilson and John Bowden. London: SCM, 1974.
Moore, Basil, ed. *Black Theology: The South African Voice*. London: C. Hurst & Co., 1973.
Morrison, Toni. *The Bluest Eye*. New York: Plume, 1994.

Morrison, Toni. *The Dancing Mind: Speech Upon Acceptance of the National Book Foundation Medal for Distinguished Contribution to American Letters on the Sixth of November, Nineteen Hundred and Ninety-Six.* New York: Alfred A. Knopf, 1996.
Morrison, Toni. *What Moves at the Margin: Selected Nonfiction.* Jackson: University of Mississippi Press, 2008.
Morse, Christopher. "Paul Lehmann as Nurturer of Theological Discernment." In *Explorations in Christian Theology and Ethics,* edited by Michelle J. Bartel and Philip G. Ziegler, 11–28. Burlington: Ashgate, 2009.
Mosala, Itumeleng. *Biblical Hermeneutics and Black Theology in South Africa.* Grand Rapids: Eerdmans, 1990.
Motlhabi, Mokgethi. *African Theology/Black Theology in South Africa: Looking Back, Moving On.* Pretoria: UNISA Press, 2008.
Moyse, Ashley John, Scott A. Kirkland, and John C. McDowell, ed. *Correlating Sobornost: Conversations between Karl Barth and the Russian Orthodox Tradition.* Minneapolis: Fortress, 2016.
Mueller, William A. "Karl Barth's View of the Virgin Birth." *Review and Expositor* 51, no. 4 (1954): 508–21.
Niebuhr, Reinhold. "Why is Barth Silent on Hungary?" *The Christian Century* 74 (1957): 108–10.
Nimmo, Paul T. "Church." In *The Oxford Handbook of Karl Barth,* edited by Paul Dafydd Jones and Paul T. Nimmo, 435–50. Oxford: Oxford University Press, 2019.
Noel, James A. "Charles H. Long Tribute". Paper read at the American Academy of Religion annual meeting held in San Diego, 2015.
Nyamnjoh, Francis B. *#RhodesMustFall: Nibbling at Resilient Colonialism in South Africa.* Mankom: Langaa Research & Publishing Common Initiative Group, 2016.
Ochs, Peter. *Understanding the Rabbinic Mind: Essays on the Hermeneutic of Max Kadushin.* Atlanta: Scholars Press, 1990.
O'Harrow Jr., Robert, Andrew Ba Tran, and Derek Hawkins. "The Rise of Domestic Extremism in America." *Washington Post,* April 12, 2021. https://www.washingtonpost.com/investigations/interactive/2021/domestic-terrorism-data/.
Opoku, Kofi Asare. "The Baobab Tree of Truth: Response to Two Papers on Barth and Comparative Theologies." Unpublished paper.
Opoku, Kofi Asare. "Standing on a Stone: Nkrumah and the African Genius." Unpublished paper.
Park, Soon-kyung. *The Kingdom of God and the Future of Minjok.* Seoul: Christian Literature Society of Korea, 1985.
Park, Soon-kyung. "The Kingdom of God, The Ultimate Revolutionary Power of World Society and History." *Korea Journal of Christian Studies* 41, no. 1 (2005).
Park, Soon-kyung. *On the Journey of Theology of Unification.* Seoul: Hanwool, 1992.
Park, Soon-kyung. *Unification of Minjok and Christianity.* Seoul: Hangilsa, 1986.
Perry, Tim. "What is Little Mary Here For?" *Pro Ecclesia* 19, no. 1 (2010): 46–68.
Petersen, Robin M. "An Analysis of the Nature and Basis of Karl Barth's Socialism." MA thesis, University of Cape Town, 1985.
Pixley, Jorge V. and Jean-Pierre Bastian, eds. *Praxis cristiana y producción teológica.* Salamanca: Ediciones Sígueme, 1979.
Prestige, George Leonard. *God in Patristic Thought.* London: SPCK, 1952.
Quinn, Philip L. *Divine Commands and Moral Requirements.* Oxford: Clarendon, 1978.
Qutb, Sayyid. *Social Justice in Islam.* Translated by John B. Hardie. Edited by Hamid Algar. New York: Islamic Publications International, 2000.

Rankine, Claudia. *Citizen: An American Lyric*. Minneapolis: Graywolf, 2014.
Reddie, Anthony G. *Is God Colour-Blind? Insights From Black Theology for Christian Ministry*. London: SPCK, 2009.
Reeling Brouwer, Rinse H. *Karl Barth and Post-Reformation Orthodoxy*. London: Routledge, 2015.
Reichel, Hanna. *Theologie als Bekenntnis. Karl Barths kontextuelle Lektüre des Heidelberger Katechismus*. Göttingen: Vandenhoeck & Ruprecht, 2015.
Report of the National Advisory Commission on Civil Disorders. Washington, DC: U.S. Government Printing Office, 1968.
Resch, Dustin. *A Sign of Mystery: Karl Barth's Interpretation of the Virgin Birth*. Burlington: Ashgate, 2012.
Reuther, Rosemary Radford. *Sexism and God-talk: Toward a Feminist Theology*. Boston: Beacon, 1993.
Rivera, Mayra. *The Touch of Transcendence: A Postcolonial Theology of God*. Louisville: WJKP, 2007.
Roberts, Hugh J. "Improvisation, Individuation, and Immanence: Thelonius [sic] Monk." *Black Sacred Music* 3, no. 2 (1989): 50–6.
Rogers, Jr., Eugene. *Thomas Aquinas and Karl Barth: Sacred Doctrine and the Natural Knowledge of God*. Notre Dame: University of Notre Dame Press, 1995.
Said, Edward W. *Orientalism*. New York: Random House, 1978.
Schleidt, Wolfgang M. and Michael D. Shalter. "Co-Evolution of Humans and Canids: An Alternative View of Dog Domestication: Homo Homini Lupus?" *Evolution and Cognition* 9, no. 1 (2003): 57–72.
Schneiders, Sandra. *Women and the Word: The Gender of God in the New Testament and the Spirituality of Women*. New York: Paulist, 1986.
Schultz, Kevin M. *Tri-Faith America: How Catholics and Jews Held Postwar America to Its Protestant Promise*. Oxford: Oxford University Press, 2011.
Seagrove, Gordon. "Blues Is Jazz And Jazz Is Blues." *Chicago Tribune*, July 11, 1915: 54.
Sedgwick, Eve Kosofsky. *Between Men: English Literature and Male Homosocial Desire*. New York: Columbia University Press, 1985.
Segal, Marcia Texler and Theresa A. Martinez, eds. *Intersections of Gender, Race, and Class*. Los Angeles: Roxbury, 2007.
Segundo, Juan Luis. *Teología de la liberación: Respuesta al Cardenal Ratzinger*. Madrid: Ediciones Cristiandad, 1985.
Shapiro, Karl. *Poems, 1940–1953*. New York: Random House, 1953.
Singgih, Emmanuel Gerrit. "Toward a Postcolonial Interpretation of Romans 13:1–7: Karl Barth, Robert Jewett, and the Context of Reformation in Present Day Indonesia." *Asia Theological Journal* 23, no. 1 (2009): 111–22.
Smit, Dirk J. "Barmen and Belhar in Conversation: A South African Perspective." In *Essays on Being Reformed: Collected Essays 3*, edited by Robert Vosloo, 325–36. Stellenbosch: SunMedia, 2009.
Smit, Dirk J. "Barths Krisentheologie in Kontexten radikaler Transformation lesen? Eine südafrikanische Reflexion." In *Theologie im Umbruch der Moderne*, edited by Georg Pfleiderer, 158–68. Zürich: TVZ, 2014.
Smit, Dirk J. *Essays in Public Theology: Collected Essays 1*. Stellenbosch: SunPress, 2007.
Smit, Dirk J. "On Adventures and Misfortunes: More Stories about Reformed Theology in South Africa." In *Vicissitudes of Reformed Theology in the Twentieth Century*, edited by George Harnack and D. van Keulen, 208–35. Leiden: Brill, 2004.

Smit, Dirk J. *Remembering Theologians—Doing Theology: Collected Essays 5*. Stellenbosch: Sun Press, 2013.
Smith, Jonathan Z. "I Am a Parrot (Red)." *History of Religions* 11, no. 4 (1972): 391–413.
Snyder, Timothy. *On Tyranny: Twenty Lessons from the Twentieth Century*. New York: Tim Duggan, 2017.
Sobrino, Jon. *Christology at the Crossroads*. Translated by John Drury. Maryknoll: Orbis, 1978.
Sobrino, Jon. *Jesucristo liberador: lectura histórico teológica de Jesús de Nazaret*. San Salvador: UCA, 1991. ET: *Jesus the Liberator*. Translated by Paul Burns and Francis McDonagh. Maryknoll: Orbis, 2003.
de Sousa Santos, Boaventura. "Public Sphere and Epistemologies of the South." *Africa Development* 37, no. 1 (2012): 43–67.
Spencer, Jon Michael. *Protest and Praise: Sacred Music of Black Religion*. Minneapolis: Fortress, 1990.
Spencer, Jon Michael. *The Rhythms of Black Folk: Race, Religion, and Pan-Africanism*. Trenton: Africa World Press, 1995.
Spencer, Jon Michael. *Theological Music: Introduction to Theomusicology*. Westport: Greenwood Press, 1991.
Spivak, Gayatri Chakravorty. *A Critique of Postcolonial Reason: Toward a History of the Vanishing Present*. Cambridge: Harvard University Press, 1999.
Spivak, Gayatri Chakravorty. *Death of a Discipline*. New York: Columbia University Press, 2003.
Stringfellow, William. *Free in Obedience*. New York: Seabury, 1964.
Strümke, Volker. "Die Jungfrauengeburt als Geheimnis des Glaubens—ethische Annmerkungen." *Neue Zeitschrift für systematische Theologie und Religionsphilosophie* 49, no. 4 (2007): 423–41.
Sugirtharajah, Rasiah S. *Postcolonial Criticism and Biblical Interpretation*. Oxford: Oxford University Press, 2002.
Sugrue, Thomas J. *The Origins of the Urban Crisis: Race and Inequality in Postwar Detroit*. Princeton: Princeton University Press, 2005.
Sumner, Darren. *Karl Barth and the Incarnation: Christology and the Humility of God*. New York: T&T Clark, 2016.
Swerling, Gabriella. "Church of England Embroiled in Racism Row for Turning Down Black Trainee Vicar." *The Telegraph*, June 16, 2020.
Tait, L. Gordon. "Karl Barth and the Virgin Mary." *Journal of Ecumenical Studies* 4 (1967): 406–25.
Tamez, Elsa. *The Amnesty of Grace: Justification by Faith from a Latin American Perspective*. Translated by Sharon L. Ringe. Eugene: Wipf & Stock, 2002.
Taylor, Keeanga-Yamahtta. *Race for Profit: How Banks and the Real Estate Industry Undermined Black Homeownership*. Chapel Hill: University of North Carolina Press, 2019.
Terry, Nicquel. "Black Jesus Statue One of Most Iconic '67 Landmarks." *The Detroit News*, July 21, 2017. https://www.detroitnews.com/story/news/religion/2017/07/21/black-jesus-statue-landmark/103908276/.
Tietz, Christiane. *Karl Barth: A Life in Conflict*. Translated by Victoria J. Barnett. Oxford: Oxford University Press, 2022.
Tignor, Robert L. *Egypt: A Short History*. Princeton: Princeton University Press, 2010.
Tillich, Paul. *Systematic Theology*. 3 vols. Chicago: The University of Chicago Press, 1951–1963.

Tonstad, Linn Marie. *Queer Theology: Beyond Apologetics*. Eugene: Cascade, 2018.
Townes, Emilie M. *Womanist Ethics and the Cultural Production of Evil*. New York: Palgrave Macmillan, 2006.
Trager, Eric. *Arab Fall: How the Muslim Brotherhood Won and Lost Egypt in 891 Days*. Washington, DC: Georgetown University Press, 2016.
Tshaka, Rothney S. "The Black Church as the Womb of Black Liberation Theology? Why the Uniting Reformed Church in Southern Africa (URCSA) is not a Genuine Black Church?" *HTS Teologiese Studies/Theological Studies* 71, no. 3 (2015): Art. no.2800.
Tshaka, Rothney S. *Confessional Theology? A Critical Analysis of the Theology of Karl Barth and its Significance for the Belhar Confession*. Cambridge: Cambridge University Press, 2010.
Tshaka, Rothney S. "Do Our Theological Methodologies Help us to Deal with Situations of Violence in Black Communities, Specifically Afrophobia." *Journal of Theology for Southern Africa* 138 (2010): 124–35.
Tshaka, Rothney S. "'Doing Theology as Though Nothing Had Happened': Reading Karl Barth's Confessional Theology in Zimbabwe Today." *HTS Teologiese Studies/Theological Studies* 72, no. 1 (2016): a3028.
Tshaka, Rothney S. "Malcolm X's the Ballot or the Bullet Speech? Its Implications for Black Liberation Theology in Present-day South Africa." *HTS Teologiese Studies/Theological Studies* 71, no. 3 (2015): Article 1420L.
Turman, Eboni Marshall. *Toward a Womanist Ethic of Incarnation: Black Bodies, the Black Church, and the Council of Chalcedon*. New York: Palgrave Macmillan, 2016.
Tutu, Desmond. *No Future Without Forgiveness*. London: Rider, 1999.
Urbaniak, Jakub. "Elitist, Populist or Prophetic? A Critique of Public Theologizing in Democratic South Africa." *International Journal of Public Theology* 12, nos. 3–4 (2018): 332–52.
Vellem, Vuyani S. "Unshackling the Church." *HTS Teologiese Studies/Theological Studies* 71, no. 3 (2015): Art. no.3119.
Villa-Vicencio, Charles, ed. *On Reading Karl Barth in South Africa*. Grand Rapids: Eerdmans, 1988.
de Villiers, E. "Editorial: Special Issue—Responsible South African Public Theology in a Global Era." *International Journal of Public Theology* 5 (2011): 1–4.
Walters, Joanna, and Jackie Renzetti. "George Floyd Killing: Sister Says Officers Should Face Murder Charge as Protests Grow." *The Guardian*, May 28, 2020.
Ward, Graham. "The Erotics of Redemption—After Karl Barth." *Theology and Sexuality* 8 (1998): 52–72.
Ward, Graham. *Ethical Life I: How the Light Gets In*. Oxford: Oxford University Press, 2016.
Webster, John. *The Domain of the Word: Scripture and Theological Reason*. London: T&T Clark, 2012.
Welker, Michael. *Gottes Offenbarung: Christologie*. Neukirchen-Vluyn: Neukirchener, 2012.
West, Cornel. *Prophesy Deliverance! An Afro-American Revolutionary Christianity*. Philadelphia: Westminster, 1982.
Weston, Randy. *African Rhythms: The Autobiography of Randy Weston*. Edited by Willard Jenkins. Durham: Duke University Press, 2010.
White, Thomas Joseph. "The *Analogia Entis* Controversy and Its Contemporary Significance." In *The Analogy of Being: Invention of the Anti-Christ or the Wisdom of God?* edited by Thomas Joseph White, 1–34. Grand Rapids: Eerdmans, 2011.

de Wilde, Laurent. *Monk*. Translated by Jonathan Dickinson. New York: Marlowe & Company, 1997.
Wilder, Amos. *Theopoetic: Theology and the Religious Imagination*. Philadelphia: Fortress, 1976.
Williams, Delores. *Sisters in the Wilderness: The Challenge of Womanist God-talk*. Maryknoll: Orbis, 1993.
Williams, Rowan. *Christ: The Heart of Creation*. London: Bloomsbury, 2018.
Williams, Rowan. *The Edge of Words: God and the Habits of Language*. New York: Bloomsbury, 2014.
Witvliet, Theo. *The Way of the Black Messiah: The Hermeneutical Challenge of Black Theology as a Theology of Liberation*. Oak Park: Meyer Stone, 1987.
Wuthnow, Robert. *The Left Behind: Decline and Rage in Rural America*. Princeton: Princeton University Press, 2018.
van Wyngaard, George Jacobus. *In Search of Repair: Critical White Responses to Whiteness as a Theological Problem—a South African Contribution*. Amsterdam: Vrie Universiteit Press, 2019.
Wynter, Sylvia. "Unsettling the Coloniality of Being/Power/Truth/Freedom: Towards the Human, After Man, Its Overrepresentation—An Argument." *CR: The New Centennial Review* 3, no. 3 (2003): 257–337.
Yoder, John Howard. *The Pacifism of Karl Barth*. Washington, DC: The Church Peace Mission, 1964.
Young, III, Josiah U. "Betwixt and Between Afrocentrism and Neorthodoxy: A Simple Call to Freedom." *The Journal of Religious Thought* 50, nos. 1–2 (1994): 72–80.
Zachhuber, Johannes. *Theology as Science in the Nineteenth Century: From F. C. Baur to Ernst Troeltsch*. Oxford: Oxford University Press, 2013.
Zachman, Randall C. "Barth and Reformation Theology." In *The Oxford Handbook of Karl Barth*, edited by Paul Dafydd Jones and Paul T. Nimmo, 101–15. Oxford: Oxford University Press, 2019.
Zagzebski, Linda Trinkaus. *Divine Motivation Theory*. Cambridge: Cambridge University Press, 2004.
Zeferino, Jefferson, Waldir Souza, and Rudolf Von Sinner, eds. "Karl Barth e a Teologia Pública." *Pistis & Praxis* 14, no. 1 (2022): 1–154.

CONTRIBUTORS

Brian Bantum is Neal F. and Ila A. Fisher Professor of Theology at Garrett-Evangelical Theological Seminary.

Faye Bodley-Dangelo is Managing Editor of the *Harvard Theological Review* and *Harvard Divinity Bulletin*.

Raymond Carr is Research Associate for the Moses Mesoamerican Archive and Research Project at Harvard University.

Meehyun Chung is Professor at the United Graduate School of Theology at Yonsei University.

David L. Clough holds the Chair in Theology and Applied Sciences at the University of Aberdeen.

Tyler B. Davis is Lecturer in Theology at St. Mary's University and University of the Incarnate Word in San Antonio, Texas.

Kaitlyn Dugan is the Director of the Center for Barth Studies at Princeton Theological Seminary.

Hani Hanna is Academic Dean at the Evangelical Theological Seminary in Cairo (ETSC).

Paul Dafydd Jones is Associate Professor of Religious Studies at the University of Virginia.

Lisa Powell is Professor of Theology and Director of Women and Gender Studies at St. Ambrose University.

Hanna Reichel is Associate Professor of Reformed Theology at Princeton Theological Seminary.

Luis N. Rivera-Pagán is Henry Winters Luce Professor Emeritus of Ecumenics at Princeton Theological Seminary.

Ry O. Siggelkow is Director of the Leadership Center for Social Justice at United Theological Seminary of the Twin Cities in St. Paul, Minnesota.

Rothney S. Tshaka is Professor of Ethics and Systematic Theology and Director of the School of Humanities, in the College of Human Sciences at the University of South Africa.

Graham Ward is Regius Professor of Divinity at the University of Oxford.

INDEX

Abdul-Nasser, Jamal 102
aesthetics 165-7, 179-85, 191-2
African theology 127-31
Agamben, Giorgio 156-7
Althaus-Reid, Marcella 42 n.21
Alt-Right 213-18, 226-31
Alves, Rubem 24-5
Anderson, Raymond 191 n.58
Apostle Paul 161-2, 164
Arab Spring 100-4
Assmann, Hugo 19, 199, 233-4
atonement, substitutionary 47-53
Awad, Najib George 114

von Balthasar, Hans Urs 181
Barth, Karl
  actualism 105, 107-10
  animals 155-9
  anthropology 88-91, 107-10
  anti-communism 88-91
  capitalism 30, 93-4, 96-7
  covenant ontology 73-8, 82
  doctrine of creation 45 n.26, 55-7, 61-8, 76-7, 95, 109-12
  doctrine of reconciliation 51-2, 141-6
  ecclesiology 219, 226-34
  The Epistle to the Romans 29-30, 43-4, 149, 153, 161-7
  Hungarian Revolution 89, 91-2
  natural theology 62, 90-1, 196-9, 202-3, 209-12
  pacifism 95-6
  political participation 104-7
  providence 110-11
  socialism 29-30, 105-6, 119-23, 125
  Soviet communism 86-92, 119
  theological method 161-2, 210-12, 218-20
  Virgin Mary 57-63, 65-8
  women and the female body 66-7

Barth studies and whiteness 147-55, 159-60, 168-9, 203-7
de Beauvoir, Simone 40
Bereczky, Albert 89-90
Black Liberation theology 25-7, 123-7, 201-3
Bloch, Ernst 16, 19-20
Boesak, Allan 6, 136-7, 141, 146
Boff, Leonardo 20-1, 23
Bonhoeffer, Dietrich 6, 117, 120, 139-40
Booth-Clibborn, Stanley 131
Brunner, Emil 86, 90-1, 119, 198, 203
Buthelezi, Manaz 124
Butler, Judith 219-20, 230-1

Carr, Raymond 201 n.31
Carter, J. Kameron 81, 151-2, 155-7, 223
Casalis, Georges 187 n.43
de las Casas, Bartolomé 22
Chacón, Jonathan Pimentel 21 n.26
Cold War theology 85-92, 97
Colenso, John William 157
Cone, James H. 8, 26, 27, 135 n.4, 148-55, 159-60, 168-9, 177-8, 182-93, 195-212, 225
Creamer, Deborah 71, 82

Detroit Rebellion 196, 199-203
dialectical theology 1, 198
Dickson, Kwesi 119 n.6, 131
Dillard, Anne 170, 173
Disability Studies 69-73, 78-82
Dussel, Enrique 36-8, 40

Eiesland, Nancy 69, 71-3, 79, 82-3

Feuerbach, Ludwig 21, 34-8, 40-50
Freire, Paulo 17, 21, 24

Gebara, Ivone 69-70
gender 39-40

gender equity 31
God as "wholly Other" 34–5, 43–53, 205, 208
Gollwitzer, Helmut 6, 205–10
Gorringe, Timothy 120–1
Gregory of Nyssa 143
Gutiérrez, Gustavo 19, 23, 25, 210

Herzog, Frederick 204 n.41
human experience 113, 224–6
Hunsinger, George 3 n.6, 7, 120–1, 180 n.10, 181, 188 n.44, 228 n.30

ideology 44, 90, 94, 97, 128, 207–10, 220–6

Jehle, Frank 119
Jenkins, Willis 56
Jennings, Willie James 155, 157, 223
Johnson, Elizabeth 224–5
Jones, Paul Dafydd 78, 81, 100

Kant, Immanuel 36, 156
Käsemann, Ernst 211
Keller, Catherine 55, 64, 223 n.41
Kierkegaard, Søren 43, 197–8
King Jr., Martin Luther 25, 167
Korean feminist theology 92–5, 97
Korean War 86–9, 97–8

Latin American liberation theology 18–25
Lehmann, Paul 7, 8, 202 n.34, 204 n.43, 206–9, 212 n.79, 229
LGBTQIA+ 124
literary theology 169–74
Lloyd, Vincent 234
Long, Charles H. 178, 186–9, 190 n.53

Machovec, Milan 88
MacKay, John 7
Malik, Ahmed Abul 183–4
Marcuse, Herbert 17 n.4
Marquardt, Friedrich Wilhelm 1, 6, 105–6, 119–21, 184 n.30, 188 n.48, 218, 234 n.43
Marx, Karl 16, 21 n.24, 30, 135, 195
Marxism 16
Mazrui, Ali 130–1

McCormack, Bruce L. 1, 69, 73–81, 219 n.14
Miranda, José Porfirio 19
Mitchell, Beverly Eileen 209 n.63
Mofokeng, Takatso 138 n.10, 139, 140 n.14
Moltmann, Jürgen 6, 25
Monk, Thelonious Sphere 178–85, 189, 192–3
Moore, Basil 123
Morrison, Toni 170 n.7, 172–4
Mozart, Wolfgang Amadeus 166, 180–1, 185, 190–2

Niebuhr, Reinhold 91, 119
Nkrumah, Kwame 130
Noel, James A. 189–90
Ntwasa, Sabelo 123

Opoku, Kofi Asare 127–8, 130
Orientalism 39–40
"otherization" 39–43, 50–3

Park, Soon-Kyung 85, 92–5, 97–8
Pityana, Nyameko 118 n.5
Pope John Paul II 23
Pope John XXIII 17–18
"preferential option for the poor" 28–9, 31

Queerness 31–2. See also LGBTQIA+
"quiet activism" 111–15

race 39–40, 122, 135–7, 148, 150–9, 222–3
Ratzinger, Joseph 23
religion 34–6, 42–6
Resch, Dustin 58 n.5
Rivera, Mayra 34 n.5, 38 n.15
Roberts, Hugh J. 180
Roberts, Sr., J. Deotis 189 n.49
Roman Catholic church 18–24
Romero, Oscar Arnulfo 22–3

Said, Edward W. 39–40
Schleiermacher, Friedrich D. E. 3, 15
Sedgwick, Eve Kosofsky 42 n.21
Segundo, Juan Luis 20
Serequeberhan, Tsenay 130 n.40

Shaull, Richard   24
Smit, Dirk   121–2
Smith, Jonathan Z.   158
Sobrino, Jon   20, 24, 210
South African liberation theology
   135–9
Spencer, Jon Michael   178 n.4, 190 n.57,
   193
Spivak, Gayatri Chakravorty   41 n.19,
   41 n.20
Sumner, Darren   78

Tamez, Elsa   34 n.4
Taylor, Keeanga-Yamahtta   200 n.25
theological discernment   210–12
"theologies of freedom"   178–9, 186–9
Tietz, Christiane   2
Tillich, Paul   104–5, 225–6
Townes, Emilie   152, 155, 170

Truth and Reconciliation Commission
   141–2
Tutu, Desmond   136, 143

universal humanity   35–9

Vatican II   17–18
Villa-Vicencio, Charles   140

Ward, Graham   56
West, Charles   119
Weston, Randy   183–4
Williams, Rowan   233
Witvliet, Theo   208–9
Wynter, Sylvia   221–2 n.19

Yoder, John Howard   95 n.31

Zimmerman, Wolf Dieter   87

www.ingramcontent.com/pod-product-compliance
Lightning Source LLC
Chambersburg PA
CBHW062126300426
44115CB00012BA/1832